T0248398

INSPIRE / PLAN / DISCOVER / EXPERIENCE

# NATIONAL PARKS
## OF THE USA

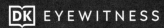

# NATIONAL PARKS
## OF THE USA

# CONTENTS

# DISCOVER 6

# EXPERIENCE 40

# NEED TO KNOW 494

Left: Avenue of the Giants in Redwood National Park
Previous page: Towering rocks of Bryce Canyon
Front cover: Bison roaming the plains in Grand Teton

# DISCOVER

Lewis's monkeyflower blooming near Paradise River, Mount Rainier

# WELCOME TO
# THE NATIONAL
# PARKS

Snow-white sand dunes. Giant redwoods towering over moss-draped trails. Verdant islets lapped by azure waters. The 63 national parks of the USA celebrate the great American wilderness. Whether you're visiting one or planning to see them all, this DK travel guide is the perfect companion.

1 Brown bear with cubs at Katmai, Alaska.

2 Hiking on the Pīpīwai Trail in Haleakalā, Hawaii.

3 Joshua Tree's namesake trees, California.

4 Watchman Mountain and Virgin River, Zion, Colorado.

Since the first park was established in 1872, the national parks of the United States have protected some of the wildest and most beautiful landscapes on Earth. These are lands of raw, elemental power: steam rises from the scorched caldera at Yellowstone, while gargantuan glaciers creak in the frozen waters of Alaska's Denali. Gaze over the depths of the Grand Canyon or hike the rugged peaks of the Rockies, and words like "epic" feel entirely insufficient. The parks have become icons of the great outdoors, promising unforgettable wilderness adventures.

They might be testament to the breath-taking force of the natural world, but the parks are incredible for their human stories, too. Long before the arrival of European settlers, these lands were home to Indigenous peoples whose legacies remain alive today. The joint efforts of centuries of conservationists, naturalists, and visionaries remind us that the parks are as delicate as they are beautiful – they are our collective gift and our joint responsibility. By exploring the parks, you can add your tale to an unfolding story spanning thousands of years.

Join the parks together and you're left with a dizzying 84-million-acre (33-million-ha) tapestry. We've broken the parks down into easily navigable chapters, with detailed itineraries, expert local knowledge, and comprehensive maps to plan the perfect trip. However many you plan to visit, this DK travel guide will ensure you have the ideal adventure. Enjoy the book, and enjoy the national parks.

# REASONS TO LOVE
# THE NATIONAL PARKS

Beautiful scenery, Indigenous heritage, incredible wildlife, and an outdoor adventure around every corner – there are endless reasons to love the national parks of the USA. Here, we pick some of our favorites.

## 1 GRAND PRISMATIC SPRING

America's first national park, Yellowstone *(p200)* remains one of the world's most spectacular places thanks to its otherworldly geyser of psychedelic colors.

## SCENIC DRIVES 2

Road trips are part of America's DNA, and the parks offer some of the country's best routes, from winding around Olympic *(p130)* to traversing Glacier's Going-to-the-Sun Road *(p190)*.

## 3 BOTANICAL MARVELS

Ranging from whimsical cactus gardens at Joshua Tree *(p76)* to some of the oldest and biggest trees on earth at Redwood *(p100)*, fantastic flora lies at the heart of the parks.

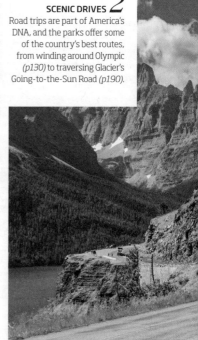

### BEAUTIFUL LANDSCAPES 4

The U.S.'s most awe-inspiring landscapes are found within its national parks: golden deserts, captivating caves, rumbling volcanoes, and lush forests are just a taste of what awaits.

### STARS IN YOUR EYES 5

Given their remote locations, many parks are blessed with little light pollution. See the aurora borealis at Isle Royale *(p366)* or join a skygazing tour at Haleakalā *(p478)*.

### PARK PROTECTORS 6

Park rangers make every visit that bit more special, whether they're leading a meteor-shower bike ride at Everglades *(p450)* or inspiring the kids on the Junior Ranger Program.

## THE MOTHER OF ALL CANYONS 7

Nothing prepares you for the unparalleled beauty of the Grand Canyon *(p262)*. Stand on the rim of this icon and gaze out at one of the most incredible vistas in the world.

## SCENE-STEALING SCENERY 8

Be it the snowy mountains of Grand Teton *(p210)* in *Rocky IV* or the enchanting forests of Redwood *(p100)* in *E.T.*, the parks have long played starring roles on the silver screen.

## 9 A HIKER'S PARADISE

To really get under the skin of the parks, pull on your boots. Numerous trails crisscross every park, with The Narrows in Zion *(p284)* one of the best for its soaring sandstone views.

## 10 INDIGENOUS CULTURE

The legacy of the Indigenous peoples who once occupied parkland is still tangible, with cliff dwellings at Mesa Verde *(p328)* and petroglyphs at Canyonlands *(p320)*.

## 11 EPIC STAYS

Even better than visiting a national park? Bedding down in one. Grab a permit and pitch your tent or book into a cosy park lodge to wake up to spectacular views.

## 12 WILDLIFE WATCHING

The thrill of spotting a humpback whale leaping from the waters of Glacier Bay *(p148)* or a black bear wandering the forests of Shenandoah *(p404)* never gets old.

Map labels:

NORTH CASCADES
OLYMPIC
WASHINGTON
MOUNT RAINIER
GLACIER
MONTANA
NORTH DAKOTA
THEODORE ROOSEVELT
SOUTH DAKOTA
PACIFIC NORTHWEST
p108
OREGON
IDAHO
YELLOWSTONE
WYOMING
WIND CAVE
BADLANDS
CRATER LAKE
GRAND TETON
THE ROCKIES AND THE GREAT PLAINS
p186
NEBRASKA
REDWOOD
LASSEN VOLCANIC
NEVADA
UTAH
ROCKY MOUNTAIN
COLORADO
CALIFORNIA
p42
GREAT BASIN
CAPITOL REEF
ARCHES
BLACK CANYON OF THE GUNNISON
KANSAS
YOSEMITE
KINGS CANYON
BRYCE CANYON
CANYONLANDS
GREAT SAND DUNES
ZION
MESA VERDE
PINNACLES
SEQUOIA
DEATH VALLEY
GRAND CANYON
NEW MEXICO
OKLAHO
CALIFORNIA
PETRIFIED FOREST
THE SOUTHWEST
p258
CHANNEL ISLANDS
JOSHUA TREE
ARIZONA
WHITE SANDS
SAGUARO
CARLSBAD CAVERNS
TEXAS
Pacific Ocean
GUADALUPE MOUNTAINS
BIG BEND

Alaska

0 km   500
0 miles   500

N ↑

KOBUK VALLEY
GATES OF THE ARCTIC
RUSSIA
ALASKA
p138
DENALI
WRANGELL-ST ELIAS
LAKE CLARK
CANADA
Bering Sea
KENAI FJORDS
GLACIER BAY
KATMAI
MEXICO
Gulf of Alaska

# EXPLORE
# THE NATIONAL PARKS

To help you discover the national parks of the USA, this guide divides the country into eight colour-coded regions, as shown on this map.

VOYAGEURS
MINNESOTA
ISLE ROYALE
Lake Superior
CANADA
0 kilometers    500
0 miles    500
N

WISCONSIN
Lake Michigan
Lake Huron
MICHIGAN
Lake Ontario
MAINE
ACADIA
VT
NH
NEW YORK

IOWA
INDIANA DUNES
Lake Erie
MA
CT    RI

ILLINOIS    INDIANA    CUYAHOGA VALLEY
OHIO
PENNSYLVANIA
NJ

**GREAT LAKES AND THE NORTHEAST**
*p358*

GATEWAY ARCH
MISSOURI
KENTUCKY
WEST VIRGINIA
NEW RIVER GORGE
SHENANDOAH
VIRGINIA

MAMMOTH CAVE

ARKANSAS
TENNESSEE
GREAT SMOKY MOUNTAINS
NORTH CAROLINA

HOT SPRINGS

**THE SOUTHEAST**
*p400*

SOUTH CAROLINA

MISSISS-IPPI
ALABAMA
GEORGIA
CONGAREE

LOUISIANA

*Atlantic Ocean*

FLORIDA

*Gulf of Mexico*

BISCAYNE
EVERGLADES
DRY TORTUGAS

CUBA

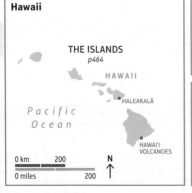

**Hawaii**

THE ISLANDS
*p464*

HAWAII

HALEAKALĀ

*Pacific Ocean*

HAWAIʻI VOLCANOES

0 km    200
0 miles    200
N

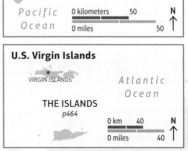

**American Samoa**

THE ISLANDS
*p464*

NATIONAL PARK OF AMERICAN SAMOA

*Pacific Ocean*

0 kilometers    50
0 miles    50
N

**U.S. Virgin Islands**

VIRGIN ISLANDS

*Atlantic Ocean*

THE ISLANDS
*p464*

0 km    40
0 miles    40
N

### ▽ Fabled Forests

Home to a stunning variety of arboreal life, America's national parks are the country's green lungs. The old growth redwoods at California's Redwood National Park *(below; p100)* are the world's tallest trees, and their verdant canopy shelters a mosaic of habitats. Further west but a whole world away, the rainforest of Olympic National Park *(p130)* is a true green haven.

### △ Canyon Country

Few images of the parks are as iconic as the chasms of Grand Canyon *(above; p262)*. Measuring an incredible 1 mile (1.6 km) deep, the canyon plummets into the Colorado River. Follow the river to find Utah's Canyonlands *(p320)*, an expanse of golden mesa and soaring arches.

# NATIONAL PARKS FOR
# NATURAL WONDERS

America's national parks are hymns to the country's wilderness, created to celebrate and protect its wild open spaces. There are few better ways to revel in the country's natural beauty than by exploring the precipitous canyons of Arizona or marvelling at California's towering redwoods.

### △ Sprawling Deserts

The southwest is home to starkly beautiful deserts, extreme landscapes rich in legend. The boiling temperatures of Death Valley *(above; p68)*, the country's hottest and driest park, have forged a basin where hardy joshua trees jut from the saltpans. Those unique trees lend their name to Joshua Tree *(p76)*, where the Mojave and Colorado deserts meet.

### ◁ Wetland Habitats

America's wetlands are some of the world's most biodiverse and ecologically delicate habitats. The subtropical Everglades in Florida *(p450)* are a seemingly enchanted wilderness of sawgrass prairies and sprawling mangrove forests. Walk the swamps and ponds to see alligators lurking in the depths. At Indiana Dunes *(p376)*, the Great Marsh is home to rare wading birds including herons and egrets.

### DELICATE ECOSYSTEMS

The parks are living climate laboratories, with scientists closely monitoring the effects of climate change. Coastal parks are seeing the thawing of permafrost and rising sea levels, while tree mortality and wildfires are on the rise further inland. The National Parks Conservation Association works tirelessly to mitigate these effects.

### ◁ Giant Glaciers

At America's extreme northwest, Alaska is a wild wonderland carved out of ice. Covering 3.3 million acres (120 thousand ha) of huge glaciers and deep fjords, Glacier Bay *(p148)* is a glimmering highlight of the state's Inside Passage. In Alaska's centre, Denali *(p154)* is scored with glacial rivers, remnants of the larger glaciers that dominated this spectacular landscape 10,000 years ago.

### ▷ Moving Mountains

These aren't your average peaks. From the soaring alpine slopes of Washington's North Cascades *(p126)* to the austere volcanic plateaus of California's Pinnacles National Park *(p90)*, America's mountains are the high points, quite literally, of its natural splendour. Feeling brave? Make for Denali *(p154)*, the highest mountain in North America, which offers breathtaking views over the roadless Alaskan wilderness.

### Beautiful Birds

Eyes to the skies! With around 900 native bird species, the U.S. has an embarrassment of riches for birders. Hawaii's Haleakalā National Park *(p478)* sits on a blissfully remote archipelago: the Hawaiian short-eared owl and Maui petrel are native. On the coast of Maine, Acadia National Park *(p390)* has a tapestry of perfect habitats: Atlantic puffin frolic on the beaches while the bald eagle parades overhead.

Atlantic puffin on a beach in Acadia, off the coast of Maine

# NATIONAL PARKS FOR
# WILDLIFE WATCHING

In the ocean, a humpback breaching; above the canopy, the startling wings of the condor; across the plain, the horns of the caribou. Unforgettable wild encounters abound in the parks, creating memories to last a lifetime.

### Watching Whales

Seeing a colossal humpback dive deep beneath the waves or an acrobatic orca leap above them is always an unforgettable spectacle. Between April and October, whales of various species glide off the frozen coast of Alaska searching for krill and other fish. A boat tour from Kenai Fjords *(p142)* or Glacier Bay *(p148)* is the best way to see them – responsible tours can be booked through trusted local organizations including Alaska Connection *(www.alaskaconnection.com)*.

A humpback breaching in front of a cruise at Kenai Fjords, Alaska

## Cavorting with Caribou

Caribou are central to the folklore of the arctic. Native peoples living within Alaska's Gates of the Arctic *(p178)* have lived in harmony with caribou for over 10,000 years. Book a tour through Arctic Wild *(www.arcticwild.com)* to see free-roaming herds.

→

Female caribou crossing the golden tundra at Gates of the Arctic

## Crocs and Gators

Crocodiles and alligators roam across the humid, swampy Southeast. The best place to see them is at Florida's Everglades *(p450)*, the largest tropical wilderness in the U.S. and the only place in the world where crocodiles and alligators can both be found. Alligators inhabit the park's freshwater swamps and marshes, but can also be found in rivers, lakes, and smaller bodies of water.

←

Alligator resting on the water's edge

### TOP 4 WAYS TO RESPECT WILDLIFE

**Every park has unique rules**
Familiarize yourself with the park's back-country guidance.

**Respect distance**
Give animals room when observing them.

**Drive slowly**
Vehicle collisions are a common cause of injury for wildlife in the parks.

**Stay on trails**
Venturing off designated trails and paths can lead to dangerous situations or disrupt wild habitats.

↑ Grizzly bear exploring with her young in Lamar Valley

## Bearing All

Bears are the unofficial symbol of America's first national park, Yellowstone *(p200)*. Grizzlies and black bears roam through the park's subalpine forest, with Lamar Valley a particularly good places to spot them. At Alaska's Katmai National Park *(p168)*, visit Brook Falls to spot brown and black bears.

### Behind the Wheel
The road trip is the quintessential American experience and the parks offer some truly iconic drives, with roads heading to the country's most beautiful spots. Stretching over 50 miles (80 km) through the heart of the Rocky Mountains *(p224)*, Going-to-the-Sun Road treats visitors to views of glacier-carved peaks, alpine lakes and lush subtropical forests. Visiting Virginia's Shenandoah *(p404)* in fall? Take the historic Skyline Drive to soak up the golden canopy in its full splendour.

→

Climbing Going-to-the-Sun Road at Glacier National Park

# NATIONAL PARKS FOR
# SCENIC JOURNEYS

Whether it's an awe inspiring drive up a winding mountain road or a leisurely cycle around a glacial lake, the national parks never fail to deliver on memorable journeys. These trips take you right to the heart of wild America.

### Riding the Rails
Railroads have long been integral to the park experience, ushering in a new age of tourism. With tracks laid in 1880, Cuyahoga Valley Scenic Railroad offers a steam-powered excursion through Cuyahoga Valley *(p382)*. To follow in the foot-steps of the pioneers, take the *Empire Builder*, which chugs along to Glacier *(p190)*.

The Cuyahoga steam train, which passes six scenic stations

## THE NATIONAL PARK-TO-PARK HIGHWAY

The National Park-to-Park Highway was conceived in 1915 to link 12 parks in the western states. In 1920, long before gas stations or fully paved roads, 12 enthusiastic motorists set out on the inaugural tour of the Highway. Their epic 5,000-mile (8,000-km) journey cemented the road trip as an iconic symbol of U.S. travel. Many of the roads that formed the original highway are still in popular use today.

### In the Saddle

What could be better than pedalling your way through America's wildest landscapes? At Oregon's Crater Lake *(p112)*, the deepest in America, you can ride the paved route around the circumference; in September, Ride the Rim *(www.ridetherim.com)* is a pedestrian-friendly group cycle. For casual cyclists, Utah's Zion *(p284)* offers a patchwork of trails along Virgin River.

→

Cycling through a fall cottonwood forest in Zion

### On the Water

To fully experience the wonders of the parks, you'll need to leave dry land. Minnesota's Voyageurs *(p362)* is a playground of expansive waterways and shimmering horizons. Book a tour through Voyageurs Outfitters *(www.voyageursoutfitters.com)*. Seeking thrills? Take a jet-propelled ride down the Colorado River near Canyonlands *(p320)*.

←

A houseboat on Lake Kabetogama in Voyageurs, Minnestota

### Foliage Walks

Fall is one of the best seasons to hike, when the climate is milder, the crowds are smaller, and the canopy burns gold, amber, and ochre. The Great Smoky Mountains *(p432)* are home to a dizzying abundance of deciduous trees; check out the Alum Cave Trail for heart-stopping views over the glowing leaves. Grand Teton National Park *(p212)* also wears its fall colors beautifully – wrap up warm and make for the banks of Lake Solitude to catch the canopy's rippling reflection.

$\rightarrow$

Fall foliage bringing color to the canopy at Great Smoky Mountains

# NATIONAL PARKS FOR
# EPIC HIKES

From migration routes carved out by Native peoples to long-distance thru-hiking paths formed in the 20th century, every trail tells a story. Exploring the grand drama of America's wilderness is as simple as choosing a route, lacing your boots, and heading for the hills.

### Scenic Ambles

Wild walking needn't be a strenuous affair, and many parks are designed to ensure accessibility for all. The Boardwalk Loop Trail in South Carolina's Congaree National Park *(p442)* is flat and fully paved, while still passing some of the park's most impressive cypress and pine trees. The Big Trees Trail in California's Sequoia National Park *(p56)* is also perfect for those with limited mobility – walkers have even been known to spot furtive brown bears from the safety of the trail.

$\leftarrow$

Strolling along Boardwalk Loop Trail at Congaree in South Carolina

### Multi-day Expeditions

The 1930s were the heyday of long-distance trail-building through the wilds of America. The most famous is the Appalachian Trail, which extends for over 2,000 miles (3,500 km), passing through 14 states and six parks; you can join in the Great Smoky Mountains *(p432)* or Blue Ridge Parkway. Then there's the John Muir Trail, which crosses Yosemite *(p46)*, Kings Canyon *(p64)*, and Sequoia *(p56)*.

← Resting on the John Muir Trail near Thousand Island Lake

### Coastal Strolls

There's something uniquely captivating about coastal walking, tracing the curve of the shore. Acadia National Park *(p390)* offers the short Ocean Path Trail along the coast of Maine, while the Ozette Triangle in Olympic National Park *(p130)* heads out along sandy beaches.

 INSIDER TIP
**Accessible Walks**

The National Park Service app includes an updated list of all the park's wheelchair accessible walkways, trails, and viewpoints *(www.nps.gov)*.

↑ The coast-hugging Ocean Path Trail in Acadia, Maine

### Explore the Skies

Whole galaxies come to life after nightfall, and many parks are certified Dark Sky spots. The kids will love rolling out a blanket in Utah's Arches *(p312)* and gazing in wonder at the Milky Way, framed by the park's namesake rocks. Not far from Arches, Capitol Reef *(p306)* offers pristine stargazing with very little light pollution.

$\rightarrow$
The Milky Way glimpsed beneath Utah's Double Arch

# NATIONAL PARKS FOR
# FAMILIES

With their abundance of gentle walking trails, wild ocean activities, and epic mountain drives, the parks can be enjoyed by the whole family. So many parks go above and beyond, providing outdoor experiences the kids will cherish for years to come.

### Celebrate the Seasons

The parks celebrate seasonal events in special ways, from stunning Christmas displays to summer gatherings. In early December, local choirs gather to sing carols in the cave at Mammoth Cave *(p412)*, a tradition dating back to 1883. Overindulged during the holidays? Join the popular First Day Hikes, joint family walks held in many national parks on the first day of January. When summer comes, visit Petrified Forest *(p280)* to join crowds toasting the summer solstice.

$\leftarrow$
Visitors warming themselves by a fire at Mammoth Cave

**TOP 4 FAMILY HIKES**

**Beaver Ponds**
This 5-mile (8-km) route passes Yellowstone's sagebrush meadows.

**Shoshone Point**
Stroll through 2 miles (3 km) of Ponderosa Pine to a picnic spot at Grand Canyon.

**Sunset Trail**
A flat 10-mile (16-km) walk in Hot Springs.

**Sand Dune Arch**
A 0.3-mile (0.5-km) stroll to one of the smaller formations at Arches.

## Become a Ranger

"Explore. Learn. Protect." The motto of the National Park Service's Junior Ranger Program captures the fun but educational ethos of the scheme. Each park has its own activities, many of which earn badges: Channel Islands *(p84)* has courses on archaeology, underwater exploring, and ecology.

→
A park ranger running the Junior Ranger Program

## Dig For Fossils

The parks provide some of America's best fossil spots. Badlands *(p240)* has a huge fossil bed, where traces of sabre-toothed cats and rhinoceroses have been found. Petrified Forest *(p280)* is named after wood from the Triassic Period, with fossils dating back 200 million years.

→
Scouring the fossil bed for traces of prehistoric life

## Black History

Too often written out of official histories, Black Americans made a lasting contribution to the parks. Yosemite's Buffalo Soldiers *(p53)* were among the first rangers; learn more at the visitor centre. At Mammoth Cave *(p412)*, you can visit the grave of Stephen Bishop, a pioneering Black American tour guide and explorer.

Buffalo Soldiers at Yosemite; around 500 served as park rangers

# NATIONAL PARKS FOR
# HISTORY BUFFS

From their Native origins *(p28)* to the arrival of the pioneers and the birth of the National Park Service, the story of the parks is a true American epic. But their natural history puts this human story in stark perspective, with landscapes whisking you back to Earth in its infancy.

## O Pioneers!

Various homesteads bring pioneer society to life. In 1880, settlers moved into Utah's Capitol Reef *(p306)*, attracted by the abundance of water. The settler village of Fruita contains a schoolhouse and traditional homestead. At Key's Ranch, in California's Joshua Tree *(p76)*, ranger-led tours teach about Native history, mining, ranching, and homesteading.

↑ A traditional pioneer community at Key's Ranch

The legacy of the Gold Rush at Death Valley ↑

## Industrial Legacies

Since the discovery of gold in California in 1848, many landscapes have been irrevocably changed by the vast structures of industry. The Harmony Borax Works in Death Valley *(p68)* went out of operation in 1888, but today the preserved site provides insights into the era of the Gold Rush. The Rocky Mountains *(p224)* were once home to around 80 mines; the vast Eugenia Mine in the park today offers excellent hiking terrain.

### Did You Know?

The second park to be founded, Mackinac, established in 1875, is no longer designated a national park.

## Magic Museums

The national parks are home to a plethora of innovative museums which assess the relationship between humans and the landscape. Mesa Verde's museum *(p330)* is one of the oldest; it explores the culture of the Ancestral Puebloans who lived in the region thousands of years ago. The Yavapai Geology Musuem, in Grand Canyon *(p262)*, features huge panoramic windows offering a fascinating perspective on the region's singular geology.

↑ Admiring a Puebloan site at Mesa Verde's museum and *(inset)* a prehistoric corn jar

### Ceremonial Dances

Many national parks strive to showcase the cultural wealth of America's Indigenous peoples. At Redwood National Park *(p100)*, dances by the Tolowa nation can be seen throughout the year; dance is an important means by which the community give thanks for the Earth's bounty. Mesa Verde National Park *(p328)* also hosts cultural dances, performances, and demonstrations by members of the Indigenous community.

→

Indigenous peoples performing a ceremonial dance at Mesa Verde

# NATIONAL PARKS FOR
# INDIGENOUS CULTURE

When exploring the wild country, it's important to remember that all national parks were originally Native lands. Thousands of years of Indigenous culture and history can be seen within the parks, with an assortment of events and exhibitions arranged to ensure the richness of Indigenous society is respected, celebrated, and preserved.

### Perfect Petroglyphs

Ancient rock art found throughout the parks' landscapes provides tantalizing clues about the country's oldest cultures. Foremost among these is the Great Gallery at Horseshoe Canyon in Canyonlands *(p320)*, with pictographs dating from 2000 BCE to 500 CE. At Arches *(p312)*, the Delicate Arch trail leads to the Ute Indian petroglyphs, startling depictions of horses, riders, and big-horn sheep.

Ute Indian petroglyphs clearly preserved at Delicate Arch, Arches

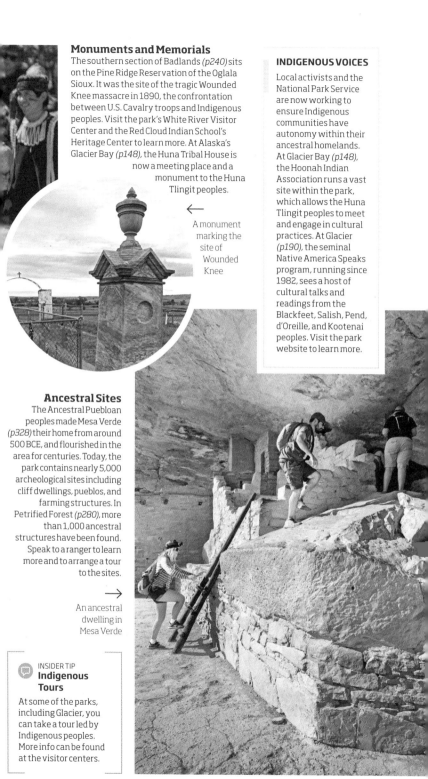

## Monuments and Memorials

The southern section of Badlands (p240) sits on the Pine Ridge Reservation of the Oglala Sioux. It was the site of the tragic Wounded Knee massacre in 1890, the confrontation between U.S. Cavalry troops and Indigenous peoples. Visit the park's White River Visitor Center and the Red Cloud Indian School's Heritage Center to learn more. At Alaska's Glacier Bay (p148), the Huna Tribal House is now a meeting place and a monument to the Huna Tlingit peoples.

← A monument marking the site of Wounded Knee

### INDIGENOUS VOICES

Local activists and the National Park Service are now working to ensure Indigenous communities have autonomy within their ancestral homelands. At Glacier Bay (p148), the Hoonah Indian Association runs a vast site within the park, which allows the Huna Tlingit peoples to meet and engage in cultural practices. At Glacier (p190), the seminal Native America Speaks program, running since 1982, sees a host of cultural talks and readings from the Blackfeet, Salish, Pend, d'Oreille, and Kootenai peoples. Visit the park website to learn more.

## Ancestral Sites

The Ancestral Puebloan peoples made Mesa Verde (p328) their home from around 500 BCE, and flourished in the area for centuries. Today, the park contains nearly 5,000 archeological sites including cliff dwellings, pueblos, and farming structures. In Petrified Forest (p280), more than 1,000 ancestral structures have been found. Speak to a ranger to learn more and to arrange a tour to the sites.

→ An ancestral dwelling in Mesa Verde

> 💬 INSIDER TIP
> **Indigenous Tours**
>
> At some of the parks, including Glacier, you can take a tour led by Indigenous peoples. More info can be found at the visitor centers.

### The Off Season

Many people first glimpse the epic Grand Canyon *(p262)* or soaring vistas of Yosemite *(p46)* from within a large crowd of tourists. To beat the crowds, and to secure cheaper accommodation in the process, visit the parks in the low season. The winter months are good for visiting desert parks, including Joshua Tree *(p76)*, with pleasant temperatures and quiet campgrounds. And Yellowstone *(p200)* is blanketed in snow during winter, with quieter trails and hotels.

$\rightarrow$

Visiting a Yellowstone hot spring in midwinter

# NATIONAL PARKS
# ON A SHOESTRING

Exploring the American wilderness should be available to everyone, regardless of budget. Some of the parks are free to enter, and there are a host of other money-saving ideas and itineraries that will ensure your backcountry adventure is big on beauty and small on cost.

### Ditch the Car

Though travelling by car has long been the most popular means of exploring, road travel can be expensive, and the parks suffer from major congestion. Yosemite, Zion, and Glacier are just a few of the country's parks offering public transportation. After decades of heavy traffic, the use of personal cars is banned on Zion's *(p284)* main road from March to November. The park now runs shuttles across the Zion Canyon. Many other parks run buses to trailheads from their visitor centers.

$\leftarrow$

The shuttle bus waiting to take passengers along the Zion Canyon Scenic Drive

Entrance fees, ranging from $10 per person to $35 per vehicle, are typically charged at many U.S. parks. These fees help fund park maintenance and support conservation efforts. But in an effort to guarantee wider accessibility, there are a number of programs that allow visitors free entry to national parks. Every year, the park service selects days (usually one per season) to offer free admission: check the NPS website for dates.

## Ranger Activities

Many of the park's best ranger talks and activities are free to enjoy. At the Grand Canyon (p262), for example, guided hikes are given by knowledgeable rangers, who shed light on the park's geology and social history. An even better way to explore the beauty of the parks (while enjoying free or cheap admission) is to volunteer yourself; there are a host of opportunities including trail maintenance and wildlife monitoring advertised on the park's websites.

↑ A park ranger giving a free talk on the ecology of the Grand Canyon

## Passes and Discounts

If you plan on visiting more than three parks or other public land sites around the U.S. in a year, the "America the Beautiful Pass" can save you money on entrance fees. The pass grants you free access to more than 2,000 recreation sites across the country for a whole year (www. nps.gov/planyourvisit/passes.htm). The park service runs a host of other discount passes, including those for 4th grader, seniors, military personnel and veterans, and volunteers. In addition, look out for the park's free entrance days.

← The "America the Beautiful Pass", a great option for those visiting more than one park

# A YEAR IN THE NATIONAL PARKS

While the parks are an inevitable hit come summer, the changing seasons bring an abundance of beauty and variety. With a host of events throughout the year, there's always a reason to visit.

## Spring

Riotous floral displays mark the arrival of spring. Follow wildflower trails during Great Smoky Mountains' *(p432)* Spring Wildflower Pilgrimage or take a self-guided tour of the blooms at Joshua Tree *(p76)*. Other events include music festivals at Haleakalā *(p478)* and National Park Week in April.

*1. Spring blooms at Joshua Tree*

## Summer

As the days lengthen and temperatures soar, crowds flock to explore the parks. Events to mark in your calendar are

> ### NATIONAL PARK WEEK
>
> In April, the National Park Service celebrates the diversity of the parks with an array of events. During the week, you can learn more about their history and ecology, while looking ahead to their future.

Glacier's Native America Speaks program and the Bryce Canyon Geology Festival. When the sun finally sets, see the stars as part of a stargazing party at Sequoia or hear the finest classical music at the Grand Teton Music Festival.

2. Exploring the rocky lanscapes of Bryce Canyon under the summer sun

## Autumn

The parks are at their most spectacular as the leaves turn during fall. See how these vibrant landscapes spark creativity at the Celebration of Art in Grand Canyon (p262) or join volunteers on National Public Lands Day, the U.S.'s largest single-day volunteer event. When November arrives, the parks host events as part of Native American Heritage Month.

3. The fall canopy burning yellow and gold at Rocky Mountain

## Winter

Winter may make some parks off-limits but plenty offer opportunities for skiing, skating, and snow-shoeing. Come Christmas, parks are lit-up with fairy lights and trees are decorated, with magical holiday themed events held at Hot Springs (p426). Visitors can also join in with the unusual Christmas tradition of cave singing at Mammoth Cave (p412) and the annual Audubon bird count.

4. Snow-shoeing on Yellowstone's Mystic Falls trail and (inset) Yosemite Chapel

3

4

### TOP 3 MUST-DO EVENTS

**National Junior Ranger Day**
Activities and events are held for budding rangers as part of the annual National Park Week held across nine days in all parks in April.

**National Trails Day**
Take part in community projects or organized hikes and rides on the first Saturday in June. On the day, tens of thousands of people come together to help maintain park trails.

**Native American Heritage Month**
Celebrate the rich ancestry and ongoing traditions of the U.S.'s Indigenous peoples at events held across the parks in November.

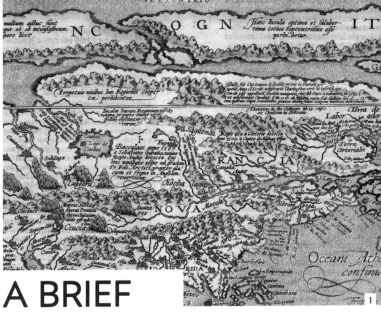

# A BRIEF
# HISTORY

Born from the desire to preserve some of the U.S.'s greatest landscapes, the national parks system has existed for some 150 years. The story of the parks spans Indigenous groups, ambitious settlers, and dedicated visionaries, resulting in what has been called "America's best idea."

## Early Days

For thousands of years, the land of the national parks was home to Indigenous peoples. Evidence of such communities can still be seen today in the stone dwellings of the ancestral Pueblo people at Mesa Verde. These Puebloans are estimated to have lived in the area for over 1,000 years, building extensive communities in the alcoves of the canyon walls. Once European settlers began to arrive in large numbers, Indigenous peoples, including the Pueblo, were obliterated by disease and war, and forced to retreat from the newly emerging settlements.

### Did You Know?
In 1832, Hot Springs became the first federal reservation, 40 years before Yellowstone was made a park.

## Timeline of events

### c.15,000 BCE
The first peoples arrive by a land bridge connecting Siberia to Alaska.

### 1776
The Declaration of Independence is adopted in Philadelphia.

### 200 CE–1400
Ancestral Puebloan culture thrives in the Four Corners region, with vast chambers built at Mesa Verde.

### 1803
The Louisiana Purchase extends the boundary of the country to the New Mexico border.

## Louisiana Purchase and Westward Pioneers

In 1803, President Thomas Jefferson doubled the size of the U.S. through the Louisiana Purchase, presenting settlers with vast tracts of supposedly "uninhabited" lands, prompting thousands of people to head west. Until the first Transcontinental Railroad was completed in 1869, the journey could take over six months. Westward movement was accelerated by the discovery of gold in 1848, and by the Homestead Act of 1862, by which anyone could claim "public land" provided they built a dwelling, cultivated the land, and resided there for five years.

## Rise of the Romantics

The move west coincided with the arrival of Romanticism, an artistic movement that placed emphasis on nature and aesthetics. Writers including Ralph Waldo Emerson and Henry David Thoreau waxed poetic about the landscape, while artists from the Hudson River School such as Thomas Cole captured the beauty of nature. Their works would influence public debates about conservation.

[1] Map of America from 1585.

[2] Illustration of the Ancestral Puebloan people, at Mesa Verde.

[3] President Thomas Jefferson, who oversaw the Louisiana Purchase.

[4] Romantic landscape painter Thomas Cole's *Indian Pass*, 1847.

### 1830

Congress passes the Indian Removal Act displacing thousands of Indigenous people from their homes and land.

### 1851

Congress ratifies the first reservations for "native" peoples through the Indian Appropriations Act.

### 1862

President Abraham Lincoln passes the Homestead Act, opening millions of acres of land to settlement.

### 1848

The Gold Rush commences after a discovery near Sacramento, California.

1

## The First National Park

Thanks in part to such newfound appreciation for the land, President Abraham Lincoln placed the Yosemite Valley under the control of the state of California through the 1864 Yosemite Grant Act. This was the first time that the government had intervened and set aside land for preservation and public use, rather than private enterprise. Eight years later, the first national park was established at Yellowstone by President Ulysses S. Grant. This act marked the land "for the benefit and enjoyment of the people" and Yellowstone quickly became a tourist attraction.

## The Question of Indigenous Peoples

The establishment of Yellowstone did much to erase the Indigenous people who had occupied the area for centuries, and were now not allowed to visit the national park. The nomadic nature of certain groups meant the government could simply take land, claiming it was "uninhabited," with new settlers and a wave of government acts forcing Indigenous peoples into assigned "Indian Territory." But even these

1 *The Grand Canyon of the Yellowstone* (1872), by Thomas Moran.

2 Illustration depicting the opening of Indigenous land to new settlers, 1889.

3 Theodore Roosevelt standing with naturalist John Muir on Glacier Point, above Yosemite Valley.

## *Timeline of events*

**1869**
John Muir first arrives in Yosemite.

**1869**
Completion of the first Transcontinental Railroad.

**1872**
President Ulysses S. Grant signs bill creating the first national park at Yellowstone.

**1864**
President Lincoln signs act ceding Yosemite Valley to California.

**1883**
The Northern Pacific Railroad is completed, bringing tourists to Yellowstone.

2

3

reservations were not safe and in 1889 the Oklahoma Land Run made just under 2 million acres (809,000 ha) of such land available to settlers. A year later, around 300 Lakota Sioux were killed or wounded by the U.S. Army on land that is now part of the Badlands National Park. Today the site is referred to as Wounded Knee.

## The Conservationist President

Considered the "conservationist president," Theodore Roosevelt was instrumental in expanding the parks system. Having always had an affinity with the natural world, Roosevelt asked the naturalist John Muir to guide him through Yosemite in 1903. The three nights the two spent camping together inspired Roosevelt into action; by the end of his presidency he had established five national parks and passed the Antiquities Act of 1906, which gave the president the authority to preserve federal lands by proclaiming them national monuments. The act also sought to preserve the cultural legacies of Indigenous peoples which were being erased following their displacement.

### JOHN MUIR

The park's story cannot be told without making mention of John Muir (1838–1914). Born in Scotland, Muir was entranced by the American wilderness as a young boy and dismayed by the destruction of land. He would devote his life to preserving nature, co-founding the conservationist Sierra Club in 1892 and helping to make Yosemite the second national park.

*1890*

President Benjamin Harrison signs a bill creating Yosemite National Park.

*1892*

A group of Californians plus John Muir co-found the Sierra Club.

*1906*

President Roosevelt signs the Antiquities Act.

*1908*

President Roosevelt declares the Grand Canyon a national monument.

## Establishing the National Park Service

By the mid-1910s, 35 national parks and monuments existed, yet there was no single body to manage them. The oversight by the Department of the Interior was often criticized, most notably by Stephen Mather, a businessman and conservationist, who was convinced of the need for a single governing body. Thanks to his pressure, Congress approved the creation of the National Park Service (NPS) in 1916, with Mather as its first director. His work to reorganize park management and promote the parks bore quick results: annual attendance grew by 700,000 in the four years after 1916.

## The Depression and Civilian Conservation Corps

The onset of the Great Depression in 1929 would bring about perhaps the greatest changes to the parks system. President Franklin Roosevelt created the Civilian Conservation Corps in 1933 to alleviate the unemployment crisis by putting people to work improving America's public lands. These programs constructed more infrastructure in the parks than in their entire history, with new roads, trails, and visitor shelters.

### THE CREATION OF PARK RANGERS

Though they may be ubiquitous today, the role of park ranger as we know it is barely a century old. During the 19th century, the parks were protected by the Army and the Buffalo Soldiers, Black infantry regiments. The first official park ranger was Harry Yount, gamekeeper at Yellowstone. It was only in 1916 that the role became more formalized.

## Timeline of events

**1916**
Congress passes a law creating the National Park Service.

**1920**
Park visitors pass 1 million for the first time.

**1933**
The National Park Service's purview is expanded to include historic sites.

**1941**
Ansel Adams is hired to photograph the national parks.

**1950**
Park visitors surpass 32 million.

4

## Mission 66

As both population and prosperity boomed after World War II, visitors to the parks skyrocketed, increasing by over 30 million between 1940 and 1956. The renewed pressure on the park system forced the NPS and Congress into action, with the passing of Mission 66 in 1956. This was a 10-year plan intended to modernize park infrastructure. Some $700 million led to necessary upgrades on infrastructure, roads, and campgrounds.

## The National Parks Today

The U.S. has changed dramatically since 1872 when the first park was established, but the love of parks and nature remains strong. Annual visitor numbers surpassed 300 million in 2015 and new parks are still being established, most recently at New River Gorge in 2020. The parks have also become more inclusive, incorporating those with ancestral ties to the land. Native American Heritage Month and partnerships with Indigenous communities have helped facilitate this learning. Today, parks seek to connect visitors with both the natural world and the country's varied Indigenous cultures.

1 Memorial plaque for Stephen Mather, Grand Canyon.

2 The Civilian Conservation Corps hard at work.

3 Visitors at Grand Canyon enjoying new facilities as a result of Mission 66.

4 A visitor enjoying a rest in the sun at Joshua Tree.

### 1955
National Park Service director Conrad Wirth proposes plans for Mission 66.

### 2016
The parks welcome an annual record of 331 million visitors.

### 2020
New River Gorge becomes the latest national park.

### 1978
Mesa Verde and Yellowstone are both among the first 12 sites to be named UNESCO World Heritage sites.

### 2018
Gateway Arch in St. Louis becomes the smallest national park.

# EXPERIENCE

Trekking along Arrigetch Creek, Gates of the Arctic

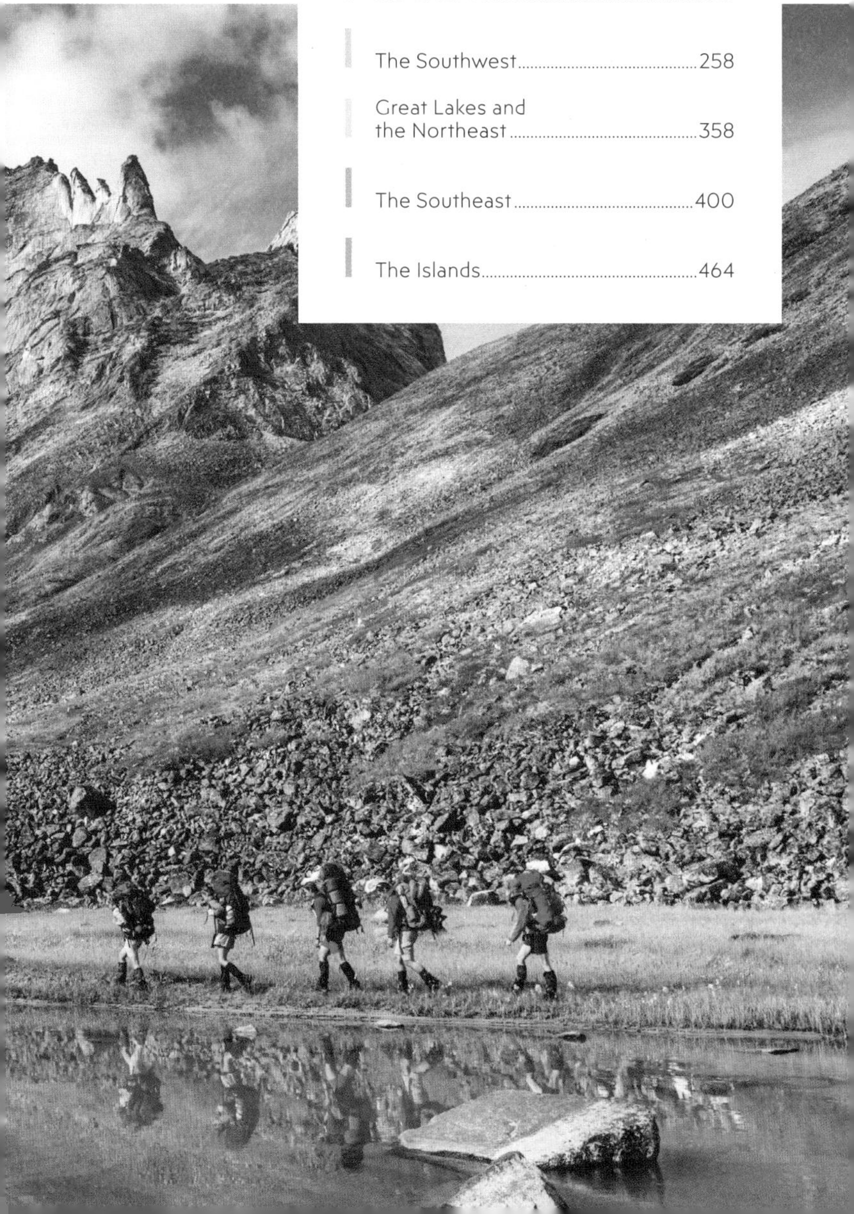

REDWOOD
*p100*

LASSEN
VOLCANIC
*p94*

YOSEMITE
*p46*

KINGS CANYON
*p64*

DEATH VALLEY
*p68*

PINNACLES
*p90*

SEQUOIA
*p56*

CALIFORNIA

CHANNEL
ISLANDS
*p84*

JOSHUA
TREE
*p76*

# CALIFORNIA

The third-largest U.S. state by area and the most populous, California extends from the rainy northern coast to the parched Colorado Desert in the south, near the border with Mexico. With nine national parks, the state boasts more than any other, each protected space a marvelous study in natural contrasts. Touring these landscapes takes you to some of the most legendary and storied spots in the U.S., from the towering rock wall of El Capitan in Yosemite to the meeting point of the Mojave and Colorado deserts in Joshua Tree.

In the state's far north, Redwood National Park is named after the tallest trees on Earth, which are found in glorious abundance within the park boundaries. The ominously named Death Valley is the largest and hottest of the state's parks, with vast salt pans, shimmering sand dunes, and sun-scorched basins. Channel Islands, meanwhile, offers the perfect escape from the bustle of the mainland. Consisting of five of the eight Channel Islands off California's Pacific coast, the park's teeming coastal waters differ markedly from the arid desert just a short boat ride away.

# 7 DAYS
## *in California*

### Day 1

Start your exploration of California's mighty Sierra Nevada at Sequoia National Park's *(p56)* southern entrance. Stop by the Foothills Visitor Center then take Generals Highway into the Giant Forest. Park your car at the Giant Forest Museum before viewing the exhibits and venturing out on the Big Trees Trail. From the museum, a shuttle bus runs to Moro Rock and Crescent Meadow (a good spot for a picnic), where you can hike to Tharp's Log, the hollowed-out sequoia once home to 19th-century pioneer Hale Tharp. Back on Generals Highway, it's a short drive to one of the park's highlights: the General Sherman Tree. End the day at the park's Lodgepole Visitor Center and Village.

### Day 2

Drive to the visitor center in Grant Grove Village in Kings Canyon National Park *(p64)*, where the General Grant Tree is known as the "Nation's Christmas Tree." Make a short detour to Big Stump – a series of gargantuan sequoia stumps, left by loggers in the 1880s – on route. From Grant Grove it's a dazzling drive into King's Canyon itself. Stop at Boyden Cavern for a tour of its stalagmites and stalactites, before lunch at Cedar Grove Visitor Center. Kings Canyon Scenic Byway continues past Roaring River Falls to terminate at Roads End, where there are trails to explore before the drive back to Grant Grove.

### Day 3

Get up early for the drive to Yosemite's *(p46)* south entrance via Fresno. Park at Mariposa Grove Welcome Plaza, where you can stroll among soaring sequoia giants. Hop back in the car and head to Wawona Visitor Center for a quick lunch, before driving north, taking the winding 16-mile (26-km) road to Glacier Point for views across Yosemite Valley and Half Dome. Stop at Bridalveil Falls before spending the evening in Yosemite Village.

### Day 4

Follow in the footsteps of park pioneer John Muir and explore Yosemite Valley on

[1] Hiking through sequoias.
[2] The epic Bridalveil Falls.
[3] Historic Ahwahnee Hotel.
[4] Scotty's Castle in summer.
[5] Flats of Badwater Basin.

foot (or by shuttle bus). Highlights include the short walk to towering Yosemite Falls, and the longer hike on the Mist Trail along the Merced River. The trek up to pretty Mirror Lake is a little shorter. There are several attractions in Yosemite Village if it's rainy: Yosemite Museum explores the history of the local Miwok and Paiute people, Ansel Adams Gallery showcases the photography of the artist, and the Valley Visitor Center screens the *Spirit of Yosemite* film. End the day with dinner at the Ahwahnee hotel.

## Day 5

Get up before dawn for a mesmerizing Yosemite sunrise at Tunnel View. There are plenty more viewpoints as you traverse the park on scenic Tioga Road (Hwy. 120), stopping at flower-dotted Tuolumne Meadows on the lesser visited eastern side of Yosemite. Aim for a late lunch in the village of Lee Vining (at Basin Café; *349 Lee Vining Ave.*) before driving south towards Death Valley. From Vining it's around three hours to the resort of Panamint Springs in Death Valley National Park (*p68*).

## Day 6

Drive the 28-mile (45-km) Emigrant Canyon Road to the Charcoal Kilns, ten eerie dome-shaped structures built in 1876. Further north are the Mesquite Flat Sand Dunes, where you can try sand-boarding, and Stovepipe Wells Village, ideal for lunch. Continue north for a guided tour of Scotty's Castle, a lavish Spanish Revival villa, and a hike around the rim of Uhebebe Crater, before driving south to Furnace Creek. Have dinner at the Old Western-themed Last Kind Words Saloon & Steakhouse in the park.

## Day 7

Explore Artist's Drive, a 9-mile (14.5-km) scenic loop through multi-hued hills known as the Artist's Palette. South of here lie the baking salt pans of Devil's Golf Course and the Badwater Basin, the lowest point in North America. Drive back to Furnace Creek to explore the old Harmony Borax Works, before a late lunch at the 1849 Restaurant. Mark the end of your trip at Dante's View, some 5,000 ft (1,500 m) above the valley floor.

# YOSEMITE

📍California 🚗$35 per vehicle, valid for seven days; reservations required on certain dates in Feb & Apr–Oct 🌐nps.gov/yose

The second-oldest national park in the United States, Yosemite is also one of the most popular. And it's easy to see why. Located in the Sierra Nevada mountains of central California, this park has it all: stunning granite formations, three of the largest waterfalls on Earth, giant sequoia trees, and mirror-like alpine lakes. The grandeur of Yosemite's glacier-carved landscape is something that needs to be experienced at least once in everyone's lifetime.

Time takes on a different meaning in Yosemite. The dramatic granite scenery of landmark sights such as Half Dome and El Capitan is the result of millions of years of glaciers slowly sculpting the rock, while the age of many of the park's signature sequoia trees is measured in thousands of years. The state of California first protected Yosemite in 1864, and thanks largely to the lobbying of the naturalist John Muir, the area became a national park in 1890. Almost 100 years later, its exceptional natural beauty and biological diversity saw it designated a UNESCO World Heritage Site, in 1984.

## Exploring the park

Hiking is the name of the game in Yosemite. The park is home to more than 750 miles (1,200 km) of trails, and the majority of visitors arrive May through October to enjoy them, when the weather is at its best and the wildflowers are in full glorious bloom. In winter, the Tioga Road – which connects Yosemite Valley with the Tioga Pass Entrance in the east and runs past Tuolumne Meadows – closes and some trails are off-limits. April offers the best balance of activities and tranquility, and the waterfalls are in flow with the spring snowmelt in full swing.

Home to many of the park's most iconic sights, Yosemite Valley is, understandably, where the vast majority of visitors spend their time – despite it occupying less than 1 percent of the park's almost 750,000 acres (300,000 ha).

## Yosemite Valley

The park's scenic highlight, Yosemite Valley is the result of glaciers melting and moving from higher elevations during the last one million years.

### GETTING AROUND

Yosemite is about 175 miles (280 km) east of San Francisco and 60 miles (95 km) north of Fresno. The park has five entrances: the South Entrance near the Wawona area; the Hetch Hetchy, Big Oak Flat and Arch Rock entrances on the west side of the park; and the Tioga Pass Entrance in the east. Arch Rock is nearest to Yosemite Valley, while Big Oak Flat passes Tioga Road (for Tuolumne Meadows and the eastern entrance) on the way to the valley; Hetch Hetchy provides access to the park's quieter northwest section. Two busy one-way roads serve Yosemite Valley itself; explore the valley on the park's free shuttle bus, which makes stops at parking areas and all the major attractions.

The sheer granite walls of wooded Yosemite Valley ↑

↑ Admiring Half Dome, bathed in the last light of the day, from the lookout at Glacier Point

# EAT

There is a range of restaurants and stores in the park as well as in all of the gateway towns.

**The Ahwahnee Dining Room**
This historic park lodge offers fine-dining dinner buffets.
🏠 Yosemite Valley
[W] travelyosemite.com
$$$

**Curry Village**
Numerous casual options including tacos, pizza, and ice cream.
🏠 Yosemite Valley
[W] travelyosemite.com
$$$

**Village Store**
This souvenir store doubles as the park's best-stocked grocery.
🏠 Yosemite Valley
[W] travelyosemite.com
$$$

→ Bathing in the cool, clear waters of Tenaya Lake, one of the largest in the park

As you enter the valley from the western or southern entrances, the looming rock formations of El Capitan and Half Dome dominate the horizon. The largest granite monolith on the planet, El Capitan (often called El Cap for short) rises more than 3,000 ft (914 m) above the valley floor, looming over its northwest side. Its sheer face attracts expert rock climbers from all over the world. At the eastern end of Yosemite Valley, Half Dome is named for the sheer face that fronts an otherwise round mountain, and is known for the popular trail that sharply ascends 4,800 ft (1,483 m) to the summit. Both iconic peaks are remnants of a long-extinct volcano, and have been shaped over the millennia by water and ice.

Providing even more wow-factor is Yosemite Falls. Tumbling in two great leaps, Upper and Lower Yosemite Falls, the waters plunge some 2,425 ft (740 m), making this the tallest falls in North America. Visit in spring, when the waters swell with snow-melt and the falls are at their most spectacular. South of Yosemite Valley, you'll find some of the park's best panoramas at Tunnel View, just east of the tunnel to Wawona, and Glacier Point, at the end of Glacier Point Road.

## Tuolumne Meadows

Above Yosemite Valley, on the north side of the park, delightful Tuolumne Meadows is defined by the Tuolumne River and the numerous creeks that originate in the

Crossing a stream on a winter's hike in Yosemite Valley ↑

IF YOU HAVE
**A day**

Make a beeline for Yosemite Valley to take in El Capitan and Half Dome from Tunnel View, then walk to Yosemite Falls.

snowpack of the High Sierra. Primarily a roadless wilderness, it is a magnet for hikers and backpackers: the Grand Canyon of the Tuolumne River cuts east–west through about 30 miles (48 km) of the back-country here, featuring numerous waterfalls and a hiking trail. Rising over the meadows' eastern fringes, Lembert Dome is another of the park's most iconic rock formations, attracting intrepid climbers to its sheer face and hikers to the varied trails that lead up its flatter back side.

## Tenaya Lake and Hetch Hetchy Reservoir

Yosemite's largest front-country body of water, Tenaya Lake is located between Yosemite Valley and Tuolumne Meadows. It is one of the most scenic spots for a picnic lunch in all of Yosemite, and is deservedly popular for sightseeing, swimming, fishing, and boating. Several hiking trailheads start here.

In the northwestern corner of the park, Hetch Hetchy Reservoir was a controversial creation when the Tuolumne River was dammed in 1923 to provide water for the residents of San Francisco. Located at the end of Hetch Hetchy Road, just outside the Big Oak Flat Entrance, the reservoir today offers uncrowded hiking trails and fishing opportunities.

## Wawona and Mariposa Grove

Just inside the South Entrance, easy-to-access Wawona is the most developed area in the park outside of Yosemite Valley, with a hotel, golf course, horse stables, the Yosemite History Center, and other popular visitor facilities. Nearby Mariposa Grove is home to the park's largest grove of giant sequoia trees, accessible via a free shuttle that runs from the South Entrance between April and November.

## Hiking

There are more than 750 miles (over 1,200 km) of trails to explore across Yosemite, most of which lead off from the five main trailhead areas, and all of which offer a great range of topography and terrain.

Hikes within the most popular trailhead area of Yosemite Valley vary from challenging climbs to walks past waterfall. The difficult 7.2-mile (11.6-km) round trip on the Yosemite Falls Trail ascends 2,700 ft (823 m) alongside the pools and water-soaked rock faces of the waterfall's three main sections. You'll reach Columbia Rock, a viewpoint about a third of the way up the trail, after 1 mile (1.6 km) of walking and a climb of 1,000 ft (328 m), with its terrific outlook down over the valley below.

The very difficult hike to the top of Half Dome is around 14 to 16 miles (23 to 26 km), depending on the

# A LONG WALK
# JOHN MUIR TRAIL

**Length** 22 miles (35 km) one-way **Stopping-off points**
Little Yosemite Valley Campground, Sunrise High Sierra
Camp **Terrain** Mountainous and challenging

One of the most ambitious treks in the western U.S.,
the John Muir Trail runs more than 200 miles (322 km)
from the floor of Yosemite Valley to the summit of Mt.
Whitney. This short stretch can be broken into day
hikes or tackled as part of a 2- to 4-day backpacking
trip (wilderness permit required) that makes the
most of the countless offshoots found along the trail.

Locator Map

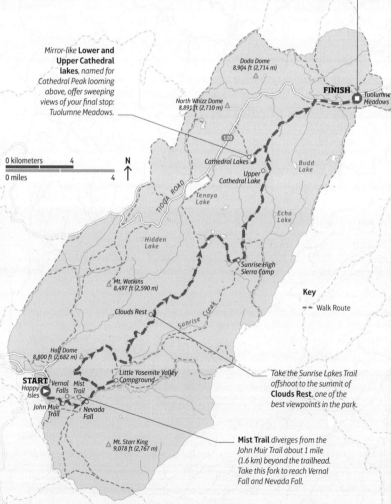

*A literal high point of the
park, **Tuolumne Meadows**
makes a great end point for
this hike. Finish the day
with a wander around the
peaceful meadows.*

*Mirror-like **Lower and
Upper Cathedral
lakes**, named for
Cathedral Peak looming
above, offer sweeping
views of your final stop:
Tuolumne Meadows.*

Doda Dome
8,904 ft (2,714 m)

North Whizz Dome
8,891 ft (2,710 m)

**FINISH** — Tuolumne
Meadows

120

Cathedral Lakes

Upper
Cathedral Lake

Budd
Lake

0 kilometers    4
0 miles    4

N

TIOGA ROAD

Tenaya
Lake

Echo
Lake

Hidden
Lake

Sunrise High
Sierra Camp

Mt. Watkins
8,497 ft (2,590 m)

Clouds Rest

Sunrise Creek

**Key**

--- Walk Route

Half Dome
8,800 ft (2,682 m)

Little Yosemite Valley
Campground

*Take the Sunrise Lakes Trail
offshoot to the summit of
**Clouds Rest**, one of the
best viewpoints in the park.*

**START**
Happy
Isles

Vernal  Mist
Falls   Trail

John Muir
Trail

Nevada
Fall

Mt. Starr King
9,078 ft (2,767 m)

**Mist Trail** *diverges from the
John Muir Trail about 1 mile
(1.6 km) beyond the trailhead.
Take this fork to reach Vernal
Fall and Nevada Fall.*

Half Dome and El Capitan towering over Yosemite Valley

route. It ascends nearly 5,000 ft (1,500 m) on the way, with cables installed on the final stretch so that hikers don't need to take climbing gear with them. A permit is required; an annual lottery for this takes place each March. If you're looking for a more manageable hike within the Valley, the 5.4-mile (8.7-km) round trip along the Mist Trail is a good option, leading up from the valley floor to the scenic cataracts at Vernal Fall and Nevada Fall. The trail to the base of Vernal Fall is moderate, but things get a bit more difficult once you pass beyond the footbridge. For fine valley views, it's hard to beat the sweeping panorama from Sentinel Dome, which is

reached on a moderate 1.8-mile (2.9-km) hike that begins on Glacier Point Road.

A natural focal point for hikes in the southern section of the park are the area's stately giant sequoia trees. The moderate Grizzly Giant Trail, near Wawona, loops for 2 miles (3.2 km) through the towering sequoias of Mariposa Grove, passing the trail's 3,000-year-old namesake – the oldest giant sequoia in the park – along the way. Another worthwhile hike while you're in the area is the difficult 8.2-mile (13.2-km) round trip on the Chilnualna Falls Trail, which culminates in the gushing five-tiered waterfall of the same name.

◉ IF YOU HAVE
**A weekend**

You can get a bird's-eye view of Yosemite Valley from Olmsted Point en route to Tuolumne Meadows for a hike in the park's high country.

Hiking in the cooler high country around Tuolumne Meadows and from the trailheads along the Tioga Road takes in mountain peaks, glacial lakes, rivers and waterfalls. Among the most popular hikes in Tuolumne Meadows itself, the Cathedral Lakes Trail is a difficult 7-mile (12.3-km) round trip to Upper and Lower Cathedral lakes, which are nestled at the foot of Cathedral Peak.

A refreshing dip awaits at the end of the Dog Lake Trail, an easy 2.8-mile (4.5-km) hike to a swimming hole. The walk also connects with trails up Lembert Dome and longer backpacking routes through Lyell Canyon.

Another much-loved Tuolumne Meadows hike is the moderate 10-mile (16-km) round trip to North Dome, near White Wolf.

### ANSEL ADAMS

Ansel Adams was 14 years old when he first visited Yosemite with his family in 1916. By age 20, he had become successful for his black-and-white images of the park, pushing physical and technical boundaries to get the perfect shot of El Capitan and the Half Dome. Ansel became one of the U.S.'s best photographers and continued to share his love for Yosemite by conducting workshops there.

↑ Cycling along a boardwalk in Yosemite Valley

A pleasant hike, it takes you to one of the best views of Half Dome in the entire park.

For a taste of the park's remote northeast corner, hit the moderate 5-mile (8-km) Wapama Falls Trail, which leads along the shore of Hetch Hetchy Reservoir to its namesake waterfall.

Boats cannot be taken on Hetch Hetchy Reservoir, but most other bodies of water in the park are open to non-motorized boats. Kayaking is popular at Tenaya Lake, and rafters take to the waters of the Merced River in Yosemite Valley. Raft rentals are available at Curry Village.

Backpacking is also very popular in Yosemite; permits are required for backcountry camping. Many visitors prefer to hike to the park's High Sierra Camps, backcountry accommodations spaced up to 10 miles (16 km) apart, with tent-cabins and dining. The spots are popular and reservations are required; a lottery is held every fall for the following summer's spots

### Rock climbing

Yosemite's granite walls are held in high regard by expert climbers. The Yosemite Mountaineering School at Curry Village offers instruction and guided climbs. A permit is required for all overnight climbs; note that few of the park's climbs are suitable for beginners.

### Cycling

More than 12 miles (19.5 km) of bike trails crisscross the Yosemite Valley, which together offer an enjoyable alternative to taking the shuttle bus. Rentals are available at Curry Village, Yosemite Village, and Yosemite Valley Lodge.

### Winter sports

Badger Pass Ski Area, on Glacier Point Road, has been operating since 1935. Five lifts serve 10 runs from mid-December to mid-March, if conditions allow. There are cross-country ski and snow-shoe trails; guide service and rentals are available.

# STAY

The park has seven lodging options, ranging from canvas tent-cabins to the luxurious Ahwahnee hotel. Rates are often lower in gateway towns.

### The Ahwahnee

Rooms at this luxury hotel have lovely views, while the Great Lounge, with its huge fireplaces, is the perfect place to relax after a hike.

🏠 Yosemite Valley
🌐 travelyosemite.com

⑃⑃⑃

### Wawona Hotel

This Victorian lodging opened in 1879 and features an outdoor pool and a golf course.

🏠 Wawona
🌐 travelyosemite.com

⑃⑃⑃

### Yosemite Bug Rustic Mountain Resort

Convivial option offering a wide range of rooms, bunks, and cabins, plus a spa.

🏠 Midpines
🌐 yosemitebug.com

⑃⑃⑃

## Camping

There are 13 campgrounds in the park, including four in Yosemite Valley. Reservations are required from May to October; a few are first-come, first-served during other times of the year. There are also numerous campgrounds in the gateways and national forests around the park.

## BUFFALO SOLDIERS

Among the first national park guardians were some 500 African American troops drawn from four all-Black regiments known as the "Buffalo Soldiers." Created in the wake of the Civil War, the regiments took on a number of military duties and performed the everyday tasks of supporting westward expansion.

The Buffalo Soldiers were responsible for keeping the peace and protecting settlers, as well as practical things like building roads and erecting telephone poles. And for three summers, between 1899 and 1904, they were dispatched to patrol the newly created Yosemite and Sequoia national parks. Drilled and disciplined, the soldiers evicted poachers, fought wildfires, tackled timber theft, and constructed the first public trails. It was hard work, often made more difficult by racial prejudice. The diplomacy, as well as the strength, with which they dealt with local trouble garnered them hard-won respect among the communities they served.

### CHARLES YOUNG

As one of the few African American officers serving in the U.S. Army, Charles Young (1864–1922) had long since proved his mettle when he was sent to Sequoia National Park in charge of his company of Buffalo Soldiers in 1903. The first Black national park super-intendent, Young galvanized his men to complete a host of infrastructure projects, including constructing roads to Moro Rock and Giant Forest. He went on to an illustrious military career, retiring as the army's highest ranked Black officer.

↑ Depiction of a group of Buffalo Soldiers, enjoying a rest beside a campfire

A park ranger dressed as a buffalo soldier, addressing park visitors ↑

# EXPLORING YOSEMITE

Located in the heart of California's Sierra Nevada, Yosemite is formed of 750,000 acres (300,500 ha) of glaciated valleys, vast meadows, jagged peaks, and vertiginous rock walls. Yosemite Valley is the most visited area, but the park extends well beyond its borders.

*Controversial with environmentalists, the* **Hetch Hetchy Reservoir** *was formed by a dam on the Tuolumne River that was completed in 1923. It is one of the park's least-visited areas.*

*The* **Yosemite Falls Trail** *scales a steep route alongside the three sections of 2,425-ft (739 m) Yosemite Falls. A mile up, Columbia Rock offers panoramic views of the valley.*

*Fronted by a nearly vertical, 3,000-ft (914-m) granite face,* **El Capitan** *is considered one of the most challenging ascents in the world for rock climbers.*

Twin Lake

Tilden Lake

Richardson Peak
9,877 ft (3,010 m)

Eleanor Creek

Mount Gibson
8,412 ft (2,564 m)

Lake Eleanor

Hetch Hetchy Reservoir

EVERGREEN ROAD

Smith Peak
7,751 ft (2,363 m)

Tuolumne Riv.

Hetch Hetchy Entrance

TIOGA ROAD

Big Oak Flat Entrance

120

Yose
Vill

Yosemite Valley Visitor Center

Yosemite Falls Trail

El Capitan
7,573 ft (2,308 m)

Cu
Vill

Tunnel View

Yosemite Valley

Ser
Do

Arch Rock Entrance

140

Nevada Fall

GLACIER POIN

Merced River

Badger Pass Ski Area

WAWONA ROAD

Chilnualna Falls

Wawona

Marip
Grove

South Entrance

41

Griz
Gia

↑ The iconic Tunnel Tree in Mariposa Grove

*The park's biggest grove of giant sequoias,* **Mariposa Grove** *has more than 500 trees, including the park's largest and oldest trees. Visitors can access the grove via hiking trail or shuttle bus.*

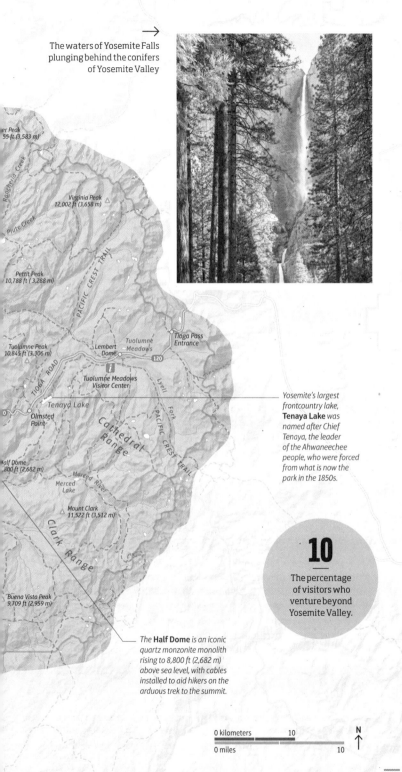

The waters of Yosemite Falls plunging behind the conifers of Yosemite Valley

er Peak
55 ft (3,583 m)

Return Creek

Virginia Peak
12,002 ft (3,658 m)

Piute Creek

Pettit Peak
10,788 ft (3,288 m)

PACIFIC CREST TRAIL

Tuolumne Peak
10,845 ft (3,306 m)

Lembert
Dome

Tuolumne
Meadows

Tioga Pass
Entrance

120

TIOGA ROAD

Tuolumne Meadows
Visitor Center

Lyell Fork

Tenaya Lake

Olmsted
Point

Cathedral
Range

PACIFIC CREST TRAIL

alf Dome
800 ft (2,682 m)

Merced River

Merced
Lake

Mount Clark
11,522 ft (3,512 m)

Clark Range

Buena Vista Peak
9,709 ft (2,959 m)

Yosemite's largest
frontcountry lake,
**Tenaya Lake** was
named after Chief
Tenaya, the leader
of the Ahwaneechee
people, who were forced
from what is now the
park in the 1850s.

**10**

The percentage
of visitors who
venture beyond
Yosemite Valley.

The **Half Dome** is an iconic
quartz monzonite monolith
rising to 8,800 ft (2,682 m)
above sea level, with cables
installed to aid hikers on the
arduous trek to the summit.

0 kilometers          10

0 miles                    10

N
↑

# SEQUOIA

 California  $35 per vehicle, valid for seven days in both Sequoia and Kings Canyon  nps.gov/seki

There's something inherently magical about a park named after the largest tree species in the world. The giant sequoia trees are the undeniable highlight of this park, but Sequoia doesn't stop there when it comes to colossal natural wonders; you'll also find Mount Whitney, the highest mountain in the Lower 48 states, along with a massive ancient cave complex deep beneath the Earth. Welcome to a land of epic proportions.

---

**IF YOU HAVE**
**A day**

Get to know the park's namesakes on the 0.7-mile (1.2-km) Big Trees Trail through Giant Forest. After, climb Moro Rock for 360-degree mountain views.

---

Established in 1980, Sequoia was America's first national park created to protect a living organism. And what a species sequoias are, some as tall as a 26-story building. Walking through groves of sequoias is awe-inspiring, but so is strolling through the rest of the park's rugged wilderness. Running through the heart of the landscape is the Great Western Divide, one of the Sierra Nevada's largest sub-ranges. Here, summits over 13,000 ft (3,960 m) pierce the sky, including Mount Whitney at a dizzying height of 14,505 ft (4,421m). These mountains overlook pristine water features, including rivers that

Best for *Gazing up at gargantuan trees*

← Giant sequoia trees, thought to be 2,200–2,700 years old

are part of the National Wild and Scenic Rivers system. Rounding out the park's geology are alluring cave systems underground.

## Exploring the park

Though jointly managed with the adjacent Kings Canyon National Park *(p64)*, Sequoia is a world unto its own. Connecting the two parks is the Generals Highway, which starts from one of Sequoia's two entrances, Ash Mountain. Most of the park's walking trails radiate out from this highway, so you can stop off at different trailheads to hike before getting back in the car to head to the next trail.

Summer is a great time to visit, when roads and trails are clear from snow (storms can occur in winter and spring). However, it's also the busiest time; fall offers a more tranquil visit, while winter sees many trails open to skiers and snowshoers.

## Giant Forest

Just off Generals Highway from Ash Mountain lies the park's most popular sight, Giant Forest. The road gains more than 5,000 ft (1,525 m) in elevation on its way here and has many switchbacks, so allow plenty of time for the drive. Once here, you'll find few sights as impressive as General Sherman, the world's largest single-stem tree.

### GETTING AROUND

Sequoia National Park is located 35 miles (56 km) north-east of the city of Visalia via Calif. Hwy. 198, which becomes the Generals Highway upon entering the park at the Ash Mountain Entrance, near the town of Three Rivers. The second entrance, Big Stump, lies farther north. From Ash Mountain, the Generals Highway sharply ascends en route to Giant Forest; this stretch often closes in winter. A free shuttle runs between Giant Forest and Lodgepole Village during the summer, as well as fall and winter holidays. The glacial Mineral King area is accessed by a dead-end road near Three Rivers. Due to road damage from winter storms, Mineral King was closed in 2023; check with the park before attempting a drive.

# EAT

There are a few dining options in the park, but many more in Three Rivers and Visalia.

### The Peaks
American fare served at Wuksachi Lodge.

🏠 Wuksachi Village
🌐 visitsequoia.com

$$$

---

### Lodgepole Café
To-go sandwiches, burgers, and burritos.

🏠 Lodgepole Visitor Center 🌐 visit sequoia.com

$$$

# STAY

Beyond the in-park lodgings below, Three Rivers and Visalia offer accommodations. There are six campgrounds in the park, too, the largest being Lodgepole and Dorst Creek north of Giant Forest.

### Wuksachi Lodge
Modern mountain lodge offering sled and snowshoe rentals.

🏠 Wuksachi Village
🌐 visitsequoia.com

$$$

---

### Silver City Mountain Resort
Cabins in a remote wooded setting with good access to trails. Serves a legendary pie in its restaurant.

🏠 Silver City, Mineral King 🌐 silvercity resort.com

$$$

To put it in perspective, this sequoia is almost 37 ft (11.3 m) in diameter at its base and weighs about 2,000 tons (1,815 metric tons). It might be hard to believe but, even at 275 ft (84 m) tall and 103 ft (31 m) around, it would be stunted by the largest sequoia ever toppled: the "Father of the Forest" was reportedly 435 ft (143 m) tall and 110 ft (34 m) in circumference.

General Sherman is far from alone here – five of the world's ten largest single-stem trees also call Giant Forest home. Take your time to explore the area, which has about 40 miles (64 km) of trails, including the easy 2-mile (3.2-km) Congress Trail, a paved loop that passes the General Sherman Tree. Another easy trail here is the 1.8-mile (2.9-km) Crescent Meadow Loop, which snakes through the forest en route to Tharp's Log, a historic cabin made from a fallen giant sequoia. For a longer hike, the Trail of the Sequoias is a moderate 6-mile (9.7-km) round trip to more remote areas of Giant Forest.

## Lakes and rivers

Beautiful water features also make up the mesmerizing landscape above ground. The park has nearly 3,200 lakes and ponds, which are essential to the survival of

→

Alta Peak, one of the park's eastern mountains and a challenging hike

wildlife, including beavers, black bears, coyotes, and the endangered yellow-legged frog. Almost at the very center of the park, Precipice Lake is quite astonishing, with other-worldly rock formations reflecting in its turquoise waters (note that getting here requires a difficult hike).

Rivers also run through the park, but these become dangerous during spring and early summer, when melting snow from nearby peaks reduces the temperature to a hazardous icy cold.

To truly immerse yourself in the park's water spectacles, embark on the Little Five Lakes Trail, a loop of around 30 miles (50 km) that starts in the subalpine glacial valley of Mineral King on the park's south side. It's worth the strenuous trek not only for the lakes, but for the dramatic waterfalls, vivid wildflower meadows, dense forests, and winding rivers along the route.

## Caves

The park astonishes below ground, too, with a network of subterranean caves and

Walking among sequoias, which have thick bark to protect them from fires ↑

tunnels. The most beloved of these is Crystal Cave, which welcomes hardy explorers from May to September. If you can bear the steep hike up through woodland and alongside ravines to the cave entrance, plus another 45 minutes of walking on the mandatory guided tour, this underground wonderland reveals its hidden pools, surreal rock formations, and a polished stream. Tours were unavailable in 2023 due to wildfire and storm damage, so check with the park for the latest information.

**IF YOU HAVE**
**A weekend**

Sign up in advance for a guided tour of Crystal Cave, then visit the General Sherman Tree. After bedding down at Wuksachi Lodge, hike the Little Five Lakes Trail from Mineral King.

### Hiking
Rounding out the park's impressive displays of nature are the surrounding mountains. The park's famed peak, Mount Whitney, sits at the eastern half of Sequoia. Although this is one of the few mountains of its size that you can hike without any mountaineering skills, the trek to the top is no mean feat. If you do attempt to tackle it, do some training at high altitudes, to prepare for the thinner air found at upper elevations.

For those up to it, summiting Mount Whitney is an experience like no other. The hike covers a distance of 22 miles (35 km) and can take up to 16 hours, so set off before sunrise. Most hikers approach from the Inyo National Forest east of the park, but others make it a 10-day trip, starting on the park's High Sierra Trail and later joining the John

↑ Putting up a tent in the clouds above Mineral King

Muir Trail. Whichever way you take, a permit is required.

Another of the park's peaks, Mount Langley is almost as high as Whitney, at 14,032 ft (4,277m), but attracts far fewer hikers due to its intense 22-mile (35-km) ascent.

For other hikes in the park (of which there are many), head west. Many multiday backpacking routes start from Mineral King or the High Sierra Trail near Giant Forest; check ahead for permits.

# EXPLORING SEQUOIA

Sequoia is a vast forested area spanning over 400,000 acres (160,000 ha) in the Sierra Nevada mountains of east California. The park is adjoined to the north by Kings Canyon National Park, with the towering Mount Whitney located on its eastern boundary.

*Named after Civil War general William Tecumseh Sherman, **General Sherman Tree** is the largest on Earth, and is still growing at 2,500 years old.*

*__Giant Forest__ is the best-known and most accessible grove of giant sequoias, the world's largest trees. A museum details the trees' ecology and ongoing decimation by logging.*

*At __Crystal Cave__, heat and pressure transformed limestone into marble over millennia. Of about 240 caves below the park's surface, this is the only one open for tours.*

Muir Grove

Wuksachi Village

Crystal Cave

Lodgepole Village

General Sherman Tree

Giant Forest

Tharp's Log

Bearpaw Meadow

GENERAL'S HIGHWAY

Middle Fork Kaweah River

Ash Mountain Entrance

Foothills Visitor Center

198

Silver City Village

East Fork Kaweah River

Lookout Point Entrance

Kaweah River

Dennison Mountain 8,650 ft (2,637 m)

← Admiring the dizzying height of the General Sherman Tree

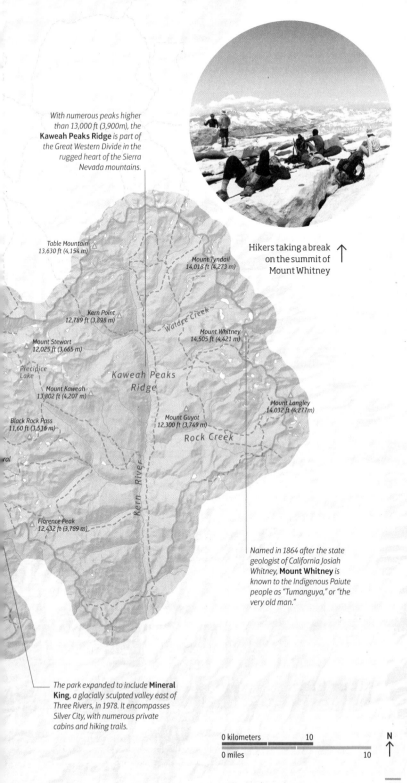

With numerous peaks higher than 13,000 ft (3,900m), the **Kaweah Peaks Ridge** is part of the Great Western Divide in the rugged heart of the Sierra Nevada mountains.

Hikers taking a break on the summit of Mount Whitney ↑

Table Mountain
13,630 ft (4,154 m)

Mount Tyndall
14,018 ft (4,273 m)

Kern Point
12,789 ft (3,898 m)

Waldee Creek

Mount Whitney
14,505 ft (4,421 m)

Mount Stewart
12,025 ft (3,665 m)

Precipice
Lake

Kaweah Peaks
Ridge

Mount Kaweah
13,802 ft (4,207 m)

Mount Langley
14,032 ft (4,277m)

Black Rock Pass
11,60 ft (3,536 m)

Mount Guyot
12,300 ft (3,749 m)

Rock Creek

ral

Kern River

Florence Peak
12,432 ft (3,789 m)

Named in 1864 after the state geologist of California Josiah Whitney, **Mount Whitney** is known to the Indigenous Paiute people as "Tumanguya," or "the very old man."

The park expanded to include **Mineral King**, a glacially sculpted valley east of Three Rivers, in 1978. It encompasses Silver City, with numerous private cabins and hiking trails.

0 kilometers        10

0 miles                        10

N ↑

## NATURE'S GIANTS

The world's largest single organism, the giant sequoia, and its even taller close cousin, the coast redwood, are surviving members of a family of trees that once thrived across the northern hemisphere, with fossil records dating relatives back more than 200 million years. Though often referred to interchangeably, these two remarkable species are quite distinct, each exploiting local conditions to reach such astonishing dimensions.

### COAST REDWOODS

The world's tallest tree, the slender coast redwood *(Sequoia sempervirens)* thrives in pockets along a narrow coastal belt that runs from Big Sur to southern Oregon, its only remaining natural habitat. Ocean fogs play an important role in the trees' prodigious growth, providing almost 40 percent of their water intake. The trees absorb moisture through their leaves, helping them replenish the water lost through transpiration – the gravity-defying process that sucks water up from the roots to the top. This clever trick enables them to reach incredible heights – only physics prevents them growing any taller.

### GIANT SEQUOIAS

Considerably more massive than the coast redwood, the giant sequoia *(Sequoiadendron giganteum)* grows naturally at altitudes of 4,000–8,000 ft (1,200–2,400 m) only on the western slopes of the Sierra Nevada. Needing vast amounts of water, giant sequoias rely on the dense snowpacks that accumulate in winter to sustain their wide root systems through the long, dry summer. Yet the dry mountain heat, and periodic fires that sweep through the forests, are also essential for their propagation. Fire clears the forest floor of competition, and the rising heat opens out the ripened cones to release seeds.

Walking among living giants in Sequoia National Park ↑

↑ Cross section of a giant sequoia tree, found in Sequoia National Park

## FOREST SENTINELS

Among the longest-living species on Earth, each capable of living over 2,000 years, redwoods and sequoias have evolved to withstand fire, infestation, and dramatic swings in climate. Unusually for conifers, coast redwoods even have the ability to regenerate after falling. But rising temperatures, drought, and ever more destructive storms and fires are placing unprecedented stresses on these battle-hardened survivors. Old-growth redwood forests store three times more carbon than any other forest, making their protection a crucial element in the battle against climate change.

### TOP 3 TUNNEL TREES

Hollowing out a living tree with a car-sized hole was once a kitsch marketing ploy.

**California Tunnel Tree**
Walk through the last surviving tunneled sequoia, in Yosemite's Mariposa Grove.

**Tunnel Log**
Carved after it fell, this tunnel tree near Moro Rock is wide enough for most cars.

**Tour-Thru Tree**
Fire-scarred but still living drive-through coast redwood off U.S. 101 in Klamath.

**Best for** *Backcountry hiking and winter adventures*

# KINGS CANYON

📍 California  🚗 $35 per vehicle, valid for seven days across both Kings Canyon and Sequoia national parks
🌐 nps.gov/seki

Kings Canyon is just one of many canyons in this park, but it certainly deserves the crown. From the canyon's depths, it's almost 2 miles (3 km) up to the summits of the surrounding peaks in the Sierra Nevada, making it the deepest in the U.S. at 8,200 ft (2,500 m). Add to that colorful alpine meadows, fast-flowing rivers, and groves of giant sequoias, and you've got a park that showcases nature at its most majestic.

What we know today as Kings Canyon National Park was initially established in 1890 as General Grant National Park. Much like its neighbor Sequoia *(p56)*, it was created to protect a small area home to giant sequoia trees, Grant Grove, at risk of logging. When naturalist John Muir *(p37)* visited the grove and its surrounds, he saw its deep valleys and epic canyon as "a rival to Yosemite," and campaigned to expand General Grant National Park to include Kings Canyon. In 1940, Muir's work paid off, with the park expanded and renamed.

## Exploring the park

Kings Canyon is largely thought of as two distinct areas: Grant Grove and Cedar Grove, the latter of which is found on the canyon floor. Roads serve the western side of the park, but the rest is pure wilderness, accessible only to hardy hikers or with rented pack-trains of horses or mules.

Given their close proximity and joint management by the National Park Service, it makes sense to combine a visit to Kings Canyon with one to adjacent Sequoia. You'll need at least a long weekend to see

---

### GETTING AROUND

Kings Canyon National Park is located about 60 miles (97 km) east of Fresno via Calif. Hwy. 180, which becomes the Generals Highway upon entering the park at the Big Stump Entrance near Grant Grove. The Kings Canyon Highway (closed in winter) culminates at Road's End on the canyon floor. The park is managed jointly with adjacent Sequoia National Park *(p56)*, which is accessible via the Generals Highway (also closed in winter) past Grant Grove. Kings Canyon Highway cuts through Giant Sequoia National Monument before reentering the park near the Grizzly Falls turnoff. Due to road damage from winter storms, Cedar Grove was closed from 2023 until summer 2024; check with the park for more information.

A picturesque stream at Darwin Bench, in the Sierra Nevada range ↑

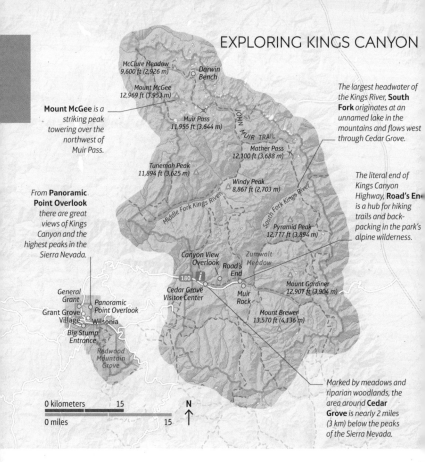

**Mount McGee** is a striking peak towering over the northwest of Muir Pass.

McClure Meadow
9,600 ft (2,926 m)

Darwin Bench

Mount McGee
12,969 ft (3,953 m)

Muir Pass
11,955 ft (3,644 m)

JOHN MUIR TRAIL

Mather Pass
12,100 ft (3,688 m)

The largest headwater of the Kings River, **South Fork** originates at an unnamed lake in the mountains and flows west through Cedar Grove.

Tunemah Peak
11,894 ft (3,625 m)

Windy Peak
8,867 ft (2,703 m)

Middle Fork Kings River

South Fork Kings River

The literal end of Kings Canyon Highway, **Road's End** is a hub for hiking trails and back-packing in the park's alpine wilderness.

From **Panoramic Point Overlook** there are great views of Kings Canyon and the highest peaks in the Sierra Nevada.

Pyramid Peak
12,777 ft (3,894 m)

Canyon View Overlook

Zumwalt Meadow

Road's End

180

Cedar Grove Visitor Center

Muir Rock

Mount Gardiner
12,907 ft (3,904 m)

General Grant

Panoramic Point Overlook

Grant Grove Village

Wilsonia

Big Stump Entrance

Redwood Mountain Grove

Mount Brewer
13,570 ft (4,136 m)

Marked by meadows and riparian woodlands, the area around **Cedar Grove** is nearly 2 miles (3 km) below the peaks of the Sierra Nevada.

0 kilometers    15

0 miles    15

N ↑

---

**IF YOU HAVE**
**A day**

See the sequoias on the short General Grant Tree Trail at Grant Grove, then drive into the canyon to hike the longer Bubbs Creek Trail.

the best of both, better yet a week or two. Plan to visit in the (albeit busier) summer months or risk contending with road closures and snow.

## Grant Grove

Here you will find some of the world's largest trees – colossal giant sequoias that are not as tall as coast redwoods, but considerably more massive. The leisurely, paved General Grant Tree Trail is an easy

0.6-mile (1-km) round trip to its namesake, the second-largest giant sequoia in the the world. At 267 ft (81 m) tall and 108 ft (33 m) in circum-ference, it's bested only by the General Sherman Tree in neighboring Sequoia. It's also known as the "Nation's Christ-mas Tree," with a ceremony held here every Christmas.

Many of the majestic trees at Grant Grove were logged in the early 20th century, and you can see the damage wrought on the easy 2-mile (3.2-km) Big Stump Loop Trail near the entrance of the same

name. The nearby Hitchcock Meadow Trail is an easy 3.5-mile (5.6-km) round trip to scenic Viola Falls.

Beyond rental cabins and dining options, Grant Grove Village also has a visitor center and a post office, as well as three campgrounds (reservations recommended).

## Cedar Grove

Though stately, Grant Grove is only a tiny fraction of the park. Almost all of the park's land area and longer trails are located in and around Kings Canyon, which stretches for

> **Here you will find some of the world's largest trees - colossal giant sequoias that are not as tall as coast redwoods, but considerably more massive.**

miles to the northeast. On the canyon floor is Cedar Grove, a gorgeous, glaciated valley and a great place to see the mighty Kings River.

On the 36-mile (58-km) drive from Grant Grove to Cedar Grove, stop for a short walk to the Panoramic Point Overlook, with views of Kings Canyon and the Sierra Crest in the distance. Then leave the car behind to take to the trails, which radiate from the highway's terminus at Road's End, 4.5 miles (7.2 km) east of Cedar Grove Village.

Highlights include the Bubbs Creek Trail, a difficult 8-mile (13-km) round trip with numerous footbridges, and the equally difficult 8-mile (13-km) round-trip hike to Mist Falls. Close by the parking lot at Road's End is the famed Muir Rock, which John Muir used as a pulpit to speak against the Sierra Nevada development.

The Cedar Grove area has lodging, dining, and three campgrounds, much like Grant Grove.

### In winter

Exploring the park is easier in spring and summer, when the roads are fully open, but that makes this time of the year busier. The winter period, which runs from late fall into late spring, has its own charms, and can be magical (road access permitting), with meadows filled with snow and sequoias dusted with swaths of white powder.

Visitors can rent skis for gentle cross-country adventures over both marked and unmarked trails. Better yet, sign up for a ranger-led snowshoe excursion. If traveling with kids, let them make the most of designated snowplay areas or sled down hills at the Big Stump area.

↑ A bridge traversing the Kings River, a 133-mile (214-km) stream of water

Admiring the view from Panoramic Point, a great place to backcountry ski ↓

## EAT

Eat at the park's two restaurants, or try the nearby city of Fresno.

**Grant Grove Restaurant**
Enjoy beef, seafood, or veggie options, with views of sequoia trees.

⌂ Grant Grove Village
[W] visitsequoia.com

$$

**Cedar Grove Grill**
Overlooking the Kings River, this place serves simple fare, like burgers and sandwiches.

⌂ Cedar Grove Village
[W] visitsequoia.com

$

## STAY

Three lodgings operate inside park boundaries.

**Cedar Grove Lodge**
Book early: this is the only lodge in the park.

⌂ Cedar Grove
[W] cedargrove.on.ca

$$

**Grant Grove Cabins**
Choose from rustic tent-cabins or modern cabins with private baths.

⌂ Grant Grove Village
[W] visitsequoia.com

$$

**John Muir Lodge**
Classic cabin hotel with open beam ceilings and a cozy fireplace.

⌂ Grant Grove Village
[W] visitsequoia.com

$$$

Photographing Zabriskie
Point, a popular spot
to capture the sunrise ↑

# DEATH VALLEY

 California   $35 per vehicle, valid for seven days
 nps.gov/deva

The lowest, hottest, and driest place in North America, Death Valley is one of the harshest environments on Earth. It's also one of the most fascinating, a long-dry ancient seabed furrowed with canyons and with millions of years of geology exposed. Despite its name, Death Valley is surprisingly biodiverse, with wildlife such as the endangered desert pupfish found here, and rainfall catalyzing colorful blooms of wildflowers in early summer.

A bleakly beautiful slice of geology laid bare, Death Valley is ringed with serpentine desert canyons below towering peaks. The geological anomalies are many, bearing foreboding names like Devils Golf Course, Hells Gate, and Dante's View.

This land of extremes has a storied human history, too. The indigenous Timbisha Shoshone called Death Valley home for about 1,000 years before the first white emigrants branded it with its current name in 1849, coined when a wagon train lost its way here during the California Gold Rush and one of the pioneers died before they found their way out of the valley again. A mining boom followed, but it wasn't until the 20th century that tourism took hold. Death Valley National Monument, established in 1933, became a national park in 1994 and now attracts more than 1 million visitors a year, despite its searingly hot summers.

### GETTING AROUND

Death Valley National Park is just west of the Nevada border in the Southern California desert, 250 miles (402 km) northeast of Los Angeles and 130 miles (209 km) west of Las Vegas. You will want a car to explore Death Valley, which at 3.4 million acres (1.4 million ha) is the largest U.S. national park outside of Alaska. Furnace Creek, the center of activity with hotels, restaurants, and other amenities, is in the heart of the park, north of Artists Palette and Badwater and south of Ubehebe Crater and Scotty's Castle. The elevation increases dramatically as you travel west, culminating at the 11,049-ft- (3,369-m-) high summit of Telescope Peak, the high point in the park.

## Exploring the park

Death Valley is the largest national park outside of Alaska, a huge area that – with more than 1,000 miles (1,600 km) of paved and dirt roads – is surprisingly accessible. The central villages of Furnace Creek and Stovepipe Wells are good places to base yourself. Both also have ranger stations, and Furnace Creek is home to the park's visitor center.

Spring is peak season for visitors, with sunny days and a carpet of gold, pink, and white wildflowers, while warm temperatures and clear skies make fall a perfect time for camping and hiking. In summer, the park becomes the hottest area in North America, when the high peaks offer a respite from the valley's blasting heat.

Badwater Basin, ↑
the lowest point
in North America

⏰ IF YOU HAVE
**A day**

Stop at Badwater Basin after an early morning canyon hike, then explore colorful Artists Palette on a 9-mile (14.5-km) scenic drive.

Note that significant floods inundated Death Valley in August 2023, closing the park at the end of the summer season. Extensive repairs to roads and facilities are ongoing; check the park website for the latest updates and information.

## Geological wonders

On the south side of the park, Badwater is an essential stop to see the seemingly endless salt flat that is the lowest place on the continent. The basin itself is desolate, but it also has numerous springs that support snails, insects, and other animals that have adapted to living in this merciless environment.

Just south of Furnace Creek, detour for the 9-mile (14.5-km) Artists Drive to see the rainbow of geology that is Artists Palette, a location for the original *Star Wars* film, and take the short side road that leads to the chaotic erosion of Devils Golf Course, the salty remnants of a long-dry lake that stretch away into the distance – the area picked up its name in 1934, when the writer of the National Park Service's guidebook to Death Valley wrote that "only the devil could play golf" on its surface, due to the clumps of rock-hard salt crystals.

On the northern side of the park, Ubehebe Crater is another geological anomaly you definitely won't want to skip. The neon orange and red crater, the result of a volcanic eruption a few hundred years ago, is a half-mile (800 m) across, and there's a short trail that takes you to its edge on a 1.5-mile (2.4-km) round trip.

The nearby Eureka Dunes, believed to be the tallest in North America, are known for the "singing" noises that occur when the sand gives way. They're reached via a 5-mile (8-km) hike. Although lacking the acoustic qualities of Eureka, the Mesquite Flat Dunes near Stovepipe Wells are easier to get to, requiring just a 2-mile (3.2-km) trek off Hwy. 190.

Perhaps one of the most mysterious places in the valley, Racetrack Playa is also one of the hardest to reach, down a 28-mile (45-km) 4WD road northwest of Stovepipe Wells. Rocks here seem to magically transport themselves across the sands, leaving tracks behind them on an ancient dry lakebed; in 2014, researchers found that the perfect combination of ice and wind allowed the rocks to move.

## Viewpoints

There are numerous lookouts in the park that afford visitors with superb views of Death Valley's banded colors and textured landscapes. Zabriskie Point, southeast of Furnace Creek, is popular with photographers aiming to capture the massive scale of their surroundings. To

### HOLLYWOOD COMES TO DEATH VALLEY

The otherworldly terrain of Death Valley has provided the background for hundreds of movies filmed here - often pinch-hitting for other worlds. *Star Wars* fans make pilgrimages to "Tatooine" and other distant planets that were actually Death Valley, a galaxy not so far away. Epics like *Spartacus* and *The Greatest Story Ever Told* were shot in and around the park, as well as dozens of Westerns, plus films including *The Doors*, *The Professionals*, and *The Godfather* trilogy.

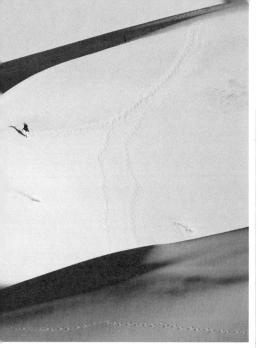

← Exploring Eureka Dunes, where the shifting sands make "singing" noises

# STAY

There's a range of lodgings in the park – at Furnace Creek, Stovepipe Wells, and Panamint Springs – as well as numerous campgrounds.

### Inn at Death Valley

Sprinkled with palm trees, this historic 1920s resort is designed in high desert style and has a picture-perfect swimming pool.

🏠 Hwy. 190
🌐 oasisatdeathvalley.com/lodging/the-inn-at-death-valley

$$$

### Ranch at Death Valley

Motel-style rooms and cottages, located in Furnace Creek and adjacent to a pool, children's playground, golf course, and horse stables.

🏠 Furnace Creek
🌐 oasisatdeathvalley.com/lodging/the-ranch-at-death-valley

$$$

### Panamint Springs Resort

Basic accommodations in a rustic property with a quirky atmosphere, on the far western edge of the park.

🏠 Panamint Springs
🌐 panamintsprings.com

$$$

---

## 134

Highest temperature in °F (56.7°C) recorded on Earth at Furnace Creek in 1913.

---

the south, above Badwater, Dante's View is another scenic overlook with dramatic valley and mountain views.

The elevation rises precipitously in the Panamint Range on the west side of Death Valley, topping out at the 11,049-ft (3,369-m) summit of Telescope Peak. You can ascend as far as 8,200 ft (2,499 m) to Mahogany Flat via Hwy. 178, where the forested terrain is much different compared to the stark valley below, and temperatures are cooler.

## Mining history

You can get a glimpse into Death Valley's mining era of the late 1800s at the ruins of Harmony Borax Works, just north of Furnace Creek, and the small but informative Borax Museum at the Ranch at Furnace Creek. Borax, or sodium borate, was used in laundry detergents, and mining operations employed teams of 18 mules and two horses to haul the wagons. One brand, 20-Mule Team Borax, even sponsored the television show *Death Valley Days* in the 1950s and 60s.

In the high country on the western side of the valley, the Wildrose Charcoal Kilns are a leftover of the silver mining that took place in neighboring Panamint Valley in the late 1800s and early 1900s. Once used to produce charcoal to refine silver ore, the ten big stone domes that remain here are in surprisingly good shape.

## Scotty's Castle

Hidden in Grapevine Canyon, Scotty's Castle has an intriguing back story – not least because it's not a castle and was never actually owned by the man after whom it's named. Built by Chicago tycoon Albert Johnson in

# EAT

Dining options can be found in the lodges in Furnace Creek and Panamint Springs *(p71)*.

### Inn Dining Room
The fine-dining option at Furnace Creek, offering steak, seafood, and pasta for dinner.

🏠 Inn at Death Valley

$$$

### Last Kind Words Saloon
Classic Western bar, with creative meals to match; open for lunch and dinner.

🏠 Ranch at Death Valley

$$$

### Ranch 1849 Restaurant
Three buffets daily, with changing entrées and a salad bar.

🏠 Ranch at Death Valley

$$$

1922, the Mediterranean-style architectural masterwork takes its moniker from the larger-than-life Walter E. Scott, the ranch's caretaker, whose tall tales – which included an imaginary gold mine and telling visitors that the castle was his own – make the building even more memorable. The castle has been closed since 2015 due to flooding and fires, but limited tours are available with advance registration.

## Hiking

Death Valley's floor is dotted with canyons, washes, and gulches that make for some excellent hiking routes. There are around two dozen trails in the park, ranging from short interpretive walks that take half an hour or so up to the difficult full-day hike up Telescope Peak and back. Experienced hikers have access to a vast area of backcountry and wilderness. Be sure to bring plenty of water (at least 2 liters for a short hike in winter, a gallon or more for longer hikes in warmer weather) and start early in the morning to avoid the midday heat.

In the valley floor, the moderate, 4-mile (6.4-km) Gower Gulch Loop starts in a canyon but ultimately

⊙ IF YOU HAVE
**A weekend**
Explore the valley floor and stay the night at Furnace Creek. Take a tour of Scotty's Castle before visiting Ubehebe Crater, and visit the park's high country on the west side.

takes hikers through a desert badlands area dominated by Manly Beacon, a monolith of sandstone; the trailhead is just south of Furnace Creek. You'll see Natural Bridge, a remarkable by-product of floods that chipped away at the rock below, just under halfway through the moderate 2-mile (3.2-km) Natural Bridge Canyon Trail, which begins farther south on Badwater Road, near the basin itself.

Stovepipe Wells is the jumping-off point for a couple of interesting canyon hikes: the moderate-to-difficult Mosaic Canyon Trail, reached off the road of the same name that runs south from the village, and the harder Grotto Canyon. The classic Mosaic Canyon route is a 4-mile (6.4-km) return hike, but many walkers only make it as far as the first set of

---

*The 20-Mule Teams*

▼ The 20-mule teams actually consisted of 18 mules and two horses at the rear. The horses' greater strength helped in starting the wagons.

▶ Three specially built wagons were hitched behind the mules. The first two each held 9 metric tons of borax, and the third hauled water and feed for a load of 33.2 metric tons.

To prevent wagons from overturning on a sharp curve, a few mules in the rear were trained to jump over the chain and pull at an opposite angle. The swamper fed the mules and cooked.

The muleskinner controlled the team by a jerkline running through the collar of each left-hand mule to the leader 80 ft (24 m) away. He guided the team with pulls.

narrows, around a quarter of the way in. Just hiking here and back reveals walls of smoothened Noonday Dolomite and patterned breccia rocks, the tiny fragments, embedded in a "natural cement," that give the canyon its name. Grotto Canyon, located east of Stovepipe Wells, is a difficult 2- to 4-mile (3.2- to 6.4-km)

hike into a ravine with numerous "grottos" carved out by raging floodwaters over the millennia.

The park's mountains offer an entirely different landscape to explore. The Telescope Peak Trail takes you on a difficult 14-mile (22.5-km) hike to the summit of the eponymous peak. The trail is only accessible from

↑ Driving along a dirt road winding through 20-Mule Team Canyon

after the snow melts in spring through late fall, and ascends nearly 3,000 ft (around 915 m) to the top of the mountain. On the way, you'll see groves of bristlecone pines, among the oldest trees on Earth. Somewhat less strenuous, Wildrose Peak Trail gains more than 2,000 ft (610 m) on a difficult 8.4-mile (13.5-km) round trip, and offers similarly stellar views of Death Valley below.

## Camping

There are seven developed campgrounds in the park, including several large ones in the Furnace Creek area; reservations are essential for all. With a high-clearance 4WD vehicle, you can also access five primitive campgrounds with free sites and limited amenities. Backpacking is also allowed; note that some routes require a park permit.

△ The man who had the idea to market a cleaning product as 20-Mule Team Borax was Stephen Mather. He would later become the first director of the National Park Service.

▽ Death Valley Days, sponsored by 20-Mule Team Borax, was a long-running television program featuring true accounts of the Old West. Past hosts included Ronald Reagan.

# EXPLORING DEATH VALLEY

Located largely within California's Inyo County, in the Great Basin east of the Sierra Nevada mountains, Death Valley is the fifth-largest park in the U.S. It spans 3.4 million acres (1 million ha), with vast portions of the park's dry basin located below sea level.

*A half-mile-diameter reminder of the volcanism underneath Death Valley, **Ubehebe Crater** is accessible via a short trail on the north side of the park.*

*Construction of the Spanish-inspired **Scotty's Castle** at the north end of Death Valley started in 1922, but the project was never fully finished. Guided tours are available today.*

Eureka Valley

Last Chance Range

Eureka Dunes

Ubehebe Crater

Sco Cas

CALIFORNIA

Dry Mountain
8,674 ft (2,644 m)

Tin Mountain
8,953 ft (2,729

White Top Mountain
7,607 ft (2,154 m)

Saline Valley

Racetrack Playa

Cotton Wood Mountains

Nelson Range

Panamint Butte
6,584 ft (2,007 m)

Panamint Springs

Ridgecrest
55 miles
(90 km)

↑ Spanish-inspired Scotty's Castle in Big Valley

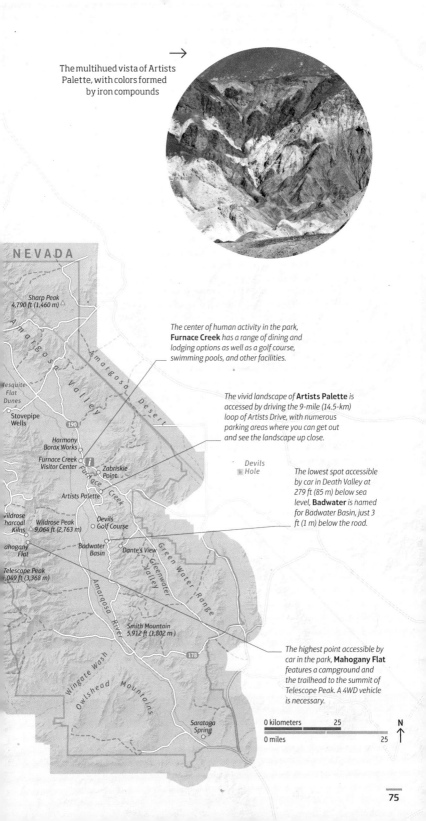

The multihued vista of Artists Palette, with colors formed by iron compounds

**NEVADA**

Sharp Peak
4,790 ft (1,460 m)

*Amargosa Valley*

*Amargosa Desert*

Mesquite
Flat Dunes

Stovepipe
Wells

Harmony
Borax Works

Furnace Creek
Visitor Center

Zabriskie
Point

Artists Palette

*Devils
Hole*

Wildrose
Charcoal
Kilns

Wildrose Peak
9,064 ft (2,763 m)

Devils
Golf Course

Mahogany
Flat

Badwater
Basin

Dante's View

Telescope Peak
11,049 ft (3,368 m)

*Green Water Valley*

*Greenwater Range*

*Amargosa River*

Smith Mountain
5,912 ft (1,802 m)

*Wingate Wash*

*Owlshead Mountains*

178

Saratoga
Spring

The center of human activity in the park, **Furnace Creek** has a range of dining and lodging options as well as a golf course, swimming pools, and other facilities.

The vivid landscape of **Artists Palette** is accessed by driving the 9-mile (14.5-km) loop of Artists Drive, with numerous parking areas where you can get out and see the landscape up close.

The lowest spot accessible by car in Death Valley at 279 ft (85 m) below sea level, **Badwater** is named for Badwater Basin, just 3 ft (1 m) below the road.

The highest point accessible by car in the park, **Mahogany Flat** features a campground and the trailhead to the summit of Telescope Peak. A 4WD vehicle is necessary.

0 kilometers 25
0 miles 25

N
↑

# JOSHUA TREE

📍 California  🚗 $30 per vehicle, valid for seven days  🌐 nps.gov/jotr

Named for the iconic yucca plant that grows here and in a few other pockets of the American Southwest, Joshua Tree National Park sits at the intersection of two vast deserts: the rugged Mojave Desert to the northwest, and the lower, hotter Colorado Desert to the southeast. Hike the trails here to see the park's fascinating desert wildlife, its signature spindly Joshua trees, and the wide array of cacti and other desert flora that manage to thrive in this landscape of baked earth.

The park is named for its numerous forests of Joshua trees, which grow densely in the open spaces of its interior. With arms outstretched, the Joshua tree earned its name from Mormon settlers exploring the Mojave Desert in the 1800s, who thought that this type of yucca plant resembled the biblical leader, Joshua. As striking as the

Joshua tree may be – especially when silhouetted against a fading, twilight sky – it is just one of a staggering variety of desert flora that is found within the park: the 750 documented plant species here include the creosote bush, wooly bluestar, shrubby honeysweet, and a number of species that are only able to flower during summer rains.

**Exploring the park**

Most visitors begin exploring Joshua Tree just outside the park itself, at one of the visitor centers in the towns of Joshua Tree or Twentynine Palms, where educational exhibits chart the area's human history and unusual plantlife. Many of the park's most famous rock formations and hiking trails are located in

← Classic Joshua tree scenery: Jumbo Rocks and the park's signature trees

its northwest section, accessed off roads that run south from the entrances near Joshua Tree and Twentynine Palms. The Cholla Cactus Garden is a popular stop on the drive to Cottonwood Springs and the park's southern entrance.

Hiking is most comfortable in the spring or fall, when temperatures range from around 70 to 85°F (21–29°C). Some trails are closed in summer, when hikes need to be started (and finished) early, to avoid the heat of the day; winter nights in the desert are often near or below freezing.

### Flora and fauna

At the Oasis of Mara at the park's North Entrance, near Twentynine Palms, a short stroll on a nature trail leads into one of the desert's rare watering holes, revealing an ecosystem of palm trees and wildlife. It's a startling departure from the arid wilderness found elsewhere.

> ⬚ IF YOU HAVE
> **A day**
>
> Hike the trails at Cap Rock and High View for the Joshua trees, then head to Keys View for a fine panoramic view of the vast Southern California desert.

→ Exploring one of the park's many strangely shaped rock formations

### GETTING AROUND

Joshua Tree National Park is located 40 miles (64 km) east of Palm Springs and 130 miles (209 km) east of Los Angeles via I-10. There are entrances in the towns of Joshua Tree and Twentynine Palms on the north side of the park, and Cottonwood Springs on the south side. A car is necessary to explore the park. From Joshua Tree, Park Boulevard leads south from the West Entrance Station to Keys View, intersecting with Pinto Basin Road near Jumbo Rocks, south of Twentynine Palms. Most of the main roads access the northwest quarter of the park, with a few rugged 4WD roads cutting through other areas. More than half of the park is designated as a roadless wilderness.

Pinto Basin Road, which bisects the park between its North and South entrances, provides easy access to a pair of hotspots for unique desert plants – the Cholla Cactus Garden (featuring a short nature trail) and Ocotillo Patch – as well as Cottonwood Springs, a lush oasis at the park's South Entrance that is a great place to spot birds.

## Rock formations and viewpoints

The central Jumbo Rocks is a good place to stop on a drive through the park, to take a look at the sculpted geological formations set among a Joshua tree forest, with wild desert stretching off in every direction.

The road beyond Jumbo Rocks leads to Sheep Pass and Ryan Mountain, at 5,456 ft (1,664 m) one of the highest peaks in the park, at which point it ends at Park Boulevard. Turning right (north) here leads to the aptly named Wonderland of Rocks, a maze of granite rocks that are a favorite with climbers.

Taking a left (south) turn onto Park Boulevard will bring you to one of the best panoramas in the West: Keys View. Here, you can see some of the lowest and highest points in Southern California, spanning the sub-sea-level lowlands of the Coachella Valley and the 11,503-ft (3,506-m) snowy peak of Mount San Gorgonio, near Palm Springs.

## Human history

Joshua Tree has a rich history. The Pinto people lived in the area for thousands of years before the idea of a park arose, and their petroglyphs mark the rocks near Barker

# EAT

There are no places to eat in the park itself, but Twentynine Palms, Joshua Tree, Yucca Valley, and Pioneertown have numerous restaurants.

**Joshua Tree Saloon**

Colorful bar and grill serving burgers, steaks, and Mexican standards.

🏠 **Joshua Tree**
[W] **joshuatreesaloon.com**

$$$

**Pappy and Harriet's Pioneertown Palace**

Legendary barbecue restaurant and live-music venue.

🏠 **Pioneertown**
[W] **pappyandharriets.com**

$$$

← Cholla Cactus Garden; the namesake cacti are native to the southwestern U.S.

# A LONG WALK
# BOY SCOUT TRAIL

Locator Map

**Length** 8 miles (13 km) one-way  **Stopping-off points** Willow Hall  **Terrain** Rocky dirt trail

In the northern reaches of Joshua Tree, this trail winds through the famed Wonderland of Rocks, a labyrinthine backcountry area with jumbles of boulders. It can be walked in a day, but an overnight backpacking trip (permit required) is recommended to experience the dark night sky of the desert wilderness. Note that the trail is very exposed, so bring plenty of water.

**Key**

-- Walk Route

Near the northern end of the Boy Scout Trail, **Indian Cove Campground** is one of the most popular campgrounds in the park.

About midway between Indian Cove and Park Blvd., **Big Pine Trail** is a 1.8-mile (2.9-km) offshoot from the Boy Scout Trail that explores the park's rugged Maze area.

BOY SCOUT TRAIL

**FINISH**

Indian Cove Campground

Maze Loop Trailhead

BIG PINE TRAIL

Maze Loop Trail

BOY SCOUT TRAIL

WILLOW HOLE TRAIL

Willow Hole

*Wonderland of Rocks*

PARK BOULEVARD

Keys Ranch

**START**

Quail Springs Trail

Keys West Trailhead

Wall Street Mill

Wonderland Ranch Ruins

Just over a mile (2 km) north of the Boy Scout Trailhead on Park Blvd. is the trail to **Willow Hole**, a rare desert oasis.

Outback Bouldering Area

Located near the trailhead off of Park Blvd., **Keys Ranch** was established in 1910 and operated for more than 60 years. It is only accessible via ranger-guided tours today.

Intersection Rock

The spectacularly craggy **Wonderland of Rocks** is a hit with climbers. The trail can be difficult to follow in this area, so use caution and follow the cairns when the trail crosses rocky areas.

0 kilometers    2

0 miles    2

N

## MINERVA HOYT

Celebrated as the first desert conservationist, Minerva Hoyt is considered the founder of Joshua Tree National Park and was a pioneer in the movement to protect the United States' wild places. A wealthy socialite from Pasadena, California, Hoyt eschewed high society in favor of the beauty of the desert. She founded the International Desert Conservation League in 1930, and in 1936 she convinced President Franklin D. Roosevelt to designate more than 800,000 acres (320,000 ha) of the California desert as Joshua Tree National Monument.

Dam and along the 4WD Geology Tour Road.

Historic Keys Ranch, near the Hidden Valley Campground on the north side of the park, was first established in the 1860s and produced livestock, fruit, and vegetables until 1969. Rangers take visitors on 90-minute guided tours of the ranch; ticket required.

The remains of several gold and silver mines dot the desert landscape around here, including a pair of mines that you can hike to on a trail: Desert Queen Mine and Lost Horse Mine.

### Hiking

By far the best way to experience Joshua Tree is hiking the park's trails. The desert wilderness begs a closer look, and that requires putting some distance between yourself and the paved road. However, this being a desert, you need to be prepared: bring plenty of water and start early to avoid the midday heat.

The California Riding and Hiking Trail runs 35 miles (56

IF YOU HAVE
**A weekend**

Base yourself in the town of Joshua Tree on the north side of the park. After exploring a Joshua tree forest and taking in Keys View, hike a longer trail: to either Lost Horse Mine or Lost Palms Oasis.

km) from Black Rock Canyon in the far northwest corner of the park to the North Entrance Station in the town of Twentynine Palms. There are six access points within the park, allowing for the trail to be split into day hikes.

Another great hike starting in Black Rock Canyon, the Hi-View Nature Trail near Yucca Valley, is a moderate 1.3-mile (2.1-km) loop that takes you past a number of big Joshua trees to a spectacular vista of the mountains and surrounding desert.

Staying in the north side of the park, the easy 1.1-mile (1.8-km) Barker Dam Nature Trail takes you to a partly

Admiring the view in the park's rocky backcountry →

Climbing Black Tide, one of over 8,000 routes in the park

humanmade remnant of the ranching area (a natural basin dammed to collect water) that continues to attract thirsty birds and other wildlife. Just to the east, at Jumbo Rocks, is the easy 1.7-mile (2.7-km) Skull Rock Nature Trail, which ends at the cranium-shaped formation of the same name.

Near Keys View, the moderate 6.2-mile (10-km) loop to Lost Horse Mine takes hikers to the ruins of one of the more productive gold-mining operations in what has since become the national park. For fine views, head for the difficult 3-mile (4.8-km) hike up steeply wooded Ryan Mountain, which starts east of here.

From Cottonwood Springs, in the south of the park, you can follow the moderate 7.2-mile (11.6-km) trail to Lost Palms, the park's largest oasis, or hike the 3-mile (4.8-km) Mastodon Peak Trail, a similarly moderate undertaking offering views of the surrounding mountains and the Salton Sea to the south.

## Rock climbing

Thanks to its unique geology, Joshua Tree is a world-class climbing destination, with more than 8,000 routes within the park's boundaries. Jumbo Rocks, Hidden Valley, and Wonderland of Rocks are among the best places to aim for. There are a number of guides who can take climbers of all skill levels on guided expeditions, including Uprising Adventure Guides *(www.joshuatreeuprising.com)*. Classes are also available.

## Cycling

There are no bike trails in the park, but cyclists are allowed on any road that is open to cars. The best places to saddle up, therefore, are often the backcountry roads, which see fewer vehicles. Ryan Campground offers a few campsites for cyclists.

## Camping

There are nine developed campgrounds in the park. Most of them are near the Jumbo Rocks and the West Entrance Station, and there's one near Cottonwood Springs at the southern entrance; some are first-come, first-served, but the largest campgrounds require advance reservations. Joshua Tree also allows backcountry camping; advance permits are required.

# EXPLORING JOSHUA TREE

Spanning the Mojave and the Colorado, two of the four deserts found in the U.S., Joshua Tree is located in southeastern California. The park's almost 800,000 acres (320,000 ha) are bordered by five mountain ranges.

*The home of a park visitor center, the beautiful **Oasis of Mara** is a non-contiguous piece of park land in the town of Twentynine Palms near Joshua Tree's North Entrance.*

*The major climbing destination of **Jumbo Rocks** captures the essence of Joshua Tree in terms of rugged geology, desert expanse, and a vast forest of the park's namesake trees.*

Twentynine Palms

Joshua Tree · Joshua Tree Visitor Center

Oasis of Mara · Oasis Visitor Center

Yucca Valley

PARK BOULEVARD

Indian Cove

North Entrance Station

Black Rock Canyon

Queen Mountain 5,677 ft (1,731 m)

Keys Ranch

Barker Dam

Mt Minerva Hoyt 5,408 ft (1,648 m)

Covington Flat

Hidden Valley

Sheep Pass

Quail Mountain 5,814 ft (1,773 m)

Cap Rock

Ryan Mountain 5,456 ft (1,664 m)

Jumbo Rocks

CALIFORNIA RIDING AND HIKING TRAIL

Little San Bernardino Mountains

Desert Hot Springs

Lost Horse Mine

Keys View 5,185 ft (1,581 m)

Pleasant Valley

Hexie Mountains

Cholla Cactus Garden

DILLON ROAD

*One of the best places for a view in Southern California, **Keys View** is well worth the drive or hike.*

Monument Mountain 4,834 ft (1,474 m)

Palm Springs 33 miles (53 km)

*Accessible via a trail, the largely intact ruins of **Lost Horse Mine** give hikers a glimpse into a different era of the park.*

Cottonwood

*You can hike a steep trail all the way to the top of the 5,456-ft (1,663-m) **Ryan Mountain** for a perfect view of the surrounding wilderness.*

← A paved trail leading through the Oasis of Mara

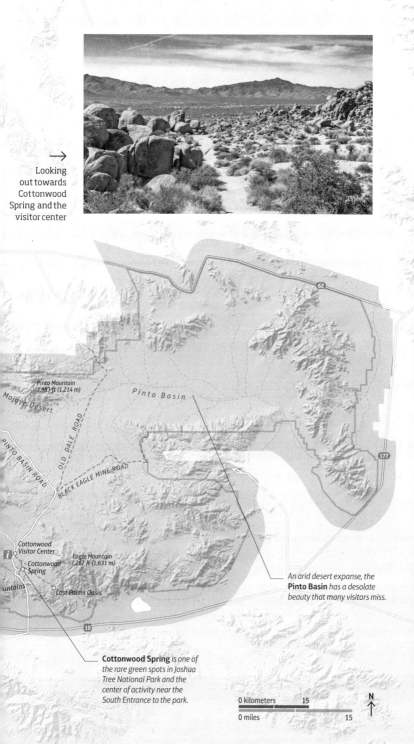

→ Looking out towards Cottonwood Spring and the visitor center

Pinto Mountain
3,983 ft (1,214 m)

Mojave Desert

Pinto Basin

PINTO BASIN ROAD

OLD DALE ROAD

BLACK EAGLE MINE ROAD

Cottonwood Visitor Center

Cottonwood Spring

Eagle Mountain
7,267 ft (1,631 m)

untains

Lost Palms Oasis

An arid desert expanse, the **Pinto Basin** has a desolate beauty that many visitors miss.

**Cottonwood Spring** is one of the rare green spots in Joshua Tree National Park and the center of activity near the South Entrance to the park.

0 kilometers    15
0 miles    15

N

*Best for Wildlife watching
and sea kayaking*

# CHANNEL ISLANDS

California  Free, but you will need to pay for transportation by boat to access the islands  nps.gov/chis

Collectively nicknamed North America's Galapagos for their unique wildlife, the Channel Islands are made up of eight biodiverse islands, all of which lie off the coast of Southern California. Five of these islands form the Channel Islands National Park, an ecological haven surrounded by stunning ocean habitats. Though the park is only a short trip from Los Angeles, it feels a world away, with vertiginous cliffs, nesting seabirds, and coastal inlets rich in marine life.

The five islands that comprise the national park – Anacapa, Santa Cruz, Santa Rosa, San Miguel, and Santa Barbara – were formed by undersea volcanic activity over the course of hundreds of thousands of years. Strung along a 40-mile (64-km) chain in the Pacific Ocean, the islands are the northernmost of the eight Channel Islands. They are surrounded by a vast marine environment with an array of rare and delicate habitats including giant kelp forests, rocky reefs, seagrass, and submarine canyons.

Such habitats mean plenty of wildlife: more than 1,000 species of fish, invertebrates, and algae are found here, and the park provides essential nesting grounds for more than 90 percent of seabirds found in Southern California.

Humans have inhabited the islands to some degree for more than 12,000 years, with the islands long home to the native Chumash peoples. Today, they offer a stunning glimpse of what coastal California could look like without development. Relatively few people visit the islands: only about 100,000 people come to the park annually, meaning you will have plenty of chances to take in the spectacular landscapes all by yourself.

## Exploring the park

The Santa Barbara Channel, which separates the islands from the mainland, can only be crossed by park boats (Island Packers) or private boat. The waters of the park see many more visitors than the islands themselves. The prime activities on solid ground are hiking and wildlife watching, while the waters offer world-class kayaking and diving.

## EAT

There are no restaurants in the park, but numerous eateries and grocery stores can be found in Ventura.

**Andria's Seafood**
A fresh seafood market that doubles as a popular restaurant near the ferry dock.

🏠 Ventura [W] andrias-seafood.com

$$$

**Sandwich Factory**
Reasonably priced box lunches for day trips.

🏠 Ventura
☎ (805) 650-0465

$$$

**Harbor Market & Liquor**
A well-stocked market that's good for sourcing lunch or camping provisions for the islands.

🏠 Ventura [W] ventura-harborvillage.com

$$$

← The Channel Islands, strung along the Pacific coast of Southern California

> **Blue and humpback whales can be seen when crossing the Channel during the summer months, as well as major populations of fish, seals, and sea lions.**

Blue and humpback whales can be seen when crossing the Channel during the summer months, as well as major populations of fish, seals, sea lions, starfish, lobsters, and various other aquatic species.

## Anacapa

Located about 15 miles (24 km) west of Ventura, Anacapa Island is the closest island (or islands: it's actually three islets) to the coast and is known for its thriving seabird population. It's notably small (just 640 acres or 259 ha), with a 2-mile (3.2-km) hiking trail, museum, and a historic lighthouse, plus campground.

## Santa Cruz

About 10 miles (16 km) west of Anacapa, Santa Cruz Island is the largest island in the park (and the state of California) and a good destination for both day and overnight trips. The eastern quarter of the island is a former ranch that has been part of the park since 1997, and the western side of the island, which features the island's highest peak, the 2,400 ft (740 m) Mount Diablo, is owned by the Nature Conservancy. It's typically not open to visitors to protect the rare species living there.

The island has a number of hiking trails, ranging from short and easy walks to scenic overlooks, to the difficult 10-mile (16-km) Montañon Ridge Loop, which explores the park's mountainous terrain. It's a good place to see the tiny island fox, only found on the Channel Islands and the smallest fox species in North America.

On the northwest side of the island, Painted Cave (or Valdez Cave) is the largest known sea cave on Earth, with a 160-ft (50-m) ceiling inside its entrance; it's a major draw for sea kayakers.

## Santa Rosa

Windy and rugged Santa Rosa Island, 6 miles (9.5 km) west of Santa Cruz, is the second-largest island in the park. It's the best island for backpackers, with numerous trails making multiday trips a fine possibility.

---

> **GETTING AROUND**
>
> This is the rare park that is not accessible by car, but there are visitor centers on the mainland in Ventura and Santa Barbara for those who don't have the time for a visit to the islands themselves. Island Packers Cruises (*www.islandpackers. com*) offers ferries to the islands from Ventura Harbor, as well as a ferry to Anacapa from Oxnard Harbor. The islands are also accessible by private boats, but once on the islands the only transportation is via foot or kayak. Crossings to Anacapa and Santa Cruz are year-round (1–1.5 hours each way), and trips to Santa Rosa and San Miguel occur April to November (3–4 hours). Due to dock damage, Island Packers has not been running trips to Santa Barbara since storms damaged the pier in 2015, but it is open to private boats.

↑ Hiking the verdant hills of Santa Rosa in summer

↑ The islands' sea lions, known to be vocal in breeding season

## STAY

There are no overnight lodging options beyond campgrounds on the islands. Visitors tend to stay in Ventura.

**Crowne Plaza Ventura Beach**
This 12-story hotel is adjacent to Ventura Pier and a short walk to downtown.

[⌂] Ventura
[W] cpventurabeach.com

$$$

**Ventura Beach Marriott**
A modern hotel conveniently located at the harbor for early morning ferries.

[⌂] Ventura
[W] mariott.com

$$$

**The Pierpont Inn**
A historic lodging with hotel rooms and cottages within walking distance of San Buenaventura Beach.

[⌂] Ventura
[W] pierpontinn.com

$$$

IF YOU HAVE
**A weekend**

Backpack to a secluded beach at Santa Rosa and learn about the culture of the Chumash people. The remains of eight villages have been found on the island.

The landscape is dotted with hundreds of archeological sites that owe their existence to the Indigenous Chumash people, who lived on the island for more than 12,000 years; the last 50 villagers were forcibly removed in the early 19th century. It also has a unique ecosystem and is one of only two locations where rare Torrey pine trees grow (the other being the San Diego area). The island has a campground near Bechers Bay on its east side and allows camping on a few remote beaches August to September (permit required).

### San Miguel

The farthest west of all of the Channel Islands, San Miguel Island is also the wildest. A former military outpost and bombing range, it sees very few visitors, the wind howls regularly, and the caliche forest, consisting of the calcified remains of trees, looks like something from another planet. The island is also home to a large population of sea lions during breeding season in late spring and early summer.

Many people visit in June to take the ranger-led 15-mile (24-km) round-trip hike to Point Bennett. Visitors have been known to see as many as 30,000 animals roaming during a single hike. There is a campground near the remnants of an old ranch on the island's east side.

### Santa Barbara

The second-smallest and southernmost island in the park, Santa Barbara Island can be explored in an afternoon, but requires a three-hour boat ride from Ventura Harbor. Most visitors come to see the resident elephant seals, the largest pinniped in the park: the males can weigh as much as 6,000 lbs (2,700 kg). There are a few hiking trails and a good campground (if you want to stay longer), as well as a historic lighthouse and a small museum.

# EXPLORING CHANNEL ISLANDS

Channel Islands National Park consists of five of the eight Channel Islands located off the Pacific coast of California. The park covers around 250,000 acres (100,000 ha), with Santa Cruz Island the largest of the eight.

*Santa Barbara Channel*

The largest sea cave on Earth, **Painted Cave** (also called Valdez Cave) is named for the colorful rocks, lichens and algae on its walls. It is about 100 ft wide and a quarter-mile (0.4-km) long.

The westernmost tip of San Miguel Island, **Point Bennett** is the summer home to about 30,000 sea lions. The point is accessible via a 15-mile (24-km) hike guided by rangers.

Harris Point

Prince Island

Cuyler Harbor

Point Bennett Trail

Caliche Forest

Point Bennett

*San Miguel*

*San Miguel Passage*

*Santa Rosa*

Lobo Canyon

Bechers Bay Pier

Torrey Pines

Soledad Peak 1,574 ft (480 m)

South Point

Painted Ca

*Santa Cruz Channel*

0 kilometers — 10
0 miles — 10

N ↑

**Bechers Bay Pier** is the point of entry for ferries arriving at Santa Rosa Island from the mainland; the pier offers easy access to the campground, ranger station and trails.

*Pacific Ocean*

← Anacapa Island Lighthouse, a beloved symbol of the park

↑ Painted Cave, named for the striking natural colors of the rock

to Santa ↓ Barbara

*Santa Cruz*

Ventura ↗

Scorpion Ranch ⌂
Montañon Ridge Loop ⊙
Montañon Peak
1,808 ft (551 m)
Scorpion Anchorage ⊙
*Smuggler's Cove*

Oxnard ↗

Landing Cove
Visitors Center ℹ︎
Anacapa Island Lighthouse
Summit Peak
936 ft (284 m)

*Anacapa*

Mount Diablo
?31 ft (741m)
Prisoner's Harbor ⊙
*Central Valley*

?orse
?int

Ranchers raised livestock at **Scorpion Ranch** on Santa Cruz Island from the 1850s to the 1990s, when the eastern part of the island became part of the national park. The ranch house, which dates to 1887, is still standing.

Operational since 1932, the fully automated **Anacapa Island Lighthouse** is an icon of the islands.

## SANTA BARBARA ISLAND

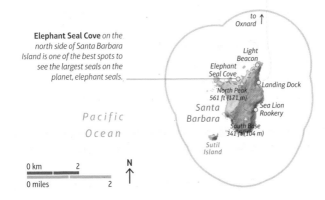

**Elephant Seal Cove** on the north side of Santa Barbara Island is one of the best spots to see the largest seals on the planet, elephant seals.

to ↑ Oxnard ↑

Light Beacon
Elephant Seal Cove
Landing Dock
North Peak
561 ft (171 m)
Sea Lion Rookery

*Santa Barbara*

South Base
341 ft (104 m)
Sutil Island

*Pacific Ocean*

0 km 2
0 miles 2

N ↑

# PINNACLES

📍 California  🚗 $30 per vehicle, valid for seven days  🌐 nps.gov/pinn

It may be one of the U.S.'s smallest national parks but Pinnacles is mighty. High in the hills above the Salinas Valley, this park preserves 16,000 acres (6,500 ha) of incredible landscape forged from the forces of volcanic eruptions and tectonic uplift, bringing you closer to California's fascinating and tumultuous geological past. Keeping watch over this landscape of rocky outcroppings, talus caves, and low valleys is the California condor, a spectacular species to watch soar and swerve around the park's trademark pinnacles.

**IF YOU HAVE**
**A day**

Set out on the park's signature High Peaks Trail, a moderate but steep walk that gives panoramic views of rock spires jutting out along the ridgeline.

Over a century ago in 1908, President Theodore Roosevelt declared this area a National Monument, to protect and preserve the unique geologic formations found here. Such amazing geology is a result of a volcano that, over a period of some 20 million years, has inched about 200 miles (320 km) north from its original location on the San Andreas Fault. This fault split the volcanic mass of the Pinnacles-Neenach volcanic field in two, while wind and water transformed the rock into superb formations.

In 2013, Pinnacles was redesignated as a national park, and is one of the smallest parks in the U.S.

←

Spire-like volcanic rock formations, formed over 20 million years ago

Today, it serves as a reminder of the volcanic and tectonic mechanics below California's often serene surface.

## Exploring the park

Given the park's rugged landscape and the solid ridge of former lava running through its center, there are no roads, so driving isn't do-able. In the place of roads are many well-maintained hiking trails, providing the only way to explore the park. As a result, visits are most pleasant in the spring, when temperatures are more appropriate for walking, and wildflowers are in bloom along the trails.

## Hiking

The Bear Gulch Day Use Area, near the East Entrance, is a good place to start exploring.

The Moses Spring and Rim trail here comprises a moderate 2.2-mile (3.5-km) loop that leads up through a superb selection of rock formations, ending at Bear Gulch Cave. The cave is typically open to the public from mid-July to mid-May (bring a flashlight if entering), but note that it's closed to hikers when bats are nesting.

Climbing the short Moses Spring and Rim trail ↑

→
Camping out under the stars at Pinnacles Campground

# EAT

There are no restaurants in the park, nor any close to the East Entrance, but you'll find a wide range of places to eat in Soledad, not far from the West Entrance.

### Cocuyos Restaurant
Mexican restaurant serving up tacos, fajitas, and other classics.

 Soledad
📞 (831) 237-5004

$ $ $

# STAY

Beyond the park's campground, you'll find motels in Soledad, as well as ranches near the East Entrance.

### Bar SZ Ranch
A large ranch with camping and glamping options as well as a cabin and Ranch House.

 Paicines
🌐 barszranch.com

$ $ $

### Inn at the Pinnacles
Comfortable and pastoral B&B with a pool outside the West Entrance of Pinnacles.

🏠 Soledad
🌐 innatthepinnacles.com

$ $ $

↑ California condors, with a distinguishing white pattern on their wings

Also found in the eastern section is the trailhead for the difficult 9-mile (14.5-km) Chalone Peak Trail, which traverses the highest mountain in the park at 3,304 ft (1,007 m).

If you're entering from the park's West Entrance, set off on a longer hike from the Old Pinnacles Trailhead. The moderate 5.3-mile (8.5-km) route to Balconies Cave takes you to another haven for the park's bats.

## Wildlife encounters
Rewarding those who hike the many trails is a sighting of the California condor, an endangered species and a prime reason for the park designation in 2013. The birds, which were nearly extinct as of 1980, have recovered to a population of roughly 300 in the wild, and about 25 of them live in Pinnacles year-round. With nearly a 10-ft (3-m) wingspan, the birds are impressive to behold while in flight, and the best place to see just that is from the High Peaks area in the heart of the park, which is accessible from both the East and West entrances but requires a long and difficult hike.

A wide range of other wildlife call Pinnacles home, including mountain lions, bobcats, gray foxes, black-tailed deer, over 20 species of raptor, acorn woodpeckers, and Townsend's big-eared bats, often found roosting in talus caves.

## Rock climbing
Forests of tangled chaparral, rolling hills, and valleys might be a magnet for wildlife, but it's the park's signature cliffs that draw many. There are climbs to suit all skill levels here, but it's best to check with the park for information and regulations; Friends of Pinnacles (*pinnacles.org*) maintains a list of outfitters.

IF YOU HAVE
### A weekend
Get closer to the park's wildlife and spend your first day hiking the Old Pinnacles Trail, ending at the Balconies Cave to see bats roosting. Bed down at the campsite, then lace up your boots the next morning for the Chalone Peak Trail – a popular haunt for the California condor.

## Camping

A colossal adventure land, Pinnacles is the kind of park to pitch a tent after an active day. Pinnacles Campground is located on the east side, and can only be accessed by vehicles from the East Entrance. RV, tent sites, and a few glamping cabins are available, but reservations are recommended; tent and RV sites can be reserved up to six months in advance. Ranger-led activities keep adventurers busy at night, too, with the likes of Star Parties and night hikes offered.

### GETTING AROUND

Pinnacles National Park is located around 113 miles (182 km) southeast of San Francisco. There are entrances on the west and east sides of the park, but no roads cross the park. Calif. Hwy. 146 enters the park on the west side from Soledad, the largest city in the area, around 10 miles (16 km) to the southwest. From the West Entrance, you can access a number of trailheads and a picnic area. The main park visitor center and campground are on the east side of the park, where Calif. Hwy. 25 enters the park as Pinnacles Parkway. Entering at the east will take you to the trailheads at Old Pinnacles and Bear Gulch. The east side of the park is much less developed, though, with the small towns of San Benito and Paicines near the entrance. To move between the entrances, the shortest route is to drive through the town of King City on Hwy. 101.

# EXPLORING PINNACLES

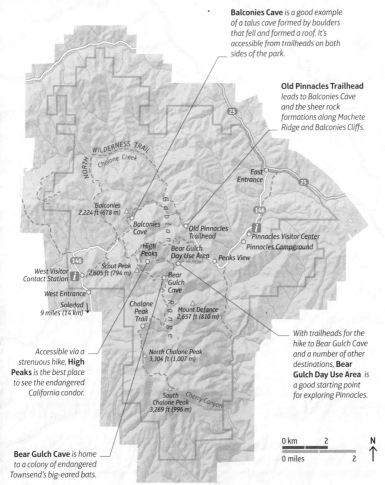

**Balconies Cave** is a good example of a talus cave formed by boulders that fell and formed a roof. It's accessible from trailheads on both sides of the park.

**Old Pinnacles Trailhead** leads to Balconies Cave and the sheer rock formations along Machete Ridge and Balconies Cliffs.

With trailheads for the hike to Bear Gulch Cave and a number of other destinations, **Bear Gulch Day Use Area** is a good starting point for exploring Pinnacles.

Accessible via a strenuous hike, **High Peaks** is the best place to see the endangered California condor.

**Bear Gulch Cave** is home to a colony of endangered Townsend's big-eared bats.

*Best for Geothermal features and volcanic sightseeing*

# LASSEN VOLCANIC

📍 California  🚗 $30 per vehicle, valid for seven days ($10 Dec–mid-April)  🌐 nps.gov/lavo

The southernmost volcano of the Cascade Mountains, which stretch from British Columbia down to northern California, Lassen Peak last roared to life over a century ago, when a series of eruptions culminated in a massive blast in 1915. Today, the park surrounding the peak is a living reminder of Earth's ever-changing and volatile landscape, home to wildflower meadows, boiling mudpots, and all four types of volcano: plug dome, shield, cinder cone, and stratovolcano.

Lassen Volcanic National Park is dominated by the world's largest plug dome volcano: Lassen Peak. For centuries, the region around the peak was a meeting place and hunting ground for the Atsugewi, Yana, Yahi, and Maidu peoples, who hunted deer and gathered plants in land that nows falls within the park's boundaries.

On May 22, 1915, an explosive eruption at Lassen Peak wreaked havoc on the surrounding flanks and nearby forests, devastating entire areas and raining volcanic ash as far as 200 miles (320 km) away. The national park was established a year later to protect the remarkable landscapes from further damage.

More than 100 years later, the area is recovering, with a wide range of trees and plants taking root. The park today is a fascinating case study in volcanism, as well as a hiker's paradise with more than 150 miles (240 km) of trails to explore. It is also home to a wide range of wildlife, including black bears, mountain lions, and mule deer. Best of all

**IF YOU HAVE**
**A day**

Take a leisurely drive (or cycle) through the park on the 30-mile (48-km) highway, stopping at viewpoints to admire the landscape.

might be the 50 serene lakes, perfect places for a walk around the shore.

## Exploring the park

Located around three hours northeast of Sacramento by car, the park has two entrance stations at both ends of the 30-mile (48-km) park highway. Most visitors begin by driving the highway, which leads past some of the park's most incredible landscapes.

Though the park is beautiful in winter, it can be incredibly hard to access by road due to heavy snowfall.

## Volcanic sights

The fiery furnace below Lassen makes itself known at several locations throughout the park. Take care when exploring: the ground above

these boiling and acidic features may be fragile and hiking off-trail is forbidden.

Bumpass Hell is a good place to start, with a short trail that starts just inside the southwestern entrance. The moderate 3-mile (4.8-km) hike takes you through the largest geothermal area in the park (and the largest this side of Yellowstone), full of steaming fumaroles, bubbling mud pots, and hot springs. Nearby, Sulphur Works is the easiest geothermal feature to access in Lassen, and you'll likely smell the vent before you arrive.

↑ Lassen's volcanic landscapes seen from the Lassen Peak Trail

In nearby Warner Valley, you can hike to Devils Kitchen, the second-largest geothermal area in the park, on a moderate 4.2-mile (6.8-km) trail, or take the easy 3-mile (4.8-km) hike to Boiling Springs Lake. Add 1.4 miles (2.3 km) each way and you can make it to the billowing steam of Terminal Geyser.

The Devastated Area offers insights into eruptions and subsequent regeneration.

### GETTING AROUND

Lassen Volcanic National Park is located 45 miles (75 km) east of Redding via California Hwy. 44. Typically open mid-June to late November, the main road (California State Route 89) loops into the heart of the park from the entrances in the northwestern and southwestern corners, with access to the park's sights including the Lassen Peak Trail as well as Bumpass Hell, Summit Lake, and Sulphur Works. Many facilities, including a camp-ground, cabins, and store, are located near Manzanita Lake at the northwestern entrance station, and the Kohm Yah-mah-nee Visitor Center is at the southwest entrance. Drakesbad Guest Ranch and Juniper Lake are accessed by Warner Valley Road and Juniper Lake Road, respectively, in the southeastern corner of the park, and the road to Butte Lake is south of California Hwy. 44 on the northeast side of the park.

Make the most of the park's scenic highway, explore Bumpass Hell's geothermal features, hike the Lassen Peak Trail, and stroll the shore of Manzanita Lake for a great trip.

Located 10 miles (16.1 km) from the northwest entrance, a short interpretive trail allows you to see the landscape up-close and read exhibits on the eruption that created it.

With their own entrances, unconnected to the main road, Juniper Lake and Butte Lake see less traffic than other areas of the park, so take the time to visit them if you're looking for solitude.

### Hiking

If you have time for just one big hike in the park, it's hard to beat Lassen Peak Trail, a difficult 5-mile (8-km) route that takes you to the 10,457-ft (3,187-m) summit of its namesake. From here, views of the lava-scarred landscape provide wider insight into the effects of volcano damage.

Just inside the northwest entrance, Manzanita Lake Trail is an easy 2-mile (3-km) route around the lake, and connects to a short trail to mirror-like Reflection Lake. From the same trailhead, you can access the Manzanita Creek Trail to the south. This 7-mile (11-km) route is a more difficult hike, but leads to an alpine meadow with great mountain views.

The easy 1.5-mile (2.5-km) Summit Lake Trail connects to a difficult 11-mile (17.7-km) loop to Echo Lake, Twin Lakes, and Cluster Lakes, which is popular for camping.

From Butte Lake, the moderate 4-mile (6.5-km) Cinder Cone Trail takes you to the top of a barren volcano surrounded by colorful dunes and lava beds.

Running from Mexico to Canada, the vast Pacific Crest Trail cuts through the park for 18 miles (29 km).

*Timeline*

*825,000 BCE*
A 9-mile (15-km) ring of plug-dome volcanoes erupts, spewing ash and lava, and forming the Lassen Volcanic Center.

*1850s*
▽ The first settlers arrive with the California Gold Rush. Pioneers Peter Lassen and William Nobles build the area's first trails.

*600,000–350,000 BCE*
The stratovolcano Mount Tehama explodes, creating a caldera 2 miles (3 km) wide.

*1500s–present*
△ For centuries, Lassen is the fertile hunting and fishing grounds for Indigenous tribes such as the Yana.

*1907*
△ Lassen Peak and Cinder Cone are established as National Monuments under President Theodore Roosevelt.

## On the water
Non-motorized boats are permitted on several lakes in the park, including Manzanita Lake and Summit Lake. Kayak, canoe, and paddle board rentals are available at the store at Manzanita Lake.

## In winter
Lassen is notoriously snowy in winter, with the main road closing in November, but the

↑ Looking out over the still surface of Manzanita Lake

park is open to snowshoers and cross-country skiers. Both entrances are open and rangers often lead guided outings; popular routes include the trails to Sulphur Works and Lake Helen.

## Camping
There are eight campgrounds in the park; some accept reservations and others are first-come, first-served. The largest is at Manzanita Lake, with a store and flush toilets, but you'll likely find more peace and quiet in Warner Valley or Butte Lake. The Southwest Campground is the only one that is open year-round.

Lassen is also a popular spot with backpackers who take advantage of the short summer season on multiday trips into the backcountry. Permits and bear-resistant food containers are required for campers.

*1914–1917*

After a 27,000-year nap, Lassen Peak Volcano awakens with a bang. A series of eruptions take place over three years.

*1916*

This active volcano park is established as a national park on August 9, in the midst of its three-year volcanic run.

# EAT

There is one restaurant in the park, but you'll find more in Chester and other nearby towns.

### Lassen Café
Sandwiches, salads, and ice cream; indoor and outdoor seating.

⌂ Kohm Yah-mah-nee Visitor Center
☎ (530) 595-3555

### Kopper Kettle Café
Hearty American fare like steaks, meat loaf, and fried chicken.

⌂ Chester 🖳 kopper-kettlecafeca.com

# STAY

The park has two overnight options; there's more choice in Chester, Mineral, and Mill Creek.

### Drakesbad Guest Ranch
An all-inclusive guest ranch offering horse riding and a pool heated by natural hot springs.

⌂ Chester
🖳 lassenlodging.com

### Manzanita Lake Camping Cabins
Basic cabins with a shared bathroom in the park's northwest.

⌂ Manzanita Lake
🖳 recreation.gov

# EXPLORING LASSEN VOLCANIC

Located in northern California, Lassen Volcanic's 100,000 acres (40,000 ha) straddle three unique biological areas: the Cascade Mountains, the Sierra Nevada Mountains, and the Great Basin.

**Did You Know?**

The Dixie Fire in 2021 burned more than half of Lassen Volcanic's total area.

*The place most impacted by the eruptions in the 1910s and 20s, the* ***Devastated Area*** *is north of Lassen Peak. A short loop trail shows you the forest's recovery.*

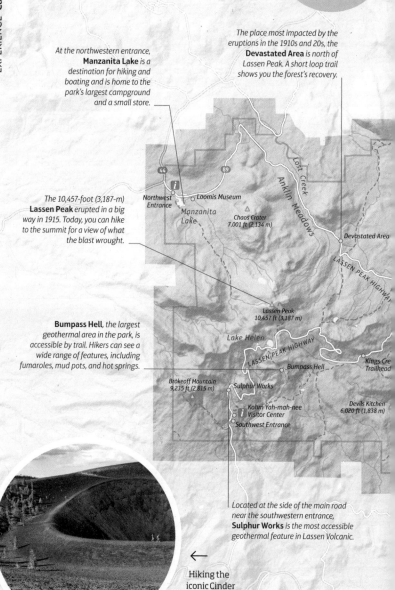

*At the northwestern entrance,* ***Manzanita Lake*** *is a destination for hiking and boating and is home to the park's largest campground and a small store.*

*The 10,457-foot (3,187-m)* ***Lassen Peak*** *erupted in a big way in 1915. Today, you can hike to the summit for a view of what the blast wrought.*

44
89
Northwest Entrance
Loomis Museum
Manzanita Lake
Chaos Crater 7,001 ft (2,134 m)
Lost Creek
Anklin Meadows
Devastated Area
LASSEN PEAK HIGHWAY
Lassen Peak 10,457 ft (3,187 m)
Lake Helen
LASSEN PEAK HIGHWAY
Bumpass Hell
Kings Cre Trailhead
Brokeoff Mountain 9,235 ft (2,815 m)
Sulphur Works
Kohm Yah-mah-nee Visitor Center
Southwest Entrance
Devils Kitchen 6,020 ft (1,838 m)


***Bumpass Hell****, the largest geothermal area in the park, is accessible by trail. Hikers can see a wide range of features, including fumaroles, mud pots, and hot springs.*

*Located at the side of the main road near the southwestern entrance,* ***Sulphur Works*** *is the most accessible geothermal feature in Lassen Volcanic.*

← Hiking the iconic Cinder Cone Rim

↑ Boardwalk leading through the hydrothermal Bumpass Hell

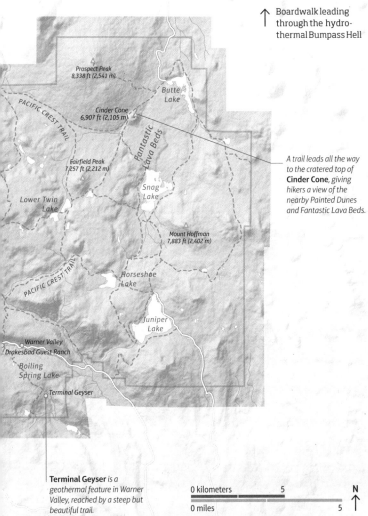

Prospect Peak
8,338 ft (2,541 m)

Butte
Lake

PACIFIC CREST TRAIL

Cinder Cone
6,907 ft (2,105 m)

Fantastic
Lava Beds

Fairfield Peak
7,257 ft (2,212 m)

Snag
Lake

Lower Twin
Lake

Mount Hoffman
7,883 ft (2,402 m)

PACIFIC CREST TRAIL

Horseshoe
Lake

Juniper
Lake

Warner Valley
Drakesbad Guest Ranch

Boiling
Spring Lake

Terminal Geyser

*A trail leads all the way to the cratered top of* **Cinder Cone***, giving hikers a view of the nearby Painted Dunes and Fantastic Lava Beds.*

**Terminal Geyser** *is a geothermal feature in Warner Valley, reached by a steep but beautiful trail.*

0 kilometers    5

0 miles    5

N ↑

Best for *Walking among giants and woodland wildlife*

# REDWOOD

📍California 🎫Free 🌐nps.gov/redw

Jointly managed by the park service and the state of California, Redwood National and State Parks protect nearly half of all remaining old-growth coast redwoods. While the redwoods, a few of which top 370 ft (113 m), take top-billing, the forests found here are also home to Sitka spruce, Douglas fir, and other trees and plants that provide a refuge for a variety of wildlife. And beyond the trees? The parks also encompass a pristine stretch of the Pacific coast, providing rugged sea views and ample opportunity for coastal hikes.

Named for their thick red bark, coast redwoods (*Sequoia sempervirens*) are the main attraction of the parks (*p62*). Words don't do justice to these magnificent trees; you need to see them for yourself to appreciate just how truly massive they are. The tallest one, Hyperion, measures 380 ft (115 m) in height. Some coast redwoods also live to be more than 2,000 years old, but there aren't that many ancient examples left. Two centuries ago, there were about 2 million acres (809,000 ha) of coast redwoods in California and Oregon. With the wood being prized by carpenters, commercial logging began in the mid-1800s, and less than 5 percent of the old-growth

forest remains today. Roughly half of it is found in the areas that make up Redwood National and State Parks, or about 40,000 acres (16,200 ha) in all.

It's not all about the trees, though. A wide variety of ferns and mosses grow under the lofty canopy, and the dynamic ecosystem supports Roosevelt elk, banana slugs, and yellow-spotted milli-pedes, plus nearly 300 species of birds, including the California condor, which was reintroduced to the area in 2022 in partnership with the local Yurok people. The parks' strip of coastline features a number of beautiful beaches and scenic overlooks that are prime whale-watching spots in early spring and late fall.

## GETTING AROUND

About 300 miles (482 km) north of San Francisco, Redwood National and State Parks are located near Crescent City, primarily along U.S. 101. There are four parks in all: Jedediah Smith Redwoods State Park is east of Crescent City; Del Norte Coast Redwoods State Park and Prairie Creek Redwoods State Park are to the south; while Redwood National Park occupies several adjacent parcels. A number of roads will take you to lesser-visited areas in the park: Howland Hill Road cuts through Jedediah Smith Redwoods State Park; Newton B. Drury Parkway accesses Prairie Creek State Park 30 miles (48 km) to the south; and Davison Road will take you to Gold Bluffs Beach, also in Prairie Creek State Park, from U.S. 101 north of the town of Orick. Nearby, Bald Hills Road will lead you to some of the tallest trees in the world.

Roosevelt elk, one of many species found in the park ↑

↑ Hikers admiring some of the park's towering coast redwoods

## Exploring the parks

U.S. 101 runs through much of the Redwood National and State Parks, but the best scenery lies off the tributary side roads and, even better still, along the many hiking trails. Fern Canyon and Tall Trees Grove (the latter accessed on a road that requires a free permit) are the most popular areas to see the parks' namesake, but there are impressive giant redwood trees in all parts of the parks – although visitors can no longer access Hyperion due to fears of degradation.

There are four visitor centers within the parks themselves, all offering ranger-led activities and programs, as well as an information center in the northern gateway town of Crescent City.

IF YOU HAVE
**A day**

Drive the 10-mile (16-km) Newton B. Drury Parkway in Prairie Creek Redwoods State Park, stopping at Big Tree Trail, and visit Lady Bird Johnson Grove.

## Old-growth forests

The easy 1.5-mile (2.5-km) loop trail through Lady Bird Johnson Grove, located off narrow and twisty Bald Hills Road in Redwood National Park, offers a stark insight into the difference between the second-growth forest at the beginning of the hike and the old-growth forest you enter after crossing the footbridge. Not only are the trees much taller, the ecosystem is radically different, with more (and more diverse) plants and animals among the old-growth redwoods. RVs, trucks, and trailers are not allowed.

To the east of Crescent City, the 10-mile (16-km) stretch of Howland Hill Road in Jedediah Smith Redwoods State Park is another gateway to old-growth forest. It's a twisty, narrow, and unpaved route; RVs, trucks, and trailers are not allowed here, either. The Grove of the Titans, with a number of 300-ft (91-m) redwoods, is just a short walk from the road on an elevated boardwalk that protects the forest floor.

The 10-mile (16-km) Newton B. Drury Scenic Parkway, which diverges from U.S. 101 just north of the turnoff to Bald Hills

↑ A dirt road cutting through the Bald Hills south of Klamath

## The Redwood Coast

Beyond the superlative trees, the parks' west side features 37 miles (60 km) of California's rugged North Coast. These stretches are great places for picnicking, hiking, tidepooling, and wildlife watching, but not swimming: the water is cold and the surf is rough. If you are visiting the parks' beaches, it's important to know the timing of the tides so you don't get cut off.

The coast is mainly accessible on foot via trails, but you can also drive to Gold Bluffs Beach in about a half-hour along Davison Road from U.S. 101 north of Orick. This is the only area in the parks where you need to pay a fee ($12) to enter. A free parking permit is also required, available via an online application. RVs and trailers are not allowed on Davison Road.

Enderts Beach, at the end of an easy 0.6-mile (1-km) trail just south of Crescent City, is a popular spot for the tidepools at its northern end, which are some of the best in the parks. If you're looking to truly get away from it all, there are two moderate hiking trails to lesser-visited Hidden Beach: a 1.4-mile (2.3-km) round trip from U.S. 101

Road, grants easy access to more coast redwoods at the Big Tree Wayside, and leads to the 3-mile (4.8-km) drive on the unpaved Cal-Barrel Road. Several short trails lead through other parts of the forest and coast here.

# EAT

There are no places to eat in the park. You'll find numerous cafés, restaurants, and grocery stores in Crescent City, and a few options in Orick and Klamath. The Historic Requa Inn *(p105)* serves breakfast and dinner.

**The Good Harvest Cafe**
Locally beloved spot for breakfast, lunch, and seafood dinners.

⌂ U.S. 101
☎ (707) 465-6028

**Abalone Bar and Grill**
Tuck into Philly cheesesteak and shrimp at one of the few restaurants in Klamath.

⌂ Klamath
☎ (707) 482-1777

**Safeway**
Modern supermarket, open 24 hours a day.

⌂ Crescent City
🖥 local.safeway.com

↑ Following a trail through a fallen tree in Redwood National and State Parks

and a 5.5-mile (8.9-km) round trip along the coast from the Wilson Creek Beach parking area. Hidden Beach itself is marked by gray sand and driftwood, and a rugged island sits just off the coast.

## Hiking

Trails for every skill level crisscross Redwood National and State Parks, wending through towering forests and along wave-lashed stretches of empty beach. Be sure to check the tides if you are hiking to the coast, and watch out for poison oak.

A great place to start is the serene Boy Scout Tree Trail, a moderate 5.5-mile (8.9-km) round-trip hike to the heart of an old-growth forest in Jedediah Smith Redwoods State Park, ending at the base of idyllic Fern Falls.

Farther south, in Prairie Creek Redwoods State Park, the easy 1.5-mile (2.5-km) Fern Canyon Trail is a perenially popular loop that starts at Gold Bluffs Beach and takes you into a lush ravine with fern-laden walls. You can continue on the moderate Friendship Ridge Trail for an 8-mile (12.9-km) round trip, but bring a map.

Another iconic hike, the Tall Trees Grove in Redwood National Park is a moderate to difficult 4.5-mile (7.2-km) round-trip ramble that takes you to some of the tallest trees in the world: many of them are 360 ft (110 m) in height. The turnoff to the trailhead is 7 miles east of U.S. 101 on Bald Hills Road. There's a gate that requires a code to unlock; online reservations are required.

The other side of U.S. 101, but still within Redwood National Park, the Trillium Falls Trail is considered by many rangers as one of the parks' best short walks: the easy 2.7-mile (4.3-km) loop

passes a waterfall before entering old-growth forest.

Backpackers gravitate to the moderate to difficult routes on the 37-mile (60-km) Coastal Trail and the 15-mile (24-km) Redwood Creek Trail.

→

Camping among the dunes at Gold Bluffs Beach in Prairie Creek Redwoods State Park

---

🕐 IF YOU HAVE
**A weekend**

Camp at Gold Bluffs Beach and hike nearby Fern Canyon, before heading inland on Howland Hill Road to Boy Scout Tree Trail. Watch the sunset from Hidden Beach.

←
An ascent on a scenic ride through the park

Permits are required for multiday adventures, but you can also take shorter day hikes on these trails.

## Cycling

Mountain biking is allowed on several old logging roads in Prairie Creek Redwoods State Park, and road biking is permitted on many of the parks' paved roads. From October to May, Newton B. Drury Scenic Parkway is closed to vehicles on the first Saturday of every month; only hikers and bikers are allowed.

## Camping

There are four developed campgrounds in the parks, including one along the coast on Gold Bluffs Beach. Reservations are advised. Backcountry camping is also allowed at seven designated sites within the parks, but it requires advance online reservations for a permit.

# STAY

There is one lodging surrounded by parkland (Elk Meadow Cabins) and more options in Crescent City, Klamath, and Orick.

**The Historic Requa Inn**
Each room is unique in this Arts and Crafts inn, built above the banks of the Klamath River in 1914.

🏠 **Klamath**
[W] **requainn.com**

$

**Curly Redwood Lodge**
This old-school motel, built from a single redwood tree in 1957, has a variety of spacious rooms.

🏠 **Crescent City**
[W] **curlyredwoodlodge.com**

$

**Elk Meadow Cabins**
Wildlife is the draw at these large cabins with kitchens; many have room for up to eight guests.

🏠 **Orick** [W] **elkmeadowcabins.com**

$$$

**Roosevelt Base Camp**
This former 1950s motel was stylishly renovated in 2022, and offers boutique suites sleeping up to six.

🏠 **Orick** [W] **rooseveltbasecamp.com**

$$

Gazing over
the rugged ↑
Enderts Beach

# EXPLORING REDWOOD

Redwood National and State Parks are a string of protected forests, beaches, and rolling grasslands along the coast of Northern California. The combined park area contains almost 140,000 acres (57,000 ha), and is comprised of Redwood National Park and three state parks: Del Norte Coast, Jedediah Smith, and Prairie Creek. Located within California's Del Norte and Humboldt counties, the four parks collectively protect 45 percent of all remaining redwood forests.

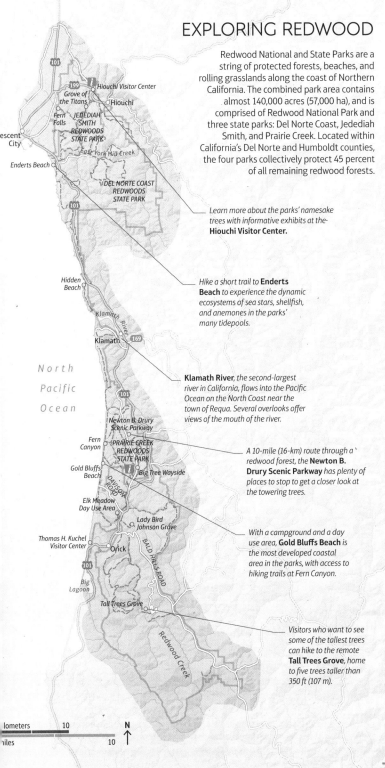

Learn more about the parks' namesake trees with informative exhibits at the **Hiouchi Visitor Center.**

Hike a short trail to **Enderts Beach** to experience the dynamic ecosystems of sea stars, shellfish, and anemones in the parks' many tidepools.

**Klamath River**, the second-largest river in California, flows into the Pacific Ocean on the North Coast near the town of Requa. Several overlooks offer views of the mouth of the river.

A 10-mile (16-km) route through a redwood forest, the **Newton B. Drury Scenic Parkway** has plenty of places to stop to get a closer look at the towering trees.

With a campground and a day use area, **Gold Bluffs Beach** is the most developed coastal area in the parks, with access to hiking trails at Fern Canyon.

Visitors who want to see some of the tallest trees can hike to the remote **Tall Trees Grove**, home to five trees taller than 350 ft (107 m).

### Map labels

Hiouchi Visitor Center
Grove of the Titans
Hiouchi
Fern Falls
JEDEDIAH SMITH REDWOODS STATE PARK
Crescent City
East York Mill Creek
Enderts Beach
DEL NORTE COAST REDWOODS STATE PARK
Hidden Beach
Klamath River
Klamath
North Pacific Ocean
Newton B. Drury Scenic Parkway
Fern Canyon
PRAIRIE CREEK REDWOODS STATE PARK
Gold Bluffs Beach
Big Tree Wayside
DAVISON ROAD
Elk Meadow Day Use Area
Lady Bird Johnson Grove
Thomas H. Kuchel Visitor Center
Orick
BALD HILLS ROAD
Big Lagoon
Tall Trees Grove
Redwood Creek

Kilometers        10
Miles              10
N

# PACIFIC NORTHWEST

The states of Oregon and Washington, along with the Canadian province of British Columbia, make up the Pacific Northwest. It's the call of the wild that draws visitors to this region, with its cloud-piercing mountain ranges, rocky coastline, and moss-draped forests. Bordered by the Pacific Ocean in western Washington, Olympic National Park shows off its prestigious UNESCO Biosphere Reserve status with its misty, primeval forests, while its northerly neighbor, the North Cascades, is home to over 300 glaciers and jagged peaks. In southwest Washington, Mount Rainier, set within its eponymous park, looms over the landscape as the fifth-highest mountain in the Lower 48. A further highlight of the region is the evocatively named Crater Lake in southwest Oregon; not only is this the state's sole national park, but it surrounds the country's deepest lake, with graded trails leading to impressive lookout points across the tranquil waters.

# 7 DAYS
## in the Pacific Northwest

### Day 1

Begin your exploration of Washington's majestic wonders at the Nisqually Entrance to Mount Rainier *(p118)*. Drive to Longmire to view the park museum and stretch your legs on the short Trail of Shadows before continuing past pretty Narada Falls to the visitor center at Paradise. Spend the rest of the day hiking the Nisqually Vista Trail, with spectacular views of Mount Rainier, before ending at the rustic gray-tiled Paradise Inn, opened in 1917.

### Day 2

In the summer you can drive Stevens Canyon Road along the southern edge of Mount Rainier to link up with Hwy. 123 and Hwy. 410. Along the route, take the spectacular spur road to the Sunrise Visitor Center on the north side of Mount Rainier – allow 2 hours from Paradise. From Sunrise it's another 3.5 hours' drive nonstop to the beginning of the North Cascades Highway in Burlington, where there's plenty of accommodations and places to eat.

### Day 3

After a filling breakfast at Billy's Café (316 E. Fairhaven Ave, Burlington), traverse the North Cascades Highway (Hwy. 20) into the mighty snaggletoothed ranges of North Cascades *(p126)*. Pause at the park visitor center at Newhalem to get oriented, before strolling the Trail of the Cedars or admiring Ladder Creek Falls. Aim to reach Diablo Lake in time for a lunch cruise, before making your way to Ross Lake Resort *(rosslakeresort.com)*. The resort offers enchanting waterside cabins, accessed via a short hike and boat ride (no road access). Spend the rest of the day hiking or paddling in the lake, surrounded by snowcapped peaks.

### Day 4

Enjoy the morning at Ross Lake before returning to your car and driving back down the Skagit Valley. It should take 4–5 hours to reach Port Angeles, taking scenic Hwy. 20 across Whidbey Island and the car ferry to Port Townshend. Aim to reach the Olympic National Park *(p130)* Visitor Center, before driving into the park itself

1 Washington Pass
in North Cascades.
2 Olympic's black-tailed deer.
3 Ruby Beach.
4 Resting by the Hoh River.
5 Sol Duc Falls.

on Hurricane Ridge Road – allow 30 minutes to get to the top, for jaw-dropping views of Mount Olympus and the central Olympic Mountains. Head back down to Port Angeles where you'll find plenty of restaurants along the Salish Sea waterfront, like Downriggers on the Water (*downriggerspa.com*).

## Day 5

In the morning, prepare to drive 40 miles (64 km) to Sol Duc from Port Angeles, stopping en route to explore the wooded shores of picturesque Lake Crescent. While at the lake, hike the easy 1.8-mile (3-km) round-trip trail to Marymere Falls, snaking through forests of emerald-green conifers, maples, sword ferns, and thick carpets of moss. Spend the rest of the day in the Sol Duc Hot Springs area in the heart of Olympic National Park, hiking up to Sol Duc Falls or Deer and Mink lakes, and ending the day with a restorative soak in the hot springs themselves. Spend the night in comfort at the picturesque Sol Duc Hot Springs Resort (*olympicnationalparks.com*).

## Day 6

Get up early and drive to the Hoh Rain Forest sector of the park – allow 2 hours to cover the 70 miles (110 km) or so. Stop at the visitor center before tackling the Hall of Mosses Trail, an easy jaunt that takes in moss-smothered trees and giant ferns. Have lunch at the Hard Rain Café (*hohrainforest.wixsite.com*), before heading to the wild coastal section of the park at Rialto Beach. Spend the night at the nearby town of Forks, best known for its connection with the *Twilight* movie and book series.

## Day 7

Begin your final day with a scenic drive along the Pacific coast to Ruby Beach, named for its red-and-black-pebble sand, before heading inland to glacier-carved Lake Quinault (where you can have lunch). This part of the park contains the lesser-visited Quinault Rainforest, best explored on foot, with trails leading to the world's largest sitka spruce. End your journey with a fresh salmon dinner at the Salmon House Restaurant (*rainforestresort.com*).

A wintry Crater Lake, which was created by snowmelt and rainfall filling a caldera ↑

# CRATER LAKE

📍 Oregon  🚗 $30 per vehicle, valid for seven days ($20 Nov–late May)  🌐 nps.gov/crla

Famous for the startling color and clarity of its lake, the caldera of what was once Mount Mazama is the showpiece of Oregon's only national park. With a depth of 1,945 ft (595 m), the lake itself is the deepest in the country (and ninth-deepest in the world) and perhaps the clearest: you can see almost 100 ft (30 m) into the water.

Crater Lake's serene surface belies its dramatic origins. Around 7,700 years ago, the monumental Mount Mazama erupted so ferociously that it created a massive caldera, 6 miles (10 km) across and 4,000 ft (1.2 km) deep. Gradually, springwater, snowmelt, and rainfall filled the caldera, making for a lake with remarkably pure and clear water.

The eruption that formed Crater Lake was cataclysmic and fast – geologists say it took hours, or at most a few days – but it wasn't the first. The Indigenous Klamath peoples who inhabited the area had witnessed thousands of years of volcanic activity. When this last violent episode occurred, they saw it as an epic battle between the sky god Skell and the god of the world below, Llao, who inhabited the mountain. The story varies, but in most versions the battle ended

↑ Enjoying views of serene Crater Lake on a gentle walk in the park

when Skell forced Llao back into the mountain, which then destroyed itself. Afterward, the Klamath considered the lake sacred; only shamans could look at it, and they kept it a secret from white settlers. Its existence wasn't recorded officially until 1862, when Oregon prospector Chauncey Nye wrote a newspaper column about seeing the lake.

## Exploring the park

Given that this national park's appeal is its lake, most visitors plan their trip here in summer, when the park's scenic Rim Drive loop is entirely open (in winter, snowfalls and snowmelt force some facilities, roads, and trails to close).

IF YOU HAVE
**A day**

Take your time (at least three hours) driving the superbly scenic Rim Drive, stopping off at the numerous overlooks along the way. After, board a shuttle boat to Wizard Island and make the short climb to the island's summit.

# EAT

Beyond options within Crater Lake, try the town of Prospect, southwest of the park.

**Crater Lake Lodge Dining Room**
Open mid-May to mid-October, this classic park lodge (dating from 1915) offers fine food, and lakeside views.
📍 Rim Village
🌐 travelcraterlake.com
$$$

**Annie Creek Restaurant**
Comforting family-favorites (pizza, salads, sandwiches) are served mid-May to September.
📍 Mazama Village
🌐 travelcraterlake.com
$$$

**Rim Village Café**
To-go sandwiches and snacks; the only option for winter visitors.
📍 Rim Village
🌐 travelcraterlake.com
$$$

Waiting for the ferry boat to cross the glassy waters of Crater Lake ↑

A must-do, the 33-mile (53-km) driving route is split into two – East Rim and West Rim – and is best traveled clockwise, so the parking areas are on the right.

### Rim Drive

Whether driving or cycling the Rim Drive, be sure to stop at any – or as many – of the 30 overlooks dotted around the lake. At Rim Village, the Sinnott Memorial Overlook is

→ Lakeside and sunset views from Crater Lake Lodge

the park's most-visited overlook, built into the caldera wall in 1931. Beyond offering lake views, the sheltered overlook houses a number of exhibits on the formation of the lake and its history.

Phantom Ship Overlook, on the southeast side of the lake, offers a view of a small island that resembles a ghostly vessel, especially on foggy days. From here, it's worth taking a detour (via Pinnacles Rd.) to The Pinnacles, towering volcanic spires in a valley in the southeastern corner of the park. A short trail leads to an overlook.

Cyclists should note the loop is a challenging ride that involves sharing the road with cars, steep grades, and limited water stops. Rentals are not available in the park so bringing your own wheels is essential.

### The lake

There is only one way to get down to lake level: the difficult 1.1-mile (1.8-km) trail to Cleetwood Cove on the lake's northeastern side. The trail descends about 700 ft (215 m) to the lake, so it's the

---

# STAY

Aside from those in the park (including Crater Lake Lodge, *p113*), find accommodations in Prospect or the Diamond Lake area.

### Cabins at Mazama Village

A basic, moderately budget-friendly option within park boundaries. Queen beds; no TVs, phones, or air-con. Open mid-May to September.

🏠 Mazama Village
w travelcraterlake.com

$$$

### Diamond Lake Resort

Year-round lakeside resort a short drive north of the park. Motel rooms, studios, cabins, and camping available. Make reservations well in advance.

🏠 Diamond Lake
w diamondlake.net

$$$

return trip uphill that can catch hikers by surprise. But making the journey is worthwhile: the trail is the only way to get to the park's popular boat tours, which typically run from July to mid-September. Narrated lake tours depart several times daily; make a day of it by catching the morning boat to Wizard Island and hiking the moderate 1-mile (1.6-km) trail to the summit of the crater at the summit of the island.

Personal watercraft are prohibited, but swimming and diving are allowed at Cleetwood Cove and Wizard Island, if you can tolerate the notably cold water, that is.

## Hiking

While the Cleetwood Cove Trail is the only trail to Crater Lake itself, there are numerous trails that lead to truly commanding views on the surrounding mountains.

The moderate 1.6-mile (2.6-km) round-trip hike to the sheltered lookout on Watchman Peak ends with great views of the lake and Wizard Island, but tends to attract crowds, especially at sunset. The summit of Garfield Peak has a view of the entire lake, accessible via a difficult 3.6-mile (5.8-km) round trip. At 8,829 ft (2,691 m), Mount Scott is the highest peak in the park. You can hike to the summit on a difficult 5-mile (8-km) round trip, and you won't run into as many people as you would on the easier hikes.

On the north side of the park is the Pumice Desert. The eruption of Mount Mazama covered this former glacial valley with a thick layer of pumice and ash; now, the mostly barren area supports a few trees and seasonal wildflowers. Pumice Flat, south of the lake, is a similar landscape, accessible by a moderate 5.4-mile (8.7-km) hiking loop that gives you a closer look at the pumice and ash plains, volcanic rocks, and slow regeneration of the forest.

For those up for a serious challenge, the epic Pacific Crest Trail, which runs from Canada to Mexico, cuts through the entire park from near the North Entrance and around the west side of the lake.

### Winter sports

When snowfall sets in, the park becomes the domain not of cars and cyclists, but cross-country skiers and snowshoers. Park rangers guide snowshoe trips from Rim Village; a limited supply of snowshoes are available to rent from the village café and shop but no skis are available.

IF YOU HAVE
**A weekend**

For an active weekend, cycle around the lake on the Rim Drive before taking in sunset views from Watchman Peak. Stay at the park's lodge or cabins, then hike Mount Scott and explore the other-worldly Pumice Desert.

---

### GETTING AROUND

Crater Lake National Park is located in southern Oregon about 250 miles (400 km) southeast of Portland via either I-5 and Ore. Hwy. 58 or U.S. 26 and U.S. 97. The southern and western entrances are open year-round, while the northern entrance is summer-only. In the park, the Rim Drive circles the entire lake, with numerous parking areas at viewpoints, trailheads, and other attractions. The scenic circuit is open as conditions allow, typically July to mid-October. On the southwestern side of the lake, Rim Village has a lodge and visitor center, with additional facilities to the south in Mazama Village. Ticketed boat tours to Wizard Island depart from Cleetwood Cove on the northeastern shore of the lake.

↑ Cycling along the Rim Drive, with the lake a constant companion

# EXPLORING CRATER LAKE

Crater Lake sits high on a crest of the Cascade Mountains, in the southwest of Oregon. The park around the lake encompasses 180,000 acres (72,000 ha), covering the wider caldera and the surrounding hills, mountain peaks, and dense forests.

**Wizard Island** *was created by a volcanic eruption after Mt. Mazama collapsed. This cinder cone jutting 760 ft (232 m) above the water resembles a wizard's hat.*

**Watchman Peak** *sits 8,000 ft (2,400 m) above sea level. The summit lookout is a popular destination for hikers because of the views of the lake, and of Wizard Island.*

**Crater Lake Lodge** *opened on the edge of the caldera in 1915, and remains a classic park hostelry, with a rustic look and stellar views of the lake.*

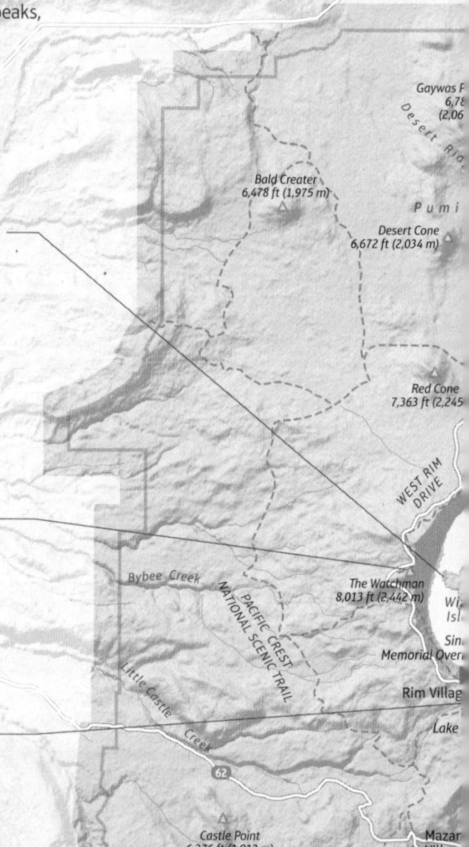

Gaywas P
6,78
(2,06

Desert Rid

Bald Creater
6,478 ft (1,975 m)

P u m i

Desert Cone
6,672 ft (2,034 m)

Red Cone
7,363 ft (2,245

WEST RIM DRIVE

Bybee Creek

PACIFIC CREST NATIONAL SCENIC TRAIL

The Watchman
8,013 ft (2,442 m)

Wi
Isl

Little Castle Creek

Sin
Memorial Over

Rim Village

Lake

62

Castle Point
6,276 ft (1,913 m)

Mazar
Villag

Annie Spring
Entrance
Station

Union Peak
7,709 ft (2,350 m)

Pumice
Flat

← Mount Scott looming over the waters of Crater Lake

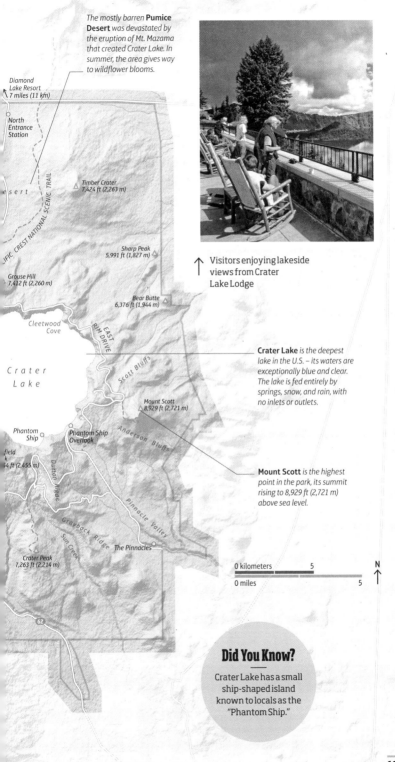

The mostly barren **Pumice Desert** was devastated by the eruption of Mt. Mazama that created Crater Lake. In summer, the area gives way to wildflower blooms.

Diamond Lake Resort
7 miles (11 km)

North Entrance Station

esert

PACIFIC CREST NATIONAL SCENIC TRAIL

Timber Crater
7,424 ft (2,263 m)

Sharp Peak
5,991 ft (1,827 m)

Grouse Hill
7,412 ft (2,260 m)

Bear Butte
6,376 ft (1,944 m)

Cleetwood Cove

EAST RIM DRIVE

Crater Lake

Scott Bluffs

Mount Scott
8,929 ft (2,721 m)

Phantom Ship

Phantom Ship Overlook

Anderson Bluffs

field
k
4 ft (2,455 m)

Dutton Ridge

Grayback Ridge

Sun Creek

Pinnacle Valley

The Pinnacles

Crater Peak
7,263 ft (2,214 m)

62

↑ Visitors enjoying lakeside views from Crater Lake Lodge

**Crater Lake** is the deepest lake in the U.S. – its waters are exceptionally blue and clear. The lake is fed entirely by springs, snow, and rain, with no inlets or outlets.

**Mount Scott** is the highest point in the park, its summit rising to 8,929 ft (2,721 m) above sea level.

0 kilometers    5
0 miles         5

N
↑

## Did You Know?

Crater Lake has a small ship-shaped island known to locals as the "Phantom Ship."

**Best for** *A healthy dose of mountain air*

# MOUNT RAINIER

◉ Washington  🚗 $30 per vehicle, valid for seven days  Ⓦ nps.gov/mora

The showpiece of Washington state, Mount Rainier gives its name to this national park, which was one of the first to be established. And make no mistake, this much-loved park is all about the mountain. Towering 14,410 ft (4,392 m) above sea level, Mount Rainier is the fifth-highest mountain in the Lower 48, though its dominance over the surrounding area places it higher in visitors' imagination.

Mount Rainier was named by George Vancouver, the British navy officer who explored and charted huge swaths of Canada and the US in the late 1700s. He saw the peak in 1792, and named it for a friend, British admiral Peter Rainier. But the mountain already had a name – several, in fact, due to the various languages spoken by the local area's Indigenous peoples. Today, debate rages about restoring traditional names to places throughout the Pacific Northwest, with some pressing for Mount Rainier to be renamed Mount Tacoma.

A still-active volcano, Mount Rainier is so massive it practically creates its own weather. That includes lots of snow: the average year sees 645 in (1,640 cm) of snowfall at Paradise (together with Sunrise, the highest car-accessible points of the park); in the winter of 1971–2, a then record 1,122 in (2,850 cm) covered the area.

All of that snow feeds the mountain's glaciers. The 28 named glaciers in the park include the largest glacier by area in the Lower 48, Emmons Glacier, as well as the lowest, Carbon Glacier.

### GETTING AROUND

Mount Rainier National Park is located about 80 miles (130 km) southeast of Seattle via I-5 and several state highways. The Nisqually Entrance in the southwestern corner of the park is the prime entry point, accessed via Wash. Hwy. 706, which becomes Paradise Rd. where it enters the park near Longmire. At Paradise, it intersects with Stevens Canyon Rd., which continues to the entrance of the same name on the southeastern side of the park at Wash. Hwy. 123. Stevens Canyon Rd. is closed in winter, while Paradise Rd. is open year-round. The White River Entrance off Wash. Hwy. 410 accesses the Sunrise area on the northeast corner of the park, and the Carbon River Entrance on the northwest side of the park is only open to hikers and cyclists. Needless to say you'll need your own vehicle (and note you must carry tire chains in winter).

Panorama Point, reached via the the Skyline Trail ↑

↑ Purple Pacific lupines, often seen in the park mid-April to August

A hazy sunset reflected in the water near Mount Rainier ↑

## Exploring the park

Mount Rainier is, naturally, the main draw for visitors to this national park and most arrive to enjoy scenic drives and hikes in its vicinity. There are four main jumping-off points: Longmire, Paradise, Sunrise, and Ohanapecosh. These are the most developed parts of the park and where you'll find visitor centers, and places to stay and eat. Mowich Lake (without a visitor center) is much quieter and mainly attracts those looking to escape the crowds.

## Longmire

For those entering the park from the Nisqually Entrance, Longmire, a designated historic district, is the first stop. It has a small museum within its visitor center, which

covers local history. Longmire is the namesake of home-steader James Longmire, who built the first guest cabins here in 1889; he later added a hotel and clubhouse, which is the area's oldest remaining building. A self-guided tour among the historic buildings leads through the district's early days. Also here is the start of the Trail of the Shadows, an accessible walk past hot springs and an early homestead.

Another trail is the moderate 4.6-mile (7.4-km) Rampart Ridge Trail, which ascends a long-hardened lava flow for stellar views of Mount Rainier and the Nisqually River. Comet Falls Trail, meanwhile, takes hikers to the second-tallest waterfall in the park. It's a moderate 3.8-mile (6.1-km) round trip, starting between Longmire and Paradise; add another 2 miles (3.2 km) to get to the glacier views in Van Trump Park.

## Paradise

Longmire is a stepping stone to Paradise, the subalpine

meadow that frames Mount Rainier with vibrant displays of wildflowers. There are a number of trailheads here, as well as roadside access to Reflection Lake and Inspiration Point, an overlook with views of Mount Rainier and the Tatoosh Range.

You can reach the top of the mountain from Paradise,

IF YOU HAVE
**A day**

Drive to Paradise, the aptly named meadow on the mountain's southern flanks, and set out on a hike along the Skyline Trail. It's a moderately difficult walk and will take the average hiker around 4–5 hours to complete.

→

Out for a hike along one of the national park's many walking trails

but shorter day hikes are perhaps more appealing to most. The supremely popular Skyline Trail is a moderate 5.5-mile (8.8-km) loop through colorful meadows to Nisqually Glacier and the well-named Panorama Point. (This is the trail to capture those much-photographed views of the mountain.) A little shorter and easier is the 2.5-mile (4-km) Bench and Snow Lakes Trail, which connects one lake to the other and provides views of wildflowers along the way.

## Ohanapecosh

It's a little over 20 miles (30 km) from Paradise to Ohanapecosh, which sits in

> ### Did You Know?
> ---
> Though it is unlikely to erupt, Mount Rainier is one of the world's most dangerous volcanoes.

the park's southeastern corner. Known to be drier and warmer than the west side of the park, it has a well-used large campground and makes a good alternative to Paradise when stormy weather hits.

The Ohanapecosh area is some of the most forested terrain in the park, and it looks particularly pretty in fall. Take the easy 1.3-mile (2.1-km) Grove of the Patriarchs Trail along the Ohanapecosh River to see sky-grazing Douglas-firs and western red cedars.

## Sunrise

Sunrise (which has its own entrance on the northeastern side of the park) lives up to its name as much as Paradise: this is the best place to watch the sun come up.

As well as early risers, Sunrise attracts its fair share of hikers, and the easy to moderate 4.8-mile (7.-km) Sunrise Rim Trail is a good hike to explore the area, with mountain and glacier views, and access to a lake and backcountry campground.

# EAT

The park has three cafés and two restaurants. Gateway towns (especially Ashford) have more options.

### National Park Inn
A casual dining room serving American classics all year.

⌂ Longmire ⓦ mtrainier guestservices.com

$ $ $

### Paradise Inn
Enjoy American fare beside the fire at this dining room, open late May to early November.

⌂ Paradise ⓦ mtrainier guestservices.com

$ $ $

---

### Sunrise Day Lodge
Grab picnic food to-go, July to mid-September.

⌂ Sunrise ⓦ mtrainier guestservices.com

$ $ $

# STAY

The park has hotels and campgrounds, with more overnight options in the gateway towns of Ashford, Packwood, and Greenwater.

### National Park Inn
Small historic hotel with trail access; some shared bathrooms.

🅰Longmire 🆆mtrainier guestservices.com

$$$

### Paradise Inn
Classic lodge near wildflower meadows and hiking trails.

🅰Paradise 🆆mtrainier guestservices.com

$$$

### Stormking Cabins and Spa
Five luxury cabins and a day spa just outside Nisqually Entrance.

🅰Ashford 🆆storm kingspa.com

$$$

A 5.5-mile (8.8-km) round trip, the moderate Mt. Fremont Lookout Trail takes you up to its namesake lookout, where you can see as far as Seattle on a clear day.

## Mowich Lake

If you want to get away from the crowds, head northwest of Mount Rainier to Carbon River and Mowich Lake, nicknamed "The Quiet Corner" of the park. Diverging south from Wash. Hwy. 410 near Enumclaw, Wash. Hwy. 165 passes the turnoff to Carbon River and ends at Mowich Lake. A 2006 flood washed out Carbon River Rd.,

which once led into the rest of the park, so any further exploration must be done on foot or by bike.

Hikers doing just that can access a difficult trail to Carbon Glacier; the round trip is 17 miles (27 km). If you have less time, or want something slightly less tricky, the Tolmie Peak Trail is a moderate 6.5-mile (10.4-km) round-trip hike that is fairly level until the final mile. As ever, hikers are rewarded with big views of Mount Rainier. Cyclists, meanwhile, will particularly enjoy pedaling along the old Carbon River Rd.

Aside from offering hiking and cycling opportunities, Mowich Lake, being the largest and deepest lake in the park, is open to fishing and nonmotorized boating.

## Mountaineering and multiday hikes

Summiting the mountain is a popular endeavor (around 10,000 tackle it yearly), but not one to be taken lightly. The snowfields and glaciers encasing its upper reaches require technical expertise and gear – ice axes, crampons, and the like. Most of those who do attempt it depart from Paradise on the 9,000-ft (2,745-m) ascent to the icy

> **Summiting the mountain is a popular endeavor (around 10,000 tackle it yearly), but not one to be taken lightly.**

↑ A stretch of the Skyline Trail, which weaves among wildflower meadows

summit. A permit is required, and an annual climbing fee must be paid. The best way to reach the summit safely is a guided climb; the park maintains a list of authorized guide services on its website.

Mountain gear and technical expertise aside, there are plenty of trails that still offer a challenge. The 93-mile (150-km) Wonderland Trail circumnavigates Mount Rainier on a difficult back-packing route that usually requires two weeks to complete. A backcountry permit is required to walk this route and because there is such demand the park runs an early access lottery to help manage the number of users competing simultaneously.

An even longer trail, the vast Canada-to-Mexico Pacific Crest Trail runs through the far eastern edge of the park.

## Winter sports

For obvious reasons, Mount Rainier is a destination for cross-country skiers and snowshoers. Rentals are available at the Longmire General Store, and rangers guide snowshoe walks at Paradise on the weekends. Sledding is allowed at Paradise and snowmobiling is permitted on a stretch of Westside Rd. near the Nisqually Entrance.

## Camping

The park has three drive-in campgrounds at Cougar Rock, Ohanapecosh, and White River. Reservations are available for Cougar Rock and Ohanapecosh, but White

🗓 IF YOU HAVE
**A weekend**

Enter the park from the northeast and spend your first day in Sunrise walking among the spectacular scenery. Let the sunrise start the day, then drive to Ohanapecosh for more time in nature, admiring seasonal foliage.

River, located at Sunrise, is first-come, first-served, as is a walk-in campground at Mowich Lake. Backcountry camping is allowed through-out the park; a permit is required year-round and must be obtained in person. Advance reservations can be made during the peak season.

# EXPLORING MOUNT RAINIER

An emblem of Washington state, the towering Mount Rainier is located around 80 miles (130 km) south of Seattle. The mountain dominates the national park, which is also home to wild-flower meadows and old-growth forest.

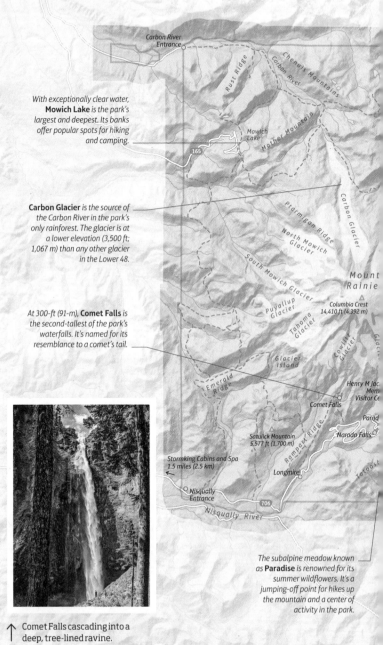

*With exceptionally clear water, **Mowich Lake** is the park's largest and deepest. Its banks offer popular spots for hiking and camping.*

**Carbon Glacier** *is the source of the Carbon River in the park's only rainforest. The glacier is at a lower elevation (3,500 ft; 1,067 m) than any other glacier in the Lower 48.*

*At 300-ft (91-m), **Comet Falls** is the second-tallest of the park's waterfalls. It's named for its resemblance to a comet's tail.*

Carbon River Entrance

Rust Ridge

Chenuis Mountains

Carbon River

Mowich Lake

165

Mother Mountain

Ptarmigan Ridge

North Mowich Glacier

Carbon Glacier

South Mowich Glacier

Mount Rainie

Columbia Crest 14,410 ft (4,392 m)

Puyallup Glacier

Tahoma Glacier

Cowlitz Glacier

Glacier Island

Emerald Ridge

Henry M Jac Mem Visitor Ce

Comet Falls

Parad

Satulick Mountain 5,577 ft (1,700 m)

Rampart Ridge

Narada Falls

Tatoost

Stormking Cabins and Spa 1.5 miles (2.5 km)

Longmire

Nisqually Entrance

706

Nisqually River

*The subalpine meadow known as **Paradise** is renowned for its summer wildflowers. It's a jumping-off point for hikes up the mountain and a center of activity in the park.*

↑ Comet Falls cascading into a deep, tree-lined ravine.

Popular among morning hikers, **Sunrise** is known for its views of Mount Rainier and other mountains as well as the many glaciers on this side of the park.

↑ The verdant banks of Mowich Lake in summer

Slide Mountain
6,339 ft (1,932 m)

Ada Creek

Grand Park

Burnt Park

Green Park

Bear Park

Huckleberry Park

Sourdough Mountains

Crystal Mountain

Dege Peak
7,008 ft (2,136 m)

Sunrise Ridge

410

Burroughs Mountain

Sunrise Visitor Center

Sunrise Day Lodge

White River Entrance

White River

Goat Island Mountain

Emmons Glacier

Tamanos Mountain
6,790 ft (2,070 m)

410

**Emmons Glacier** *is the largest glacier in the Lower 48 in terms of surface area, spanning 2,752 acres (1,114 ha).*

Barrier Peak
5,933 ft (1,808 m)

Buell Peak
5,933 ft (1,808 m)

Seymour Peak
6,337 ft (1,932 m)

Whitman Glacier

Ohanapecosh Park

123

Double Peak
6,199 ft (1,890 m)

Cowlitz Rocks
7,454 ft (2,271 m)

Cowutz Park

Panther Creek

Steven Ridge

Cowlitz Divide

Stevens Canyon Entrance

Stevens Peak
6,510 ft (1,984 m)

i

Ohanapecosh Visitor Center

123

*From the* **Stevens Canyon Entrance**, *visitors can join a number of the park's eastern trailheads.*

0 kilometers 5

0 miles 5

N
↑

# NORTH CASCADES

📍 Washington 🎟️ Free 🌐 nps.gov/noca

A bastion of untamed wilderness, this barely developed park is a fantastic place to escape the modern world. Here is an unmediated experience of nature: rugged backcountry hikes, awesome scenery little changed in centuries, and primitive camping in remote places. There are endless backcountry adventures to be had, with hundreds of miles of trails finding their way to unspoiled pockets, which you may well have to yourself.

---

📅 IF YOU HAVE
**A weekend**

Take the *Lady of the Lake* ferry (around four hours) from Chelan across to the village of Stehekin, your base for the weekend. Get back to nature by hiking in the South Unit and boating on the lake.

---

Nicknamed the "American Alps" and characterized by a series of jagged ridges, spires, and pinnacles, North Cascades National Park encompasses some of the most imposing alpine wilderness in the Lower 48. Here are more than 300 glaciers and a lengthy list of biodiverse plant life (more than most other parks). Wildlife abounds, too: the lack of civilization means this is one of the few places outside of Yellowstone and Glacier national parks with populations of both gray wolves and grizzly bears, though both are rarely seen.

The national park was established in 1968 and is divided into the North Unit and South Unit, separated by Wash. Hwy. 20 and the Skagit River. Unusually, the park also

Best for *Backcountry adventures and going off-grid*

← The snowy Mount Shuksan, captured from Picture Lake

includes a pair of adjacent national recreation areas, Lake Chelan on the park's southern boundary and Ross Lake, wedged between the park's northern and southern units.

**Exploring the park**

Both the North and South units are dominated by wilderness, with plenty of trails snaking up, down, and through glaciated peaks, unspoiled meadows, and dense forests. The Pacific Crest Trail cuts through the Lake Chelan National Recreation Area and the South Unit en route to the Canadian border. Many visitors come to drive along Wash. Hwy. 20., otherwise known as the North Cascades Highway, journeying through the park from Marblemount in the west to the Washington Pass Overlook. But this is really a park for getting out into the wilderness, whether hiking, cycling, on horseback or on the water.

## Did You Know?
—
Beatnik writer Jack Kerouac spent 63 days at the park's Desolation Peak fire lookout in 1956.

→ Hiking through larch trees on the Pacific Crest Trail, which runs through the park

The park has neither restaurants nor lodgings, but you'll find options in Stehekin, Ross Lake, Winthrop and Marblemount.

## EAT

**Stehekin Pastry Company**
Pastries, sandwiches, and assorted baked goods. Rental cabins are also available. Open May to November.
🏠 Stehekin
[W] stehekinpastry.com
$

**Old Schoolhouse Brewery**
Open year-round, this Winthrop craft brewery serves lunch and dinner made largely from local ingredients.
🏠 Winthrop
[W] oldschoolhouse brewery.com
$$

## STAY

**North Cascades Lodge at Stehekin**
Lakeside lodge with a variety of rooms and cabins; only full-service dining in Stehekin.
🏠 Stehekin
[W] lodgeatstehekin.com
$$$

**Ross Lake Resort**
Only accessible by boat, this resort has 15 lakeside cabins (no restaurant or store).
🏠 Ross Lake
[W] rosslakeresort.com
$$$

Mount Shuksan, named for the Lummi word said to mean "high peak" ↑

### North Unit

The wildest area in the park complex, the North Unit is where you'll find Mount Shuksan, perhaps one of the most photographed features of the park, and the turquoise Diablo Lake. There are numerous designated backcountry campsites here (permits required), making multiday hikes an exciting possibility. One standout is the 25-mile (40-km) Big Beaver Trail, accessed from Ross Dam.

### South Unit

The rugged South Unit is accessible via Cascade River Road, which leads to the Cascade Pass Trailhead. From here, it's a moderate 7.5-mile (12-km) round trip to the top of Cascade Pass, but you can add a difficult 2.2 miles (3.5 km) each way to the base of Sahale Glacier or continue along to High Bridge, where you can board the shuttle bus to the small and picturesque village of Stehekin, with houses set among the trees (note there is no access to Stehekin on Wash. Hwy. 20).

### Lake Chelan

Stretching some 50 miles (80 km) from Stehekin to Chelan is Lake Chelan. Visitors often make a day trip across the lake to the village, to enjoy boating, fishing, and numerous easy day hikes. One favorite sight is Rainbow Falls, accessed by a 7-mile (11-km) hike, bike, or bus ride from Stehekin. At the falls is a very short accessible trail leading through ponderosa pine. The paved route climbs steadily, offering an excellent vantage over the waterfall.

### Ross Lake

This is the best spot for day hiking in the park complex. Numerous trails start at Ross and Diablo dams, and the moderate to difficult hikes to Pyramid Lake (4 miles; 7 km) and Fourth of July Pass (10 miles; 16 km) are well worth the effort.

The lake also offers great paddling and boating opportunities. Boats of various types can be rented from Ross Lake Resort *(www.rosslakeresort.com)* and two cement boat ramps at Hozomeen on the lake's banks are normally usable from mid-June through September. Note, however, that Ross Lake is a reservoir with naturally changing water levels. The lake is generally at full capacity from July to September, when all of the docks are in use.

## GETTING AROUND

North Cascades National park is around 2–3 hours' drive northeast of Seattle via I-5, Wash. Hwy. 530, and Wash. Hwy. 20 (the North Cascades Highway). The road to the trail up Cascade Pass diverts from Wash. Hwy. 20 at the Skagit River in Marblemount. If arriving by train, there are two Amtrak options. The Amtrak Cascades arrives in Mount Vernon, about an hour's drive from the park. The grand *Empire Builder* from Chicago can get visitors as close as Seattle, which is a 2-hour drive from the park. The North Cascades Highway separates the north and south units of the park and accesses Ross Lake National Recreation Area on its way west to the town of Winthrop. The ferry on Lake Chelan to Stehekin leaves from the town of Chelan, which is about 60 miles (96 km) south of Winthrop. A shuttle bus provides transportation up the Stehekin Valley Road, with no reservations required. Bicycles are allowed on some ferries, but cars must remain at the dock.

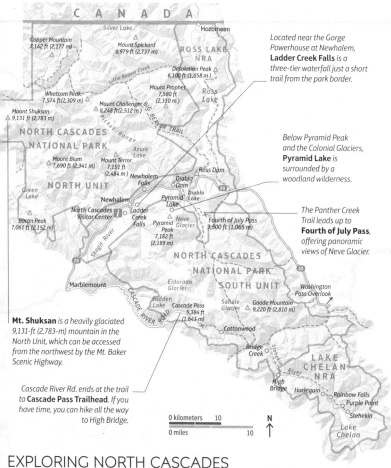

Located near the Gorge Powerhouse at Newhalem, **Ladder Creek Falls** is a three-tier waterfall just a short trail from the park border.

Below Pyramid Peak and the Colonial Glaciers, **Pyramid Lake** is surrounded by a woodland wilderness.

The Panther Creek Trail leads up to **Fourth of July Pass**, offering panoramic views of Neve Glacier.

**Mt. Shuksan** is a heavily glaciated 9,131-ft (2,783-m) mountain in the North Unit, which can be accessed from the northwest by the Mt. Baker Scenic Highway.

Cascade River Rd. ends at the trail to **Cascade Pass Trailhead**. If you have time, you can hike all the way to High Bridge.

0 kilometers 10

0 miles 10

N

# EXPLORING NORTH CASCADES

Best for *Immersing in nature at its best*

# OLYMPIC

📍Washington 🚗$30 per vehicle, valid for seven days
🌐nps.gov/olym

From fairytale forests to coastal wilderness, Olympic National Park protects places that are wildly diverse and like nowhere else in the country. Visitors are treated to what feels like three parks in one: on the western fringe of the Olympic Peninsula, a string of untamed beaches; in the interior, a mountainous and glaciated landscape crowned by Mount Olympus; and on the west side, some of the only temperate rainforests in the U.S.

↑ Grazing black-tailed deer, commonly seen in the national park

The Pacific Northwest is known for its rainfall and perhaps nowhere is that more true than in Olympic National Park. The west side of the park is among the wettest spots in North America, giving life to a rainforest and an abundance of plant species (more than 1,450). The park claims a giant fir tree that lives up to its name (it stands 246 ft/75 m high) and the world's largest Sitka spruce, which has stood for a millennium. All around the land is alive and vibrant: moss clings and ferns drape in hues of green; fertile tidepools house starfish and anemones; and jagged mountains are topped with ancient glaciers.

Wildlife abounds: over 60 species live on the land, around 300 types of birds fly above, and the likes of gray whales and sea otters swim off the coast. Fortunately, over 95 percent of the park is designated wilderness, protecting this almost primeval landscape for years to come.

## GETTING AROUND

Located on the Olympic Peninsula on the west side of Puget Sound, the park is best accessed via ferry from the Seattle area or car from Olympia, Washington state's capital city, via U.S. Hwy. 101. The coastal part of the park is not connected to the interior, but U.S. Hwy. 101 skirts the western edge of the park's interior on its way north from Kalaloch before hooking east to Sol Duc, Lake Crescent, Elwha, and Hurricane Ridge en route to Port Angeles, the largest city on the peninsula. The interior itself is not accessible by car so while a vehicle is essential to travel around the park, to explore the interior you'll need to set off on foot.

↑ Finding peace on the beach, a tiny stretch of the park's 73-mile (117-km) coastline

# STAY

There are campgrounds and lodges in the park, with many more options in the vicinity.

### Lake Crescent Lodge

Historic lakeside lodge with rooms, cabins, and cottages.

🏠 Port Angeles
🌐 olympicnational parks.com

$ $ $

### Kalaloch Lodge

Cedar lodge and cabins perched above the rugged Pacific coast.

🏠 Forks 🌐 thekalaloch lodge.com

$ $ $

### Sol Duc Hot Springs Resort

Cabins in an isolated setting with hiking trails and soaking pools.

🏠 Port Angeles
🌐 olympicnational parks.com

$ $ $

↑ The coniferous and deciduous trees, mosses, and ferns in Hoh Rainforest

## Exploring the park

Given the make-up of this park – the coast, the rainforest, and the interior – there's inevitably a lot to take in, so it's worth deciding ahead where you want to spend your time. Visitor centers are located in Port Angeles (a logical first stop) and Hoh Rain Forest, and there's a ranger station at Kalaloch on the coast.

## The rainforest

The park's temperate rainforests are some of the rarest (and wettest) ecosystems in the entire country. The Hoh Rain Forest, 19 miles (31 km) east of U.S. 101 on the Hoh River Rd., is accessible and favored by many. This is where you'll find the Hoh River Trail, a 17-mile (27-km) hike that starts off easy, but increases in difficulty as it ascends Mount Olympus in its final stretch. On the way, you'll pass through the moss-covered Hoh, home to giant Sitka spruce trees and wandering elk, and alpine meadows on the flanks of the mountain, before arriving at Blue Glacier near the peak.

North on U.S. 101, the Bogachiel River Trail offers a similar experience to the Hoh, but attracts far fewer hikers. The trail runs 24.4 miles (39.3 km) from the trailhead at the end of Undi Rd., about 10 miles (16 km) southeast of Forks, to Mink Lake Junction near Sol Duc. The trail has several river crossings that can be impassable during times of high flow.

To the south of the Hoh is the Queets Rainforest, another old-growth rainforest. The Queets River Trail here is difficult to navigate except in the dry season of late summer due to numerous river crossings (and no footbridges). When the rivers are rushing, opt for the moderate 2.8-mile (4.5-km) Sam's River Loop Trail, which also begins at the Queets River Ranger Station, but doesn't cross the river.

## The mountains and interior

With commanding views and numerous trails, Hurricane Ridge is a good place to start exploring the park's interior. The moderate 3.2-mile (5.1-km) round-trip hike on the Hurricane Hill Trail takes you to stunning views of both Mount Olympus and the waters of the Strait of Juan de Fuca. Another option is the Klahhane Ridge Trail, a 7.6-mile (12.2-km) round trip; it's moderate at first, but the last mile is a steep climb, well rewarded by a panorama of mountains, glaciers, and the saltwater below. For overnighters, the Heart O' the Hills Campground is near the base of the ridge. In winter, the Hurricane Ridge Ski and Snowboard Area operates on weekends.

Northwest of Hurricane Ridge, deep, blue Lake Crescent is one of the most popular places in the park, with lodging, dining, and a campground on its shores.

## Did You Know?

More than 200 inches (508 cm) of rain can fall in the Hoh Rain Forest in a given year.

# A LONG WALK
# HOH RIVER TRAIL

**Length** 17.4 miles (28 km) one-way  **Stopping-off points**
There are various backcountry campsites along the trail
**Terrain** Rocky dirt trail

From its source on Mt. Olympus, the milky-colored
Hoh River tumbles downstream to the Pacific Ocean.
This trail tracks the waterway's journey in reverse,
starting in one of the largest and wettest rainforests
in North America before meandering upstream
through subalpine meadows and old-growth forest.

**Locator Map**

*Hoh River Trail*

**OLYMPIC**

**Key**

– – Walk Route

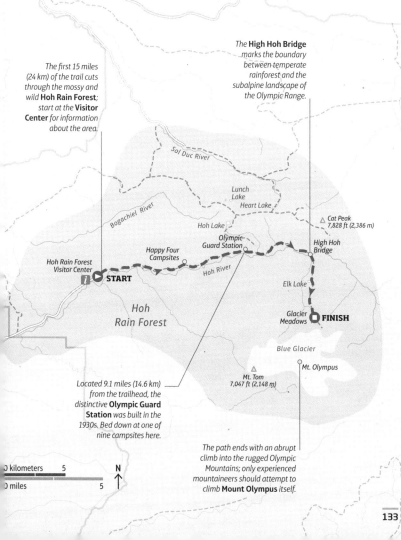

*The first 15 miles
(24 km) of the trail cuts
through the mossy and
wild **Hoh Rain Forest**;
start at the **Visitor
Center** for information
about the area.*

*The **High Hoh Bridge**
marks the boundary
between temperate
rainforest and the
subalpine landscape of
the Olympic Range.*

Sol Duc River

Lunch
Lake

Heart Lake

Bogachiel River

Hoh Lake

△ Cat Peak
7,828 ft (2,386 m)

Olympic
Guard Station

High Hoh
Bridge

Happy Four
Campsites

Hoh Rain Forest
Visitor Center

**START**

Hoh River

Elk Lake

*Hoh
Rain Forest*

Glacier
Meadows

**FINISH**

*Blue Glacier*

△
Mt. Tom
7,047 ft (2,148 m)

Mt. Olympus

*Located 9.1 miles (14.6 km)
from the trailhead, the
distinctive **Olympic Guard
Station** was built in the
1930s. Bed down at one of
nine campsites here.*

*The path ends with an abrupt
climb into the rugged Olympic
Mountains; only experienced
mountaineers should attempt to
climb **Mount Olympus** itself.*

0 kilometers          5

0 miles               5

N
↑

## A weekend

Make your first stop Kalaloch Beach and its surroundings, and plan to overnight here in a lodge or campground. Spend time finding tidal pools and peaceful pockets. Then head to Hurricane Ridge for a hike on the second day.

You can rent kayaks, canoes, and paddleboards at Lake Crescent Lodge and Log Cabin Resort. Beyond the lodges, there is a campground on the western tip of the lake.

The Sol Duc Valley, located south of Lake Crescent, is one of the most developed areas of the park, with the Sol Duc Hot Springs Resort and a campground. It's also a hub for trails heading in every direction. Day hikers can pick from trails to Sol Duc Falls, an easy 1.7-mile (2.7-km) round trip, or Mink Lake, a moderate 5.2-mile (8.4-km) round trip. There are also numerous

multiday backpacking routes that start here, including the 18.2-mile (29.3-km) loop around Seven Lakes Basin.

The largest watershed in the park, the Elwha Valley was returned to its natural state with the removal of two dams between 2011 and 2014. The work was among the largest ecosystem restoration projects in the history of the National Park Service. Today, the area is open to hikers and bicyclists, but not cars: a flood washed out Olympic Hot Springs Rd. in 2015 and it has since been closed to motorized vehicles for the forseeable future.

On the east side of the park, you'll find numerous isolated areas to explore, including Deer Park, Staircase, and Dosewallips. Because of their location in the "rain shadow" of the Olympic Mountains, they're much drier than other parts of the park, but note reaching them requires long drives down rough roads. All three areas have campgrounds and a variety of hiking trails, inclu-

Kayaking on the tranquil waters of Crescent Lake ↑

ding the moderate trail along the Main Fork of the Dosewallips River, which runs 15.5 miles (24.9 km) and connects with trails to Staircase.

## On the coast

From South Beach to Shi Shi Beach, you won't have any trouble finding solitude on the park's western coast. Make sure you check the tides

Oil City Trailhead, a moderate to difficult 15.7-mile (25.3-km) hike; a permit is required.

You'll find plenty of peace if you're willing to wander even further from the roadside. The easy 9.2-mile (14.8-km) Ozette Triangle, which starts at Ozette Lake, takes you to the beach at Cape Alva, then returns inland to the lake at Sand Point. You can camp on the beach, but a permit is required. There is also a park campground and a private cabin complex at Ozette Lake.

ahead; you may have to take a trail above the beach during high tides.

Below the lodge of the same name is Kalaloch Beach, top of most visitor lists. You can continue north on U.S. 101 to lesser-visited Ruby Beach. Whichever you pick, both are easy to get to from the highway and are home to campgrounds.

Further north, you'll find four beaches clustered around the Teahwhit Head near the Mora area: Rialto Beach and First, Second, and Third beaches. Rialto and First are close to the roadside, but Second and Third require an easy hike of 0.7 miles (1.1 km) and 1.4 miles (2.3 km) respectively. Many backpackers continue south from Third Beach to the

# EAT

There are numerous dining options in the park and in Forks and Port Angeles.

### Roosevelt Dining Room

At the Lake Quinault Lodge, find hearty fare for breakfast, lunch, and dinner.

🏠 Quinault 🌐 olympic nationalparks.com

---

### Fairholme Store

Grab-and-go sandwiches, groceries, and camping supplies near Lake Crescent.

🏠 Port Angeles 🌐 olympicnational parks.com

---

### Sully's Drive-In

Old-school place serving no-frills food (burgers, burritos, hot dogs, fries) just right.

🏠 Forks 📞 (360) 374-5075

$$$

←
Sea stacks at Shi Shi Beach, in the top corner of the national park

# EXPLORING OLYMPIC

With its remarkable array of landscapes, Olympic packs a lot into its 900,000 acres (360,000 ha). It encompasses a Pacific coast, vast alpine areas, temperate rainforest to the west, and the forests of the drier east side.

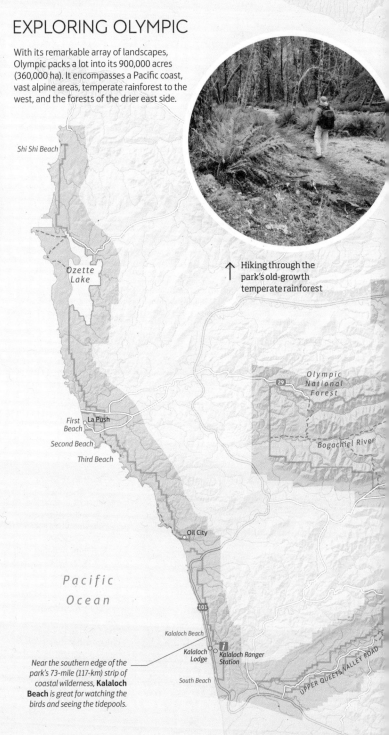

↑ Hiking through the park's old-growth temperate rainforest

*Shi Shi Beach*

*Ozette Lake*

*Olympic National Forest*

29

*Bogachiel River*

*First Beach* — La Push

*Second Beach*

*Third Beach*

Oil City

*Pacific Ocean*

101

*Kalaloch Beach*

*Kalaloch Lodge*  ℹ Kalaloch Ranger Station

*South Beach*

UPPER QUEETS VALLEY ROAD

*Near the southern edge of the park's 73-mile (117-km) strip of coastal wilderness, **Kalaloch Beach** is great for watching the birds and seeing the tidepools.*

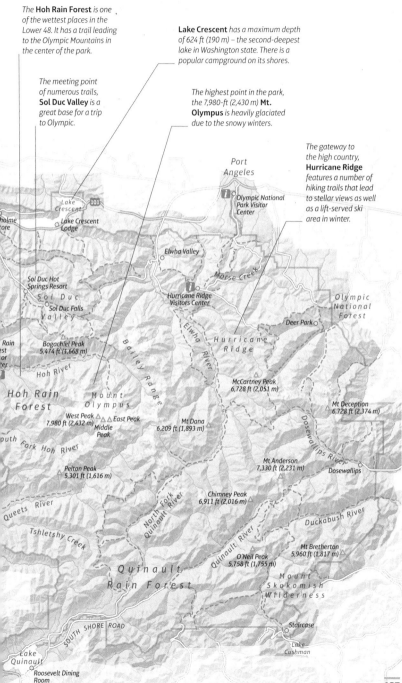

The **Hoh Rain Forest** is one of the wettest places in the Lower 48. It has a trail leading to the Olympic Mountains in the center of the park.

**Lake Crescent** has a maximum depth of 624 ft (190 m) – the second-deepest lake in Washington state. There is a popular campground on its shores.

The meeting point of numerous trails, **Sol Duc Valley** is a great base for a trip to Olympic.

The highest point in the park, the 7,980-ft (2,430 m) **Mt. Olympus** is heavily glaciated due to the snowy winters.

The gateway to the high country, **Hurricane Ridge** features a number of hiking trails that lead to stellar views as well as a lift-served ski area in winter.

Port Angeles

Olympic National Park Visitor Center

Lake Crescent

101

holme
est
ore

Lake Crescent Lodge

Elwha Valley

Morse Creek

Sol Duc Hot Springs Resort

Sol Duc

Sol Duc Falls

Valley

Hurricane Ridge Visitors Center

Olympic National Forest

Deer Park

Rain
st
or
er

Bogachiel Peak
5,474 ft (1,668 m)

Hoh River

Bailey Range

Elwha River

Hurricane Ridge

Hoh Rain Forest

Mount Olympus

West Peak △ △△ East Peak
7,980 ft (2,432 m)  Middle Peak

Mt Dana
6,209 ft (1,893 m)

McCartney Peak
6,728 ft (2,051 m)

Mt Deception
6,728 ft (2,374 m)

outh Fork Hoh River

Pelton Peak
5,301 ft (1,616 m)

Dosewallips River

Mt Anderson
7,330 ft (2,231 m)

Dosewallips

Queets River

Tshletshy Creek

North Fork Quinault River

Chimney Peak
6,911 ft (2,016 m)

Duckabush River

Mt Bretherton
5,960 ft (1,817 m)

Quinault Rain Forest

Quinault River

O'Neil Peak
5,758 ft (1,755 m)

Mount Skokomish Wilderness

SOUTH SHORE ROAD

Staircase

Lake Cushman

Lake Quinault

Roosevelt Dining Room

0 kilometers     10

0 miles          10

N

KOBUK
VALLEY
*p182*

GATES OF
THE ARCTIC
*p178*

ALASKA

DENALI
*p154*

WRANGELL-
ST. ELIAS
*p162*

LAKE CLARK
*p174*

KATMAI
*p168*

KENAI
FJORDS
*p142*

GLACIER BAY
*p148*

# ALASKA

Home to the country's only Arctic ecosystem and 17 of
North America's tallest mountains, Alaska is a land of epic
proportions. The state's diverse and fragile ecosystems
are protected by some of the wildest parks in the U.S.,
each defined by their extremes: in the far north, the
Gates of the Arctic, abundant in boreal woodland of
birch, spruce, and aspen; to the west, majestic sand
dunes rise from the tundra at Kobuk Valley; at Mount
Denali, the park's namesake peak is the tallest in the
country. The state's glacier-scoured coastlines, vast
alpine tundra, and arboreal forests are roamed by some
of the world's most beautiful animals: salmon-hungry
brown bears prowl the icefields and herds of caribou
migrate in their thousands. These wild landscapes have
long been maintained by Alaska's ancestral peoples, and
Indigenous communities now work with the park service
to ensure their cultural legacy is protected.

The country's largest and least densely populated
state, Alaska provides the ultimate adventure for
explorers. With parks larger than entire countries, it
would take many lifetimes to explore its wonders.

1 Hiking the McKinley Trail, Denali.

2 Kayaking in Kenai Fjords.

3 The *Denali Star*.

4 Shops along the dock in Seward Harbor.

# 5 DAYS
## *in Alaska*

### Day 1

Begin your Alaska adventure at Denali National Park *(p154)*, 240 miles (386 km) north of Anchorage. Get oriented at the visitor center before hopping on a green transit bus to traverse the 92-mile- (148-km-) long Denali Park Road. Take the bus all the way to Wonder Lake, with great views of Denali, the U.S.'s tallest mountain. If there's time, consider hiking the McKinley Bar Trail to the McKinley River, or stroll to tiny Reflection Pond with its iconic reflection of Denali. Grab the bus to the final stop at Kantishna, where you can view pioneer Fannie Quigley's historic cabin and stay in the Kantishna Road-house *(kantishnaroadhouse.com)*.

### Day 2

Today you'll slowly make your way back to the park entrance, soaking up the vistas of taiga forest, blasted tundra, and saw-toothed peaks. Popular stops include the Eielson Visitor Center, where you can explore the short Gorge Creek Trail, and Toklat River, where you might spot curly-horned Dall sheep. Accommodations can be found close to the park entrance on Hwy. 3. If you have the energy, Denali Raft Adventures *(denaliraft.com)* offers evening rafting on the Nenana River.

### Day 3

This morning, round off your Denali experience by participating in ranger programs, seeing a sled-dog demon-stration, or strolling the easier trails around the visitor center. Alaska Railroad's *Denali Star (alaskarailroad.com)* usually departs the station (opposite the visitor center) for Anchorage at 12.30pm, arriving at 8pm – it's a wonderfully scenic journey, with a dining car on board and plenty of hotels on arrival.

### Day 4

Get up bright and early for another epic train ride, this time the *Coastal Classic* to the port town of Seward. Dump your bags at your hotel in Seward and grab lunch before visiting Kenai Fjords *(p142)* Visitor Center at the harbor. In the afternoon, head to Exit Glacier, 12 miles (19 km) out of town and the only part of the park accessible by land. From the Exit Glacier Nature Center, it's a short walk on the Glacier View Loop Trail through cotton-wood forests to a captivating vista of the glacier. Back in Seward, the SeaLife Center *(alaskasealife.org)* is usually open in summer. End the day sampling seafood at The Cookery *(cookeryseward.com)*.

### Day 5

The best way to appreciate Kenai Fjords is from the water. Book a full-day cruise *(majormarine.com)* that takes in the wildlife-rich waters of Resurrection Bay, Aialik Bay, pristine Northwestern Fjord, and the seabird rookeries of the Chiswell Islands. For a more intimate experience of these majestic natural wonders book a kayaking tour *(kayakak.com)* to Aialik Glacier. Mark the end of your Alaskan journey with an evening of live music and beers at Yukon Bar (201 4th Ave, Seward).

# KENAI FJORDS

📍Alaska 🎟Free 🌐nps.gov/kefj

Alaska's smallest national park is a Tolkien-like land, offering a foray into a complex wilderness that crosses ice, land, and sea. The crown jewel is the Harding Icefield from where glaciers flow outward, cutting through mountain ridges and valleys before meeting the ocean. On the coastal perimeter, dramatic cliffs reach skyward. Because of the park's accessibility and amenities in nearby Seward, there are many activities for visitors of all ages, skill levels, and interests.

IF YOU HAVE
**A day**

Spend your time on the water. Take a day-long National Park Service boat tour, pushing off from the Seward waterfront to spy local fauna: seals, porpoises, and even whales.

On the leeward edge of Alaska's rugged Kenai Peninsula sits one of the best arctic maritime parks in the world. While the fjords here give the park its name, it's the massive icefields and glaciers that have carved the region over thousands of years, creating an epic, and beautiful, landscape.

The park is cut into four distinct ecosystems, and glaciers (now receding due to the effects of the climate crisis) feed the whole of the environment. The craggy mountains they rest upon act as channels feeding the water downward. Lush forests sit at the bast of the mountains and are filled with alder, sedges, and salmonberry that in turn support wildlife, like black

←
Hiking, with Exit Glacier
an imposing presence
in the background

and brown bears, moose, and mountain goats. The fjords also provide a habitat for aquatic mammals, puffins, and tens of thousands of coastal birds.

## Exploring the park

While there are several multi-day guided trips available with regional tour companies, part of the beauty of this national park is its accessibility, opportunities to travel on your own schedule, and the variety of adventures available. There are two information points in the park: a visitor center in Seward and a nature center in Exit Glacier. The former is a great first stop to get information, pick up memorabilia, and arrange ranger-guided boat tours. The Exit Glacier Nature Center is the unofficial trailhead for hikes in Exit Glacier, including the Harding Icefield Trail.

## On the water

No trip to Kenai Fjords would be complete without seeing the fjords themselves and the icy waters that splash at their bases. There are half- and full-day boat tours available that either stay close to picturesque Seward or venture farther afield to Aialik Bay. Aboard, keep your eyes fixed on the water to catch sight of Stellar sea lions, Dall's porpoises, and migratory whales surfacing. Look out, too, for local birdlife: cormorants, kittiwakes, oyster-catchers, puffins, and the like.

### GETTING AROUND

Kenai Fjords is located around 130 miles (210 km) from Anchorage and is one of the most accessible parks in Alaska. If you're not arriving by car, driving the scenic Seward Highway, hop aboard Seward Bus Lines from Anchorage for a three-hour ride (each way). The Alaska Railroad is another option, a great way of transiting southern Alaska (May–September). Many visitors arrive by cruise ship. Once in the park, the only area accessible by car is Exit Glacier. Water taxis, air-taxi, and helicopters can be arranged for transportation to designated areas throughout the park or for journeys with a view.

→ Enjoying the view from an alpine hut along the Harding Icefield Trail

# EAT

Dubbed the "Gateway to Kenai Fjords National Park", Seward has plenty of excellent restaurants featuring fresh-off-the-boat seafood. If you are camping in a tent or RV, follow mandatory food storage requirements. The park service provides bear cans and metal storage food lockers to protect wildlife.

### Ray's
This place is something of an institution. The food (seafood, steaks, sandwiches) is tasty but the views of the harbor are the real highlight.

⌂ Seward
W rayswaterfront.com

$ $ $

---

### Chinooks Waterfront Restaurant
Casual waterfront restaurant serving fresh seafood. Open March through December.

⌂ Seward
W chinooksak.com

$ $ $

---

### Zudy's Café
An easy choice for sandwiches and cakes.

⌂ Seward
W zudyscafe.com

$ $ $

---

↑ A moose and her calf, animals commonly sighted in Kenai Fjords

Aialik Bay is home to the Aialik Glacier, an active tidewater glacier that regularly calves, sending boulders of ice into the waters with an almighty noise. Motorized boats and self-propelled watercraft can get you up close to the action.

Another way of exploring the park's waters is by paddle. Sea kayaking is a popular pursuit here, with Resurrection Bay, Northwestern Lagoon, and Nuka Bay all stellar paddle locations, along with the bays and coves that hug their shores. To extend the adventure, set out on a

multiday kayak trip, stopping at public-use cabins or camping on remote beaches. Kayaks can be rented and tours booked at outfitters in Seward.

## Glacier exploration
Ready to get up close and personal with Kenai Fjords' famed glaciers? Strap on some crampons, grab a helmet, and head out with a tour company (or solo if you are an experienced mountaineer) to hike across

---

🕐 IF YOU HAVE
**A weekend**

Camp at Exit Glacier and pair with a challenging hiking excursion on the Harding Icefield Trail, which leads to views of a glacier landscape.

---

Kayakers exploring a natural ice bridge around Aialik Bay ↑

vast blue ice on Exit Glacier. These adventures are tailored for novice ice-climbers and moderately experienced mountaineers. Regardless of your experience, safety training is required prior to exploring such notoriously unpredictable terrain.

## Hiking

The park has only a few well-maintained trails. The short Glacier View Loop Trail on the valley floor of Exit Glacier is an easy trail. Starting at the Exit Glacier Nature Center, the 1-mile (1.6-km) route travels through forest to lookout points of the outwash plain. The 7.5-mile (12-km) Harding Icefield Trail hike (a round trip) is strenuous, gaining 1,000 ft (300 m) as it climbs through meadows and forest. The reward is sprawling views of America's largest icefield.

## Mountain running

If you are a runner, consider participating in the 3.1-mile (5-km) "Mount Marathon", which runs each July. This steep, rocky climb has been called the most challenging race in the world. It's open to around 800 people with entry available by lottery.

## In winter

Through the summer, Exit Glacier Road is accessible by car. But in winter? From November until the snow melts around May the road becomes a thoroughfare for cross-country skiing, snowmobiling, snowshoeing, and fat biking. The winter months also bring opportunity to spot moose, common in the area. A warming hut (facilitated by the park) and a winter-use cabin are available when the cold weather gets too much.

Always check in advance of your trip for weather reports, information on closures, and how to best navigate the park. Adventure Sixty North, a park concessionaire, provides authorized scenic shuttle tours and guided snowshoe walks. Some boat tours to tidewater glaciers and among the fjords may be available with private companies but the unpredictable weather can prompt cancellations.

# STAY

Stay in Seward, or use the park's limited cabins and campground.

### Kenai Fjords Glacier Lodge

The only lodge in the park, located in a wildlife sanctuary.

⌂ Kenai Fjords
🅦 alaskawildland.com

Ⓢ Ⓢ Ⓢ

### Willow Public Use Cabin

A winter-use cabin accessible by skis, bicycle, snowshoes, and snowmobile. Reservations required.

⌂ Exit Glacier
🅦 nps.gov/kefj

Ⓢ Ⓢ Ⓢ

# EXPLORING KENAI FJORDS

Covering around 608,000 acres (246,000 ha), the Kenai Fjords National Park takes in some of Alaska's finest coastal scenery and glacial landscapes. Some 51 percent of the land is covered in ice, with many tidewater glaciers in the process of shedding their outer layers.

*The 70-mile- (113-km-) long and 30-mile- (48-km) wide **Harding Icefield** is the largest icefield located entirely within the U.S. Hikers can access it via a trail from Exit Glacier.*

↑ Looking out over the vast expanse of the impressive Exit Glacier

Harding

Northwestern Glacier

Northwestern

McCarty Glacier

Black Mountain
2,028 ft (618 m)

Dinglestadt Glacier

McCarty Fjord

Ho

Iceworm Peak
5,800 ft (1,767 m)

Storm Mountain
3,793 ft (1,156 m)

Surok Point

Gulf of Alaska

Yalik Glacier

North Arm

Petrof Glacier

West Arm

Steep Point

Pye Islands

Nuka Island

| 0 kilometers | 10 |
| 0 miles | 10 |

The **Exit Glacier Nature Center** is the starting point for hikes in the Exit Glacier area. Rangers can lend advice here before you set off.

The **Kenai Fjords National Park Visitor Center** in Seward is open daily during the summer season, and issues backcountry permits.

Resurrection River

Exit Glacier Nature Center

Harding Icefield Trail

Exit Glacier

Phoenix Peak 5,155 ft (1,571 m)

The Kenai Fjords Visitor Center

Seward

Icefield

Bear Glacier

Resurrection Bay

Skee Glacier

State Park Cabins

Callisto Peak 3,223 ft (983 m)

Aialik Glacier

Bear Glacier Lagoon

Addison Glacier

Slate Island

Pedersen Glacier

Aialik Bay Cabin

Aialik Bay Ranger Station

Wildlife cruises take in **Resurrection Bay**, where you might spot seabirds, sea lions or even whales, depending on the season.

**Aialik Glacier** is the largest glacier in Aialik Bay. It is known for its high activity, with glacier calving frequently occurring during May and June.

Aialik Peninsula

Aialik Bay

Harris Peninsula

Chiswell Islands

Granite Island

On the rocky outcrops of the **Chiswell Islands**, day cruises approach one of Alaska's Steller sea lion rookeries.

→ Cruise passengers spotting a humpback whale leaping

**Did You Know?**
—
Huna Tlingit society is matrilineal, with descent and rights passed from mother to child.

The mighty Lamplugh Glacier, ↑ which descends from the Brady Icefield into the bay

# GLACIER BAY

📍 Alaska  🎟 Free  🌐 nps.gov/glba

Little compares to seeing a house-sized block of ice crashing into the water or a huge humpback whale seemingly defying gravity as it breaks the water's surface, but these scenes are common in Glacier Bay National Park. A biosphere reserve and binational UNESCO World Heritage Site, this park is a sprawling landscape of glaciers, snowcapped mountains, icy seascapes, and scores of wildlife. On top of that, it's also a living laboratory for scientists researching glacier retreat.

Best known for its tidewater glaciers and deep fjords, Glacier Bay is predominantly wilderness. Its forests and alpine peaks are habitats for bears, wolves, moose, and mountain goats, and the water is home to humpback whales and the occasional orca. As impressive as the wildlife is the native flora and bio-organisms that grow from areas where glaciers once existed.

Home to Huna Tlingit groups for centuries, the bay has been a prime destination for visitors since naturalist and national park advocate John Muir made his way here in the 1800s. When the park was made a national monument in 1925, however, the native Huna Tlingit lost access to natural resources, all but devastating the way of life they and their ancestors had relied upon for centuries. Over the last 30 years, the park service has heeded repeated calls to right this wrong, and has worked with Indigenous groups to help the Huna Tlingit reconnect with their homeland.

## Exploring the park

Learning about Glacier Bay and how to navigate the park is made easy at the Visitor Information Station and Backcountry Office located in Bartlett Cove, 10 miles (17 km) from the town of Gustavus. There you can get boating and camping permits and take a safety orientation before heading out to explore

### GETTING AROUND

The only way to get to Glacier Bay is by small plane or boat. Unless arriving by cruise ship, private boat, the Alaska Marine Hwy., or air-taxi, visitors typically start in the town of Gustavus. From there it's a 10-mile (17-km) drive by taxi or shuttle bus to Bartlett Cove. Once in the heart of the park visitors get around on foot, or by plane or boat (the park has barely any roads). Glacier Bay's high visitor count can largely be attributed to travelers passing through on cruise liners between May and September – the prime time to see humpback whales migrating

# EAT

The park has only one dining option, the Fairweather Dining Room located in Glacier Bay Lodge (also home to the visitor center). Nearby Gustavus has several dining options though availability is more limited during the off-season.

# STAY

There is one lodge and one established campground in the park. Backcountry travelers have near unlimited places to pitch a tent. Gustavus has several inns, lodges, and bed-and-breakfasts.

### Glacier Bay Lodge

Cozy rooms, full dining, and in a prime location by the visitor center, Huna Tribal House, hiking trails, and push-off points into the cove and surrounding waters. Open mid-May to mid-September.

 Bartlett Cove
Ⓦ visitglacierbay.com

Ⓢ Ⓢ Ⓢ

### Bartlett Cove Campground

A free, walk-in, tent-only campsite (permit required) with a fire pit, bear-proof food storage, and warming shelter near the shore.

 Bartlett Cove
Ⓦ visitglacierbay.com

Ⓢ Ⓢ Ⓢ

on your own. Also in Bartlett Cove (a scattering of buildings that comprises the park's only sign of development) is the Glacier Bay Lodge Visitor Center, a beautiful facility with large windows peering onto the bay. The center has exhibits and films, and helpful rangers.

## Huna Tribal House

Xunaa Shuká Hít (the Huna Tribal House), located in Bartlett Cove, was created to provide a place for the Huna Tlingit to engage with their history and culture. Here, visitors can learn more about Indigenous history and enjoy performances, presentations, and demonstrations.

## Boating

The Glacier Bay Tour Boat, operated by the park service, is a wonderful way of getting to grips with the park. It departs Bartlett Cove each morning during the summer season. Day-long trips (lasting around seven hours) passage 130 miles (210 km) into Glacier Bay, which was made up entirely of ice until just 250 years ago. Aboard, passengers can marvel at marine life, birds, and the tidewater glaciers the park is named after. Park guides narrate the trip and are there to answer questions. The voyage is a family favorite and an opportunity for young explorers to earn a Junior Ranger badge. Be sure to bring your cameras and binoculars to get a better view of all you are seeing.

Private boats are allowed in the park but a (free) permit must be secured in advance of your arrival. Permits go

A paddle-and-pitch, one way of exploring the park's vast wilderness ↑

↑ Margerie Glacier, one of several tidewater glaciers at Glacier Bay

quickly; only 25 private vessels are allowed inside the park each day (June–August). See the park website for details.

## Active glaciers

Glacier Bay is home to, among others, the Grand Pacific Glacier and the Margerie Glacier, one of the park's most active. Around 300 ft (90 m) tall, 1 mile (1.5 km) wide, and 20 miles (30 km) long, the glacier regularly calves, shedding boulders of ice into the waters with echoing booms that permeate the otherwise quiet surroundings.

## Sea kayaking

Kayaking Glacier Bay is another way of exploring the park, and seeing both wildlife and glaciers. Muir Inlet is closed to motorized boats during the summer, making it a popular place to paddle. Visitors can also arrange for boat drop-off to backcountry shores, where they can paddle in more remote areas and camp overnight.

## Fishing

Deep-sea fishing is at its best in Glacier Bay where you can drop a line for salmon, halibut, and other local favorites. Private charters are available; if going solo, an Alaska State Fishing License is required, which you can pick up during the summer at the Glacier Bay Lodge Visitors Center. These outings also provide great opportunities to spot, if you are lucky, orca ( or "killer") whales when farther out in the waters.

## Hiking

Hiking through spruce-hemlock forests and along the shores of Glacier Bay allows for sightings of wildlife such as bears and moose, ducks and geese, and otters and harbor seals.

The park has only four established trails, crossing just 10 miles (17 km). One such trail is the easy Tlingit Trail (0.5 miles/1 km), which takes walkers along the shore to the Huna Tribal House. The longest of the four trails is the 8-mile (13-km) Bartlett Lake Trail (round trip). Winding through woodland, the trail runs to the lake, providing beautiful views of the mountains. Bears and moose are often sighted in this area, so do exercise caution.

Beyond the established trails are backcountry trails, which provide endless adventures. The scenery is diverse, crossing alpine meadows, rugged coastlines, and deglaciated areas that quietly tell the ecological history of the region. You are unlikely to see others while traveling the backcountry and the solitude is part of its undeniable beauty.

## Cruises

Luxury ships operated by Carnival, Holland America, Norwegian, and Princess Cruise Lines, as well as smaller companies, make trips to the park during the summer season. Voyages often start in Seattle and Vancouver, B.C. and prices range from moderate to expensive.

---

 IF YOU HAVE
**A weekend**

Take the park boat tour for wildlife sightings and up-close views of active glaciers. Spend the rest of the time walking in the wilderness, perhaps to Bartlett Lake, and pay a visit to Huna Tribal House.

# EXPLORING GLACIER BAY

Located in Southeast Alaska, Glacier Bay National Park comprises 3.2 million acres (1.3 million ha) of pristine mountains and waterways. You'll find some of the purest air on the planet here, as well as seven tidewater glaciers that calve icebergs into the bay.

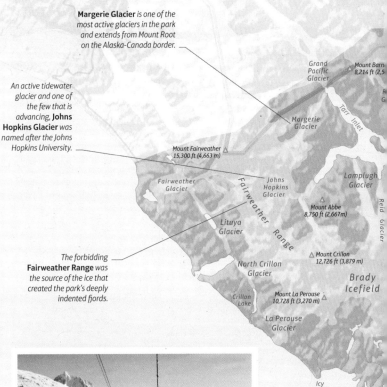

**Margerie Glacier** *is one of the most active glaciers in the park and extends from Mount Root on the Alaska-Canada border.*

*An active tidewater glacier and one of the few that is advancing,* **Johns Hopkins Glacier** *was named after the Johns Hopkins University.*

*The forbidding* **Fairweather Range** *was the source of the ice that created the park's deeply indented fjords.*

Grand Pacific Glacier

Mount Barn 8,214 ft (2,5...

Tarr Inlet

Margerie Glacier

Mount Fairweather 15,300 ft (4,663 m)

Fairweather Glacier

Johns Hopkins Glacier

Fairweather Range

Lamplugh Glacier

Reid Glacier

Lituya Glacier

Mount Abbe 8,750 ft (2,667m)

△ Mount Crillon 12,726 ft (3,879 m)

North Crillon Glacier

Brady Icefield

Crillon Lake

Mount La Perouse 10,728 ft (3,270 m)

La Perouse Glacier

Icy Point

Gulf of Alaska

↑ Keeping an eye out for marine mammals on a cruise through Glacier Bay

→

Enjoying a trail through Bartlett Cove, one of many easy hikes

Takhinsha Mountains

Muir Glacier

Cushing Glacier

Mount Brock
4,990 ft (1,521 m)

Sitth-gha-ee Peak
5,870 ft (1,789 m)

Carroll Glacier

Casement Glacier

Muir Inlet

Mount Rice
5,658 ft (1,725 m)

Mount Merriam
5,083 ft (1,549 m)

Mount Wright
5,139 ft (1,566 m)

Beartrack Mountains

Glacier Bay

Drake Island

Willoughby Island

Wood Lake

Bartlett River

Excursion Ridge

Excursion River

*The **Muir Inlet** in Glacier Bay was named after the naturalist John Muir (p37) who studied the region. It's a popular place to kayak.*

Dundas River

Glacier Bay Lodge
Visitor Center
Bartlett Cove

Bartlett Lake

Gustavus

Pleasant Island

Lemesurier Island

Inian Island

Cross Sound

*Once the home of a 100-mile (161-km) long glacier, **Bartlett Cove** is now the only developed area within the park, home to several easy hikes, a lodge, and a campground.*

*The village of **Gustavus** outside the southeast corner of the park offers lodging and visitor services, and operators run tours from here.*

0 kilometers        20
0 miles             20

N
↑

153

# DENALI

📍 Alaska 🔁 $15 per person, valid for seven days 🌐 nps.gov/dena

First established as Mount McKinley National Park, Denali was designated to protect the rare wildlife of the Alaska Range. This park is nature at its most awesome: wildlife roam here, the landscape bursts into vivid hues of purple, green, and orange. And when the high clouds part, and the towering massif of North America's tallest peak reveals itself, it's a no-holds-barred showstopper. Little wonder, then, that a trip to Denali makes it onto so many people's bucket lists.

IF YOU HAVE
**A day**

Venture into the park along Denali Park Road. Book a narrated tour or make a reservation for a park-led shuttle. Expect scenic views of both the landscape and the park's wildlife.

Denali is one of Alaska's most visited parks, with hundreds of thousands of visitors flocking here each year to witness wildlife in its natural habitat, and explore landscapes sprawling with soft tundra, braided rivers, spruce forests, and high mountains. The pinnacle of the park is Mount Denali, the highest mountain in North America

at 20,310 ft (6,190 m) and a dream climb for high-altitude mountaineers from around the world.

**Exploring the park**

Most summer visitors to Alaska have Denali on their itineraries, so a smooth visit requires pre-booking and advance planning. In the June to August peak season, it is

←
The dramatic scenery of Denali National Park, seen from the air

not uncommon to have to wait several days for shuttle tickets or campsite bookings.

The Denali Visitor Center at the park entrance is a good place for information about park history, wildlife, and general activities. By the Denali Bus Depot (secure shuttle tickets and camp-ground reservations here) is the Backcountry Information Center, where you can get backcountry permits. Visitors exploring off Denali's roads are required to watch a bear safety presentation.

The Murie Science and Learning Center, a short walk away, is designed for hands-on science education related to the park's geology, wildlife, and conservation efforts.

Near the park headquarters are working sled dog kennels, where the National Park Service's only team resides. These hardy dogs spend the winter patrolling the park's backcountry for weeks on end, and enjoy the summer months playing host to scores of visitors.

Many visitors will be happy exploring the park along the Denali Park Road and around the main entrance area, but it's worth remembering this park is vast. Exploring beyond the main draws need only take a bit of planning and some imagination.

→
A Dall ram; protecting these wild sheep was a key factor in creating the park

## Mount Denali

This soaring peak was named Mount McKinley in 1896, in support of then-presidential candidate William McKinley. It remained so for more than 100 years until 2016, when it was officially redesignated Denali, which means "The High One" in native Athabascan. The high-elevation peak creates its own microclimate and is frequently hidden by cloud systems, so consider it lucky if you catch a decent view. Some of the best places in the park to see it are from Mountain Vista near the parking lot and at Wonder Lake (mile marker 85 on the Denali Park Road). The colorful region around Wonder Lake, characterized by expanses of tundra and blueberry bushes, is also favored grizzly habitat; you might also spot caribou and beavers.

Climbing the mountain is an activity reserved for highly skilled and experienced mountaineers only.

## Denali Park Road

There is only one road in Denali's epic wilderness

and it leads into the heart of the park. You can explore it solo in your private vehicle – but only to mile marker 15. Beyond that, concessionaire operated shuttle bus tours bring travelers up to 92 miles (148 km) to where the park ends at Kantishna, before turning back to the main park visitor center. There are stops at scenic markers and visitor centers along the way, as well as at drop-off points for backcountry hikes into the park's interior. Some shuttles are narrated by rangers, who

tell stories of the park's natural and cultural history, and help guests see the wildlife Denali is so famous for. Reservations can be made at the park's Wilderness Access Center (see also Getting Around for further information).

To extend your scenic drive, why not leave the park on the Denali Highway? This spectacular route extends for 135 miles (217 km) from Cantwell on the park's east side to Paxson, providing near-endless views of the Alaskan landscape. Note the surface ranges from smooth to rough to rutted, and the road can sometimes be closed by snowfall.

### Wildlife watching

In a park established explicitly to protect wildlife, it is no surprise that seeing park fauna in their natural habitat is at the heart of almost every adventure in Denali.

Early efforts to protect the park's wildlife were spearheaded by a naturalist named Charles Sheldon who was passionate about keeping grizzly bears, wolves, moose, Dall sheep, and birdlife safe from poachers eager to make

 A shuttle bus driving along the supremely scenic Denali Park Road

The snowy peaks of Mount Denali, an intrepid adventure for two explorers

a profit. These species and others, including around 170 species of birds, still thrive in the park.

Your best opportunities to see wildlife are on Denali Park Road shuttle trips, in the Savage River area, and on foot in the backcountry. Bring binoculars or a zoom lens for your camera to get the best views, remembering to keep a safe distance to avoid causing animals and birdlife undue stress.

## Guided walks
Heading out on an independent hike requires a bit of skill and experience, given the park's dense vegetation and uneven terrain, and plenty of wildlife roaming around. Here's the good news: the park offers two types of

guided trips on foot. Ranger-led walks and hikes, offered May–September, are relatively short (about two hours) and set at an easy pace. American Sign Language interpretation is available on request, too, which the park service always strives to accommodate.

Discovery Hikes, venturing off-trail and into the wilderness, are labeled as moderate to strenuous and last about 10 hours, so do take stock of your skill and ability. Sign up in advance and in person at the Denali Visitor Center; here, rangers will explain what you can expect from the walk and where you'll go.

## Hiking
Those who do venture off on their own are in for a treat. Part of the beauty of exploring the Denali backcountry is the solitude you will find in such a truly unforgettable natural setting. There are no designated routes (the park's few maintained trails are short and located near visitor centers, and usually very crowded) nor backcountry campgrounds, meaning you and your group can create your own adventure.

## -100
The coldest temperature in °F (-73°C) recorded in Denali

## EAT

Finding somewhere to purchase food within the park is tricky, with just one sit-down restaurant (May-Sep) and a couple of places selling snacks (at the Denali Bus Depot and the Riley Creek Mercantile). Your best bet is to bring your own supplies or plan to fuel-up in places along Hwy. 3 on the park border; Healy is an obvious choice.

**Morino Grill**
Located next to the Denali Visitor Center at the park entrance, this is the only sit-down restaurant in the park. Coffees and cafeteria-style meals.

🏠 Denali
🌐 nps.gov/dena
$ $ $

Cycling along Denali Park Road, a challenging undertaking for some ↑

> **From above you can easily spot large mammals peppering the soft tundra below ... and braided rivers glistening under the glow of the midnight sun**

Be sensible, of course. Plan for unpredictable weather, uneven terrain, river crossings, and wildlife encounters. Backcountry permits are required for all overnighters in the park and are issued at the Backcountry Information Center from mid-May to mid-September; during the winter you can pick them up at the main park visitor center. Prior to obtaining a permit, you will need to attend a backcountry orientation briefing. One vital takeaway will be the Leave No Trace principles that helps keep the Denali wilderness as pristine as you found it.

### Cycling

Rent a bicycle at the Denali Outdoor Center or bring your own and pedal through Denali's front country. There are only a few areas open to bicycles (e-bikes too, with some restrictions) including portions of Denali Park Road, the Roadside Bike Path, and campground loops. If you're up for it, bicycle camping is a fun and unique multisport adventure. The park shuttle to the campgrounds has a two-bicycle maximum load capability so plan in advance and make reservations.

### On the water

If cruising down a river is your game, half-day rafting excursions are operated by private outfitters on the 10-mile (17-km) Nenana River, taking you on whitewater rapids, then to still sections where you can take in your surroundings. Extended river adventures can be arranged too, with

---

**IF YOU HAVE**
**A weekend**

Prepare well ahead for a backcountry camping experience. Take the shuttle bus along Denali Park Road and into the park, disembarking for a two-day adventure into the wilds. End your trip with a pre-booked flightseeing tour.

---

→

The ethereal aurora borealis seen in the park after dark

multiday paddle trips venturing onward on the Talkeetna River.

## Flightseeing

Witnessing Denali National Park from the sky is a wonderful way of experiencing the park's beauty.

Flights climb to eye level of Denali peak where in its folds, mountaineers make technical climbs ascending and descending unforgiving terrain. From above you can easily spot large mammals peppering the soft tundra below, as they move from one area to the next, and braided rivers glistening under the glow of the midnight sun. There are four authorized air-taxi operators in the park offering multiple itineraries lasting varying lengths of time.

### In winter

Winter in Denali is cold, dark, and covered in snow. At the same time, a calmness blankets the park, making it a great time of year to set off on snowshoes, skis, and winter-equipped bicycles. Winter is also the best time of year to see the awesome aurora borealis (also known as the Northern Lights), colorful green, pink, and orange ribbons that dance across the skies.

# STAY

While the NPS doesn't operate lodging facilities within the park there are a number of accommodations within the park boundary on private land. There are also a number of options in the nearby towns of Healy and Cantwell.

### Kantishna Roadhouse

An Alaskan Native enterprise and historic landmark, this privately run roadhouse offers all-inclusive amenities including planning and guided experiences (Jun–Sep).

🅰 End of Denali Park Road 🆆 kantishna roadhouse.com

### Camp Denali

A family-owned and operated wilderness lodge with 18 cabins, meals, and naturalist-guided programs and activities (Jun–Sep).

🅰 Wonder Lake area 🆆 campdenali.com

### National Park Service Campgrounds

Summer-only campgrounds equipped for tents and RVs. Reservations open in December ahead of the following summer season; some sites are first-come, first-served.

🅰 Along Denali Park Road 🆆 reservedenali. com/camping

# EXPLORING DENALI

The expansive Denali National Park sprawls across more than 6 million acres (2.4 million ha) and is larger than the entire state of New Hampshire. Denali, North America's highest peak, dominates the landscape, while remote lakes, glistening glaciers, and carpets of wildflowers leave visitors just as awestruck.

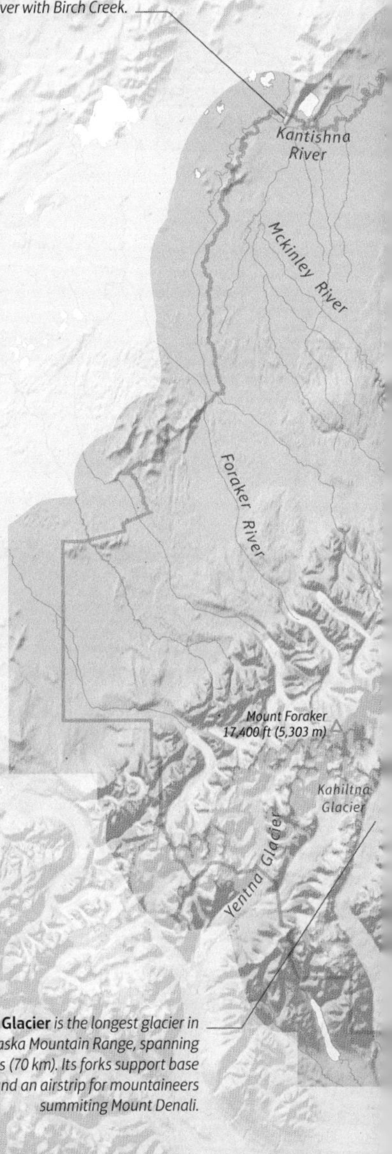

*From the north, the park can be reached by river boat on the **Kantishna River**, which is formed by the confluence of the McKinley River with Birch Creek.*

Kantishna River

Mckinley River

Foraker River

Mount Foraker
17,400 ft (5,303 m)

Kahiltna Glacier

Yentna Glacier

↑ Mountaineering on a narrow ridge above the Kahiltna Glacier

0 kilometers    30

0 miles    30

N ↑

**Kahiltna Glacier** *is the longest glacier in the Alaska Mountain Range, spanning 44 miles (70 km). Its forks support base camps and an airstrip for mountaineers summiting Mount Denali.*

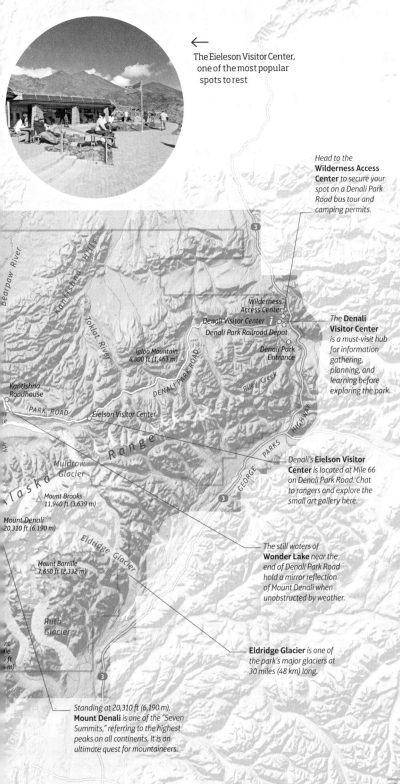

The Eieleson Visitor Center, one of the most popular spots to rest

Head to the **Wilderness Access Center** to secure your spot on a Denali Park Road bus tour and camping permits.

Wilderness Access Center

Denali Visitor Center

Denali Park Railroad Depot

The **Denali Visitor Center** is a must-visit hub for information gathering, planning, and learning before exploring the park.

Denali Park Entrance

Igloo Mountain, 4,800 ft (1,463 m)

Riley Creek

Bearpaw River

Kantishna Hills

Toklat River

DENALI PARK ROAD

Kantishna Roadhouse

PARK ROAD

Eielson Visitor Center

GEORGE PARKS HIGHWAY

Denali's **Eielson Visitor Center** is located at Mile 66 on Denali Park Road. Chat to rangers and explore the small art gallery here.

Range

Muldrow Glacier

Alaska

Mount Brooks 11,940 ft (3,639 m)

Mount Denali 20,310 ft (6,190 m)

Eldridge Glacier

Mount Barrille 7,650 ft (2,332 m)

The still waters of **Wonder Lake** near the end of Denali Park Road hold a mirror reflection of Mount Denali when unobstructed by weather.

Ruth Glacier

**Eldridge Glacier** is one of the park's major glaciers at 30 miles (48 km) long.

nt ie s ft m)

Standing at 20,310 ft (6,190 m), **Mount Denali** is one of the "Seven Summits," referring to the highest peaks on all continents. It is an ultimate quest for mountaineers.

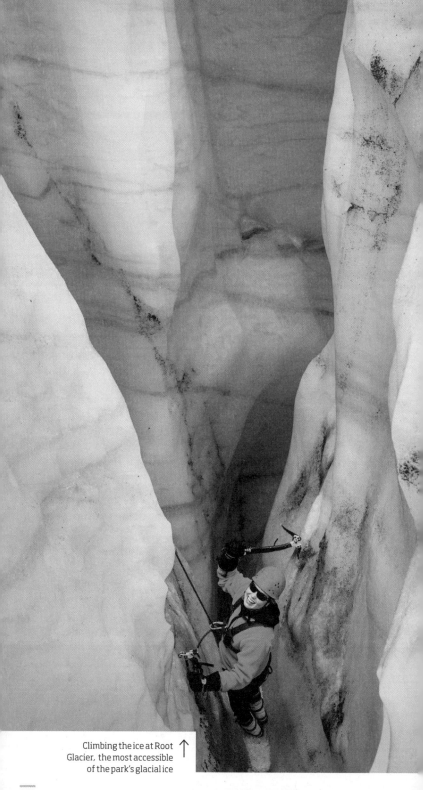

Climbing the ice at Root Glacier, the most accessible of the park's glacial ice ↑

# WRANGELL-ST. ELIAS

📍 Alaska and Canada  💲 Free  🌐 nps.gov/wrst

Bigger than Yellowstone, Yosemite, and the state of Maryland combined, Wrangell-St. Elias is the nation's largest national park. A vast wilderness of rugged mountains, fast-flowing rivers, and expansive glaciers, it is also one of the most remote parks in the country, with only a few road-based access points. Alaskan Tlingit and Eyak communities have lived along the coasts and in the Copper Basin for more than a thousand years, but the region remained little known until scientific research began here in the late 1800s.

Located in the sprawling area that is Alaska's southeastern mainland section, this park wears the adjective "epic" well. Describing it takes a list of numerous superlatives. The park has nine of the 16 highest mountains in the U.S., and a few of the largest glaciers on Earth, including the Nabesna Glacier, the longest nonpolar valley glacier in the world. It's also one of few protected wilderness areas to be designated a binational UNESCO World Heritage Site (it stretches from Alaska into Canada). There's a volcano, too. Dominating the landscape at 14,163 ft (4,316 m), Mount Wrangell is one of the largest active volcanoes in the U.S.

Natural wonders aside, the park also serves up a slice of Alaskan history. Within the park are the Kennecott Mines, a National Historic Landmark. Here visitors can explore the restored buildings of a once-booming copper-mining company town.

This park may take some effort to reach but it pays high return for adventurous travelers and history buffs looking to explore Alaska's dazzling backcountry.

## Exploring the park

The Copper Center Visitor Center near Glennallen is a must first stop. Here, you'll find information on exploring the backcountry (essential for even the most intrepid),

## EAT

Other than that provided by lodges, there are few dining options in the park.

**The Golden Saloon**
Serving lunch and dinner mid-May to mid-September, this saloon is a go-to for the locals. Expect U.S. classics on the menu and live music on weekends.

📍 McCarthy  🌐 golden-saloon.com

**The Roadside Potatohead**
Open mid-May to mid-September, this is a great place to stop and fill up while exploring Kennicott. Vegetarian and vegan friendly.

📍 McCarthy  🌐 theroadsidepotatohead.com

A national park on a grand scale: the Wrangell Mountains ↑

← A floatplane at one of the park's creeks, a thrilling start to a rafting trip

← Backpacking on the Kennicott Glacier with a canine companion

All offer a spectacular taste of lowland terrain with views of the mountains and glaciers. A standout is a half- or full-day guided hike on Root Glacier, the most accessible glacier in the park, located just 1.5 miles (2.4 km) from Kennecott.

Two other trails are the Bonanza Trail and the Skookum Volcano Trail. The former is a steep one, with 3,800 ft (1,160 m) of vertical gain. The reward, though, is a spectacular view of the Root and Kennicott glaciers. The short Skookum Volcano Trail, just 2.5 miles (4 km), takes walkers along an eroded volcanic system, which leads to a high alpine pass. Look out for Dall sheep as you go.

### Glacier exploration
Ice climbing up vertical walls, repelling into crevasses, and glacier hiking expeditions are among the favorite ways to get on the ice. And while no experience is necessary for guided tours on Root Glacier, for example, these natural wonders are active and dangerous. Set upon volcanic plates, the estimated 150 glaciers here are constantly moving, calving, and cracking. Needless to say, responsible exploration and proper outfitting is key, and traveling with an experienced guide is always the best way forward.

An alternative to hiking or climbing a glacier is to fly over one; flightseeing tours can be booked in gateway towns around the park.

> Ice climbing up vertical walls, repelling into crevasses, and glacier hiking expeditions are among the favorite ways to get on the ice.

exhibits, a store, and ranger talks. Visitor information can also be found at ranger stations along McCarthy Road in Chitina and at the entrance to the Nabesna Road in Slana.

Given the wildness of this park, booking guided tours – especially for hiking glaciers and rafting along the river – is highly recommended. For those going it alone, take necessary precautions and always leave your itinerary with a responsible person.

### Cultural history
Before embarking on a park adventure, pay a visit to the Ahtna Cultural Center, which sits just next door to the Copper Center Visitor Center. Detailing local Indigenous history, it's owned by 2,000 shareholders, the majority of whom are of Alaska Native or Ahtna Athabascan descent. Ahtna communities have long lived off the land in the Copper River region – fishing, trapping, hunting, and gathering plants and berries.

### Hiking
Maintained hiking trails, doable in a day, are mostly concentrated in three areas: Copper Center, Kennecott, and along Nabesna Road.

## On the water

A land of glaciers inevitably forms networks of rivers and whitewater float expeditions (single-day or multiday trips available) beckon river-runners from around the world. Popular locations include the Copper, Chitina, and Tana Rivers. Trips are challenging with changing water levels, frigid temperatures, and high levels of silt clouding the river bottom from view, but this is some of the best rafting in the state.

### GETTING AROUND

Wrangell-St. Elias's rocky gravel roads are not easy roads to travel: bring spare tires or opt instead for a seat on the summer-only Kennicott Shuttle (reservations required). Note that some rental car companies don't allow their fleet to traverse these roads so check ahead. Starting in Chitina, the 60-mile- (97-km-) long McCarthy Road leads to the heart of the park at Kennecott, where the main visitor center is located. The shorter Nabesna Road begins in Slana, north of the park. Both are reachable from Anchorage with a half- to full-day drive. Air-taxis offer drop services from Anchorage and other towns in the region, and flightseeing tours in small bush planes are popular ways of getting around the park.

# EXPLORING WRANGELL-ST. ELIAS

The **Copper Center Visitor Center** at Mile 106.8 on the Richardson Highway is where most visits begin, home to scenic overlooks and trails.

Built in 1933 to access the Nabesna Mine, the 42-mile (67-km) **Nabesna Road** leads through hills to the eponymous village.

One of the main draws to the park, **Kennecott** is home to an abandoned copper-mining camp.

The **McCarthy Road Entrance** begins in the town of Chitina.

The old mining town of **McCarthy** is accessed via a short walk or shuttle ride. It must be passed through to reach the town of Kennecott.

The **Bagley Icefield** is the second-largest nonpolar icefield in North America.

Sea kayaking trips on **Icy Bay** are a great way to see marine life.

Nabesna Road Entrance

Copper River

Chistochina

Noyes Mtn
8,147 ft
(2,483 m)

USA

Gakona

Alaska Range

Wellesley Mountain
4,960 ft (1,512 m)

Mount Sanford
16,237 ft (4,949 m)

Chisana

Nutzotin Mountains

Copper River Visitor Center Complex

Mount Wrangell
14,163 ft (4,317 m)

Mount Jarvis
13,421 ft (4,091 m)

Wrangell Mountains

Wiki Peak
7,655 ft (2,333 m)

CANADA

Copper Center

Copper River

Mount Blackburn
16,390 ft (4,996 m)

Root Glacier

White River

Chitina

McCarthy Road Entrance

Kennicott Glacier

McCarthy

Kennicott

Mount Bona
16,421 ft (5,005 m)

Hanagita Peak
8,504 ft (2,592 m)

Chitina River

Goodlata Peak
8,166 ft (2,489 m)

Granite Range

St. Elias Mountains

Chugach

Bagley Icefield Mountains

Jefferies Glacier

Mount Miller
8,875 ft (2,705 m)

Seward Glacier

Mount Saint Elias
18,008 ft (5,489 m)

Point Glorious
5,000 ft (1,524 m)

Icy Bay

Malaspina Glacier

0 km          50

0 miles          50

N

# GLACIERS OF ALASKA

Glaciers develop when mountain snow builds up into masses of ice, in areas where it is cold enough for winter snowfall to survive the summer thaw. Some areas of Alaska, like the Harding Icefield in Kenai Fjords, receive around 400 inches (10 m) of snow each year. Layers of snow compress into glacial ice and move downhill due to gravity.

Over hundreds of thousands of years, glaciers have had a huge impact on the landscape around them, changing the shape of valleys, eroding the landscape through glacial floods, and forming steep-sided fjords.

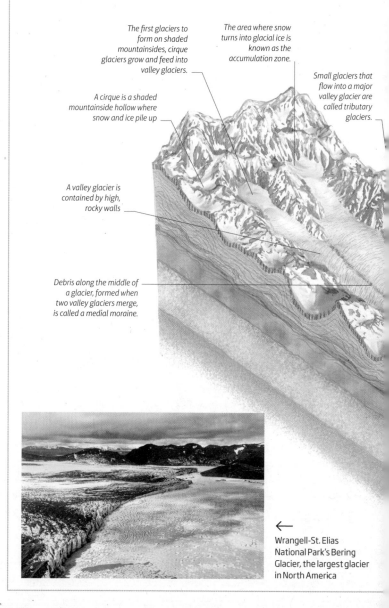

The first glaciers to form on shaded mountainsides, cirque glaciers grow and feed into valley glaciers.

The area where snow turns into glacial ice is known as the accumulation zone.

Small glaciers that flow into a major valley glacier are called tributary glaciers.

A cirque is a shaded mountainside hollow where snow and ice pile up

A valley glacier is contained by high, rocky walls

Debris along the middle of a glacier, formed when two valley glaciers merge, is called a medial moraine.

← Wrangell-St. Elias National Park's Bering Glacier, the largest glacier in North America

## GOING, GOING...

Alaska is one of the most heavily glaciated areas in the world (it has over 19,400 glaciers) – and it's warming twice as fast as the rest of the U.S. From 1985 to 2020, glacier-covered areas in Alaska decreased by some 13 percent. The loss has been greatest in the mountainous coastal regions of the state. Glacier cover in Wrangell-St. Elias, for example, which has the most glaciers of any park, has decreased by over 370 sq miles (950 sq km).

1 Kennicott Glacier is thinning, with lakes that didn't exist in the 1990s growing ever larger.

2 Hubbard Glacier, a tidewater glacier, is actually getting bigger.

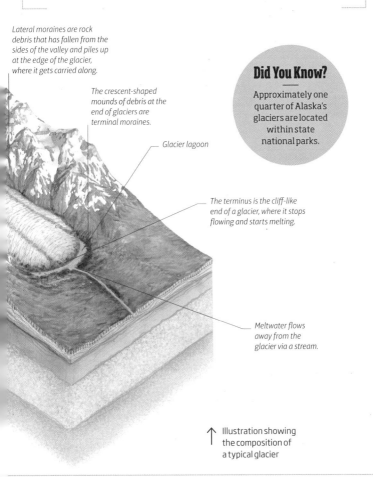

*Lateral moraines are rock debris that has fallen from the sides of the valley and piles up at the edge of the glacier, where it gets carried along.*

*The crescent-shaped mounds of debris at the end of glaciers are terminal moraines.*

*Glacier lagoon*

*The terminus is the cliff-like end of a glacier, where it stops flowing and starts melting.*

*Meltwater flows away from the glacier via a stream.*

↑ Illustration showing the composition of a typical glacier

### Did You Know?

Approximately one quarter of Alaska's glaciers are located within state national parks.

Best for *Bear spotting and salmon fishing*

# KATMAI

**Alaska** · **Free** · **nps.gov/katm**

Positioned on a peninsula between the Gulf of Alaska and the Bering Sea, isolated Katmai is the definition of "wild." There are only a few miles of established trails here, but a world of wilderness to explore: watch brown bears scoop salmon from rushing rivers, admire a landscape irrevocably changed by one of the planet's largest volanic eruptions, and paddle waters – rivers, lake, the surrounding sea – plied by numerous species of fish and abundant marine life.

This remote national park offers a front-row seat to one of nature's most storied hunting events. Each year, hulking brown bears converge on Katmai National Park to feast on the million-plus salmon that make their journey here. If you're after that classic image of wild Alaska, this is the place to come. Not that it's easy to get here, mind. Access to the park is only by plane, and if you want to explore beyond the bears you'll need to be backcountry and boat ready – or book onto a guided tour.

Summer is the best – and therefore busiest – time to visit the park, when the salmon are running, wildflowers are blooming, and the bears are hungry.

## Exploring the park

Navigating such an intensely wild ecosystem can be daunting and safety must be thought of at every step, from pre-planning, to carrying the essentials, to understanding how to stay safe in bear country. Fortunately, the National Park Service and regional expedition companies are

McNeil River, one of the best places for watching brown bears hunting

passionate about helping visitors have safe experiences that are memorable in all the right ways.

Katmai has three main visitor centers: Brooks Camp, where you will get safety training in advance of bear-viewing trips at the legendary Brooks Falls; Robert F. Griggs, which overlooks the Valley of the Ten Thousands Smokes; and the King Salmon Visitor Center, the best first stop to obtain general information, pick up bear cans, and get advice from rangers.

## Bear watching

Katmai is best known for its enormous population of brown bears with more than 2,200 estimated in the park. They are massive in size too, feeding on five species of Pacific salmon that "run" through the region annually, and that have sustained Indigenous communities in the region for more than 9,000 years. Bear viewing at Brooks Falls is by far the most popular activity in the park – and one that all can witness from the comfort of their own home by watching seasonal "bear cams" on the National Park Service website.

Bear viewing is best in July and September, inevitably making these months busy.

Crossing the Katmai River on a backcountry hiking adventure

## GETTING AROUND

Katmai comprises more than 3.8 million acres (1.5 million ha) of wilderness and there are no access roads to (or in) the park. Access is made possible by seaplane (landing on water) or tundra plane (landing on solid terrain) depending on where you are going. The town of King Salmon is around 300 miles (485 km) west of Anchorage as the crow flies. It is the jumping-off point for most Katmai adventures including to Brooks Falls, which can be reached in under 30 minutes by seaplane, dropping you into the heart of the action at Naknek Lake.

Be prepared to wait to cross the bridge at Brooks River and for access to the four viewing platforms; your viewing time may also be limited to an hour.

## Wildlife spotting

Beyond the park's famous bears, there are endless wildlife viewing opportunities regardless of where you go. Guided adventures in less frequently visited areas like the Shelikof Strait yield sightings of bears, moose, fox, coastal birds, and marine life such as sea lions, otters, and migrating whale species.

## The Valley of the Ten Thousand Smokes

Katmai was established because of significant scientific and scenic interest that came following the most devastating volcanic eruption of the 20th century. In 1912, the Novarupta stratovolcano

**IF YOU HAVE**
**A weekend**

Aim for Brooks Lodge, to see bears from one of several viewing platforms perched atop the Brooks River. Then, book onto the Valley of the Ten Thousand Smokes tour, and explore this impressive landscape.

sent ash 20 miles (32 km) into the sky for three days straight in the region surrounding Mount Katmai, driving Native Alaskans and wildlife from the area and turning it into a barren wasteland. Today, the 56-mile (90-km) area – now known as the Valley of the Ten Thousand Smokes – is vibrantly colored by volcanic ash deposits and is beloved by backcountry hikers.

To explore the valley, book onto a tour (daily tours are

# EXPLORING KATMAI

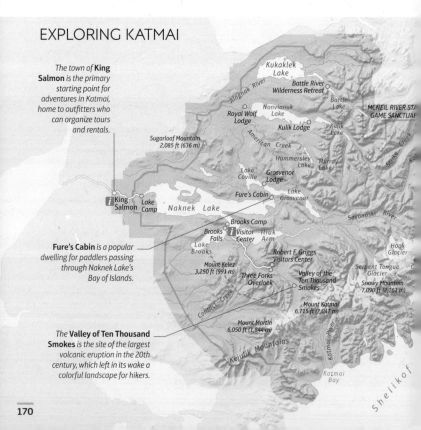

The town of **King Salmon** is the primary starting point for adventures in Katmai, home to outfitters who can organize tours and rentals.

**Fure's Cabin** is a popular dwelling for paddlers passing through Naknek Lake's Bay of Islands.

The **Valley of Ten Thousand Smokes** is the site of the largest volcanic eruption in the 20th century, which left in its wake a colorful landscape for hikers.

→ Fly-fishing for salmon in Hallo Bay, also a popular site for bear viewing

offered by concessionaire Katmailand through Brooks Lodge). A bus runs to the valley, stopping for a couple of terrific viewpoints and with an onboard park ranger providing information. Once at the valley visitor center, you'll have the opportunity to hike the area. There are a number of river crossings here, so exercise real caution; water depths are tricky to estimate due to volcanic ash and sediment.

### On the water

Easily accessible (by road, from King Salmon, or from Brooks Camp), the massive Naknek Lake is Katmai's go-to body of water. Launch a kayak, canoe, or packraft and explore; the 80-mile (130-km) Savonoski Loop is a popular choice for those with boating experience, and starts and ends at Brooks Camp.

Sport fishing is hugely popular, with anglers arriving from around the world to cast a line in the park's salmon-rich waters. Read up on rules and regulations on the NPS website and ensure you have the correct licenses – and be alert to your rival hunters, the park's bears. The Kulik River and Hallo Bay are two good places to cast off.

> Sport fishing is hugely popular, with anglers arriving from around the world to cast a line in the park's salmon-rich waters.

0 km                    25

0 miles                  25

N ↑

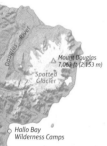

Douglas River

△ Mount Douglas
7,064 ft (2,153 m)

Spotted Glacier

Hallo Bay
Wilderness Camps

Hallo
Bay

ai
erness Lodge

**Hallo Bay** *is an excellent place to spot bears feeding on sedges in the shadow of the Aleutian Range.*

Strait

*The* **Shelikof Strait** *teems with birds, aquatic animals, and colorful flora including lichen and fireweed.*

## THE BEARS OF ALASKA

Most visitors to Alaska's parks want to see bears, and nearly everyone does. With the exception of the Aleutian Islands, Alaska is prime bear habitat and home to three species of bears: black, brown, and polar. Active in summer, many bears become dormant in winter, retreating to dens and living on fat reserves; it is often at this time that cubs are born. Bears can sometimes be aggressive, particularly when protecting cubs or competing with each other during the breeding season.

↑ A black bear resting in open grassland

### BROWN BEARS

Alaska brown bears *(Ursus arctos)* are split into three types: the rangier grizzlies of the Interior, coastal brown bears, and the huge Kodiak bears of Southwest Alaska. The Kodiak are not a true subspecies, however, and the size variations are due only to differences in diet. The grizzlies eat more vegetation, whereas coastal browns eat lots of high-protein fish. Brown bears are resident from the Southeast to the Arctic, mostly spotted in summer and fall.

### BLACK BEARS

Black bears *(Ursus americanus)* are the smallest Alaska bears, measuring an average of 5 ft (1.5 m) in length. These predominantly vegetarian creatures are found everywhere in Alaska except the Arctic tundra and the Aleutian Islands. They are recognizable by their black or cinnamon coat and pointed muzzle, and can be seen in the wild from spring through to fall.

↑ A female brown bear with her cubs in Katmai National Park

## POLAR BEARS

Polar bears *(Ursus maritimus),* which inhabit the Arctic Ocean coastline, subsist mainly on marine mammals. Swimming across open water, they spend most of their lives roaming the ice floes in search of seals, but come ashore in the fall to breed. In addition to their creamy coat, they are also distinguishable from Alaska's other bear species by their longer neck. Visitors to Alaska's national parks are unlikely to see polar bears.

↑ Polar bear cubs on a snowy beach next to the Beaufort Sea

## BEAR SAFETY

Staying safe in bear country involves a trifecta of preparation, awareness, and protection. Remember the following points at all times.

**Be Aware of Your Surroundings**
Take note of any environmental factors (brushy areas, rushing water) that may impede sounds, and look out for evidence of bears (scat, tracks, flattened vegetation). Pay attention to all posted warning signs.

**Take a Guide** Do not hike or walk in polar bear country without a trained guide.

**Make Noise** Sing, rattle stones in a can, or talk loudly to let bears know you are entering their territory.

**Travel in Groups** Hike or walk with other people. Instruct children to stay within an arm's reach at all times.

**Carry Bear Spray** Studies show that capsaicin-based aerosol spray is most effective in deterring bears. Make sure to read all directions for safe use.

**Do Not Run** If you see a bear closer than 550 yd (500 m) away, keep your eyes on it and back away slowly. Do not ever run.

**Stay Together** If a bear approaches you, group all individuals together, raise your arms, and talk to the bear in a firm, calm voice. Ready your bear spray, and if the bear continues to approach, spray it in a sweeping motion toward the bear's nose. Once the bear walks away, leave the area and report the encounter to the nearest park ranger.

Best for *Choosing your own backcountry adventure*

# LAKE CLARK

📍Alaska $ Free 🌐nps.gov/lacl

**Alaska is often called The Great Land, and perhaps there's little greater than untamed Lake Clark National Park, a wilderness of more than 3.8 million acres (1.5 million ha) filled with volcanoes, rivers, and lakes. Spotting the park's resident bears might be top of the list for most visitors but, really, there isn't one sole reason to come here. Rather, the beauty of this park is in the full experience: floating on turquoise lakes, watching the trees for local birdlife, or hiking the tundra.**

When the Alaska National Interest Lands Conservation Act was passed in 1980, Lake Clark National Park came into being to protect the 50-mile- (80-km-) long Lake Clark and its surrounding ecosystems. This impressive patch of wilderness includes the shores of Cook Inlet, which is prime bear territory, and the glaciated heights of the Chigmit Mountains and the Aleutian Range. The twin volcanoes Mount Iliamna and Mount Redoubt are also within its boundaries. The park is home to an array of wildlife, most prominently brown bears and migrating herds of caribou.

IF YOU HAVE
**A weekend**

Take a floatplane to the Twin Lakes area and make it your base. Set up camp on the shores and set off on day hikes, exploring the area where Dick Proenekke made a home.

## Exploring the park

Given that access to the park is primarily through Port Alsworth, it makes sense to start with a trip to the community's visitor center, open May–September.

Lake Clark itself is as good a place as any to spend your time, but the Twin Lakes area provides boundless outdoor activities, and is where you'll find one of the park's must-see spots: Richard "Dick" Proenekke's Cabin.

Mount Redoubt volcano, part of the Aleutian Range ↑

# STAY

The park has lodges and some public-use cabins (reserve in advance). There are no official campgrounds.

**Kontrashibuna Lake**
Camping is permitted 100 yards (90 m) from the shore.
📍Port Alsworth area
$

**The Farm Lodge**
Modern waterfront lodge with activity packages (Jun-Sep).
📍Port Alsworth area 🌐thefarmlodge.com
$$$

**Silver Salmon Creek Lodge**
Lodges and camping with outdoor activities on offer (Jun-Sep).
📍Cook Inlet 🌐silver salmoncreek.com
$$

↑ Kayaks on the shores of Lake Clark, known as Qizhjeh Vena by early Alaskans

# EAT

Aside from lodges in Port Alsworth, the park has no dining services. Non-lodge visitors will need to carry camping and cooking gear, as well as all food, bear canisters, and methods of sourcing safe water.

Preparing food at Proenneke's Cabin must be done away from the cabin (the nearby beach is a good spot) and picnicking is prohibited at the upper portion of Chinitna Bay during the summer.

## Cultural history

For 12,000 years, the migrating Dena'ina Athabascan people have lived at Lake Clark, which in their language translates as "a place where people gather." In the early 1900s, the largest population of Athabascans still living in the region abandoned the 1,000-year-old Kijik village. This ghost town is the largest Athabascan archeological site in Alaska and is listed on the National Register of Historic Places.

### Richard "Dick" Proenneke's Cabin

Having first visited the Twin Lakes area of Lake Clark in 1962, amateur naturalist, filmmaker, and craftsman Richard "Dick" Proenneke returned in 1968, to build his own handhewn log cabin. While staying in the park he wrote daily in journals, which have since become icons of wilderness homesteading. Proenneke donated the cabin to the National Park Service after his final visit there in 2000, offering it as a way for visitors to better understand the value of Alaska and the park, and as a means to get to know oneself.

The cabin is open only during summer and, unless you are hiking here, access is by floatplane.

## Bear viewing

Imagine standing on saltwater shores while families of bears hunt for razor clams burrowed into the sandy beach and fish the tidal waters. At Lake Clark, this scene becomes reality. Bears

> Imagine standing on saltwater shores while families of bears hunt for razor clams burrowed into the sandy beach and fish the tidal waters.

are common here, due in large part to plentiful food: thousands of salmon migrate to the lake annually, creating a steady source of protein. Bear viewing is best achieved by chartering a floatplane to areas like Chinitna Bay, Crescent Lake, and Silver Salmon Creek.

## Hiking

Adventures on foot abound in Lake Clark. While there are only a handful of maintained trails (the four-trail Tanalian trail system starting in Port Alsworth and the 3-mile/5-km Portage Creek Trail), a hike can be enjoyed by anyone who has the inclination, equipment, and backcountry navigation skills.

Hardy multi-hikers might be interested in the long-distance Telaquana Route. Following in the footsteps of the Dena'ina people, the hike runs loosely from Telaquana Lake to Kijik village. There's no set trail so this is one for hikers to plan their own route; prepare for challenging terrain, which includes tricky river crossings.

↓ Tanalian Falls, seen on a 4-mile (6.5-km) round-trip walk from Port Alsworth

↓ Brown bears, often sighted in Chinitna Bay or Silver Salmon Creek

# EXPLORING LAKE CLARK

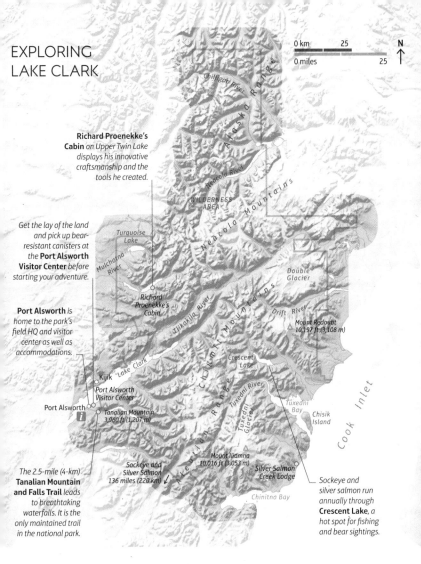

**Richard Proenekke's Cabin** on Upper Twin Lake displays his innovative craftsmanship and the tools he created.

Get the lay of the land and pick up bear-resistant canisters at the **Port Alsworth Visitor Center** before starting your adventure.

**Port Alsworth** is home to the park's field HQ and visitor center as well as accommodations.

The 2.5-mile (4-km) **Tanalian Mountain and Falls Trail** leads to breathtaking waterfalls. It is the only maintained trail in the national park.

Sockeye and silver salmon run annually through **Crescent Lake**, a hot spot for fishing and bear sightings.

*Map labels:*
Chilligan River
Alaska Range
Neacola River
WILDERNESS AREA
Neacola Mountains
Turquoise Lake
Mulchatna River
Double Glacier
Richard Proenekke's Cabin
Tlikakila River
Drift River
Mount Redoubt 10,197 ft (3,108 m)
Crescent Lake
Chigmit Mountains
Kijik
Lake Clark
Port Alsworth Visitor Center
Tuxedni River
Tuxedni Bay
Port Alsworth
Tanalian Mountain 3,960 ft (1,207 m)
Tuxedni Glacier
Chisik Island
Cook Inlet
Sockeye and Silver Salmon 136 miles (220 km)
Mount Iliamna 10,016 ft (3,053 m)
Silver Salmon Creek Lodge
Aleutian Range
Chinitna Bay

0 km    25
0 miles    25
N

## On the water

Bears aren't the only ones interested in the park's salmon; sport fishing is a popular activity for many. You must have a license and comply with state regulations.

Skilled paddlers can ply the waters of Lake Clark, or three of Alaska's National Wild and Scenic Rivers: Chilikadrotna, Tlikakila, and Mulchatna. You will need to bring your own equipment (check your inflatable canoes or kayaks can be accommodated on your air-taxi). Alternatively, book a guided kayak tour.

### GETTING AROUND

There are no roads into Lake Clark National Park and most adventures begin in the small settlement of Port Alsworth, which can be reached by air-taxis from Anchorage in just a couple of hours. From the hub of the park, Port Alsworth, you can arrange flight drops and pick-ups to different locations in the vast wilderness. Lake Clark Air is the top service in the area with regular flights between Anchorage, Merrill Field, the Iliamna area, and to destinations throughout the national park. Lake and Peninsula Airlines is another solid option, offering flightseeing, charters, and gear drops to backcountry locations. Once in the park proper, get around by chartered plane, guided tour, or under your own steam, either by hiking or paddling (wilderness skills are essential).

**IF YOU HAVE**
**A day**

Arrange a flightseeing
tour to take in Gates of
the Arctic's sprawling
wilderness and geologic
wonders (and stop at
Kobuk Valley, too).

Hiking with the
Arrigetch and Camel
peaks in the distance ↑

# GATES OF THE ARCTIC

📍Alaska 💲Free 🌐nps.gov/gaar

Located in the Central Brooks Range entirely north of the Arctic Circle, the U.S.'s second-largest national park remains one of the least visited, year after year. It's a land of rugged beauty and extreme solitude. Despite the unforgiving landscape, several small communities inhabit resident subsistence zones here, areas where descendents of Alaskan Athabascan and Iñupiat people continue the traditions of their ancestors, freely fishing and hunting caribou for food, to build tools, and to construct clothing.

A visit to Gates is not for the faint of heart – there are no roads, maintained trails, designated campgrounds, or services within the park. There is also no cell service and limited means of communications; visitors need to be prepared and have proficient knowledge of outdoor survival skills if planning solo expeditions. Many of the landmarks don't have official names but descriptors passed down by Indigenous communities and early surveyors conducting research here. But this storied landscape and lack of infrastructure is what makes experiences here so special, allowing focus to remain on the exemplary natural backdrop enfolded by glacial cirques, dense forests, and sprawling Arctic tundra.

## Exploring the park

Planning your trip in detail is an essential component of exploring the vast Gates of the Arctic; even the most experienced of outdoor enthusiasts will find the going tough here.

## EAT

The only dining options here are those you bring yourself. If on a guided trip, you can count on three meals plus snacks each day. If on your own, stock up on supplies in nearby Bettles, Coldfoot, or Kotzebue; options will be limited, and because of transportation costs, provisions are guaranteed to be pricey. Your best bet is to tote food in from Fairbanks. Bear-resistant containers are mandatory.

As well as the Northwest Arctic Heritage Center in Kotzebue *(p183)*, there are ranger stations in Bettles (a tiny settlement southeast of the park) and at Anaktuvuk Pass. The Arctic Interagency Visitor Center in Coldfoot and

↑ Rafting along the Noatak River, one of six Wild and Scenic Rivers in the park

the Fairbanks Alaska Public Lands Information Center in Fairbanks are both useful places to stop, for exhibits, to seek advice and plan trips, and to rent bear cannisters.

### GETTING AROUND

The isolated yet scenic Dalton Highway (AK-11) is the closest access point to the park by car, taking drivers 5 miles (8 km) from the park's eastern boundary. Driving this road is an undertaking, however, with plenty of hazards to contend with (few services, bad weather, potholes, and a mostly dirt and gravel track). Air-taxi is the most common mode of transportation into the park with charter flights from Fairbanks International Airport to the smaller towns of Bettles, Coldfoot, and Kotzebue (which is also a jumping-off point to neighboring Kobuk Valley National Park). Once in the park, get around on foot or by floating on the river, being mindful of private land boundaries, leaving no trace, and navigating with care.

Many visitors combine a visit to Gates of the Arctic with Kobuk Valley (p182), organizing flightseeing tours that stop at both. Seeking the guidance of an expert is recommended, for safety but also to experience the best the park has to offer.

### On the water

The rivers of Gates of the Arctic have served as transportation routes for wildlife and humans for thousands of years. And with six of Alaska's 13 designated Wild and Scenic Rivers, it is no surprise that paddling trips

## EXPLORING GATES OF THE ARCTIC

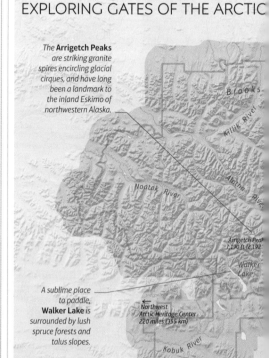

The **Arrigetch Peaks** are striking granite spires encircling glacial cirques, and have long been a landmark to the inland Eskimo of northwestern Alaska.

Brooks

Killik River

Alatna River

Noatak River

Arrigetch Peak 7,190 ft (2,192

Walker Lake

A sublime place to paddle, **Walker Lake** is surrounded by lush spruce forests and talus slopes.

← Northwest Arctic Heritage Center 220 miles (355 km)

Kobuk River

**IF YOU HAVE**
**A weekend**

Charter a small plane to take you and your canoe or kayak into the park, then spend your time floating through the park, stopping to watch wildlife and camp overnight.

are one of the most popular ways of exploring the park. Because boats are transported by small plane, collapsible boats, inflatable rafts and canoes, and packrafts are the most common types of watercraft.

Rapids average Class I and II (slow moving), increasing to Class III–IV rapids in some areas. Conditions can abruptly change so unless you are an experienced river paddler, it's recommended that you join a guided trip. Floating through

the heart of the park on bending waterways, you are guaranteed to see plenty of wildlife along the way while taking in the contoured mountains and boreal forests en route.

## Hiking and camping

Overland adventures are one of the best ways to truly immerse yourself in this backcountry wilderness. But it's not as simple as setting out for a walk in the park; there are no established trails here and progress is slow considering the terrain (water crossings are inevitable). As with any out-there expedition, take the necessary precautions to protect both yourself and the natural environment; group hikes are limited to 10 people to minimize impact on the land, and the park service recommends sticking to "game trails" where possible.

# STAY

While opportunities for backcountry camping abound, there are no accommodations within the park (note that Gold Rush-era cabins are not open to the public). Settlements beyond the park's borders have options.

**Iniakuk Lake Wilderness Lodge**
Beautiful all-inclusive fly-in lodge on the edge of the park.
⌂ Iniakuk Lake
Ⓦ gofarnorth.com

$ $ $

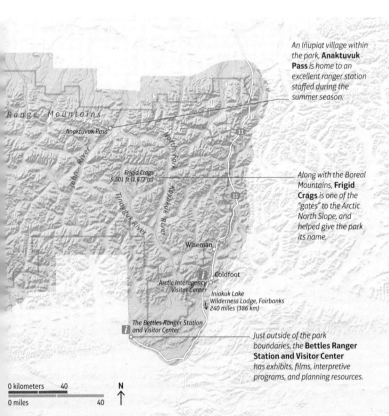

An Iñupiat village within the park, **Anaktuvuk Pass** is home to an excellent ranger station staffed during the summer season.

Along with the Boreal Mountains, **Frigid Crags** is one of the "gates" to the Arctic North Slope, and helped give the park its name.

Just outside of the park boundaries, the **Bettles Ranger Station and Visitor Center** has exhibits, films, interpretive programs, and planning resources.

0 kilometers 40
0 miles 40
N ↑

181

# KOBUK VALLEY

📍Alaska 💲Free 🌐nps.gov/kova

Like its neighbor Gates of the Arctic *(p178)*, Kobuk Valley offers Arctic wilderness in abundance. Far fewer people make it here, largely due to it being so hard to reach, expensive to navigate, and potentially dangerous to explore. But those who do are richly rewarded: Kobuk Valley is a land of astonishment, featuring rare Arctic sand dunes, crawling rivers, and one of the world's finest wildlife displays, the annual migration of thousands of caribou. Willing to brave it? This remote, wild land is waiting.

### Did You Know?

Caribou are the only member of the deer family where both females and males grow antlers.

Kobuk is a park so remote that visitors are unlikely to see any trace of humanity on the sandy dunes that sprawl between lush tundra, forest, and rivers. This is the domain of gray wolves, grizzly bears, lynx, and caribou. You might spot their tracks but they, like yours, can be washed away in an instant by winds and water

that have chiseled this land's mountains and glaciers, creating more than 19,000 acres (7,700 ha) of active dunes ,some of which stand more than 100 ft (30 m) high.

### Exploring the park

Visiting a park such as Kobuk Valley takes self-sufficiency and a healthy amount of

← The Great Kobuk Sand Dunes, the largest active sand dunes in the Arctic

gumption. There are no roads, or services, and you're unlikely to come across many fellow travelers. Careful planning, therefore, or booking on a guided tour, is essential.

The Northwest Arctic Heritage Center in Kotzebue (the gateway town to the park) serves as the park's headquarters and visitor center. Staff here can advise on places to hike, camp, see wildlife, and visit the sand dunes. It also runs ranger programs and has a museum.

## The caribou migration

The Western Arctic Caribou crossing is one of the greatest migrations in North America. Twice each year, in spring and fall, more than half a million caribou transit between their summer calving grounds to their winter breeding grounds

↑ Kayaking on the slow-running Kobuk River, which traverses the park

Caribou bulls, with their distinctive antlers, crossing the river

# EAT

Like other remote national parks in Alaska, there are no services in the park. Guided tours will usually provide food and water; otherwise bring food from Anchorage, Fairbanks, Kotzebue, or Bettles.

# STAY

The only way to stay overnight inside the national park is by camping in the backcountry. As well as Kotzebue, the villages of Ambler and Kiana, located outside of the park on the eastern and western side respectively, have basic accommodations.

### Kobuk River Lodge
A remote lodge, open June to September. Day trips and camping adventures focused on fishing, wildlife watching, boating, and hiking can be arranged.

🏠 Ambler 🌐 kobuk riverlodge.com

$$$

### Nullaġvik Hotel
Neat hotel with a restaurant that serves American-style food with an Alaskan twist.

🏠 Kotzebue 🌐 kobuk riverlodge.com

$$$

↑ A flightseeing plane, the best way to access and see the park

(and back again), just as they have done for thousands of years. Iñupiat communities make their way to Paatitaaq (or Onion Portage), a stretch of the Kobuk River, as the herd migrates south, hunting to support a way of life passed down from their ancestors. This is the best place to observe the migration, if not from a flightseeing plane above.

## Arctic sand dunes
The park's most visited attraction is the Great Kobuk Sand Dunes, which lie along Kavel Creek. Covering miles upon miles, the dunes were created when glacier-ground rock built up in an area where vegetation could not take hold. The dunes present a grand illusion: an environment that seems to stand still but, on closer look, reveals the movement of time. Peppered through the dunes are deposits of jade and schist.

Sprouting from their surface are grasses, wild rye, and colorful wildflowers that appear delicate but are sturdy enough to withstand the region's unforgiving weather systems.

To see the dunes, book a flightseeing tour from Kotzebue; some tours will merely fly over the dunes while others will set down to allow hiking or camping.

### Hiking and camping
There are no set trails within the park but that's part of the adventure for hardy hikers. Opt to walk the sands of the Great Kobuk Sand Dunes, explore the vast tundra, or brave the peaks of the Baird Mountains, stopping to camp overnight along the way. Hikers will inevitably spot some of the park's impressive

---

🕐 IF YOU HAVE
**A weekend**

Most organized tours of this park also stop in Gates of the Arctic, so make it an extended weekend and plan for a five-day trip. How much time you spend in each park (camping overnight, of course) depends on the tour; spots are limited so book well in advance.

residents and visitors: caribou, Dall sheep, wolves, and bears, and migrating loons, cranes, and Arctic terns (traveling from Antarctica on the world's longest bird migration).

## On the water

Book a tour or arrange for your own gear to be flown in and float along the Kobuk River or Salmon River in a kayak or similar to see the park from a different angle. Fishers can try for the likes of salmon, pike, sheefish, and Dolly Varden (fishing license required).

### GETTING AROUND

Like neighboring Gates of the Arctic, Kobuk Valley is extremely remote and there are no roads into or within the park. Commercial airlines fly from Alaska's two largest airports to park border towns; from Anchorage to Kotzebue west of the park, and from Fairbanks to Bettles positioned east of Gates of the Arctic. Kotzebue is home to the Northwest Arctic Heritage Center, so most visitors opt to start their trip here. Access to the park itself is predominately by small plane on a chartered flight or an organized tour. Arrangements can be made to access the park by authorized watercraft during the summer and by snowmobile during the winter. Hiking into the park is possible but is not recommended unless you are an experienced traveler trained in outdoor survival. Once in the park, getting around is on foot or by paddling.

# EXPLORING KOBUK VALLEY

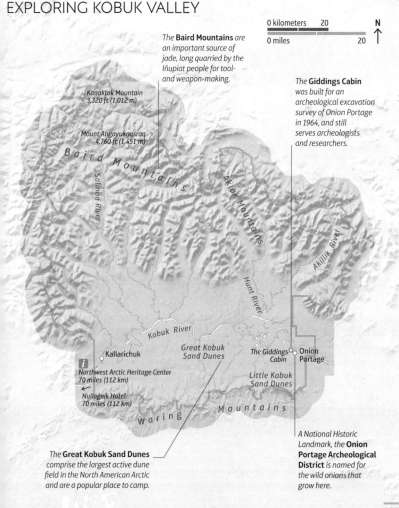

0 kilometers 20

0 miles 20

N

The **Baird Mountains** are an important source of jade, long quarried by the Iñupiat people for tool- and weapon-making.

The **Giddings Cabin** was built for an archeological excavation survey of Onion Portage in 1964, and still serves archeologists and researchers.

Kanaktok Mountain 3,320 ft (1,012 m)

Mount Angayukaqsraq 4,760 ft (1,451 m)

Baird Mountains

Salmon River

Akiak Mountains

Akillik River

Hunt River

Kobuk River

Kallarichuk

Great Kobuk Sand Dunes

The Giddings Cabin

Onion Portage

ℹ️ Northwest Arctic Heritage Center 70 miles (112 km)

Little Kobuk Sand Dunes

Nullagvik Hotel 70 miles (112 km)

Waring Mountains

The **Great Kobuk Sand Dunes** comprise the largest active dune field in the North American Arctic and are a popular place to camp.

A National Historic Landmark, the **Onion Portage Archeological District** is named for the wild onions that grow here.

GLACIER
p190

MONTANA

NORTH
DAKOTA

THEODORE
ROOSEVELT
p246

YELLOWSTONE
p200

WIND
CAVE
p252

SOUTH
DAKOTA

GRAND TETON
p212

BADLANDS
p240

WYOMING

NEBRASKA

ROCKY MOUNTAIN
p224

COLORADO

BLACK CANYON OF
THE GUNNISON
p220

GRAND SAND
DUNES
p234

KANSAS

# THE ROCKIES AND THE GREAT PLAINS

The largest mountain chain in North America, the Rocky Mountains snake 3,000 miles (4,800 km) from the deserts of New Mexico through the verdant forests of Montana into Canada. The range is bordered on its east by the Great Plains, a huge expanse of semi-arid grassland draped across a high plateau. The soaring peaks and plunging valleys of the region are home to some of the U.S.'s most iconic parks: the geothermal wonderland of Yellowstone; the shifting, wind-blown dune fields of Great Sand Dunes; the vertiginous pinnacles of Badlands. Each park is testament to nature's power, but the startlingly beautiful region also speaks of America's human story: of Indigenous peoples negotiating the wilderness, of ranchers transforming the plains, and of conservationists protecting the country's marvelous but delicate natural legacy.

# 7 DAYS

## *in the Northern Rockies*

### Day 1

Begin your Rockies road trip in Moose, the southern entrance to Grand Teton National Park *(p212)*. Stop at the Craig Thomas Discovery and Visitor Center and explore the nearby Menors Ferry Historic District; if it's hot, take a float trip along the Snake River, or rent a kayak or canoe from Dornans *(dornans.com)*. Back on dry land, detour to Mormon Row, framed by the snowcapped Tetons. Drive north to Colter Bay Village for a late-afternoon cruise on Jackson Lake, before ending the day at Jackson Lake Lodge, a 1950s hotel with grand panoramas of the Tetons.

### Day 2

After breakfast, drive south on Teton Park Road, making a short detour to Signal Mountain for dizzying views of the fang-like Tetons. Follow scenic Jenny Lake Drive before leaving your car at Jenny Lake Visitor Center. You can join scenic cruises of the lake from here, or take the shuttle across to the other side for hikes deep into the Tetons; you can also trek up to Inspiration Point. Leave the park via the north entrance on U.S. 191, staying at Headwaters Lodge & Cabins at Flagg Ranch *(100 Grassy Lakes Rd., Moran)*.

### Day 3

Get up early to begin your trip to Yellowstone *(p201)*, entering from the south. Stop at Grant Village Visitor Center and explore nearby West Thumb Geyser Basin for a taster of the park's iconic steaming pools and geysers. Continue north around the lake, stopping for lunch at Lake Yellowstone Hotel Dining Room. In the afternoon, drive 16 miles (26 km) north to Canyon Village, the gateway to the awe-inspiring Grand Canyon of the Yellowstone, where you can explore the Canyon Visitor Education Center. Allow an hour or so for the scenic drive to Mammoth Hot Springs in the evening.

### Day 4

Today is all about Yellowstone's thermal wonders. Begin at the Albright Visitor Center, then wander through the terraces formed by the Mammoth

1 Boats on Jackson Lake.

2 Canyon Visitor Education Center.

3 Inspiration Point.

4 Logan Pass in Glacier.

5 Bison at Firehole River.

Hot Springs themselves. Norris Geyser Basin, 21 miles (34 km) south, is a bubbling, smoking landscape that includes Steamboat, the world's tallest geyser. Farther south lies Grand Prismatic Spring and Old Faithful. Have lunch at the Old Faithful Inn, and explore the trails and boardwalks along the Firehole River. From here it's an easy 30-mile (48-km) drive to the resort town of West Yellowstone, over in Montana.

## Day 5

After a breakfast at Running Bear Pancake House *(538 Madison Ave., West Yellowstone)*, it's time for the drive north to West Glacier, the gateway to Glacier National Park *(p190)*. The journey should take 6–7 hours, but you'll need a break on the way; Grant-Kohrs Ranch National Historic Site at Deer Lodge is about halfway and makes for an excellent stop. Once you've arrived at Glacier, pop into the Apgar Visitor Center to get oriented, then spend the evening admiring the views of mountain peaks, cedars, and hemlock forests across Lake McDonald.

## Day 6

Forget the car today and traverse Glacier on Going-to-the-Sun Road with a Red Bus Tour. The first bus runs from Apgar Visitor Center to Avalanche Creek, where it's worth hiking the short Trail of the Cedars or the longer path to Avalanche Lake before hopping on the next bus to Logan Pass. Enjoy the views at Logan Pass Visitor Center before continuing to Sun Point via St. Mary Falls. From here, hop on the final bus at Rising Sun to eat at Two Dog Flats Grill, or take a boat trip on St. Mary Lake. Make sure you get back to Logan Pass in time to catch the last shuttle to Apgar.

## Day 7

Drive U.S. 2 around the southern edge of the park to lesser-visited Two Medicine Lake, where there are beautiful trails. Farther north you can travel past Lake Sherburne up the Swiftcurrent Valley to Many Glacier, where there are more lakes and pristine waterfalls to explore. End your Rockies journey with dinner and drinks at the Ptarmigan Dining Room in Many Glacier Hotel on Swiftcurrent Lake.

# GLACIER

📍 Montana 🚗 $35 per vehicle, valid for seven days 🌐 nps.gov/glac

The dramatic geological legacy of the Ice Age is etched into Glacier National Park's fearsomely beautiful mountains. The distinctive grooves were scored by the weight of glaciers receding down these peaks as they carved the U-shaped valleys into the landscape you see today. Despite global temperatures leading to a decline in the park's namesake features over the past half century, exploring the icy wonders of Glacier will leave you awestruck at nature's power.

 IF YOU HAVE
**A day**

Spend at least three hours exploring Going-to-the-Sun Road on the park's free shuttle tour, getting off at overlooks en route. Leave the bus at Logan Pass to hike the Hidden Lake Trail.

Named Ya·qawiswitxuki ("the place where there is a lot of ice") by the Indigenous Kootenai people, Glacier National Park was shaped by its glaciers scouring the rock over the course of millions of years. The ice here was once 1 mile (1.6 km) thick, finally retreating at the end of the most recent Ice Age approximately 10,000 years ago.

Today, this park is a crucible for the changing climate. When it was established in 1910, Glacier National Park was home to more than 100 glaciers; today, three-quarters of them are gone. The 25 active glaciers left are still a huge draw, but many are tucked away in remote locations that require considerable hiking chops.

← Fresh snowfall topping Sinopah Mountain's peak in Two Medicine Valley

Fortunately, the "Crown of the Continent" offers a bounty of other natural wonders, including turquoise lakes formed when age-old glaciers scraped hollows in the land.

## Exploring the park

Glacier encompasses more than 1 million acres (400,000 ha) of land. West Glacier is the most accessible of the park's entrance points. From here, it's just 3 miles (4.8 km) to Apgar Village at the foot of Lake McDonald. To the north-east of the park is Many Glacier, another popular point to base yourself at with its trail access to dense forests.

Glacier is often appreciated from the heights of Going-to-the-Sun Road, an engineering marvel that snakes along the valley wall and accesses many of the park's sights. It's fully open in the summer, when a free shuttle runs along the road. Cycling or walking parts of the route at quieter times is also memorable.

### Did You Know?

The park is home to 762 lakes, of which Lake McDonald is the largest.

→ Hiking the Hidden Lake Trail, one of the most popular shorter adventures

← Logan Pass, the park's highest point reachable by car or bus

# EAT

There are a number of dining options at the lodgings in the park, plus more restaurants in East Glacier, West Glacier, Columbia Falls, and Whitefish.

### Russell's Fireside Dining Room

Local fare served in a former hunting lodge.

◨ Lake McDonald Lodge
ⓦ glaciernationalpark lodges.com/dining

$$$

### Great Northern Dining Room

Enjoy a buffet at breakfast and hearty American fare.

◨ Glacier Park Lodge
ⓦ glacierpark collection.com/lodging

$$$

### Ptarmigan Dining Room

Scenic mountain and lake views accompany dishes such as duck breast and king salmon. Vegan dishes available.

◨ Many Glacier Hotel
ⓦ glaciernationalpark lodges.com/dining

$$$

### Eddie's Cafe

Ideal for an ice cream after a long hike.

◨ Agpar Village
ⓦ eddiescafegifts.com

$$$

↑ Mountain goats with their protective double-layer wool coats

## Going-to-the-Sun Road

For many visitors, this iconic stretch is the reason to visit Glacier. Spanning the width of the park at 50 miles (80 km), it traverses everything from lush valleys to waterfalls.

Starting in the town of West Glacier, the road almost instantly runs parallel to the 10-mile (16-km) Lake McDonald, the park's largest lake; a number of roadside overlooks offer great views of the lake's waters. Just past the lake is a stop for McDonald Falls, one of the few waterfalls in the park you can see without hiking.

After passing through the West Side Tunnel, the road makes its only switchback on its precipitous 3,493-ft (1,065-m) ascent from the lake to the Continental Divide. This sharp turn is known as "The Loop," and features a parking area to stop and take in Heavens Peak.

The road then passes an overlook where you can see 492-ft (150-m) Bird Woman Falls in the distance, quickly followed by Haystack Creek Falls, which flows directly under the road. Just 1 mile (1.6 km) later is Weeping Wall, which often douses cars driving by in the early summer with snowmelt.

At mile marker 30, Big Bend is another overlook with

↑ The Loop viewpoint on Going-to-the-Sun Road

a sweeping view of the park's mountains. Here, you're just 2 miles (3.2 km) west of Logan Pass, where Going-to-the-Sun Road intersects with the Continental Divide. At 6,646 ft (2,026 m) above sea level, Logan Pass is the highest point on the route, with a visitor center and several trails into the alpine tundra above timberline. Note that the parking lot often fills to capacity early in the morning.

On the road goes, through the East Side Tunnel before the parking areas at Siyeh Bend, Jackson Glacier Overlook, and Sunrift Gorge. The last stretch follows the north shore of St. Mary Lake before it exits the park.

While it's easy to access, Going-to-the-Sun Road is prone to traffic that can detract from the beautiful mountan scenery. When the road is busy and the lots are full, try one of the other entrances, or take the opportunity to explore a different way.

### GETTING AROUND

Glacier National Park is located along the U.S.-Canada border in northwestern Montana, about 140 miles (225 km) north of Missoula and 25 miles (40 km) northeast of Whitefish. The park has seven entrances. Going-to-the-Sun Road, the only road that traverses the park, runs for 50 miles (80 km) through the heart of the park from the West Glacier Entrance to the St. Mary Entrance. U.S. 2 runs alongside the park's southern boundary. There are three entrances that don't connect with Going-to-the-Sun Road: Many Glacier and Two Medicine on the east side of the park and Polebridge on its west side. From the Camas Creek Entrance south of Polebridge, Camas Rd. runs 11 miles (18 km) to Going-to-the-Sun Road at Apgar at the western tip of Lake McDonald. A free shuttle runs on Going-to-the-Sun Road in the summer; it is typically open only between West Glacier and Lake McDonald in winter.

### Guided tours

By driving alone, you often miss the chance to learn about the park's long history and those who once called the landscape home. St. Mary Valley, the eastern entrance, borders the Blackfeet Indian Reservation, home to around 16,000 members. This area has a rich history of Blackfeet, Salish, Kootenai, and Pend d'Oreille cultures, and each summer, members of the Blackfeet Nation and Confederated Salish and Kootenai peoples share their knowledge of local history and culture through "Native America Speaks," the longest-running Indigenous speaker series in any national park.

# A LONG WALK
# HIGHLINE TRAIL

**Length** 7.6 miles (12.2 km) one-way **Stopping-off points**
Granite Park Chalet has rooms to stay at overnight; reserve
ahead **Terrain** Rocky dirt trail

A jewel of a trail atop the "Crown of the Continent",
the Highline provides some of the best views of
Glacier National Park. The fairly moderate route hugs
the Garden Wall cliffside, where alpine meadows and
glacier-sculpted mountains define the landscape. The
entire trail takes a few hours to tackle.

**Locator Map**

**Key**

-- Walk Route

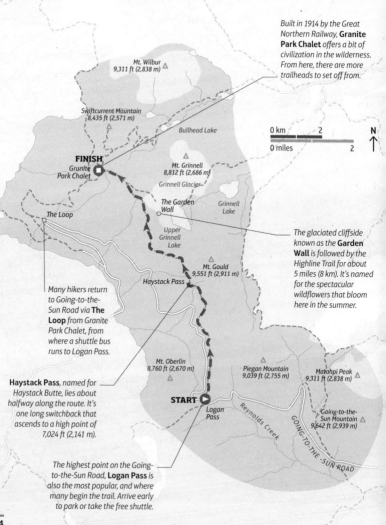

Built in 1914 by the Great
Northern Railway, **Granite
Park Chalet** offers a bit of
civilization in the wilderness.
From here, there are more
trailheads to set off from.

The glaciated cliffside
known as the **Garden
Wall** is followed by the
Highline Trail for about
5 miles (8 km). It's named
for the spectacular
wildflowers that bloom
here in the summer.

Many hikers return
to Going-to-the-
Sun Road via **The
Loop** from Granite
Park Chalet, from
where a shuttle bus
runs to Logan Pass.

**Haystack Pass**, named for
Haystack Butte, lies about
halfway along the route. It's
one long switchback that
ascends to a high point of
7,024 ft (2,141 m).

The highest point on the Going-
to-the-Sun Road, **Logan Pass** is
also the most popular, and where
many begin the trail. Arrive early
to park or take the free shuttle.

A Jammer bus, named for the sound they once made when drivers "jammed" the gears ↑

The talks are held at park campgrounds and lodges as well as locations in Blackfeet Nation. There are also interpretive bus tours of the park that shed light on the rich history and culture of the Blackfeet, who historically lived in the prairies on the park's east side. Pickups are on the east and west side of the park, and reservations through Sun Tours *(www. suntours.co)* are required.

Glacier is also famous for its narrated "Jammer" tours, which are held in vintage red buses on Going-to-the-Sun Road, and to Many Glacier and Two Medicine. The buses, which have rollback roofs, are a deluxe way to see the glacier terrain, with drivers providing fun anecdotes and stories of folklore at stops along the way. Different itineraries are offered, with pickups at lodgings in the park and gateway towns. Reservations are required.

If you prefer to forego the road and get out on the silvery water, Glacier Park Boat Company *(www.glacier parkboats.com)* offers scenic tours in wooden boats on Lake McDonald, St. Mary Lake, and lakes in Many Glacier. The company also rents kayaks, row boats, paddleboards, motorboats, and canoes at Apgar, Lake McDonald, Two Medicine Lake, and Swiftcurrent Lake. For a wilder experience, Flathead River offers excellent rafting.

## Hiking and backpacking

For many, getting out into the wild on two feet is the main draw to this park. After all, Glacier is home to more than 700 miles (1,127 km) of trails, making it one of the best parks for hiking and backpacking in the system. A pair of backcountry chalets also allow hikers to eschew big packs for overnight trips. Further, most of the park's best-known glaciers, including Grinnell Glacier and Sperry Glacier, require a hike to get to a viewpoint, so if you want to see the park's namesakes, you'll need to lace up your boots.

Across from the Lake McDonald Lodge, the Sperry Trailhead on the park's west side is the main starting point for numerous day hikes and overnight treks. This includes the moderate 5.4-mile (8.7-km) round trip to Fish Lake, or you can continue to Sperry Chalet, a slighty longer circular route. On the northeast end of the lake, the very short Johns Lake Loop allows for a view of the Sacred Dancing Cascade, a river waterfall. Nearby, the trailhead to the moderate 4.6-mile (7.4-km) hike to Avalanche Lake also takes in the easy and wheelchair-accessible Trail of the Cedars, which passes partly along flat boardwalks.

←

Rafting on Middle Fork of the Flathead River, forming the park's southwestern border

# STAY

The park has six lodgings, as well as one just outside the southeast entrance. You can find further accommodations in West Glacier, Columbia Falls, and Whitefish.

### Lake McDonald Lodge

This classic lakeside lodge has both hotel rooms and cabins. It's a great base for boat tours from its dock.

🏠 Lake McDonald
🌐 glaciernationalpark lodges.com

$$$

---

### Many Glacier Hotel

Swiss chalet-inspired hotel on picturesque Swiftcurrent Lake.

🏠 Many Glacier
🌐 glaciernationalpark lodges.com

$$$

---

### Glacier Park Lodge

Stately log hotel built by the Great Northern Railway in 1913, near the park's southeast entrance.

🏠 East Glacier
🌐 glacierparkcollection.com/lodging

$$$

---

### Cedar Creek Lodge

Just outside the park, this comfortable mountain lodge is the gateway to Columbia Falls.

🏠 Columbia Falls
🌐 glaciernationalpark lodges.com

$$$

↑ Hiking the Grinnell Glacier Trail, popular in the fall when the park has fewer visitors

In Logans Pass, hikers will find one of the most popular routes in the park: Hidden Lake Overlook Nature Trail, an easy round trip on a boardwalk to its namesake lake. The legendary Highline Trail also starts here, a moderate 12-mile (19-km) one-way hike along Garden Wall to the Granite Park Chalet which is a stepping stone to other hiking routes.

If you're starting at Many Glacier, the challenging 5.3-mile (8.5-km) trek to the Grinnell Glacier Viewpoint is consistently rated one of the most spectacular in the U.S. Though strenuous, you'll be rewarded with incredible scenery, a famous glacier, and the chance to spot mountain goats and possibly black bears along the route.

There are numerous trailheads at Two Medicine, too, including the easy 1.2-mile (1.9-km) round-trip hike to Appistoki Falls; you can add a difficult 3 miles (5 km) one-way to get to a scenic point with a bird's-eye view of the valley. Many of the trailheads on Two Medicine Lake are accessible by boat.

Several multiday back-packing routes begin in Polebridge, a 35-mile (56-km) drive on the rough North Fork Rd. from Columbia Falls. It is by far the least-visited area in the park, home to Bowman Lake and other untouched bodies of water, as well as plenty of uncrowded trails. Starting at Bowman Lake, the Numa Overlook Trail is a difficult 11.2-mile (18-km) hike that ascends 2,930 ft (893 m) on its way to a lookout on Numa Peak; the view is worth the effort.

For backpacking, a permit is required and reservations are recommended, although the park reserves a portion of backcountry campsites for walk-up permits. For those who prefer roofs over their heads, the hostel-style Granite Park Chalet and full-service Sperry Chalet are accessible only by trail; reservations are required.

---

### IF YOU HAVE
## A weekend

Spend your first day hiking to Grinnell Lake and Grinnell Glacier, trying to spot bighorn sheep and mountain goats along the way. Rest at Many Glacier Hotel, then get on the road to Lake McDonald. From here, take the Fish Creek Trail along the west shore.

The cascading Triple Falls, one of over 200 waterfalls in the park ↑

# EXPLORING GLACIER

Glacier National Park is made up of more than 1 million acres (400,000 ha), with two sub-ranges of the Rocky Mountains inside its borders and more than 130 lakes to explore.

Glacier's mountains, lakes, and valleys are the products of the region's namesake glaciers; they make for a rugged but wonderful area to hike, climb, drive, and ski.

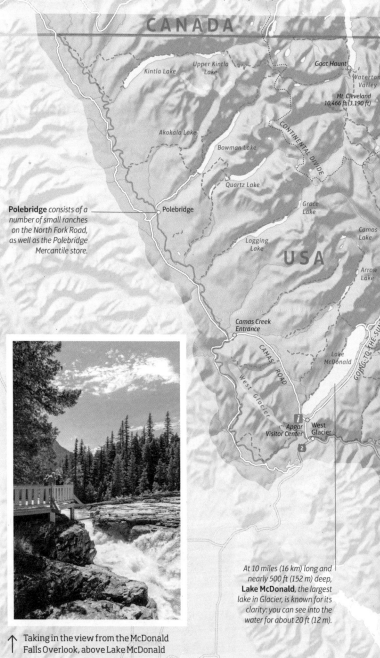

CANADA

Kintla Lake

Upper Kintla Lake

Goat Haunt

Waterton Valley

Mt. Cleveland
10,466 ft (3,190 ft)

CONTINENTAL DIVIDE

Akokala Lake

Bowman Lake

Quartz Lake

Grace Lake

Camas Lake

**Polebridge** *consists of a number of small ranches on the North Fork Road, as well as the Polebridge Mercantile store.*

Polebridge

Logging Lake

Arrow Lake

USA

Camas Creek Entrance

CAMAS ROAD

West Glacier

Lake McDonald

GOING-TO-THE-SUN

Apgar Visitor Center

West Glacier

*At 10 miles (16 km) long and nearly 500 ft (152 m) deep,* **Lake McDonald**, *the largest lake in Glacier, is known for its clarity: you can see into the water for about 20 ft (12 m).*

↑ Taking in the view from the McDonald Falls Overlook, above Lake McDonald

198

Nicknamed the "Switzerland of North America," **Many Glacier** has its own entrance, lodging, and hiking trails.

Walking the boardwalk through Logan Pass

Actually a by-product of Going-to-the-Sun Road's construction, the **Weeping Wall** seeps snowmelt, and often sprays water onto passing traffic early in the summer.

**Logan Pass** is the highest point on Going-to-the-Sun Road at 6,646 ft (2,026 m) above sea level.

One of the most scenic roads in the country, the 50-mile (80-km) **Going-to-the-Sun Road** crests the Continental Divide.

**Jackson Glacier Overlook** is one of the only places you can see a glacier from a park road.

Iceberg Lake

Many Glacier

Lake Sherburne

Swiftcurrent Lake

St. Mary Visitor Center

St Mary Lake

89

Logan Pass 6,646 ft (2,026 m)

West Side Tunnel

Jackson Glacier Overlook

Gunsight Lake

Lake Ellen Wilson

coln Lake

Blackfoot Glacier

CONTINENTAL DIVIDE

Atlantic Creek

arrison ake

Lower Nyack Creek

Beaver Woman Lake

Two Medicine Lake

Upper Two Medicine Lake

Cobalt Lake

Lake Isabel

Oig Lake

2

2

Marias Pass

Scalplock

Ole Creek

Walton

0 kilometers    10

0 miles    10

N

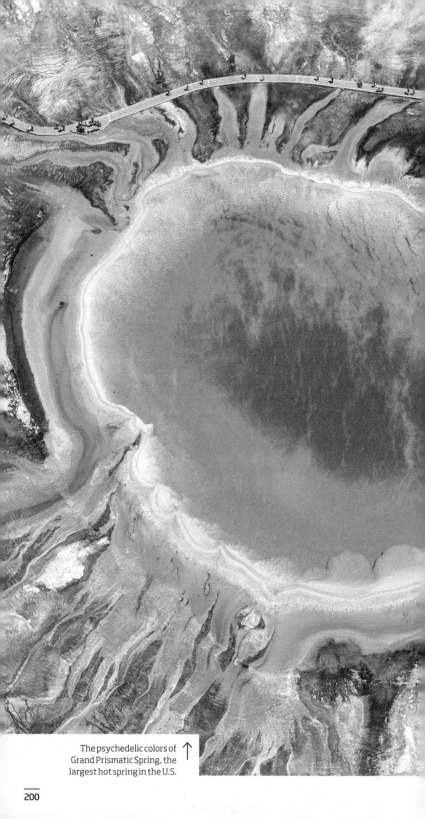

The psychedelic colors of Grand Prismatic Spring, the largest hot spring in the U.S. ↑

# YELLOWSTONE

📍 Wyoming, Montana, Idaho  🎫 $35 per vehicle, valid for seven days  🌐 nps.gov/grte

Yellowstone is not only one of the oldest national parks in the world, it's also one of the largest and wildest, with sprawling forests, vast mountains, and green meadows. But it's what lies underneath this beautiful wilderness that makes Yellowstone truly unique: the park sits atop an ancient supervolcano. Though the volcano hasn't fully erupted for 640,000 years, it continues to power the park's geysers, hot springs, mud pots, and steam vents – the greatest concentration of thermal features on Earth.

With wolves, bears, and bison roaming Yellowstone's vast forests and meadows, the park is one of the wildest places in the Lower 48 states. For thousands of years prior to its designation as the first national park in the U.S., Indigenous peoples foraged, hunted, and quarried the lands at the convergence of the Great Plains, Great Basin, and Columbia Plateau. Formal expeditions by trappers in the late 19th century led to calls to legally protect the area's beautiful otherworldly landscapes, replete with hot springs and geysers. Reports of huge waterfalls, dizzying canyons, and a host of geo-thermal features captured the American imagination,

↑ Visitors at the Bunsen Peak overlook on the Grand Loop Road

 IF YOU HAVE
**A day**

Watch the park's most famous geyser, Old Faithful, erupt before exploring the surrounding board-walks. You can then hike the nearby rim of the Grand Canyon of the Yellowstone, near the Yellowstone Falls.

and the park was eventually signed into law by President Ulysses S. Grant in 1872. At a time when large tracts of land were being parceled off and sold to developers, the intention was to ensure Yellowstone was preserved for the enjoyment and appreciation of future generations. Its protected status has ensured the park remains home to a wonder-fully diverse array of large fauna, including bison, elk, grizzly bear, and cougar.

← Blue pools seen along the Artists' Paintpot Trail

> **A great way to experience the park is on its hiking trails, of which there are more than 900 miles (1,400 km) snaking through the vast and diverse wilderness.**

## Exploring the park

Encompassing more than 2 million acres (800,000 ha) stretching across the states of Wyoming, Montana and Idaho, the park is a glorious example of America's diverse and beautiful wilderness. A great way to experience the park is on its hiking trails, of which there are more than 900 miles (1,400 km) snaking through the vast wilds. Many of these trails run along wooden boardwalks which make for easier accessibility.

Yellowstone also has over 300 miles (480 km) of paved roads that run near all of the park's most popular sights. If visiting the park by car, note that summer can be very busy, so be prepared for traffic at popular areas and lines at the entrance gates, in construction areas, and at wildlife sighting areas on the roadside. A car is necessary for visiting certain regions and attractions within the park, as there is little public transportation offered within the park's borders. Note, however, that roads often close for snowfall and maintenance work, so it's best to check updates posted on the National Park Service website before you hit the road. Gas stations are also limited inside Yellowstone, so it's worth filling up in advance.

### Old Faithful

Yellowstone has more thermal features than the rest of the world combined. The best-known and still the most

→ Steam rising from the Norris Geyser Basin in winter

recognizable geyser in the park, Old Faithful continues to erupt every 90 minutes or so. The benches around the geyser tend to fill up quickly with spectators. You'll have more elbow room walking the Upper Geyser Basin Trail (p205) to Castle Geyser, Grand Geyser, Riverside Geyser, and the ethereal blue waters of Morning Glory Pool. You can walk up to 6 miles (9.7 km) on the trail; Morning Glory Pool is a 3-mile (4.8-km) round trip from Old Faithful.

## The Geyser Basins

About 7 miles (11.3 km) to the north of Old Faithful is rainbow-hued Grand Prismatic Spring, the largest hot spring in the U.S. and the third-largest in the world. It can be accessed from a roadside viewing area (which is often very busy), or you can hike 1.2 miles (1.8 km) to an overlook on the Fairy Falls Trail. Grand Prismatic is part of the Midway Geyser Basin,

### GETTING AROUND

Yellowstone National Park is spread across northwestern Wyoming, southern Montana, and eastern Idaho just north of Grand Teton National Park. There are five entrances that lead to a central pair of roadways that are collectively known as the "Grand Loop," with access to Old Faithful, Yellowstone Lake, the Grand Canyon of the Yellowstone, and other attractions. Yellowstone Lake is on the south side of the lower loop, to the east of Old Faithful. Canyon Village and Norris Geyser Basin are in the middle, and Mammoth Hot Springs is in the north. U.S. 89/191/287 enters the park from Grand Teton; U.S. 89 enters from Gardiner, Montana, at the North Entrance; and U.S. 191/287 enters from West Yellowstone, Montana. With the exception of the route from Gardiner to Cooke City, roads close in winter, but snowcoaches run.

which can be further explored via an easy and flat loop across the boardwalks. The nearby Lower Geyser Basin has the 3-mile (4.8-mile) Firehole Lake Drive, with roadside geysers and a short boardwalk, and the 0.6-mile (1-km) loop on the Fountain Paint Pot Trail. Norris Geyser Basin, 22 miles (35 km) north of Lower Geyser Basin, is the

park's oldest, hottest, and most active geothermal area, with the world's tallest geyser in Steamboat Geyser, with eruptions of up to 400 ft (120 m). You can explore the area on 2.3 miles (3.7 km) of gentle trails and flat boardwalks. Nearby, the Artists' Paintpot Trail is an easy 1-mile (1.6-km) loop passing by a number of

The powerful 110-ft (30-m) Upper Falls of the Yellowstone River

From the lake, the Yellowstone River cuts north into the Grand Canyon of the Yellowstone, with scenery rivaling that of the more famous Grand Canyon in Arizona. Along the canyon rims are a number of overlooks with views of the Upper Falls and Lower Falls.

curious babbling mudpots and steaming fumaroles. At Mammoth Hot Springs, you can walk among the pale travertine terraces that have accumulated over the millennia here on 3 miles (5 km) of boardwalks. The lakeside West Thumb Geyser Basin is one of the park's most scenic geothermal areas, with features on the lake's shores and in its waters and a 1-mile (1.6-km) boardwalk loop.

There are also a number of geysers and other thermal features spread across the park's vast backcountry. Note that all visitors are required to stay on the trails and boardwalks in thermal areas. Never throw anything into a thermal feature or attempt to swim in a hot spring.

## Yellowstone Lake

The geysers and hot springs are just one facet of the park's many natural wonders; there are also glimmering lakes and rivers across the park. Not only is Yellowstone Lake the largest in the park, it's the largest alpine lake in North America at over 83,000 acres (33,000 ha), and it has the continent's largest population of native cut-throat trout. Spanning the Yellowstone River (the lake's only outlet) just to the north, Fishing Bridge is a great place to watch the fish spawn in late spring and early summer, although fishing is no longer allowed from the bridge. The notably cold lake freezes over every winter; swimming is not recommended in the colder months.

## Hiking and backpacking

There are a number of walks aside from the geyser basins. North of Old Faithful, the round trips on the easy Mystic Falls Trail and the moderate Fairy Falls Trail are good options without the crowds of the Upper Geyser Basin. You can extend both routes: if you continue 0.2 miles (0.3 km) on

---

**IF YOU HAVE**
**A weekend**

Spend a busy couple of days exploring the Norris Geyser Basin and Mammoth Hot Springs. In the early mornings and late evenings, look out for rare wildlife in the beautifully tranquil Lamar Valley.

---

Bison grazing the vast plains as steam rises in the Upper Geyser Basin ↑

# A SHORT WALK
# UPPER
# GEYSER BASIN

**Length** Up to 5 miles (8 km) **Stopping-off points** Old
Faithful Inn, Old Faithful Snow Lodge **Terrain** Boardwalks,
pavement, and a dirt trail make this easy to moderate

This is one of the busiest areas in the park, and with
good reason: Upper Geyser Basin contains the world's
densest concentration of geysers, with more than
150 in 1 sq mile (2.6 sq km). Take a couple of hours
to wander the boardwalks and trails here to see the
thermal features in this hotspot.

**Locator Map**

**Key**

-- Walk Route

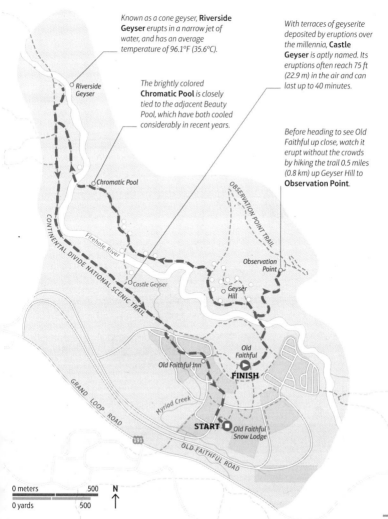

Known as a cone geyser, **Riverside
Geyser** erupts in a narrow jet of
water, and has an average
temperature of 96.1°F (35.6°C).

The brightly colored
**Chromatic Pool** is closely
tied to the adjacent Beauty
Pool, which have both cooled
considerably in recent years.

With terraces of geyserite
deposited by eruptions over
the millennia, **Castle
Geyser** is aptly named. Its
eruptions often reach 75 ft
(22.9 m) in the air and can
last up to 40 minutes.

Before heading to see Old
Faithful up close, watch it
erupt without the crowds
by hiking the trail 0.5 miles
(0.8 km) up Geyser Hill to
**Observation Point**.

Riverside
Geyser

Chromatic Pool

OBSERVATION POINT TRAIL

CONTINENTAL DIVIDE NATIONAL SCENIC TRAIL

Firehole River

Observation
Point

Castle Geyser

Geyser
Hill

Old
Faithful

Old Faithful Inn

**FINISH**

GRAND LOOP ROAD

Myriod Creek

**START** Old Faithful
Snow Lodge

191

OLD FAITHFUL ROAD

0 meters    500    N
0 yards    500

the Mystic Falls Trail, you'll be rewarded with a view of Old Faithful to the south. From Kepler Cascades south of Old Faithful, the Lone Star Geyser Trail is an easy 4.6-mile (7.4-km) round trip to a geyser that erupts for a half-hour multiple times a day. From here, you can backpack to the backcountry geyser basin on the west side of Shoshone Lake, but it's a bit long to do on a day trip.

On the north side of the park, the Bunsen Peak Trail is

**On the north side of the park, the Bunsen Peak Trail is a moderate 4.2-mile (6.8-km) hike up and down the beautiful slopes of the route's namesake mountain.**

a moderate 4.2-mile (6.8-km) hike up and down the beautiful slopes of the route's namesake mountain. A favorite for wildlife-watchers, the Slough Creek Trail starts at a trailhead about 25 miles (40 km) east of Mammoth in the Lamar Valley and continues north for 11 miles (18 km) past the park's northern boundary. Most hikers turn around after a few miles. Between Tower and Canyon, Mount Washburn has a moderate 6-mile (10-km) round-trip trail to its summit that gains 1,400 ft (430 m) to one of the very best views in the park.

Starting near Canyon Village, Seven Mile Hole Trail is the easiest way to tread the floor of the Grand Canyon of the Yellowstone, but it's still a difficult 10-mile (16-km) round trip that gains more than 2,000 ft (610 m) on the

way out. There are easy trails which allow walkers to marvel at the canyon from above on both canyon rims. The moderate 5.1-mile (8.2-km) loop along the rim to Clear Lake starts at Artist Point on South Rim Dr. For a photoworthy view of Yellowstone Lake, the moderate 3.6-mile (6-km) Elephant Back Loop Trail begins near Lake Village.

The park has numerous multiday backpacking routes; permits are required. Be sure to check with the park about backcountry regulations and safety in grizzly bear country.

### Wildlifewatching

Yellowstone is known for its wonderful array of wildlife as much as its geysers. The park is home to grizzly bears, gray wolves, bison, moose, elk, deer, as well as otters, martens, and bald eagles. Called "The Serengeti of North America," the Lamar Valley inside the Northeast Entrance is considered the best wildlife-watching area. It helps to have a spotting

← A gray wolf in the wild backcountry of Yellowstone

*Park wildlife*

**Bison**

▽ From fewer than 50 individuals in 1902, the free-ranging Yellowstone bison herd now numbers 5,900.

**Gray wolf**

Reintroduced here in 1995, the gray wolf now roam freely, and are best seen at sunrise and sunset in the northern range.

**Canadian lynx**

▽ The Canadian lynx, noted for its silver-brown fur and black-tufted ears, lives in the forests and preys on the snowshoe hare.

**Grizzly bear**

△ The park is one of the last refuges for grizzlies. Look for them in the Hayden and Lamar valleys, and from Fishing Bridge to the east entrance.

↑ Walking the Old Faithful boardwalk in the Upper Geyser Basin in winter

scope; rentals are available just outside the park at Silver Gate Cabins.

When watching wildlife, remember to respect the animals in their natural habitats. If traveling on foot, never get within 100 yards (90 m) of bears or wolves, or within 25 yards (20 m) of other wildlife.

## Tours and programs

Yellowstone National Park Lodges offers a wide variety of tours in the park, including narrated drives in historic yellow buses that depart from Old Faithful, Mammoth, and Lake Village in summer. Yellowstone Forever, based out of the historic Lamar Buffalo Ranch, conducts field seminars and private tours of the park, some of which include lodgings.

## Boating and fishing

Motorized and non-motorized boats are allowed on both Yellowstone Lake and Lewis Lake. Boat rentals are available at Bridge Bay Marina, and Yellowstone National Park Lodges has a regular schedule of scenic cruises in summer. Fly-fishing is popular in the Yellowstone River, Madison River, and Lamar River, as well as Soda Butte Creek and other bodies of water in the park. Fishers must secure a park fishing permit; inspections and permits are also required for private boats.

## In winter

Only a tiny fraction of visitors come to Yellowstone in the winter, when the roads are open only to snowcoaches and guided snowmobile tours. The Old Faithful Snow Lodge and Mammoth Hot Springs Hotel are the only lodging options in the park during the colder months. The trails to Lone Star Geyser and Fairy Falls (see "Hiking," earlier in this chapter) are popular for cross-country skiing in the winter.

## Camping

There are more than 2,000 campsites at a dozen camp-grounds all over the park, many close to the best hiking trails. Reservations are required at all except Mammoth, which is first-come, first-served from mid-October to early April.

**300**
The number of bird species found within the park's boundaries.

# STAY

Yellowstone has a wide range of lodging options found across the park.

### Old Faithful Inn

This typical national park lodge offers geyser views and shared baths.

🏛 Old Faithful Historic District
ⓦ usparklodging.com

$$$

### Lake Yellowstone Hotel and Cabins

A historic Colonial Revival hotel, with fine dining and lake views.

🏛 Lake Village
ⓦ yellowstonenational parklodges.com

$$$

### Roosevelt Lodge Cabins

Popular with families, this lodge hosts cowboy cookouts and horseback riding.

🏛 Tower-Roosevelt
ⓦ yellowstonepark.com

$$$

# EXPLORING YELLOWSTONE

Spread across northwestern Wyoming and parts of southern Montana and eastern Idaho, the landscape of Yellowstone has been volcanically and seismically active for millions of years. The park is the largest in the U.S., spanning over 2 million acres (800,000 ha).

*For thousands of years, hot springs like **Mammoth Hot Springs** have bubbled up and created intricate and strangely beautiful terraces across the landscape.*

*An ever-changing geothermal area that's the park's hottest, **Norris Geyser Basin** is home to the world's largest active geyser, Steamboat Geyser.*

*__Old Faithful__, the best-known and most predictable geyser on Earth, has erupts every 90 minutes or so.*

Gardiner
North Entrance

Mammoth
Mammoth Hot Springs

Phantom

Blackt
Deer Pla

Grizzly Lake

Roaring Mountain

Norris Geyser Basin
Steamboat Geyser
Beryl Spring
Gibbon River
Artists Paintpot

Central Plateau

WYOMING

MONTANA

Gallatin Range

191

West Entrance
West Yellowstone Visitor Center
20

Midway Geyser Basin
Great Fountain Geyser
Biscuit Basin
Black Sand Basin
Old Faithful
Old Faithful Geyser
Firehole River

West Thumb Geyser Basin

Lone Star Geyser
Grant Villa

Shoshone Lake

Lewis Lake

Caldera Boundary

Lewis Falls
M
Sher
10,3
(3,14

IDAHO

Pitchstone Plateau

Lewis River

Union Falls

Cave Falls

South Entrance

↑ The Yellowstone River stretching across the flat expanse of Lamar Valley

*The park's **South Entrance** is located near Grand Teton National Park (p212) and the Jackson Hole Valley.*

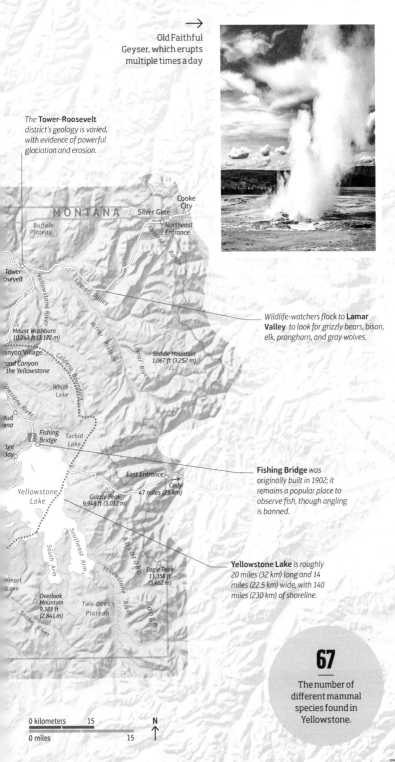

→

Old Faithful Geyser, which erupts multiple times a day

The **Tower-Roosevelt** district's geology is varied, with evidence of powerful glaciation and erosion.

MONTANA

*Buffalo Plateau*

Silver Gate

Cooke City

*Northeast Entrance*

*Absaroka Range*

Tower-Roosevelt

*Yellowstone River*

*Lamar Valley*

*Mirror Plateau*

*Mount Washburn 10,243 ft (3,122 m)*

*Canyon Village*

*Grand Canyon of the Yellowstone*

*Caldera Boundary*

*Lamar River*

*Saddle Mountain 1,067 ft (3,252 m)*

Wildlife-watchers flock to **Lamar Valley** to look for grizzly bears, bison, elk, pronghorn, and gray wolves.

*Yellowstone River*

*White Lake*

*Mud Volcano*

*Fishing Bridge*

*Bridge Bay*

*Turbid Lake*

*East Entrance*

*Cody 47 miles (75 km)*

**Fishing Bridge** was originally built in 1902; it remains a popular place to observe fish, though angling is banned.

*Yellowstone Lake*

*Grizzly Peak 9,948 ft (3,032 m)*

*Southeast Arm*

*South Arm*

*Heart Lake*

*Overlook Mountain 9,321 ft (2,841 m)*

*Snake River*

*Two Ocean Plateau*

*Absaroka Range*

*Yellowstone River*

*Eagle Peak 11,358 ft (3,462 m)*

**Yellowstone Lake** is roughly 20 miles (32 km) long and 14 miles (22.5 km) wide, with 140 miles (230 km) of shoreline.

0 kilometers    15

0 miles    15

N
↑

# 67

The number of different mammal species found in Yellowstone.

# GEOTHERMAL ACTIVITY

Set atop a dormant supervolcano, Yellowstone contains more than half the world's geysers and hydrothermal features. Early 19th-century explorers described it as a place of fire and brimstone, and their reports of boiling mud and petrified trees were dismissed as tall tales or a touch of lunacy. Later, when the unique features and environmental importance of this incredible landscape were realized, Yellowstone became the first national park. The landscape is something of a wizard's cauldron: sulfurous gases belch from bubbling mudpots; minerals and bacteria turn rolling hot springs a rainbow of colors; and geysers erupt into the sky.

## GEYSERS

Yellowstone National Park has more geysers than anywhere else on Earth. The most famous is Old Faithful, which, as the name suggests, predictably erupts every 45 minutes to two hours, as it has done since 2000. But what is a geyser? Geysers are formed in deep, vertical, flooded vents known as pipes. The water at the bottom of the pipe comes into contact with hot rock and boils, expanding upward, while the cooler water at the surface of the geyser forms a kind of lid, trapping the rising water, until so much pressure builds up that the geyser explodes skyward. The eruption only stops when the water is depleted or the temperature cools.

↑ Old Faithful, in Yellowstone's Upper Geyser Basin

## SAFETY TIPS

The extraordinary geothermal features of Yellowstone attract millions of visitors every year, but it's important to remember that these incredible sights are signs of an active and changeable landscape. Heed the advice of park rangers and safety notices, and stick to designated trails or boardwalks; what might look like solid earth is most likely a thin, breakable crust. Hot springs can have temperatures of 200°F (94°C), so to avoid fatal or severe burns don't swim, soak, or put your hand in thermal features.

**Did You Know?**

Geothermal energy is created when groundwater comes within range of hot rocks or magma.

Grand Prismatic ↑ Spring, the largest hot spring in the U.S.

↑ Travertine terraces at Mammoth Hot Springs, created by deposits of calcite

TOP 5 YELLOWSTONE GEYSERS

**Old Faithful**
The big attraction, Old Faithful can erupt for 1.5–5 minutes and shoot up to 184 ft (56 m) high.

**Riverside**
In a picturesque setting, this geyser erupts every 5.5–7 hours.

**Steamboat**
The world's tallest active geyser, Steamboat can erupt more than 300 ft (90 m) high.

**Grand**
Expect spectacular, if infrequent, eruptions (every 8–12 hours) from this fountain geyser.

**Great Fountain**
Not to be confused with Fountain Geyser, this geyser might erupt 200 ft (60 m) high.

## HOT SPRINGS

The most common feature in Yellowstone is the hot spring. Hot springs start as rainwater, which then seeps through the Earth and is heated by the volcanic system below. The water is able to circulate, with currents preventing it from getting too hot to cause eruptions. When a hot spring rises up through limestone, it can create a travertine terrace, like those found at Mammoth Hot Springs.

## THE SCIENCE OF COLOR

The variety of incredible colors seen in geothermal areas comes from minerals and micro-organisms. Yellow deposits are generally sulfur, white ones are gypsum, while clumps of metallic gray or rusty red earth or particles of rock are hematite. The water itself can take on a variety of quite beautiful colorings, as seen at Yellowstone's Grand Prismatic Spring. The color is caused by different kinds of thermophiles, organisms that thrive at high temperatures, such as reddish-purple archaea and *Cyanidium caldarium*, a heat-loving green algae.

# GRAND TETON

📍 Wyoming 🚗 $35 per vehicle, valid for seven days
🌐 nps.gov/grte

The sublime panorama of Grand Teton, Middle Teton, and Mount Owen is one of the most unforgettable sights of the western U.S. These purple-tinged, snowcapped peaks seemingly shoot straight out of the valley floor, furrowed by glacial canyons and fronted by a chain of picture-perfect lakes. Grand Teton National Park encompasses the mountain range and the surrounding valley of Jackson Hole, which is roamed by majestic wild animals including bison, elk, and grizzly bears. The park offers a timeless snapshot of the American West – and a nature playground for outdoor enthusiasts of all stripes.

The incomparable Teton Range looms over the west side of Jackson Hole, the valley that is home to Grand Teton National Park and the town of Jackson. Formed by the opposing forces of the valley floor dropping and the mountains thrusting skyward over millions of years, the peaks were further shaped by glaciers receding down the vast canyons.

It's hard not to be spell-bound by the beauty of these mountains, from Mt. Moran to South Teton, as you explore the park. There are numerous roadside overlooks from which to admire the views, but it's even better to hike to a panorama that you'll have all to yourself.

## Exploring the park

The park is located in northwestern Wyoming, north of the town of Jackson and south of Yellowstone. Teton Park Road and Hwy. 191/89/26 comprise a 42-mile (67-km) loop that winds past several of the park's best viewing points. The Craig Thomas Discovery Center offers excellent opportunities to learn more about the park's history and ecology.

Hiking the mountain trails above Lake Solitude →

## EAT

There are eateries at Jackson and Jenny lakes, Moose, and Jackson.

**Jenny Lake Lodge Dining Room**
One of the park's best-reviewed restaurants, housed in a log cabin.
📍 Jenny Lake
🌐 gtlc.com
$$$

**The Mural Room**
Fine dining with stunning views of the Teton Range.
📍 Jackson Lake Lodge Rd 🌐 gtlc.com
$$$

**Deadman's Bar**
Casual lakefront bar offering great tacos.
📍 Signal Mountain
🌐 signalmountain lodge.com
$$$

↑ The Grand Teton Range,
with slopes draped in
fall colors

→ Taking in the wooded backcountry of the park

## Lakes and boating

There are 44 beautiful lakes to explore within the park, many offering excellent fishing, hiking, and boating. On the far north side of the park, the Snake River flows into Jackson Lake, a large reservoir that is a particularly popular boating and fishing destination, with a number of trails in the Jackson Lake Lodge area. Heading south from Jackson Lake Junction on Teton Park Rd., Signal Mountain is one of the best spots to view the Teton Range and other nearby peaks. You can drive or hike to the Jackson Point Overlook to see as far as Yellowstone.

Just south of Signal Mountain Rd., the Mt. Moran Turnout features a great view of the flat-topped mountain that's named for landscape artist Thomas Moran. You'll soon reach Jenny Lake, one of several snowmelt-fed lakes strung along the base of the Tetons to the south of Jackson Lake. This is a major center of

↓ Leaping into the clear waters of Phelps Lake

activity in the park, with the trailhead for a hike that circles the lake and the dock for the Jenny Lake Boating Company tours that will take you to the mouth of Cascade Canyon.

Motorized boats are allowed on Jackson Lake and Jenny Lake, but the latter has a maximum of 10-horsepower engines. Non-motorized craft are allowed at these and a number of backcountry lakes. If you bring your own boat, park permits are required.

Besides providing shuttle service for the trailhead for Cascade Canyon, Jenny Lake Boating Company offers scenic cruises on Jenny Lake and rents kayaks and canoes from its location on the east side of the lake. Grand Teton Lodge Company conducts cruises on Jackson Lake and raft trips on the Snake River, and rents boats at Colter Bay.

In addition to the park's sublime lakes, many visitors are keen to visit its glaciers. About 3 miles (4.8 km) south of Jenny Lake on Teton Park Rd., Teton Glacier Turnout has views of its namesake glacier, the park's largest.

## Moose

The southern entrance to the park is named for Moose, a village home to the main

 IF YOU HAVE
**A day**

Hike around (or take a scenic boat journey across) Jenny Lake to reach the trail leading to Hidden Falls. From here, you can take in the magnificent views from the summit of Inspiration Point.

# A LONG WALK
# CASCADE CANYON TRAIL

**Length** 13.3 miles (21.4 km)  **Stopping-off points**
Jenny Lake Lodge, Jenny Lake Visitor Center
**Terrain** Rocky dirt trail

Hike directly into the postcard view that is the Tetons
on this iconic trail, just west of Jenny Lake. Known as
one of the easiest routes to access the park's backcountry, the trail gains height gently on the way to
the Forks of Cascade Canyon, which each lead to
longer routes popular with backpackers. For a fitting
end to the hike, take the boat across Jenny Lake.

**Locator Map**

**Key**

-- Walk Route

*After 6.7 miles (10.8 km), at the*
**Forks**, *Cascade Canyon Trail*
*diverges into Lake Solitude*
*Trail to its namesake alpine*
*lake, a popular overnight trek.*

0 kilometers    2

0 miles    2

N

*Enjoy spectacular views of*
*Jenny Lake, Jackson Hole,*
*and the Teton Range from*
**Inspiration Point**.

*Snowmelt feeds the*
*cascades of **Hidden**
**Falls**, found near the*
*boat dock and trailhead.*

*With Mt. Owen, **Teewinot** comprises*
*the southern wall of Cascade Canyon.*
*Its name comes from the Shoshoni*
*word for "many pinnacles."*

*The second-highest peak of the*
*Teton Range, **Mt. Owen** is part of*
*the Cathedral Group, along with*
*Grand Teton and other mountains.*

→ Camping on the high ground along the Teton Crest Trail

# STAY

In-park lodgings range from rustic to luxury, and you'll find many options in Jackson.

### Jenny Lake Lodge

An all-inclusive guest ranch with log cabins and complimentary cruiser bikes.

 Jenny Lake
w gtlc.com

$$$

---

### Jackson Lake Lodge

Enjoy outdoor pools at these lodge rooms and cottages.

 Jackson Lake
w nationalpark reservations.com

$$$

---

### Colter Bay Village

These one- and two-room units are on Jackson Lake, close to boat rentals and trailheads.

 Colter Bay Village
w gtlc.com

$$$

You can leave the park for Jackson at Moose or take the Moose-Wilson Rd. (closed winter) to the Laurence S. Rockefeller Preserve, a former dude ranch on the southern shores of Phelps Lake that was donated to the park in 2001. It now features a trail network and exhibits on nature at the preserve center. Moose-Wilson Rd., which exits the park near the town of Wilson, is an excellent place to see moose.

## Hiking and backpacking

The Jenny Lake area has a number of hiking options, starting with the Jenny Lake Loop Trail, a moderate 6.5-mile (10.5-km) loop around the lake. You can hike the loop or get a ride across the lake with the Jenny Lake Boating Company to get to the west shore of the lake and the trailhead to Hidden Falls and Inspiration Point, a 1.8-mile (2.9-km) route.

South of Jenny Lake, the Taggart Lake Trail will take you on an easy 3-mile (4.8-km) round trip to Taggart Lake. On the north side of Jenny Lake, the easy 3.7-mile

(6-km) String Lake Loop takes you to a pair of idyllic mountain lakes. East of Jackson Lake, the moderate 5.8-mile (9.3-km) round trip on the Two Ocean Lake Trail ascends 600 ft (183 m) to Grand View Point.

The canyons on the west side of the park are entry points for routes connected

visitor center, a grocery store, restaurants, and rental cabins; many finish their journeys here when visiting the park. Just west of the visitor center is Menor's Ferry, a historic district where a ferryboat once transported wagons and horses across the Snake River, and the Chapel of the Transfiguration, where the tallest Tetons are visible through the altar window.

→ Cycling one of the many highways leading through Grand Teton

**IF YOU HAVE**
**A weekend**
Explore the Laurence S. Rockefeller Preserve with a trek to Death Canyon, followed by a gentle hike to Phelps Lake. Come evening, enjoy the sunset from Signal Mountain.

by the Teton Crest Trail, a 40-mile (65-km) high country hike. Many hikers combine Paintbrush and Cascade canyons into a multiday loop, or Granite and Death canyons off Moose-Wilson Rd.

## Climbing and mountaineering

The Tetons attract expert climbers and mountaineers from all over the world, but the terrain and climate are very challenging for even the most experienced athletes. Jackson Hole Mountain Guides and Exum Mountain Guides offer instruction and guide service in the park.

## Winter sports

The park draws backcountry downhill skiers, but preparation and safety are key; check with the park for current conditions. Cross-country skiing and snow-shoeing are popular on a number of the park's trails in winter, including the Jenny Lake Loop and the Taggart Lake Trail. The Moose-Wilson Rd. and Signal Mountain Summit Rd. are also open to skiers and snowshoers.

## Camping

There are five campgrounds, as well as the Headwaters Campground off the John D. Rockefeller, Jr. Memorial Parkway. Jenny Lake Campground is picturesque, and only allows tents. Gros Ventre Campground is the largest and typically the last to fill. Permits are required for all backcountry camping.

## GETTING AROUND

Grand Teton National Park is located in northwestern Wyoming between Yellowstone and the town of Jackson. From the South Entrance of Yellowstone near Flagg Ranch, southbound U.S. 89/191/287 (also known as the John D. Rockefeller, Jr. Memorial Parkway) enters the park near Jackson Lake. From here, the highway exits the park to the east as Teton Park Rd. (closed in winter) and continues to Jenny Lake and the south side of the park. Jackson is 13 miles (21 km) south of Moose via U.S. 26/89/191. You can also take the narrow Moose-Wilson Rd. and exit near Jackson Hole Mountain Resort.

# EXPLORING GRAND TETON

Grand Teton National Park is located in north-west Wyoming, near the border of Idaho. The park's 310,000 acres (130,000 ha) encompass the Teton mountains, the 13,000-ft (4,000-m) Grand Teton peak, and the valley known as Jackson Hole.

← Hiking the Cascade Canyon Trail

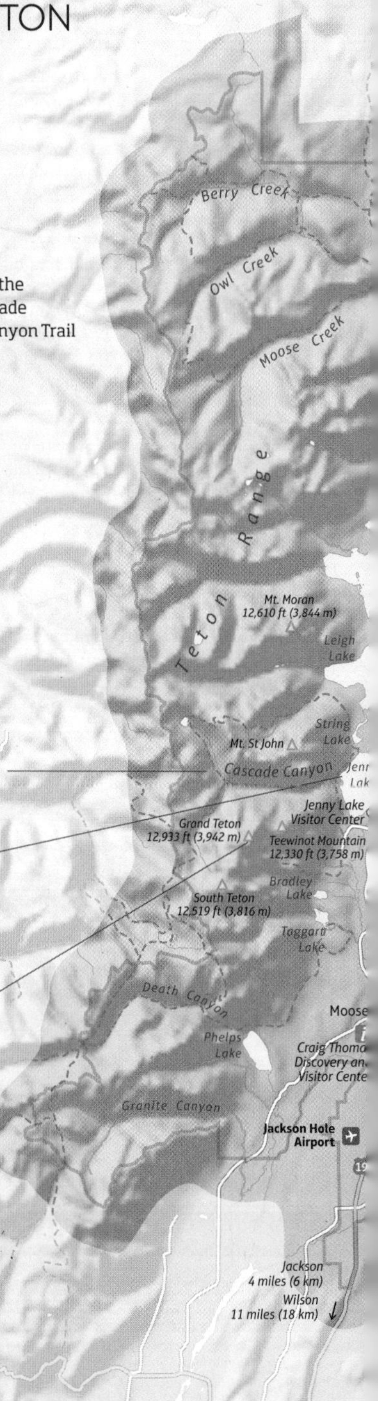

**Cascade Canyon** *runs between Teewinot Mountain and Mt. St. John from the western banks of Jenny Lake.*

The idyllic **Jenny Lake** *sits at the base of the Tetons, and owes its existence to rocky glacial moraine that was pushed out of Cascade Canyon.*

The highest peak in the Teton Range, 13,775-ft (4,199-m) **Grand Teton** *rises more than 7,000 ft (2,100 m) above Jackson Hole.*

Berry Creek

Owl Creek

Moose Creek

Teton Range

Mt. Moran
12,610 ft (3,844 m)

Leigh Lake

String Lake

Mt. St John △

Cascade Canyon

Jenny Lake

Jenny Lake Visitor Center

Grand Teton
12,933 ft (3,942 m)

Teewinot Mountain
12,330 ft (3,758 m)

Bradley Lake

South Teton
12,519 ft (3,816 m)

Taggart Lake

Death Canyon

Moose

Phelps Lake

Craig Thomas Discovery and Visitor Centre

Granite Canyon

Jackson Hole Airport

Jackson
4 miles (6 km)
Wilson
11 miles (18 km)

**0 kilometers** 8

**0 miles** 8

N ↑

**Jackson Lake** has been enlarged by a dam to provide irrigation water to farmers in Idaho, but it also provides excellent boating and fishing.

The marshy banks of the **Emma Matilda lake** offer excellent hiking, with great views of the Teton Range.

With one of the best Teton views, the 7,727-ft (2,355-m) summit of **Signal Mountain** was a favorite of painter Thomas Moran.

Cutting a serpentine path through Jackson Hole, the **Snake River** winds around the park for 27 miles (43 km) and attracts rafters and anglers.

Colter Village

ℹ️ Colter Bay Visitor Center

Two Ocean Lake

Emma Matilda Lake

Donaho Island

Signal Mountain 7,727 ft (2,355 m)

26

191

Snake River

Antelope Flats

ROCKEFELLER JR. MEMORIAL PARKWAY

TETON PARK ROAD

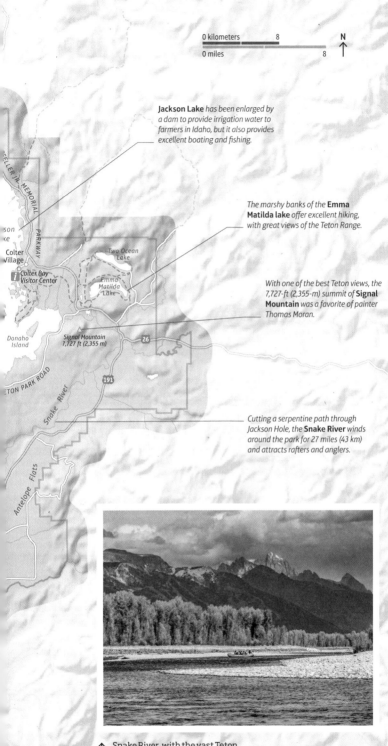

↑ Snake River, with the vast Teton Range looming in the background

Some of the steepest cliffs,
oldest rock, and craggiest
spires in North America ↑

# BLACK CANYON OF THE GUNNISON

📍 Colorado 🎫 $30 per vehicle, valid for seven days 🌐 nps.gov/blca

One of Colorado's best-kept secrets, the Black Canyon emerges as if from nowhere. Over the last 2 million years, the Gunnison River has carved this dizzyingly steep and deep abyss into the land – one of the sheerest, narrowest gorges on the continent. The sheer-walled canyon, which ranges from 1,730 ft (527 m) to 2,700 ft (823 m) in depth, is so narrow in places that its walls block sunlight for more than 23 hours a day, thus the name: the Black Canyon.

With its awe-inspiring combination of deep gorges, narrow passages, and steep drops, the Black Canyon of the Gunnison is a worthy peer of the more famous Grand Canyon. The remarkable geology of the region is dramatic testament to the erosive powers of water: the Gunnison River cuts through volcanic and sedimentary rocks forming the park's vertiginous gorge. As the river cascades down one of the steepest mountain descents in North America, it forcibly alters the landscape at a faster rate than the Colorado River's work scouring the Grand Canyon. The erosion has created such geological spectacles as the 2,250-ft (686-m) Painted Wall, the tallest cliff in Colorado, and the slim strait known as the Narrows.

---

🕐 **IF YOU HAVE**
**A weekend**

Spend the first day tackling the North Vista Trail, keeping an eye out for peregrine falcons. Camp in the North Rim, then walk the Cedar Point Nature Trail for views of Painted Wall.

---

# EAT

There are no restaurants in the park. The towns of Montrose and Crawford have numerous places to eat and grocery stores.

**Camp Robber**
Enjoy steaks, seafood, and New Mexican fare, all made using local ingredients, at this popular restaurant.

🏠 Montrose
🌐 camprobber.com

**Colorado Boy Pizzeria and Brewery**
A family-friendly craft brewery serving pizza and sandwiches in downtown Montrose.

🏠 Montrose
🌐 coloradoboy montrose.com

↑ The Gunnison River, which is responsible for the canyon's existence

↑ Studying the cliff walls from a pinnacle that seems to hang over the void

## Exploring the park

The park is split into two sections: the North Rim and the South Rim, with most visitors confining their visit to the South, arriving along the paved and scenic South Rim Rd. South Rim Rd. has a dozen overlooks that require a short walk from the parking lots. Near the South Rim Visitor Center, Gunnison Point gives a good perspective of the canyon's near-vertical walls and their colorful geology, and Sunset View has a picnic area to watch the landscape as the light fades.

The North Rim might be less frequented, but it's equally spectacular. North Rim Rd. has five overlooks,

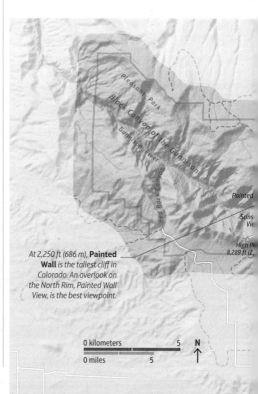

*At 2,250 ft (686 m),* **Painted Wall** *is the tallest cliff in Colorado. An overlook on the North Rim, Painted Wall View, is the best viewpoint.*

0 kilometers 5
0 miles 5

N ↑

**IF YOU HAVE**
**A day**

Drive the South Rim, stopping at various overlooks along the way, then hike the difficult Oak Flat Loop, exploring below the rim. Stay in the park until dark to skygaze.

but you'll find more on the trails here. The North Rim is also a rock-climbing destination, and the starting point for canyon hikes.

## Hiking

The best way to study the cliffs is on a hike. On the South Rim, Cedar Point Nature Trail leads to views of Painted Wall on an easy 0.7-mile (1.1-km) round trip, while the steep and narrow 2-mile (3.2-km) Oak Flat Loop Trail takes you below the rim.

For a longer hike, the North Vista Trail on the North Rim is a moderate to difficult 7-mile (11.2-km) round trip. The trail takes you to Exclamation Point, which offers some of the best views of the inner canyon, and then leads up Green Mountain.

Backpackers regularly descend to the canyon floor. The Gunnison Route, which requires a permit, starts on the Oak Flat Loop Trail on the South Rim and descends 1,800 ft (549 m). Chain is installed along the wall on a particularly difficult area midway down. There are two other routes that begin on the South Rim and three more on the North Rim; you can also hike in from East Portal in the Curecanti National Recreation Area.

## Stargazing

A certified International Dark Sky Park, the park is ideal for stargazing thanks to its lack of light pollution. An astronomy festival is held in September, with a host of activities.

**GETTING AROUND**

Black Canyon of the Gunnison National Park is located about 250 miles (402 km) southwest of Denver. The turnoff to the South Rim is 8 miles (13 km) east of the city of Montrose on U.S. 50, and the North Rim is 11 miles (18 km) south of the town of Crawford on Colo. Hwy. 92. The 7-mile (11-km) South Rim Dr. features stops at 12 overlooks with canyon views, and the 8-mile (13-km) North Rim Rd. has five overlooks. There is no bridge across the canyon; the drive between the rims takes about two hours. Both roads are closed in winter, but you can access the visitor center on the South Rim year-round.

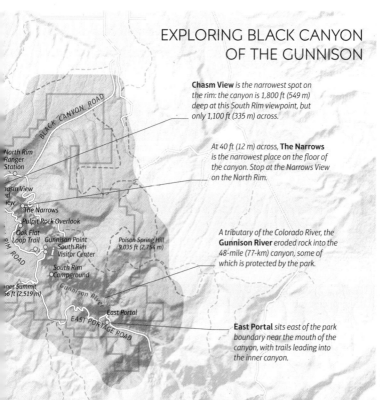

# EXPLORING BLACK CANYON OF THE GUNNISON

**Chasm View** is the narrowest spot on the rim: the canyon is 1,800 ft (549 m) deep at this South Rim viewpoint, but only 1,100 ft (335 m) across.

At 40 ft (12 m) across, **The Narrows** is the narrowest place on the floor of the canyon. Stop at the Narrows View on the North Rim.

A tributary of the Colorado River, the **Gunnison River** eroded rock into the 48-mile (77-km) canyon, some of which is protected by the park.

**East Portal** sits east of the park boundary near the mouth of the canyon, with trails leading into the inner canyon.

*Map labels:* BLACK CANYON ROAD · North Rim Ranger Station · Chasm View · The Narrows · Pulpit Rock Overlook · Oak Flat Loop Trail · Gunnison Point · South Rim Visitor Center · South Rim Campground · Poison Spring Hill 9,035 ft (2,754 m) · Gunnison River · Summit 8,265 ft (2,519 m) · East Portal · EAST PORTAL ROAD

A trickling creek not far from Estes Park, the wild gateway to Rocky Mountain ↑

# ROCKY MOUNTAIN

◉ Colorado ⬙ $35 per vehicle, valid for seven days; reservations and timed-entry permit required
Ⓦ nps.gov/romo

The startling grandeur of the Rockies is on glorious display at Rocky Mountain, one of the most wildly beautiful parks in the U.S. With 60 huge peaks towering above 12,000 ft (3,600 m), the park offers unrivaled mountain adventures. The vertiginous and ruggedly beautiful high country is dominated by alpine tundra, while verdant meadows and valleys nestle below, intersected by some of the country's wildest trails.

The undulating terrain and soaring elevations of the Rocky Mountains mean the namesake national park is home to three distinct ecosystems. The park's lower levels and sunnier, south-facing slopes are defined by biodiverse montane landscapes, with open meadows, woodland glades, and trickling rivers. Here, the long-lived ponderosa pine tree dominates, an abundant feature across the western U.S.

Above the gentle lowland greenery, the slopes give way to a subalpine ecosystem, defined by its rich coverage of spruce and fir trees. Snow is known to last longer in

↑ Climbing a precarious arête high in the Rocky Mountains

these reaches, sheltered by the forest canopy.

Finally, at the very highest points, well beyond the treeline, the park is dominated by sparse alpine tundra, redolent of landscapes seen beyond the Arctic Circle. This treeless expanse covers more than one third of the park, and makes for wild hiking: the high winds and freezing temperatures here stunt tree growth, with only the hardiest flora on Earth surviving.

---

📅 IF YOU HAVE
**A day**

Drive 48-mile (77-km) Trail Ridge Road, first stopping at the Alpine Visitor Center. When driving, look out for the remarkable changing ecosystems on either side of the Continental Divide as you head into the mountains.

A viewing platform near Trail Ridge Road, the highest paved road in the U.S.

## EAT

There is one place you can eat in the park, and many more choices in nearby Estes Park and Grand Lake.

**Trail Ridge Store**
Café and coffee bar, offering soups, salads, and sandwiches.
 Alpine Visitor Center
ⓦ shop.trailridge giftstore.com

$⑤⑤

---

**Rock Inn**
Pastas, pizzas, and sandwiches in a historic tavern, with craft beer and a cocktail menu.
🄰 Estes Park
ⓦ rockinnestes.com

$$⑤

---

**Seven Keys Lodge**
Fine dining at a historic mountain lodge near Longs Peak, serving creative western fare.
🄰 Estes Park
ⓦ sevenkeyslodge.com

$$$

### Exploring the park
Most people visit the park in the summer, a relatively brief season given the park's location and altitude. The vast majority of visitors explore the park by car, arriving from the nearby town of Estes Park (note that the town can become highly congested during the summer). Many of the park's higher roads become impassable during the winter months.

Though Trail Ridge Road is the only route to cross the entire park, the Bear Lake Road Corridor is the park's most popular section. This road provides a gateway to some of the most awe-inspiring views and dramatic

A narrow, elevated section of the Trail Ridge Road

hikes. A shuttle bus runs the length of the route in summer, dropping guests off at trailheads and the most popular viewpoints.

## Trail Ridge Road

Often described as a highway to the sky, Trail Ridge Road is a spectacular route through the park. From the Fall River Entrance, it takes an exhilarating 48-mile (77-km) route through the heart of the park, ascending about 3,000 ft (914 m) on either side of the Continental Divide. Allow 4–6 hours for the epic drive from Estes Park to Grand Lake.

Just beyond where U.S. 34 and U.S. 36 merge at Deer Ridge Junction is Many Parks Curve. Here you'll find one of the first overlooks with a sweeping mountain view, followed by Rainbow Curve and Forest Canyon Overlook. At the road's high point at Rock Cut, you can explore the delicate alpine tundra via an easy 1.2-mile (1.9-km) round trip around the Tundra Communities Trail. The park's alpine tundra ecosystem begins around 11,500 ft (3,505 m) in elevation and is marked by cold temperatures, heavy winds, and rocky soil. Alpine tundra occurs at lower and lower elevations the farther north you go, before it ultimately transitions into polar tundra in the lowlands above the Arctic Circle. Most plants are dwarfed to survive in this extreme climate, with tiny flowers and long taproots, and colorful lichens find purchase all over the exposed rock. Bighorn sheep are specially adapted for life in the tundra, along with hare-like pikas, marmots, and ptarmigans.

### GETTING AROUND

Rocky Mountain National Park is about 70 miles (113 km) northwest of Denver via U.S. 36. There are two entrances near Estes Park on the east side of the park: U.S. 34 enters at the Fall River Entrance and U.S. 36 enters at the Beaver Meadows Entrance. The routes merge together as Trail Ridge Road at Deer Ridge Junction. The 48-mile (77-km) Trail Ridge Road connects the east and west sides of the park, rising to 12,183 ft (3,713 m) in elevation at its highest point at Rock Cut, near the Alpine Visitor Center, before descending to the Grand Lake Entrance on the park's southwestern corner. The park runs free shuttle buses in the summer, as well as a hiker's shuttle bus (reservations required) from Estes Park. Trail Ridge Road closes in the winter months; it typically remains open from early May to October.

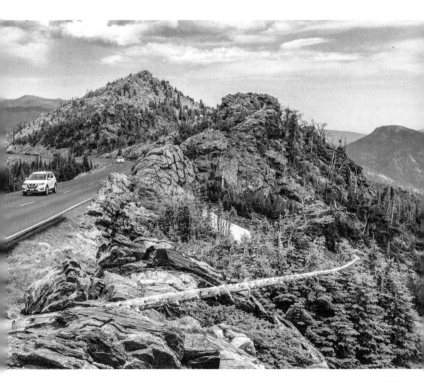

Holzwarth Historic Site,
home to traditional
log buildings ↑

From Rock Cut, Trail Ridge Road leads to the Gore Range Overlook and the Alpine Visitor Center, which has exhibits on the park's tundra ecosystem. Alternatively, you can take the unpaved, one-way Old Fall River Road (closed in winter) from near the Fall River Entrance 9 miles (14.5 km) to the visitor center.

A little more than 4 miles (6.4 km) west of the visitor center, the road crosses the Continental Divide at Milner Pass. The divide is the pass that runs north-south down the Rocky Mountains; any rain or snowmelt on its west side will eventually flow into the Pacific, and any water running down its eastern slopes will end up in the Atlantic. Upon descending from the tundra on the west side of the park, Trail Ridge Road passes the Farview Curve Viewpoint, with a panoramic perspective on the Kawuneeche Valley and the Never Summer Mountains. The road turns south from here and parallels stretches of the nascent Colorado River through the valley on its way to exiting the park near the town of Grand Lake. A former dude ranch in Grand Lake, Holzwarth Historic Site preserves several log buildings from the 1920s in the valley.

## Hiking

Hikers have more than 350 miles (560 km) of trails to choose from in Rocky Mountain National Park. The Bear Lake area is a great place to start. Beyond the easy 0.5-mile (0.8-mile) loop on the Bear Lake Nature Trail, the moderate 5-mile (8-km) round-trip Mills Lake Trail rewards hikers with one of the best views of Longs Peak in the park, and there are numerous other trailheads in the vicinity.

To the north at Deer Ridge Junction, the moderate 6-mile (9.6-km) Deer Mountain Trail ascends about 1,000 ft (305 m) to the summit of its namesake mountain for sweeping views of the mountains and meadows.

For a deeper dive into the alpine tundra, the Ute Trail starts across from the Alpine Visitor Center on Trail Ridge Road, with great views of the surrounding peaks but little in the way of tree cover. The moderate 8-mile (12.9-km) round trip is steep and tough on the return.

The tallest mountain in the park, Longs Peak is about 10 miles (16 km) south of Estes Park via Colo. Hwy. 7 on the southeastern edge of the park. The iconic mountain

←

Overlooking Bear Lake from the nature trail that runs along its banks

# A DRIVING TOUR
# OLD FALL RIVER ROAD

**Length** 11 miles (17.7 km) one-way **Stopping-off points** Endovalley Picnic Area is great for a lunch stop if you've got food supplies **Terrain** Gravel and dirt road

Before Trail Ridge Road's completion in 1932, this was the first automobile route into the park's upper elevations, and it's now a less hectic alternative with similarly superlative views. Note that the road is narrow in spots and has no guardrails, and is opened seasonally, typically from July to October.

**Locator Map**

**Key**

-- Drive Route

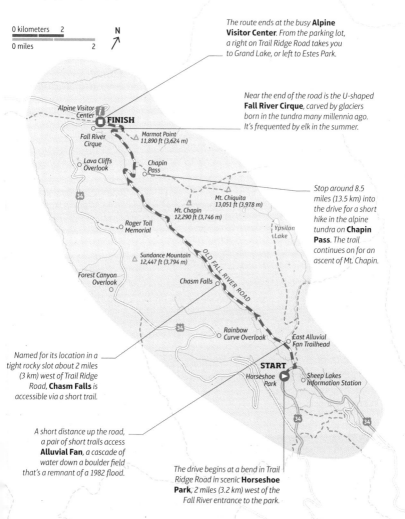

The route ends at the busy **Alpine Visitor Center**. From the parking lot, a right on Trail Ridge Road takes you to Grand Lake, or left to Estes Park.

Near the end of the road is the U-shaped **Fall River Cirque**, carved by glaciers born in the tundra many millennia ago. It's frequented by elk in the summer.

Stop around 8.5 miles (13.5 km) into the drive for a short hike in the alpine tundra on **Chapin Pass**. The trail continues on for an ascent of Mt. Chapin.

Named for its location in a tight rocky slot about 2 miles (3 km) west of Trail Ridge Road, **Chasm Falls** is accessible via a short trail.

A short distance up the road, a pair of short trails access **Alluvial Fan**, a cascade of water down a boulder field that's a remnant of a 1982 flood.

The drive begins at a bend in Trail Ridge Road in scenic **Horseshoe Park**, 2 miles (3.2 km) west of the Fall River entrance to the park.

0 kilometers 2
0 miles 2

N

Alpine Visitor Center
**FINISH**
Fall River Cirque
Marmot Point 11,890 ft (3,624 m)
Lava Cliffs Overlook
Chapin Pass
Mt. Chiquita 13,051 ft (3,978 m)
Mt. Chapin 12,290 ft (3,746 m)
Roger Toll Memorial
Ypsilon Lake
Sundance Mountain 12,447 ft (3,794 m)
OLD FALL RIVER ROAD
Forest Canyon Overlook
Chasm Falls
Rainbow Curve Overlook
East Alluvial Fan Trailhead
**START**
Horseshoe Park
Sheep Lakes Information Station

# STAY

Aside from camping, there are no lodgings within the park, but you'll find overnight options in Estes Park and Grand Lake.

### Stanley Hotel

Grand historic hotel near eastern park entrances, said to have inspired Stephen King's *The Shining*.

🏠 Estes Park
🌐 stanleyhotel.com

$$$

### Grand Lake Lodge

Famed for having "Colorado's favorite front porch," with rocking chairs and swings.

🏠 Grand Lake
🌐 grandlakelodge.com

$$$

### Allenspark Lodge B&B

Historic log lodge found near Wild Basin, offering shared and private baths and comfortable private apartments.

🏠 Allenspark
🌐 allensparklodgebnb.com

$$$

↑ Intrepid alpine mountaineering on the winter slopes of Longs Peak

advanced planning and the required equipment.

Just north of the turnoff to the Longs Peak Trailhead is Lily Lake, where you'll find a fishing pier, a wheelchair-accessible loop trail, and a picnic area, and the rocky duo known as the Twin Sisters.

The Twin Sisters Trail is a good pick for intermediate hikers, a difficult 7.4-mile round trip that gains 2,338 ft (716 m) up to the top of Twin Sisters East, and a short rocky scramble takes you to the summit of its western sibling.

From the Wild Basin Trailhead, a moderate 5.4-mile (8.7-km) trek will get you to scenic Ouzel Falls and back, or you can add 2.2 miles (3.5-km) one way to reach the forested shores of Ouzel Lake, a favorite for fly-fishing.

On the west side of the park, the Colorado River Trailhead starts an easy 6.2-mile (10-km) round trip to Lulu City, the ruins of a mining town that was abandoned in the 1880s. Near the town of Grand Lake, the East Inlet Trail passes Adams Falls en route to a picture-perfect valley, culminating in Lake Verna. The 7-mile (11.3-km) hike to Lake Verna is difficult, but the first half of the trail is not as steep as the latter. Many of the park's trailheads

connect to longer back-packing routes.

## Climbing and mountaineering

With 17 peaks above 13,000 ft (3,962 m), the park has plenty of mountains to summit and rocks to climb. Note, however, that all climbs in the park have difficult sections suitable for experienced climbers only. The Estes Park-based Colorado Mountain School (www.colorado-mountainschool.com) offers guide services and lessons. Permits are required for those on overnight climbing or mountaineering trips.

## Winter sports

The trails at Bear Lake, Kawuneeche Valley, and

---

IF YOU HAVE
**A weekend**

Explore the routes around Wild Basin before taking a trip around the length of the park. While on the west side, explore the East Inlet Trail near Grand Lake. After a relaxing break here, you can take the strenuous but beautiful walk to Lake Verna.

---

lures mountaineers to the very difficult 16-mile (25.7-km) trek up and down the mountain. The trail gains 4,855 ft (1,480 m) en route to the summit on experts-only terrain. The park service calls Longs Peak "much more than a hike," admitting that it's a classic mountaineering route that should not be undertaken without

Wild Basin are open for snowshoeing and cross-country skiing in winter, and rangers conduct guided snowshoe talks on both sides of the park. Sledding is allowed at Hidden Valley, 7 miles (11.3 km) inside the Beaver Meadows Entrance.

## Wildlife watching

The park's iconic bighorn sheep can be seen in the tundra along Trail Ridge Road, especially at higher elevations, along with marmots, pikas, and small ptarmigans. Herds of elk congregate in the meadows at lower elevations from fall to spring. Moose, black bears, mule deer, beavers, and otters are also found in the park, along with more than 250 species of birds. Clark's nutcrackers, Steller's jays, golden eagles, and prairie falcons are often seen along Trail Ridge Road.

## Camping

There are five campgrounds in the park, with three around the east side. The Longs Peak Campground is first-come, first-served, but the others require booking. Backcountry camping requires a permit.

$\rightarrow$

Meadow of wildflowers in the park's montane fields and *(inset)* a moose in the high country

# EXPLORING ROCKY MOUNTAIN

Rocky Mountain is in northeast Colorado, with the towns of Estes Park on its eastern border and Grand Lake to the west. The park's 260,000 acres (105,000 ha) encompass some of the U.S.'s finest mountain landscapes.

**Rock Cut** *is the highest point on Trail Ridge Road at 12,183 ft (3,713 m) above sea level; it's prone to howling winds and freezing temperatures.*

*Trail Ridge Road crosses the Continental Divide at the 10,759-foot (3,297-m)* **Milner Pass**.

*The 48-mile (77-km)* **Trail Ridge Road** *between Estes Park and Grand Lake is the country's highest paved road, ascending about 3,000 ft (914 m).*

Mirror Lake

Long Draw Reservoir

Flatiron Mountain 12,335 ft (3,760 m)

Alpine Visitor Center

ALPINE RIDGE

Lulu City

Tundra Communities Trail

Never Summer Mountains

Milner Pass

Rock Cut

TRAIL RIDGE

Colorado River

Farview Curve

Arrowhead Lake

Inkwell Lake

Timber Lake

CONTINENTAL DIVIDE

TRAIL RIDGE ROAD

Kawuneeche Valley

34

Grand Lake Entrance
Kawuneeche Visitor Center

Grand Lake

INLET TRAIL

Shadow Mountain Lake

↑ Hiking across the precipitous Ledges on Longs Peak

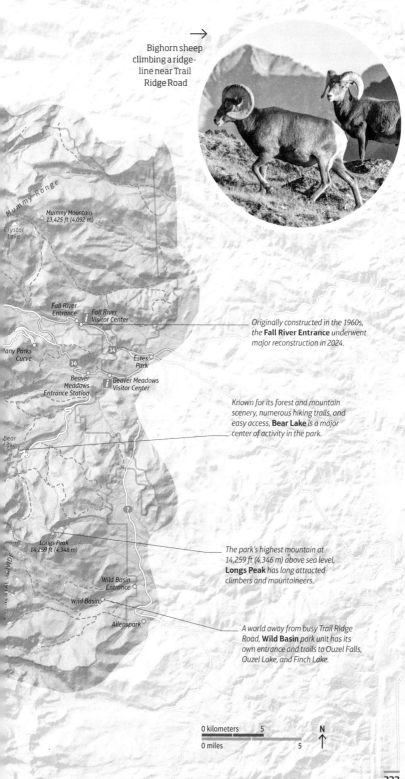

Bighorn sheep climbing a ridge-line near Trail Ridge Road

Mummy Range

Mummy Mountain
13,425 ft (4,092 m)

Crystal Lake

Fall River Entrance

Fall River Visitor Center

Many Parks Curve

34

Estes Park

36

Beaver Meadows Entrance Station

Beaver Meadows Visitor Center

Bear Lake

7

Longs Peak
14,259 ft (4,346 m)

CONTINENTAL DIVIDE

Wild Basin Entrance

Wild Basin

Allenspark

Originally constructed in the 1960s, the **Fall River Entrance** underwent major reconstruction in 2024.

Known for its forest and mountain scenery, numerous hiking trails, and easy access, **Bear Lake** is a major center of activity in the park.

The park's highest mountain at 14,259 ft (4,346 m) above sea level, **Longs Peak** has long attracted climbers and mountaineers.

A world away from busy Trail Ridge Road, **Wild Basin** park unit has its own entrance and trails to Ouzel Falls, Ouzel Lake, and Finch Lake.

0 kilometers        5

0 miles                 5

N

# GREAT SAND DUNES

**⬚ Colorado 🔁 $25 per vehicle, valid for seven days ⬚ nps.gov/grsa**

From a distance, the landscape is hard to believe; in the dune field itself, it's even more quizzical. Like a lost piece of the Sahara Desert that's been dropped into a Colorado valley, the Great Sand Dunes are equal parts baffling and beautiful. The tallest sand dunes in North America rise about 750 ft (229 m) above the floor of an alpine valley ringed by Rocky Mountains, and offer a sandbox playground for downhill sledding sprees.

When you first see the dunes, the obvious question is: how did they get here? Nestled between the San Juan and Sangre de Cristo mountains, the dunes are a by-product of a huge lake that once covered the San Luis Valley. A sand sheet was left behind when the lake disappeared, and winds from two opposing directions caused the sand to form (over thousands of years) vertical dunes.

The dune field now occupies about 19,200 acres (7,770 ha). Vegetation across the valley floor has since slowed the process, but the landscape is far from static. Even today, parabolic dunes form in the sand sheet and migrate toward the dune field. And while they might look barren, the dunes support a surprising amount of life. Only the top few inches are dry; rainfall keeps the lower layers moist and allows hardy plants like Indian ricegrass, blowout grass, and scurfpea to thrive, as well as animals such as kangaroo rats, tiger beetles, and pronghorn.

Beyond the dunes, there's even more diverse flora and fauna in the park's wetlands, lakes, rivers, and tundra.

Young pronghorn grazing in the park tundra

## EAT

There are no restaurants in the park, but you'll find a variety of places to eat in nearby Alamosa, as well as supermarkets to stock up on camping and picnic supplies.

**The Friar's Fork**
This award-winning restaurant serves upscale Italian dinners in a historic former church.
⬚ Alamosa
⬚ friarsfork.com

$$$

**San Luis Valley Brewing Company**
A brewpub that cooks up Mexican and American fare for lunch and dinner.
⬚ Alamosa
⬚ slvbrewco.com

↑ The dune field, estimated to contain more than 1.2 cubic miles (5 cubic km) of sand

↑ Hiking the Mosca Pass Trail through forest, a good place to spot songbirds and grouse

## STAY

You can camp in the park at the Piñon Flats Campground (Apr–Oct) or in designated backcountry areas with a permit, but there are no lodgings within park boundaries. Alamosa has chain motels and hotels, and the San Luis Valley has lodgings.

### Great Sand Dunes Lodge
Motor lodge at the park entrance offering motel rooms and a camper suite, open March to early November.

🅰 Mosca 🆆 gsd lodge.com

$$$

### Frontier Drive-Inn
Unique huts and yurts make up this inn, set in a former mid-century drive-in movie theater park.

🅰 Center 🆆 frontier driveinn.com

$$$

## Exploring the park

Despite its name, the park in fact consists of a variety of habitats and ecosystems alongside the eponymous dunes, including lakes, meadows, and forests. The dune field is open to hiking, but there are no trails. Pick a dune and a route, and keep in mind that walking on sand is slower than walking on solid ground. Many visitors set their sights on High Dune, one of the park's tallest dunes and the easiest to hike to – expect to spend about 90 minutes hiking from the Dunes Parking Lot to the top.

For more solitude, the Medano Pass Primitive Rd. – the only road to access the dune field – takes drivers to the Eastern Dune Ridge. If you don't have a 4WD vehicle, park at the Point of No Return trailhead and hike to the picnic areas at Sand Pit or Castle Creek.

A note of caution: the sand can heat up to 150°F (66°C) on summer afternoons, and thunderstorms with lightning are common. Start hiking early and bring plenty of water.

## Hiking

While there aren't any designated trails in the dunes, there are several on more solid ground on the valley floor and the adjacent Sangre de Cristo Mountains. The Montville parking area near the visitor center has trailheads for all skill levels, from the easy 0.5-mile (0.8-km) Montville Nature Trail, a shady loop with good views of the dunes, to the difficult Mosca Pass Trail, a 7-mile (11.3-km) round trip through a woodland up more than 1,400 ft (427 m) to its namesake mountain pass. From the main Dunes Parking Lot, you can hike Medano Creek to Castle Creek, a moderate 5-mile (8-km) round trip along the ever-steeper eastern edge of the dune field. The Sand Ramp Trail, accessible from the campground or the Point of No Return parking area, is a difficult 11-mile (17.7-km) round trip that connects to a number of longer backpacking routes in the Sangre de Cristos.

To hike the dunes themselves, prioritize Star Dune, tied for the tallest dune in the park with Hidden Dune at 741 ft (225 m). It takes six hours to hike the 6 miles (9.7 km) to Star Dune and back, but the effort is worth the reward of idyllic views of both the dune field and the

→ Hiking the dunes, which can take surprising effort to climb

IF YOU HAVE
**A weekend**

Scurry up High Dune, one of the park's tallest dunes at 650 ft (198 m), then sled down, before hiking the Mosca Pass Trail. The next day, make for the shaded Montville Nature Trail.

surrounding mountains. Find the trailhead by hiking 2 miles (3 km) south along Medano Creek to the dune's base, then follow a ridge to the summit. Hidden Dune, meanwhile, is named for its remote location; it's not visible from many areas in the park. To embark on a hike to this dune, start from the main Dunes Parking Lot and walk north for six hours, at a distance of 7 miles (11 km).

For something extra special, hike the dunes under a full moon. In 2019, the Great Sand Dunes was named an International Dark Sky Park, and the nighttime stargazing is epic here; it's so bright on evening treks that no flashlight is needed.

## Sand sports

For many, hiking is a means to an end for sledding and "sandboarding." Unlike many fragile natural environments, the dunes suffer no ill effects from being sledded down. Of course, to come down, you first have to hike up, and this can feel like a tough task. The payoff is the invigorating downhill spree.

Many enthusiasts hike up High Dune and sled down, while others make for the Castle Creek Picnic Area; it's best to practice a bit near the Dunes Parking Lot before trying both areas. Board and sled rentals are available at the Great Sand Dunes Lodge just outside the entrance and at several other businesses in the valley; the park keeps a list of nearby rental shops.

## GETTING AROUND

Great Sand Dunes National Park and Preserve is located on the east side of the San Luis Valley, about 200 miles (322 km) southwest of Denver via U.S. 285 or I-25. The biggest city nearby is Alamosa, 30 miles (48 km) southwest of the dunes via Colo. Hwy. 150 and U.S. 160. The park itself has very few roads; the main entry road, Colo. Hwy. 150, enters the park from the south and ends at the campground, while Medano Creek Rd. accesses the dune field. There's also an unpaved 4WD road leading north from the campground that will take you to Medano Pass to the east of the park.

# EXPLORING GREAT SAND DUNES

Located in Colorado, Great Sand Dunes National Park sits within the San Luis Valley, near the base of the Sangre de Cristo mountains. The park stretches for 150,000 acres (60,700 ha), offering a unique mix of high desert, shimmering grasslands, and rolling alpine landscapes.

Liberty Gate

*From **Liberty Gate** in the north, an array of cross-country trails and backpacking routes can be accessed.*

San Luis Valley

*The beautiful alpine landscapes around **Sand Creek** differ markedly from the nearby dune fields.*

Sand Creek

Sand Sheet

Big Spring Creek

Sabkha

← Hikers resting on the summit of High Dune

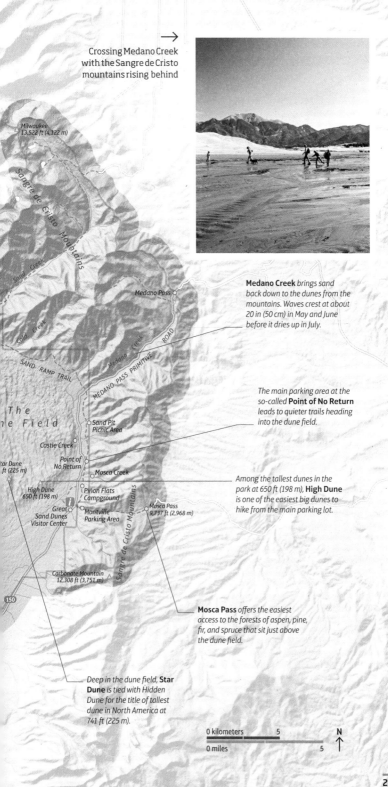

Crossing Medano Creek
with the Sangre de Cristo
mountains rising behind

**Milwaukee**
13,522 ft (4,122 m)

Sangre de Cristo Mountains

Sand Creek

Cold Creek

Medano Pass

MEDANO PASS PRIMITIVE ROAD

SAND RAMP TRAIL

The
ne Field

Sand Pit
Picnic Area

Castle Creek

tar Dune
ft (225 m)

Point of
No Return

Mosca Creek

High Dune
650 ft (198 m)

Piñon Flats
Campground

Mosca Pass
9,737 ft (2,968 m)

Great
Sand Dunes
Visitor Center

Montville
Parking Area

Sangre de Cristo Mountains

Carbonate Mountain
12,308 ft (3,751 m)

150

**Medano Creek** *brings sand
back down to the dunes from the
mountains. Waves crest at about
20 in (50 cm) in May and June
before it dries up in July.*

*The main parking area at the
so-called* **Point of No Return**
*leads to quieter trails heading
into the dune field.*

*Among the tallest dunes in the
park at 650 ft (198 m),* **High Dune**
*is one of the easiest big dunes to
hike from the main parking lot.*

**Mosca Pass** *offers the easiest
access to the forests of aspen, pine,
fir, and spruce that sit just above
the dune field.*

*Deep in the dune field,* **Star
Dune** *is tied with Hidden
Dune for the title of tallest
dune in North America at
741 ft (225 m).*

0 kilometers          5

0 miles                    5

N

↑ The famous colorful sedimentary rocks spread across Badlands

Best for *Exploring the ancient fossil bed*

# BADLANDS

[location] South Dakota [ticket] $30 per vehicle, valid for seven days
[W] nps.gov/badl

Badlands National Park is famous for its striking rock formations, naturally shaped over millions of years and spread across the largest mixed-grass prairie in the U.S. Bison, bighorn sheep, and prairie dogs roam these remarkable landscapes between otherworldly spires, canyons, and buttes. Beneath it all lies one of the richest fossil beds on Earth, with ancient deposits yielding insights into the area's prehistory. In short? This park offers a stark natural beauty little found elsewhere.

Badlands is so much more than an evocative name. Sprawling across nearly 250,000 acres (11,0000 ha), these rugged landscapes of sedimentary rock reveal layers of geological time stretching back eons. Away from the rocks, the mixed grasses feel like a different planet, supporting a variety of plant and animal species, including the endangered and elusive black-footed ferrets that were classified as extinct in the 1980s. The park is also a haven for paleontologists, with ancient fossils testament to the wild horses, rhinos, and saber-toothed cats that once roamed the plains.

### Exploring the park

Whether hiking, cycling, or driving the scenic park road, adventures at Badlands offer plenty of variety.

Badlands is divided into three units: the North Unit, the Stronghold (also called the South), and Palmer Creek Unit. Most visitors confine their visit to the North Unit, where the main Ben Reifel Visitor Center and the Fossil Discovery Trail can be found. The Stronghold and Palmer Creek Units consist of backcountry trails with little infrastructure, and are typically visited only by those planning longer hiking or camping trips.

← A bison on the rolling prairies within the park

## EAT

There is one dining option near the Ben Reifel Visitor Center in the North Unit, but the Big Foot Pass Overlook and Conata picnic areas are good places to refuel.

**Cedar Pass Lodge**
A sit-down restaurant serving local and regional dishes and freshly baked bread; it also provides snacks for purchase.
[⌂] North Unit
[W] cedarpasslodge.com
$

**Wall Drug Store**
This historic shop in the nearby town of Wall has a popular restaurant.
[⌂] Wall
[W] walldrug.com
$

← Mountain biking on the gravel trails in Badlands

managed by members of the Oglala Sioux, a subgroup of the Lakota Nation. These Lakota communities gave the park its name long before it was established as a national park. *"Mako sica,"* meaning "bad lands," was a nod to the brutal winters, strong winds, blaring sun, and lack of water.

The White River Visitor Center is a must-visit in the south, where you can learn from rangers about the history and ecology of the park, including the story of the early French fur-trappers, as well as the unique treaties formed between the National Park Service and the local Lakota community.

## STAY

There is one lodging accommodations at the Cedar Pass Lodge in the north of the park which allows for easy access to Badlands Loop Road. There are other options on the edge of the park, as well as two park campgrounds.

### Cedar Pass Lodge
Eco-friendly cabins built of pine from the Black Hills, modeled after designs from the 1920s. The Lodge also offers RV and tent camping.

⌂ North Unit
ⓦ cedarpasslodge.com

$$$

### Badlands Frontier Cabins
Located just north of the park, these 33 log cabins are custom-built and spacious.

⌂ North Unit
ⓦ frontiercabins.com

$$$

### North Unit
The North Unit of the park is the most developed in terms of infrastructure and offers numerous ways to explore the landscape and see a range of prairie wildlife.

The Ben Reifel Visitor Center on the eastern edge of the park provides useful information to help you shape your plans and provides opportunities to learn about the park's history through a range of exhibits and installations. Here you can also learn about fossils from paleontologists and other researchers at the park's Fossil Preparation Lab.

Built in 1938, Badlands Loop Road is the most popular feature in the park, covering almost 40 miles (65 km) of paved roadway between the east and north entrances of the North Unit. It's best to drive slowly, both to marvel at the surrounding landscapes and to ensure wildlife is safe to cross. The roadway starts at the eastern entrance near the visitor center or the Pinnacles entrance on the north edge. Head to Sage Creek Rim Road to enjoy views of sedimentary rock formations.

### Stronghold Unit
The Stronghold Unit lies entirely on the Pine Ridge Indian Reservation and is

## Hiking and cycling
The park has a host of official hiking trails for all abilities. The short and popular Door Trail in the North Unit takes in some of the park's best rock

Boardwalk of the Door Trail, offering excellent rock panoramas ↑

IF YOU HAVE
**A day**

Explore the North Unit on one of the many scenic drives that run past 11 of the park's best overlook viewpoints, as well as many trailheads. Finish at the Ben Reifel Visitor Center.

formations but can be completed in just half an hour. Many hikers make for the North Unit's Deer Haven Wilderness for an array of unmarked backcountry trails. There are no marked trails in the Stronghold Unit, only a wide expanse of wilderness. Ensure you map a route before heading off.

While bicycles are allowed only on designated roads within the park, there are a number of excellent loops.

## Fossil hunting

If you're fascinated by fossils, you're in for a treat at Badlands. The park has one of the most concentrated

mammal fossil beds on Earth, with finds dating back 12,000 years. Ancient bones of bison are believed by archaeologists to be a remnant of traveling hunters who once passed through the area. There are 300 additional sites where ancient campfires, tools, and pottery relics have been identified throughout the park, particularly in and around the Stronghold Unit.

There are ranger-guided hikes at Fossil Exhibit Trail in the North Unit around the Cedar Pass area, where undiscovered fossils remain today. If you find one, leave it in place, take a picture and share it with the park service for cataloging.

## Stargazing

The remote location and geographic position of the Badlands makes it a wonderful place to view the night sky. There are ranger-led outings throughout the summer months where you can learn more about celestial objects, stars, and galaxies. These usually run from the visitor

### GETTING AROUND

Badlands National Park is located 75 miles (120 km) east of Rapid City. The most common entry is from I-90 north of the park. There is a scenic drive from the town of Interior located southeast of the park. Once in Badlands, there are three main roadways. Badlands Loop Road (paved) and Sage Creek Rim Road (gravel) are located in the North Unit. Sheep Mountain Table is a dirt road that borders the North and South units. The latter two roads may be closed in winter due to rain or snow.

center. The park also hosts an annual astronomy festival, usually in early July, bringing together astronomers, park rangers, and visitors for a fun night of activities celebrating the wonders of the cosmos.

# EXPLORING BADLANDS

The vast canyons and expansive mixed-grass prairie that form Badlands National Park are located in southwestern South Dakota. The park protects over 240,000 acres (98,000 ha) of pinnacles, fossil beds, and prairies.

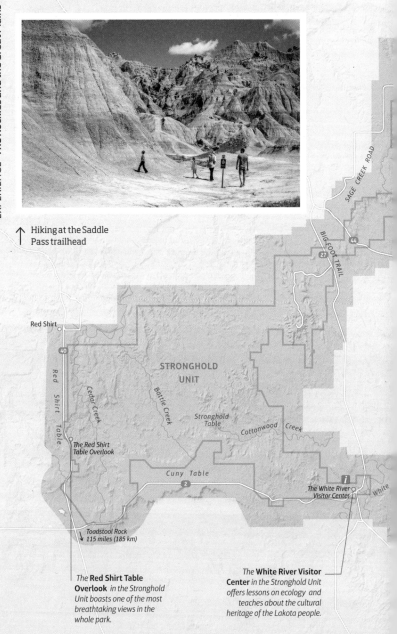

↑ Hiking at the Saddle Pass trailhead

STRONGHOLD UNIT

Red Shirt

Cedar Creek

Battle Creek

Stronghold Table

Cottonwood Creek

Red Shirt Table

The Red Shirt Table Overlook

Cuny Table

The White River Visitor Center

White

↓ Toadstool Rock
115 miles (185 km)

SAGE CREEK ROAD

BIGFOOT TRAIL

The **Red Shirt Table Overlook** in the Stronghold Unit boasts one of the most breathtaking views in the whole park.

The **White River Visitor Center** in the Stronghold Unit offers lessons on ecology and teaches about the cultural heritage of the Lakota people.

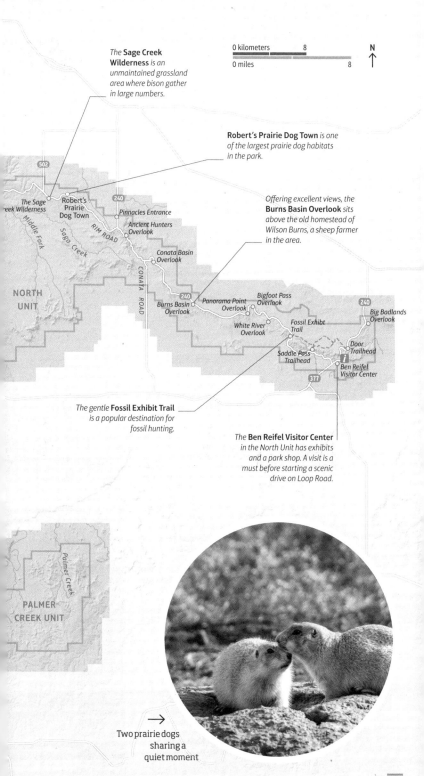

The **Sage Creek Wilderness** is an unmaintained grassland area where bison gather in large numbers.

**Robert's Prairie Dog Town** is one of the largest prairie dog habitats in the park.

Offering excellent views, the **Burns Basin Overlook** sits above the old homestead of Wilson Burns, a sheep farmer in the area.

502

The Sage Creek Wilderness

Middle Fork

Sage Creek

240

Robert's Prairie Dog Town

Pinnacles Entrance

RIM ROAD

Ancient Hunters Overlook

Conata Basin Overlook

CONATA ROAD

NORTH UNIT

240

Burns Basin Overlook

Panorama Point Overlook

Bigfoot Pass Overlook

240

Big Badlands Overlook

White River Overlook

Fossil Exhibit Trail

Door Trailhead

Saddle Pass Trailhead

377

Ben Reifel Visitor Center

The gentle **Fossil Exhibit Trail** is a popular destination for fossil hunting.

The **Ben Reifel Visitor Center** in the North Unit has exhibits and a park shop. A visit is a must before starting a scenic drive on Loop Road.

Palmer Creek

PALMER CREEK UNIT

0 kilometers 8
0 miles 8

N
↑

Two prairie dogs sharing a quiet moment

# THEODORE ROOSEVELT

📍 North Dakota 🚗 $30 per vehicle, valid for seven days
🌐 nps.gov/thro

"It was here that the romance of my life began." So said Theodore Roosevelt when musing on the time he spent in the Dakota Territory. Explore here and it's easy to share the love. Tucked away on the prairie grasslands, Theodore Roosevelt National Park harbors some of Earth's great natural treasures: colorful badlands follow the bends of a crooked river, while fabled Great Plains animals thrive in diverse microclimates, from dry slopes to wet woodlands. Prepare to swoon.

After being elected to the highest office in the U.S. in 1901, Theodore Roosevelt become known as "the Conservationist President," establishing five national parks among many other federally protected sanctuaries. Following his death in 1919, there were many proposals to establish a memorial in his honor, given his life pursuit to protect wild lands and threatened animal and bird species. This national park was eventually established by President Harry Truman in 1947, allowing Roosevelt's legacy to live on and for future generations of nature and national park lovers to enjoy the fruits of his accomplishments. And it makes sense that it was this park that bears his name, since he returned to the region many times throughout his life to seek solace in the wilderness. The landscape is as heavenly today as it was when Roosevelt spent time here. The Little Missouri River, which began life more than 23 million years ago, carves colorful stripes into a rolling landscape that looks like it's been brushed onto canvas by a master painter.

### Exploring the park

Bound by the Little Missouri River, this park stretches more than 70,000 acres (28,328 ha) across the Great Plains, and is made up of three sections: the South Unit, the North Unit, and Elkhorn Ranch. Many visit the park with grand ambitions to explore all three areas, but the most widely visited and accessible is the South Unit thanks to a scenic loop drive that showcases the park's many treasures.

---

📅 IF YOU HAVE
**A day**

Visit the Maltese Cross Cabin, where Theodore Roosevelt lived, then embark on the 48-mile (77-km) South Unit scenic drive. Stretch your legs on the Painted Canyon Trail, looking out for sightings of bison in the fields.

---

↑ The craggy, rugged landscape of the badlands stretching for miles

Bison grazing as cars skirt along the North Unit scenic drive ↑

## The South Unit

The scenic drive in the South Unit is an iconic 48-mile (77-km) route, hugged by lush badlands and forested scenery. Along the road are many overlook stops and trailheads, so it's worth stretching your legs along the drive – you may even be forced to stop mid-journey when herds of bison decide to flock down the paved road. American Bison are now protected, but long ago were the focus of hunting expeditions. While wildlife watching can be done from the car, it's exhilarating to see bald and golden eagles fly overhead, or wild horses roaming grassy expanses while on a hike.

The Painted Canyon Trail is one of the South Unit's most popular hikes, a moderate 4.2-mile (6.7-km) route that offers spectacular views of the badlands and sightings of bison grazing in the fields. For a quick and easy amble, hike the 20-minute Wind Canyon Trail for views of the Little Missouri River. Longer backcountry trails are also available, but you'll need to pick up a permit from the South Unit Visitor Center. If you're in the center vicinity, check out the Maltese Cross Cabin right outside; this is where Roosevelt first lived in the area, and his personal belongings are preserved inside the picturesque cabin.

## North Unit

If you're after a quieter experience, the North Unit offers this in abundance. It was here that Roosevelt and those who lived in the Dakotas in the late 1800s would travel on horseback, and the area still maintains a

South Unit's Maltese Cross Cabin, used by Theodore Roosevelt ↑

remote, rugged setting. A great way to get a lay of the land is by traveling the 14-mile (23-km) paved scenic drive, tracing the base of dramatic badland formations. Nestled within these features are large deposits of ancient petrified wood and concentrations of fossils, creating a living laboratory for scientific researchers and paleontologists. The road is suitable for cars, RVs, and cyclists, and can be completed in just over an hour, but you'll want to make stops along the way. The pinnacle viewpoint is at the River Bend Overlook where you can view a stone structure with the Little Missouri River snaking through the valley below.

Here you'll also find great camping and backcountry trails; you can pick up a permit at the North Unit Visitor Center. For an epic trail, try the 18-mile (30-km) Achenbach route that leads deep into the wilderness;

## GETTING AROUND

This park is separated across three units: the South Unit, the North Unit - about an hour's drive apart - and the remote Elkhorn Ranch unit positioned between the two. The main entrance to the South Unit is in the town of Medora, while the entrance to the North Unit is 14 miles (23 km) south of Watford City. Elkhorn Ranch is hidden in an off-road area and can be difficult to find - ask the park rangers at the visitor center how to best find your way. Note that you may need a high-clearance vehicle to get there. Many also make the journey to the park on a road trip from the national parks and monuments in neighboring South Dakota. Both the South and North units have designated scenic drives that pass by popular trailheads. Many hikes are accessed via Colo. Hwy. 7 along the east side of the park.

start early and aim to cross the Little Missouri River at daybreak to see the sun rise.

## Elkhorn Ranch

This is the most off-the-beaten-path of the park's three units, with its unspoiled, wide-open landscape – exactly what drew Roosevelt here in the first place. With no visitor centers, services, or scenic roads, it's a challenge to find, and you're left to your own devices to plot your path amid this peaceful countryside. Wander the grounds of Roosevelt's beloved ranch, now marked only by a few remaining foundation stones, and chill out beneath the towering cottonwood trees. It's little wonder Roosevelt chose this spot to relax.

# EXPLORING THEODORE ROOSEVELT

Found in the badlands of western North Dakota, Theodore Roosevelt National Park contains three park units spread over more than 70,000 acres (28,000 ha). The park is home to steep cliffs, deep gullies, and towering hills.

The **Peaceful Valley Ranch** area houses the only original remaining ranch house from the Roosevelt era.

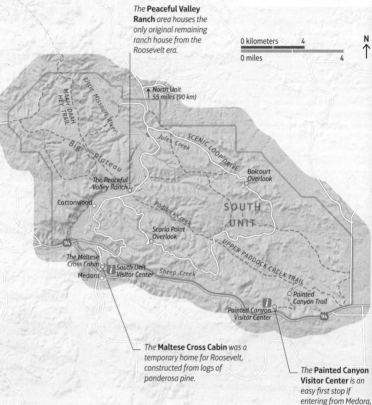

The **Maltese Cross Cabin** was a temporary home for Roosevelt, constructed from logs of ponderosa pine.

The **Painted Canyon Visitor Center** is an easy first stop if entering from Medora, with excellent views of the badlands.

The site of Elkhorn Ranch, the base of Theodore Roosevelt

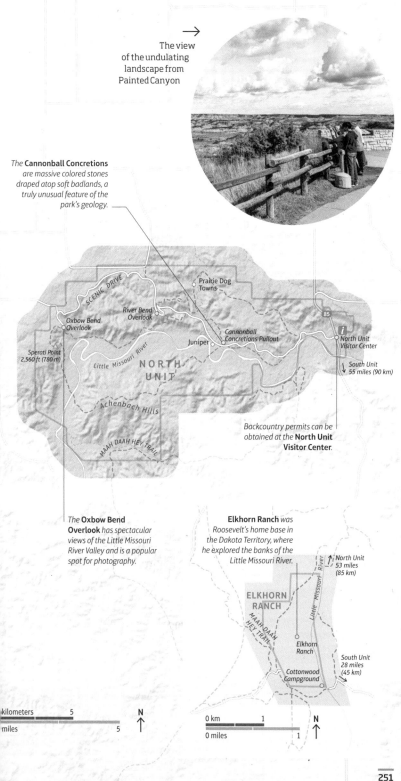

The view of the undulating landscape from Painted Canyon

The **Cannonball Concretions** are massive colored stones draped atop soft badlands, a truly unusual feature of the park's geology.

Prairie Dog Towns

SCENIC DRIVE

River Bend Overlook

Oxbow Bend Overlook

Cannonball Concretions Pullout

Juniper

85

*i* North Unit Visitor Center

Sperati Point 2,560 ft (780 m)

Little Missouri River

**NORTH UNIT**

South Unit 55 miles (90 km)

Achenbach Hills

MAAH DAAH HEY TRAIL

Backcountry permits can be obtained at the **North Unit Visitor Center**.

The **Oxbow Bend Overlook** has spectacular views of the Little Missouri River Valley and is a popular spot for photography.

**Elkhorn Ranch** *was Roosevelt's home base in the Dakota Territory, where he explored the banks of the Little Missouri River.*

North Unit 53 miles (85 km)

Little Missouri River

**ELKHORN RANCH**

MAAH DAAH HEY TRAIL

Elkhorn Ranch

South Unit 28 miles (45 km)

Cottonwood Campground

kilometers 5

miles 5

N

0 km 1

0 miles 1

N

# WIND CAVE

 South Dakota 🎫 Free; cave tours range from $7 to $45
🌐 nps.gov/wica

Wind Cave is home to two different ecosystems rolled into one incredible park. Below ground is one of the oldest cave systems on Earth, a peculiar world of vast caverns housing rare calcite structures. Above ground, grasslands and prairies are home to a diverse wildlife population. Exploring the plains is wonderful, but heading below the surface is the best way to get a taste of South Dakota's hidden gem.

---

📅 IF YOU HAVE
**A day**

Tour the vast cave system with a park service cave ranger. Then head above ground to drive the two paved park routes, looking out for bison, elk, and rare birds above.

---

The first cave to be officially designated a national park, Wind Cave is a place of superlatives. It's among the longest and most complex caves in the world, where you can find 95 percent of Earth's rare boxwork formations clinging like lace to the cavern walls and ceilings. The first record of Wind Cave was cited by Lakota people living in the Black Hills. They believed that wisdom from spirits in the underworld flowed with the dry-wind systems, bestowing life to the land. The region was later known for settlers and prospectors who came to the area during the Gold Rush to source valuable materials from the land.

Today, many visitors to the park come to explore the far

← The sweeping prairies and undulating hills above Wind Cave

reaches of the caves, but the area's wonders aren't confined to the subterranean. Above ground, almost 34,000 acres (14,000 ha) of forest and prairie provide a haven for wildlife including bison, elk, and prairie dog.

## Exploring the park

If you're keen to explore above ground at Wind Cave, the park has over 30 miles (48 km) of hiking trails, providing visitors with a perfect chance to view the hills and valleys.

Though Wind Cave is one of the smaller national parks, it helps to know the right areas to visit when looking for wild-life. To see bison, it's best to head to the wide expanse of Bison Flats, just off Hwy. 385. The roadside in this area is also a good place to see prairie dogs. To spot the park's elk herds, it's best to head to Boland Ridge. The excellent Boland Ridge Trail, accessed from NPS 6, runs through the eastern valleys.

### Did You Know?
—
Wind Cave is named for the powerful gusts of air that blow in and out of its entrance.

→ A prairie dog peering out from a burrow in the park

→
One of the vast caverns within Wind Cave

There are no dining or lodging options in the park, though both can be found in the nearby towns of Hot Springs (to the south) and Custer (to the north).

# EAT

### Sage Creek Grille
Local food, including seafood and bison, prepared fresh on the premises daily. Sandwiches and salads can be taken away.

🏠 Custer
🌐 mhme.nu

$$$

### Big Time Pizza
Inexpensive, family-owned joint serving pizza and sub sandwiches with beer, wine, and many non-alcoholic beverages.

🏠 Hot Springs
🌐 btpizza.com

$$$

# STAY

### Rocket Motel
Situated off Hwy. 16, this retro-themed motel is laid-back and comfortable, and provides good access to the park and other attractions.

🏠 Hot Springs
🌐 rocketmotel.com

$$$

→
The honeycomb formation of the boxwork caves

To gain access to the cave, a ticket must be purchased in advance. All trips underground are led by trained rangers and all tours leave from the visitor center.

## Wind Cave
Wind Cave is a remarkable example of a boxwork cave system. Boxwork is formed of calcite spread across the cave's walls and ceilings, arranged in a striking honeycomb pattern; the feature is a draw for geologists and researchers from around the world.

Once you have booked onto a tour from the visitor center, you will journey among intense examples of geological forces in the cave, where age, climate, erosion, moisture, and microscopic organisms are actively forming unique subterranean features. Stalactites drip from the ceilings, while the earth's floor cradles stalagmites, and flowstone, popcorn, curtains, and cave bacon (gracefully curved strips of calcite).

On the tour, tales from the cave's ancient and more recent past are recounted by rangers. You are likely to hear the fascinating story of a young explorer named Alvin McDonald who explored the cave system extensively, with hundreds of hours spent searching for its end – a point he would never find. He

became one of the most noted cave guides before the turn of the 20th century.

Note that due to high demand, long waits are common for cave visits during spring, summer, and fall.

## The prairies

Wind Cave's diverse wildlife population has made a remarkable comeback over the past century. Excessive hunting, along with intensive farming and ranching, became common across the area in the late 19th century, threatening the area's elk and bison populations. Taking quick action, the U.S. government established the area as a game reserve to help restore mixed-grass prairie, pine forest, riparian zones, and the wildlife and birdlife that rely upon these landscapes to survive.

Scenic drives provide the best way to see a lot of this wildlife in a short amount of time. A favorite sighting is the American bison – a symbol emblazoned on the national park insignia, and emblematic

### GETTING AROUND

Most visitors arrive at Wind Cave driving in from U.S. Hwy. 385 on the west side of the park or on South Dakota Hwy. 87. Both routes offer wildlife viewing opportunities along the paved roads. You will also find many overlooks with excellent views as well as wayside exhibits teaching you about the ecology and flora and fauna of the park. The only park visitor center is just off of Hwy. 385 and is well marked - this is where all cave tours start. To explore the quieter and more rugged parts of the park in the north and east, follow NPS 5 and NPS 6 along fairly steep gravel roads.

of the Dakota region. You may also see elk, pronghorn (North America's fastest animal, and the second-fastest mammal on the planet), deer, coyotes, and prairie dogs (prey for larger animals and the park's birds of prey). A less likely spotting is the critically endangered nocturnal black-footed ferret.

If you are interested in ancient archaeology, stop along scenic Hwy. 87 in the western part of the park to see Precambrian Peg-matites (a form of igneous rock, about which you can learn at the Ancient Found-ations wayside exhibit on the right side of Hwy. 87).

## Hiking

Hiking along 30 miles (48 km) of established trails in the park reveals an enthralling landscape where lush hills roll as wide as the horizon. Weather during the summer brings some unpredictability, with thunderstorms that create enormous hail pellets and severe lightning. It's important to take shelter during these occurrences but keep your cameras close as they may result in electric-colored skies and rainbows.

↑ Bison roaming the prairies of Wind Cave

# EXPLORING WIND CAVE

Wind Cave National Park is located in South Dakota, north of Hot Springs and south of Custer. The park's surface spans 34,000 acres (14,000 ha) above ground, with more than 80 miles (130 km) of explored passages across the cave system.

*The **Lookout Point Trail Loop** makes for an excellent walk in its own right, or it can be joined with the longer Centennial Trail.*

↑ A National Park Service guide speaks about the park's ecology

*The **Wind Cave National Park Visitor Center** is an excellent place to learn more about the cave and prairie ecosystems.*

**Cold Brook Canyon Trail** *is a 2.8-mile (5-km) out-and-back hike in the Cold Brook Canyon leading through ponderosa pine forests. Falcons can be spotted en route.*

**East Bison Flats Trail** *is a strenuous route leading to a lookout with panoramic views of the Buffalo Gap and Black Hills.*

Lookout Tower

R a n k i n   R i d g e

CENTENNIAL   TRAIL

Limestone

Beaver

Lookout Point Trail

Prairie Canyon

Elk Mountain Campground

Elk Mountain Trail

Elk Mountain 4,504 ft (1,373 m)

ℹ Wind Cave Visitor Center

COLD BROOK CANYON TRAIL

B i s o n   F l a t s

EAST BISON FLATS TRAIL

CENTENNIAL

0 kilometers    2
0 miles    2

N
↑

**The Centennial Trail** is a 111-mile (178-km) trail that begins in Wind Cave and ends in Bear Butte State Park farther north.

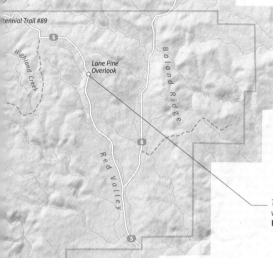

Centennial Trail #89

Highland Creek

5

*Lone Pine Overlook*

Boland Ridge

6

Red Valley

5

There is a small parking spot with excellent views at **Lone Pine Overlook.**

→ Wind Cave Visitor Center, a helpful first stop

# THE SOUTHWEST

The staggering scale of the Grand Canyon; the red sandstone mesas of Mesa Verde; the silent prairies of Petrified Forest: the Southwest is defined by its spectacular landscapes. The region's national parks are home to some of the world's most remarkable geological features, from the sculpted hoodoos of Utah's Bryce Canyon to the towering domes, bridges, and needles of Canyonlands.

For more than 15,000 years, the region was inhabited by Indigenous peoples who left complex cliff dwellings and beautiful rock art; the Ute petroglyphs at Arches are testament to the vision of the region's ancient inhabitants. Today, exploring the Southwest brings the epic myths of the American frontier to life, with cactus-studded deserts evoking the landscape of the cowboy. Whether hiking the Saguaro desert or hunting for fossils in the Guadalupe Mountains, the parks of the Southwest provide an epic image of the American wilderness.

# 6 DAYS
## *in the Southwest*

### Day 1

Your Southwestern adventure kicks off in style at the Grand Canyon *(p262)* – you'll want a full day to experience this wonder in all its glory. Arrive early to take a North Rim Mule Trip *(www.canyonrides.com)* – it's the best way to appreciate the scale of the place. Later you can visit the North Rim Visitor Center and hike the short trail to Bright Angel Point for iconic views of the whole canyon. Grab lunch at Deli in the Pines *(6225 AZ-67, North Rim)*, before taking scenic drives to Point Imperial and Cape Royal, or hiking one of the many trails along the rim. Stay at the Grand Canyon Lodge.

### Day 2

Allow three hours for the drive from the North Rim to Kolob Canyons Visitor Center at Zion National Park *(p284)*. Spend the afternoon exploring the less-visited Kolob Canyons section of Zion; the best hike for the afternoon is Taylor Creek Trail, which follows Taylor Creek into a narrow box canyon and the Double Arch alcove, a stunning natural amphitheater

with two sandstone arches. Drive to Springdale this evening, where there are plenty of hotels and restaurants.

### Day 3

Pack a picnic and set off early, parking your car at the Zion Canyon Visitor Center. Take the free park shuttle to the Temple of Sinawava at the end of Scenic Drive; from here follow the short Riverside Walk to the end of the gorge where the Virgin River enters a narrow slot canyon. Walk back to Scenic Drive to hop on the shuttle, stopping at the steep but short Weeping Rock Trail, or tackling the trek to Angels Landing via the West Rim Trail, which ends up high above the canyon floor (allow four hours, with a lunch break). Board the shuttle once more, back to Zion Lodge, where there are restaurants, trails to the Emerald Pools, and horseback rides to the Court of the Patriarch.

### Day 4

Drive the spectacular Zion-Mount Carmel Highway (aka Hwy. 9) early this morning,

1 Grand Canyon Lodge.
2 Zion-Mount Carmel Hwy.
3 Double Arch alcove.
4 Angels Landing, Zion.
5 The famous Delicate Arch.

stopping before the tunnel to view the Great Arch, and hiking the short Canyon Overlook Trail. Back on the road, you should arrive at Bryce Canyon National Park (p294) within two hours or so. Take the free park shuttle from the visitor center along the edge of Bryce Amphitheater and stroll the Rim Trail between Sunrise Point, Sunset Point, and Inspiration Point to view the "hoodoo" pinnacles. Later, hike the Navajo Loop Trail, which switchbacks steeply through the canyons known as "Wall Street." You'll need to get back in the car to drive the remaining 13 miles (21 km) of scenic park road to Rainbow Point, where the Bristlecone Loop Trail is an easy 1-mile (1.6-km) stroll through ancient groves of bristlecone pines. Spend the night in Bryce Canyon City, sampling the live country music at Ebenezer's Barn and Grill (www.ebenezersbarnandgrill.com).

## Day 5

Arches National Park (p312) is a 4–5 hour drive northeast of Bryce. Arrive by late afternoon and get oriented at the visitor center, exploring the array of outdoor exhibits, before heading into nearby Moab for the evening. Moab Diner is an excellent place to eat, while World Famous Woody's Tavern (221 Main St.) is always fun for a beer or two.

## Day 6

Today is all about the otherworldly landscapes of Arches – make sure you bring lots of water and head off early to avoid the traffic jams. The trail to view famous Delicate Arch up close is a 3-mile (4.8-km) round trip, passing the historic Wolfe Ranch and a striking wall of petroglyphs. After the walk, drive to the Devils Garden trailhead, where an easy 1.8-mile (2.9-km) gravel trail leads to the awe-inspiring span of Landscape Arch, the longest arch in the park. On the way back to the entrance, explore the sandstone labyrinths of the Fiery Furnace, and stop at the iconic Windows section. From here, a half-hour stroll leads to the Double Arch, the tallest arch in the park – a fitting place to end your tour of the landscapes of the Southwest.

# GRAND CANYON

📍 Arizona 🎫 $35 per vehicle, valid for seven days
🌐 nps.gov/grca

One of the world's great natural wonders, the Grand Canyon is an instantly recognizable symbol of the American Southwest. This is a place of awe-inspiring beauty: sweeping views of banded cliff faces; the ever-shifting patterns of light and shadow; and the deep hues of weathered rock, bleached white at midday, bathed in red and gold at sunset. A UNESCO World Heritage Site, the area has been home to Indigenous communities for more than 10,000 years.

Carved out by the Colorado River over millions of years, the Grand Canyon is 277 miles (448 km) long, 10 miles (16 km) wide and a mile (1.5 km) deep. It stretches along the Colorado Plateau, in the Southwest's Four Corners region, a geological wonder that has been eroded down into vast cliffs, pinnacles, and buttes made of limestone, sandstone, and shale, which recede as far as the eye can see. These magnificent rock formations are ringed in vibrant colors, their shades shifting throughout the day with the changing light. This stunning sight draws over 5 million visitors each year, and makes the Grand Canyon one of the most popular national parks in the U.S.

The Colorado River, winding through the Grand Canyon

## Exploring the park

Grand Canyon National Park is split into three main sections: the popular South Rim, the quieter North Rim, and the canyon floor, where you can stand on the edge of the fast-flowing Colorado River. Walking trails along the North and South rims offer staggering views, but to experience the canyon at its most fascinating, you need to explore the more challenging trails that lead down to the canyon floor.

The park has two main entrances, one on either rim. Most visitors use the South Entrance, which can become very congested during the peak summer season; to avoid the queues, park in nearby Tusayan and take the free shuttle bus from there to Grand Canyon Village and the South Rim. Summer is by far the most popular time to visit, but temperatures in the spring and fall shoulder seasons are more comfortable, and make for a much better (and safer) time to hike into the canyon.

## The South Rim

Most visitors spend all their time at the South Rim, which is open year-round, has the most services, and is easily accessible along the main highways from Flagstaff and Williams. Grand Canyon Village serves as a central hub, with accommodation, cafés, restaurants, and a market. At the village's Grand Canyon Visitor Center, rangers provide information and advice on the park and you can pick up detailed maps of driving routes and hiking trails. There are also exhibits on the park's geology, flora, and fauna at the Verkamp's Visitor Center and the Backcountry Information Center.

> **IF YOU HAVE**
> **A day**
>
> Take the South Rim shuttle buses and hop off at places along the way, such as the Grand Canyon Visitor Center, Yaki Point, and Maricopa Point.

The park's scenic main roads run along the South Rim from Grand Canyon Village; traditional mule trips, which have been descending into the canyon for over a century, start here too.

### Scenic drives on the South Rim

Starting at Grand Canyon Village, Hermit Road and Desert View Drive run in either direction along the South Rim, taking in museums, ruins, trailheads, and several viewpoints that between them offer some of the finest vistas in the park.

The park's free shuttle bus provides access to Hermit Road, which weaves west along the South Rim for 7 miles (11 km) to Hermits Rest. Buses run from March to November (no private vehicles allowed), departing from Grand Canyon Village frequently from an hour before dusk to an hour after sunset. Stop-offs include the popular viewpoints at Trailview Overlook, Maricopa Point, and Hopi Point. You can also walk the route, along the Rim Trail *(p271)*, and hop on a shuttle bus at any time. Hermit Road also makes a great cycle ride – bike rental is available near the Grand Canyon Visitor Center.

Running for 60 miles (97 km) east from Grand Canyon Village to Desert View, the Desert View Drive is open all year, conditions permitting, and offers breathtaking views of both the central and eastern canyon. Twelve miles (19 km) from Grand Canyon Village, you'll reach the aptly titled Grandview Point, where Spanish explorers caught their first glimpse of the canyon in 1540 CE. Ten miles (16 km) farther on lies the pueblo remains of Tusayan Ruin, where a small museum has exhibits highlighting the history of the Ancestral Puebloans. The road ends at Desert View near Mary Colter's Desert View

← The South Rim's free shuttle bus stationed at Grand Canyon Village

←
Mary Colter's Desert View
Watchtower, home to (*inset*)
20th-century Hopi murals

Watchtower, its upper floor decorated with early 20th-century Hopi murals.

## The North Rim

At 8,000 ft (around 2,440 m) above sea level, the North Rim is higher, cooler, and greener than the South Rim, with dense forests of ponderosa pine, aspen, and Douglas fir. There's a better chance of spotting wildlife here, too, such as mule deer, Kaibab squirrel, and wild turkey. The North Rim is closed from mid-October to mid-May, part of the reason why just 10 percent of the park's annual visitors make it here.

Although there are fewer viewpoints and access areas on the North Rim than there are on the South Rim, its location – twice as far from the river as its southern counterpart – provides some stellar views, with the canyon stretching out farther from the overlooks and thus giving a different perspective on its massive width.

There are about 30 miles (48 km) of scenic roads, as well as hiking trails to viewpoints or down to the canyon floor – the north section is beloved by backcountry explorers and is the preferred starting point for the famous Rim to Rim hike *(p266)*. Staying at the North Rim Campground or the Grand Canyon Lodge is a wonderful way to explore this area on overnight trips; the patio of the lodge offers epic views of the canyon's curves and is a great place to capture the sunset while enjoying a meal. Cape Royal viewpoint,

> **Hermit Road and Desert View Drive take in museums, ruins, trailheads, and several viewpoints that between them offer some of the finest vistas in the park.**

at the end of Cape Royal Road, is another spot to take in the sweeping landscape, including the incredible arch known as Angels Window.

Rangers at the North Rim Visitor Center and the Roaring Springs Overlook kiosk can give advice, and help with trip-planning and preparing for hikes. Nearby is the Backcountry Information Center, as well as a gas station, post office, gift shop, and laundry and medical services.

↑ The landmark El Tovar hotel, perched near the edge of the South Rim

## Scenic drives on the North Rim

The picturesque Cape Royal Drive starts north of Grand Canyon Lodge and travels 23 miles (37 km) to Cape Royal on the Walhalla Plateau. From here, several famous buttes and peaks can be seen, including Wotans Throne and Vishnu Temple; there are also

### MARY COLTER

At a time when there were few women architects in the U.S., Mary Colter was the chief architect for the Fred Harvey Company from 1902 to when she retired in 1948. Taking her inspiration from the surrounding landscape, she designed six distinctive buildings at the South Rim of the Grand Canyon: Hopi House, Hermits Rest, Lookout Studio, Desert View Watchtower, Bright Angel Lodge, and, at the bottom of the canyon, Phantom Ranch. The first four of these are now National Historic Landmarks.

# STAY

There are many places to stay on the South and North rims, as well as a couple of options on the canyon floor.

**Phantom Ranch**
The only lodging at the bottom of the canyon, offering cabins and dorms with meal service. Reservations are run on a lottery program.

🏠 Bottom of the canyon
🌐 grandcanyonlodges.
com/lodging/
phantom-ranch

$$$

**El Tovar**
This historic and luxurious lodge, right on the canyon rim, was built in 1905.

🏠 South Rim
🌐 grandcanyonlodges.
com/lodging/
el-tovar-hotel

$$$

several short, easy walking trails around Cape Royal. A 3-mile (5-km) detour leads to Point Imperial, the highest point on the North Rim, while the nearby Vista Encantada has delightful views and picnic tables.

## Hiking to the canyon floor

The canyon floor is accessed on two kinds of hikes: the Rim to Rim, the classic trail through the park, which commonly starts at the North Rim; and the Rim to River to Rim, a truncated but still challenging up-and-downer that begins and ends at the South Rim. The bottom of the canyon

→
The start of the North
Kaibab Trail, which winds
down to the canyon floor

# THE GEOLOGY OF THE GRAND CANYON

The Grand Canyon's multicolored layers of rock provide the best record of the Earth's formation anywhere in the world. Each stratum of rock reveals a different period in the Earth's geologic history beginning with the earliest, the Precambrian era, which covers geologic time up to 570 million years ago. Almost two billion years of history have been recorded in the canyon, although the most dramatic changes took place five to six million years ago, when the Colorado River began to carve its path through the canyon walls. The sloping nature of the Kaibab Plateau has led to increased erosion in some parts of the canyon.

## HOW THE CANYON WAS FORMED

About 5 million years ago the Colorado River changed its course. But why? According to one theory, it was encompassed by another, smaller river that flowed through the Kaibab Plateau. The force of these combined waters are responsible for carving out the deep Grand Canyon.

While the Colorado River accounts for the canyon's remarkable depth, its width and distinctive formations are the work of even greater natural forces. Strong winds rushing through the canyon erodes the limestone and sandstone a few grains at a time. Rain pouring over the canyon rim, meanwhile, cuts deep side canyons through the softer rock. Perhaps the greatest canyon-building force is ice. Water from rain and snowmelt slowly works itself into cracks in the rock. When frozen, this water expands, forcing the rock away from the canyon walls. The resulting canyon layers vary in hardness. Soft layers erode quickly into sloped faces, while harder rock resists erosion, leaving sheer vertical faces.

## THE ASYMMETRICAL CANYON

The North Rim of the Grand Canyon is considerably more eroded than the South Rim. The entire Kaibab Plateau, part of the broader Colorado Plateau, slopes to the south, so rain falling at the North Rim flows toward the canyon and over the rim. This ongoing flow creates deep side canyons and a wide space between the rim and the river running its course below.

↑ Looking out over the deep canyon, formed by powerful natural forces

↑ The spectacular cliffs and pinnacles of the
Grand Canyon's beautiful South Rim

## RECORD OF LIFE

The fossils found in each layer of the Canyon
tell the story of the development of life on
Earth. One of the oldest layers in the canyon,
the Vishnu Schist, was formed in the Proterozoic
era, when the first bacteria and algae were just
emerging. Many of the layers were created by
billions of marine creatures, whose hard shells
eventually built up into thick layers of limestone.

### Did You Know?

The three main types
of sedimentary rocks
at the Grand Canyon
are sandstone, shale,
and limestone.

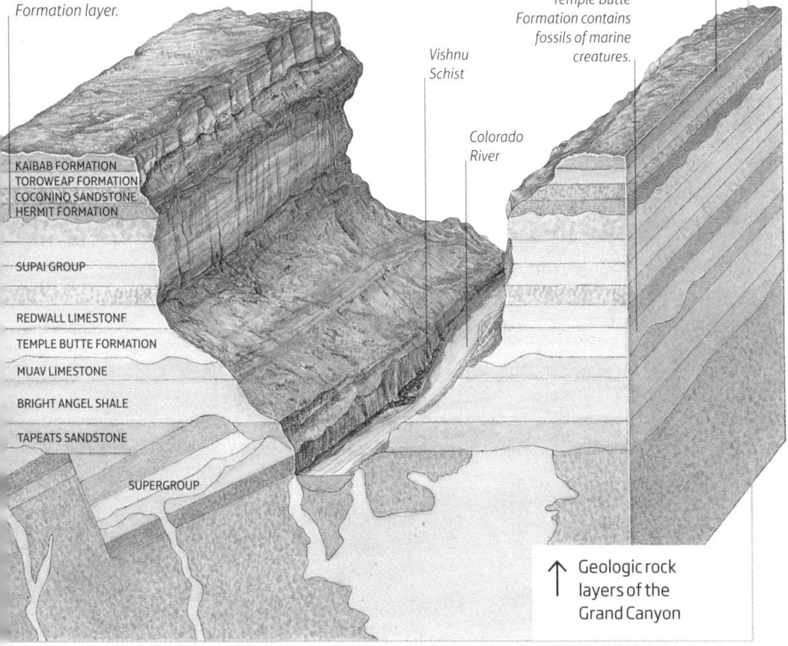

*Fish plate fossils
are found in the
Kaibab Formation.*

*Seedfern leaf fossils
are found in the Hermit
Formation layer.*

*North Rim*

*Temple Butte
Formation contains
fossils of marine
creatures.*

*Vishnu
Schist*

*Colorado
River*

KAIBAB FORMATION
TOROWEAP FORMATION
COCONINO SANDSTONE
HERMIT FORMATION

SUPAI GROUP

REDWALL LIMESTONE
TEMPLE BUTTE FORMATION
MUAV LIMESTONE

BRIGHT ANGEL SHALE

TAPEATS SANDSTONE

SUPERGROUP

↑ Geologic rock
layers of the
Grand Canyon

↑ A guided kayak tour on the Colorado River

offers a one-of-a-kind experience, with beautiful green vegetation fringing the Colorado River. The trails cross the river on a suspension bridge, from where you might see river runners coursing through on whitewater rafting trips – several operators in the area run guided 1- to 25-day trips along the river.

On the Rim to River to Rim, hikers usually work their way down into the canyon along the Bright Angel Trail, the most popular trail in the park. It's a descent of 4,460 ft (1,360 m) over 7.8 miles (12.6 km), with plenty of switch-backs, so plan for a full-body workout to get there.

After a night at the Bright Angel Campground or perhaps the Phantom Ranch (with advance reservations, sometimes reaching full capacity in the high season), hike back up to the South Rim along the South Kaibab Trail, which features a slightly steeper climb (4,860 ft or 1,480 m) over a slightly shorter distance (6.3 miles or 10.1 km). The Rim to River to Rim can be done in reverse, descending the South Kaibab Trail and hiking back up the steep Bright Angel Trail, or by hiking down and back up the North Kaibab Trail, the only trail that descends to the canyon floor directly from the North Rim.

The longer Rim to Rim hike is a bucket-list traverse that usually follows the North Kaibab Trail down from the North Rim, dropping 5,850 ft (1,780 m) in 14.2 miles (22.9 km) to the canyon floor. After a night here, climb up the Bright Angel Trail or South Kaibab Trail to the South Rim.

Both are challenging hikes, particularly the Rim to Rim, which many hikers spend months training for in advance – know your limits, as access to the route is limited and emergency help can only arrive by helicopter. Take plenty of water with you, and pack several layers: the temperature at the bottom of the canyon is considerably cooler than it is at the top.

> **IF YOU HAVE**
> **A weekend**
>
> Hike the famous Rim to Rim trail, starting from the North Rim, and spend a night sleeping beside the Colorado River at the bottom of the canyon.

*Timeline*

### 1903

△ President Theodore Roosevelt visits the Grand Canyon and says it "fills me with awe." He declares it to be "the one great sight that every American should see."

### 1906-08

Roosevelt establishes the Grand Canyon Game Preserve and the Grand Canyon National Monument, vowing to keep this natural treasure unspoiled.

### 1933-42

During the Depression, President Franklin D. Roosevelt's Civilian Conservation Corps of unemployed men builds park trails and roads that are still in use today.

### 2019

▽ Grand Canyon National Park, a UNESCO World Heritage Site, celebrates its centennial with a year-long "100 Years of Grand" showcase of park highlights.

# A LONG WALK
# RIM TRAIL

**GRAND CANYON**

*Rim Trail*

**Locator Map**

**Length** 13 miles (20.9 km) one-way **Stopping-off points**
El Tovar Hotel and Dining Room, Bright Angel Lodge,
Thunderbird Lodge **Terrain** Mostly flat and paved

Punctuated by numerous overlooks with spectacular
views, this trail parallels the South Rim of the Grand
Canyon from South Kaibab Trailhead to Hermits Rest.
It runs through Grand Canyon Village, the center of
the park's human activity, with easy access from the
park's main roads. While private vehicles are not
allowed for most of the year, a free shuttle bus runs
along Hermit Rd. west of Grand Canyon Village, and
many of the stops are easily accessible from the trail.

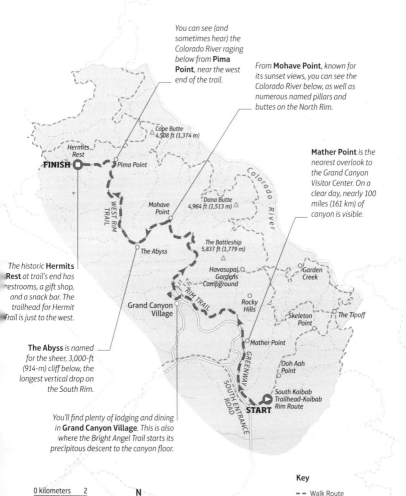

*You can see (and sometimes hear) the Colorado River raging below from* **Pima Point**, *near the west end of the trail.*

*From* **Mohave Point**, *known for its sunset views, you can see the Colorado River below, as well as numerous named pillars and buttes on the North Rim.*

**Mather Point** *is the nearest overlook to the Grand Canyon Visitor Center. On a clear day, nearly 100 miles (161 km) of canyon is visible.*

*The historic* **Hermits Rest** *at trail's end has restrooms, a gift shop, and a snack bar. The trailhead for Hermit Trail is just to the west.*

**The Abyss** *is named for the sheer, 3,000-ft (914-m) cliff below, the longest vertical drop on the South Rim.*

*You'll find plenty of lodging and dining in* **Grand Canyon Village**. *This is also where the Bright Angel Trail starts its precipitous descent to the canyon floor.*

Cope Butte
4,508 ft (1,374 m)

Hermits Rest
**FINISH**
Pima Point

Mohave Point

Dana Butte
4,964 ft (1,513 m)

WEST RIM TRAIL

The Abyss

The Battleship
5,837 ft (1,779 m)

Havasupai Gardens Campground

Garden Creek

Grand Canyon Village

RIM TRAIL

Rocky Hills

Skeleton Point

The Tipoff

Mather Point

Ooh Aah Point

GREENWAY

SOUTH ENTRANCE ROAD

South Kaibab Trailhead-Kaibab Rim Route

**START**

Colorado River

0 kilometers 2
0 miles 2

N

**Key**

-- Walk Route

# EXPLORING GRAND CANYON

The Grand Canyon was carved out by the path of the Colorado River. The Canyon's northeast end starts at Lake Powell on the Utah-Arizona border; the west end is where the Colorado River empties into Lake Mead on the Arizona-Nevada border. The national park stretches for over one million acres (490,000 ha).

← Looking out over the canyon at sunset

*Tuweep is the ancestral home of the Southern Paiute people. Toroweap Overlook offers excellent views over the Colorado River.*

*The Grand Canyon Skywalk is a horseshoe-shaped sky bridge located on the Hualapai reservation, offering east-facing views of the canyon.*

0 kilometers 18
0 miles 18

N ↑

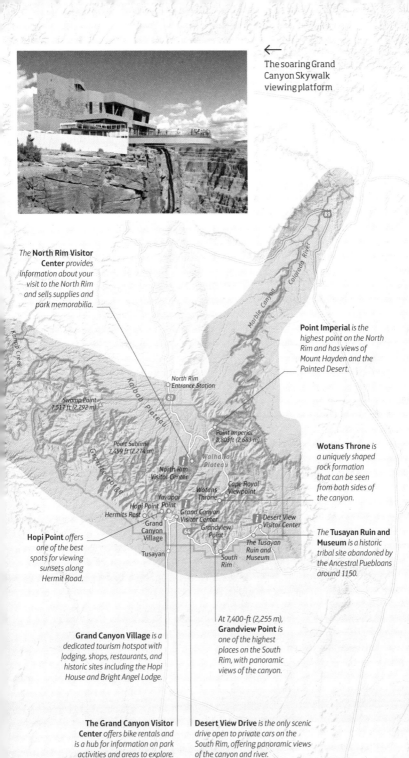

← The soaring Grand Canyon Skywalk viewing platform

The **North Rim Visitor Center** *provides information about your visit to the North Rim and sells supplies and park memorabilia.*

**Point Imperial** *is the highest point on the North Rim and has views of Mount Hayden and the Painted Desert.*

**Wotans Throne** *is a uniquely shaped rock formation that can be seen from both sides of the canyon.*

**Hopi Point** *offers one of the best spots for viewing sunsets along Hermit Road.*

The **Tusayan Ruin and Museum** *is a historic tribal site abandoned by the Ancestral Puebloans around 1150.*

**Grand Canyon Village** *is a dedicated tourism hotspot with lodging, shops, restaurants, and historic sites including the Hopi House and Bright Angel Lodge.*

*At 7,400-ft (2,255 m),* **Grandview Point** *is one of the highest places on the South Rim, with panoramic views of the canyon.*

The **Grand Canyon Visitor Center** *offers bike rentals and is a hub for information on park activities and areas to explore.*

**Desert View Drive** *is the only scenic drive open to private cars on the South Rim, offering panoramic views of the canyon and river.*

Kamb Creek

Marble Canyon

Colorado River

89

Kaibab Plateau

North Rim Entrance Station

67

*Swamp Point 7,517 ft (2,292 m)*

*Point Sublime 7,459 ft (2,274 m)*

*Point Imperial 8,803 ft (2,683 m)*

*Walhalla Plateau*

Granite Gorge

North Rim Visitor Center

*Yavapai Point*

*Wotans Throne*

*Cape Royal Viewpoint*

*Hopi Point*

Hermits Rest

Grand Canyon Visitor Center

Grand Canyon Village

*Grandview Point*

Desert View Visitor Center

Tusayan

64

*South Rim*

*The Tusayan Ruin and Museum*

The park's namesake cacti standing like sentinels across the desert ↑

# SAGUARO

📍 Arizona  🎫 $25 per vehicle, valid for seven days
🌐 nps.gov/sagu

The vast Saguaro (pronounced "sa-WAH-roh") was established to protect its namesake cactus, which grows across the Sonoran Desert and has been known to live for longer than 200 years. And while the park continues to be symbolized by this prickly pronged plant (the largest cactus in the U.S.), they aren't the only draw: split into two sections situated on either side of the city of Tucson, Saguaro offers some of the finest landscapes in the Southwest, and plenty of desert adventures.

The silhouette of a towering saguaro, stretching its arms skyward against a blazing sunset, is as iconic a South-western image as it gets. Surprisingly though, this regal cactus grows only in the Sonoran Desert of southern Arizona and northern Mexico. Saguaro National Park is the very best place to enjoy these plants, with cacti spread across the desert.

The fascinating saguaro grows to 60 ft (18m) tall. Beneath its thick, spiny skin is a reservoir of water that it drinks in during the rainy season. When the larder is full, a mature cactus can weigh up to an incredible 4,800 pounds (2,175 kg).

↑ Climbing to the summit of Wasson Peak in the Tucson Mountains

## Exploring the park

Saguaro West, on one side of Tucson, has a denser concentration of saguaro cacti and welcomes more visitors drawn to the stark desert landscape. Saguaro East is at a higher elevation, with increasingly rugged terrain as the desert ascends into the Rincon Mountains.

Most visitors confine their experience to Saguaro West, arriving from the north of Tucson along Interstate 10. For those looking to visit Saguaro East, head out of Tucson and make for Old Spanish Trail.

**IF YOU HAVE**
**A day**

Explore Saguaro West's plethora of short trails that lead out among the Saguaro cactus forests. Start with the Desert Discovery Nature Trail.

Once inside, the desert's trails are perfect for horseback rides, hikes, or mountain biking. Saguaro West has the Red Hill Visitor Center and Saguaro East has a small visitor center at the entrance.

## Scenic drives

Driving or biking the scenic roads in both Saguaro districts allows you to appreciate the delicate beauty of the park's landscape. Note that the loop drives in both sides of the park have some length and size restrictions for RVs and trailers. Check with the visitor centers before heading out along particular routes.

The Bajada Loop Drive (Saguaro West) travels one-way on a well-maintained 6-mile (9-km) dirt road and can be both driven and cycled in a counterclockwise direction. Bikes can travel beyond the road on two multi-use trails including the short Belmont and Golden Gate trails.

Cactus Forest Drive (Saguaro East) starts at the main visitor center and travels an 8-mile (12-km) one-way loop with pull-outs and lookouts positioned along the way. There are several popular stops where you can stretch your legs, admire the desert flora and fauna, and hop onto boulders offering views of the park landscape. If cycling, note that Bajada Loop Drive is gravel and Cactus Forest Drie is paved.

## Hiking

The park has more than 150 miles (240 km) of designated trails stretching across East and West, which you can explore solo or on park-facilitated guided walks and hikes. Hikers are required to stick to these designated trails (if you want to head off-trail, you must be above 4,500 ft/1,370 m in elevation in the East Rincon district). Pick up a topographic map and learn more about planning a route at either of the visitor centers.

## Hiking Saguaro West

The Desert Discovery Nature Trail is a wonderful way to get a taste of the park, with educational stops along the 0.5-mile (0.8-km) route, teaching you about the

IF YOU HAVE
**A weekend**

Camp overnight at the base of the Rincon Mountains, explore the loop drive by car or bicycle, then hit some big trails in the high country.

↑ A spiral-design petroglyph at the top of Signal Hill

desert plants, wildlife, and surrounding ecosystem.

The Valley View Overlook Trail is just under a mile (1.5 km) and is an easy and accessible way to see cactus, prickly pear, agave, and other desert plants and roots, with views of the forests from Hohokam Road.

The Signal Hill Petroglyphs trail is a half-mile (0.8-km) hike off of Bajada Loop Drive, leading to a viewpoint with a collection of petroglyphs that were carved into the rock by Hohokam communities more than 800 years ago.

The Wasson Peak Trail is a strenuous 8-mile (12-km) adventure leading to stunning views of the national park from its apex. There are several other networks that feed into the trail including the Sendero Esperanza Trail and the Hugh Norris Trail.

## Hiking Saguaro East

The Mica View Trail is the area's most accessible route, crossing 2 miles (3 km) on flat terrain while providing many opportunities to spot birds including greater road-runners, Gila wood-peckers, and Gambel's quail. There are plenty of opportunities to walk among towering saguaro cacti, too, with epic views of the Rincon Mountains a welcome sight.

The short Desert Ecology Trail is a 0.3-mile (0.5-km) paved path located at the foot of Cactus Forest Drive. On this enjoyable short stroll among vegetation, look out for local birdlife as you go.

Another option is the Tanque Verde Trail. It's a little under 2 miles (3 km), with some steep rocky sections leading to a powerful waterfall.

←
Cycling uphill on the beautiful Cactus Road Loop

# EAT

There are no dining options in either park district in an effort to mitigate disposable product use. Tucson has plenty of wonderful dining options, featuring all types of cuisine.

### Saguaro Corners Restaurant
Comfort food and cocktails with plenty of outdoor seating.

🏠 Tucson 🌐 saguaro-corners-restaurant-bar.business.site

### Guadalajara Original Grill
Tasty Mexican food, often accompanied by live mariachi music.

🏠 Tucson 🌐 guadalajaraoriginalgrill.com

$$$

# STAY

The Rincon Mountain District has six camping areas, all in close proximity to a network of backcountry trails. There are many other lodging options in Tucson.

### Gilbert Ray Campground
RV and tent camping a short drive from the western section of the park, with beautiful views in all directions.

🏠 Tucson 🌐 pima.gov

# EXPLORING SAGUARO

Saguaro National Park surrounds Tucson, Arizona, at the heart of the Sonoran desert. The park is comprised of 92,000 acres (37,000 ha) of dry desert landscapes and consists of two separate areas: the Tucson Mountain District west of Tucson, and the Rincon Mountain District east of the city.

RINCON MOUNTAIN DISTRICT

Tucson

TUCSON MOUNTAIN DISTRICT

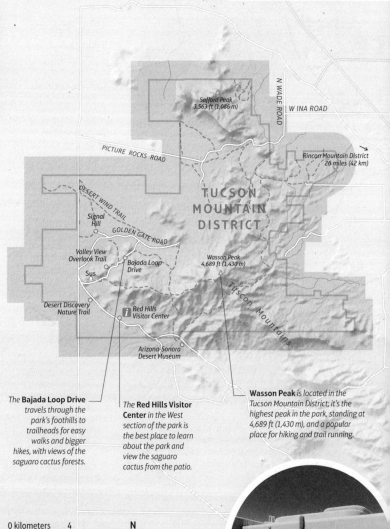

Safford Peak
3,563 ft (1,086 m)

N WADE ROAD

W INA ROAD

PICTURE ROCKS ROAD

Rincon Mountain District
26 miles (42 km)

TUCSON MOUNTAIN DISTRICT

DESERT WIND TRAIL

Signal Hill

GOLDEN GATE ROAD

Valley View Overlook Trail

Sus

Bajada Loop Drive

Wasson Peak
4,689 ft (1,430 m)

Tucson Mountains

Desert Discovery Nature Trail

Red Hills Visitor Center

Arizona-Sonora Desert Museum

The **Bajada Loop Drive** travels through the park's foothills to trailheads for easy walks and bigger hikes, with views of the saguaro cactus forests.

The **Red Hills Visitor Center** in the West section of the park is the best place to learn about the park and view the saguaro cactus from the patio.

**Wasson Peak** is located in the Tucson Mountain District; it's the highest peak in the park, standing at 4,689 ft (1,430 m), and a popular place for hiking and trail running.

0 kilometers    4

0 miles    4

N ↑

→ The Red Hills Visitor Center, in the park's west

The iconic saguaro, a common sight within the park

The **Douglas Spring Campground** in the Rincon District is home to oaks and cottonwoods and is located near great hiking, with views of Tanque Verde Falls.

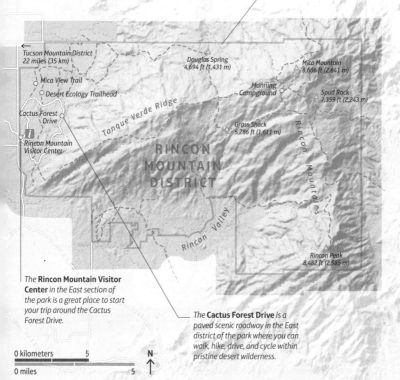

Tucson Mountain District
22 miles (35 km)

Mica View Trail

Desert Ecology Trailhead

Cactus Forest Drive

*i* Rincon Mountain Visitor Center

Tanque Verde Ridge

Douglas Spring
4,694 ft (1,431 m)

Manning Campground

Grass Shack
5,286 ft (1,611 m)

Mica Mountain
8,666 ft (2,641 m)

Spud Rock
7,359 ft (2,243 m)

RINCON MOUNTAIN DISTRICT

Rincon Mountains

Rincon Valley

Rincon Peak
8,482 ft (2,585 m)

The **Rincon Mountain Visitor Center** in the East section of the park is a great place to start your trip around the Cactus Forest Drive.

The **Cactus Forest Drive** is a paved scenic roadway in the East district of the park where you can walk, hike, drive, and cycle within pristine desert wilderness.

0 kilometers 5
0 miles 5

N ↑

# PETRIFIED FOREST

📍 Arizona 🚗 $25 per vehicle, valid for seven days
🌐 nps.gov/pefo

Sheltering the largest concentration of petrified wood on the planet, this epic national park delivers scenic and scientific wonders in equal measure. The otherworldly landscape is the result of a toppled forest, which saw its unique features carved by bustling winds and trees turn to stone. Add to that the rainbow hued Painted Desert that runs the length of the forest and you've got one of Arizona's most unusual attractions.

The plant and animal fossils unearthed at this national park tell the story of a time when the world was young. Over 200 million years ago, the terrain of northeastern Arizona was nothing like you see today. Instead of high, dry grasslands, this landscape was a humid forested basin slashed by winding rivers and streams, with small dinosaurs roaming among towering conifers and leafy ferns.

As the trees here died, they were swept downstream into swamps and buried beneath mud and volcanic ash. Entombed in the sediment layer known as the Chinle Formation, the wood absorbed silica from minerals in the groundwater; over time, these crystallized within the wood's structure, forming a stone-like material, badlands in colorful hues, and sculpted buttes. The most iconic of these buttes is

> **IF YOU HAVE**
> **A day**
> Drive between the north and south entrances on the main park road, stopping to walk Blue Mesa and the Longs Log Trail.

the Painted Desert, an area of colored bands of sand and rock changing from blues to reds as light catches mineral deposits.

## Exploring the park

The best way to take in these wonders is via the 28-mile (45-km) main park road, which cuts north to south. You can drive or cycle the long stretch, but this is a landscape best appreciated up close, so be sure to make stops at the nine overlooks, hiking trailheads, and roadside highlights along the road. For instance, a

segment of America's Historic Route 66 once crossed through this area, and you can still see remnants of the route such as road imprints and decommissioned telephone poles from Vista Point, one of the overlooks.

## Hiking

The landscape might be otherworldly, but traversing it is easy. There are relatively few hiking trails here, with the majority coming in at under

> **The most iconic of these buttes is the Painted Desert, an area of colored bands of sand and rock changing from blues to reds as light catches mineral deposits.**

← Layers of rock at Blue Mesa, which chronicle a million years of history

3 miles (4.8 km), but that's no bad thing; part of the joy is slowing down to really take in the dazzling displays. As an added bonus, a lot of the trails here allow you to bring dogs, as long as they're leashed and Leave No Trace practices are followed.

Lying at the park's center is one of the most popular hiking spots, Blue Mesa, with blue, gray, and purple bentonite clay and petrified wood scattered on the badlands.

### GETTING AROUND

The closest major airports to Petrified Forest are in Albuquerque, New Mexico, and Las Vegas, Nevada, and where you come from will determine how to best enter the park. If possible, start in the town of Holbrook, southwest of the park. From there, Hwy. 40 runs to the north entrance and Hwy. 180 leads to the south entrance; there are visitor centers at each side. There is only one park road, which stretches 28 miles (45 km) between the two entrances, and with no shuttle service or transportation within the park, you'll need to rely on a rental car or your own vehicle; bikes and e-bikes are also an option.

# EXPLORING PETRIFIED FOREST

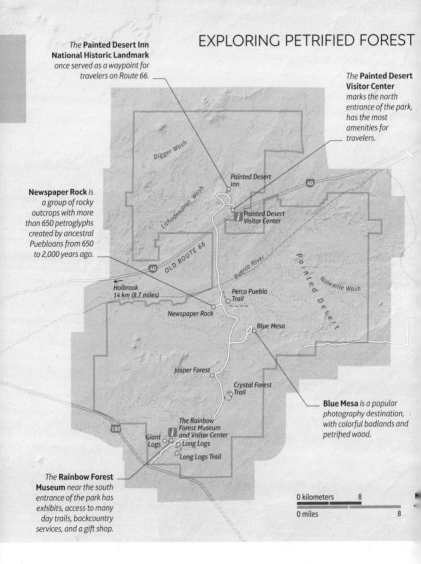

The **Painted Desert Inn National Historic Landmark** once served as a waypoint for travelers on Route 66.

The **Painted Desert Visitor Center** marks the north entrance of the park, has the most amenities for travelers.

**Newspaper Rock** is a group of rocky outcrops with more than 650 petroglyphs created by ancestral Puebloans from 650 to 2,000 years ago.

Digger Wash

Lithodendron Wash

Painted Desert Inn

Painted Desert Visitor Center

OLD ROUTE 66

Puerco River

Painted Desert

Ninemile Wash

Holbrook 14 km (8.7 miles)

Perco Pueblo Trail

Newspaper Rock

Blue Mesa

Jasper Forest

Crystal Forest Trail

**Blue Mesa** is a popular photography destination, with colorful badlands and petrified wood.

The **Rainbow Forest Museum and Visitor Center**

Giant Logs

Long Logs

Long Logs Trail

The **Rainbow Forest Museum** near the south entrance of the park has exhibits, access to many day trails, backcountry services, and a gift shop.

0 kilometers 8
0 miles 8

## PETRIFIED WOOD

Petrified Forest cradles the world's largest collection of petrified wood: quartz that is vibrant in color and smooth in texture on one side, with the appearance of hardened tree bark on the other. Hundreds of millions of years ago rivers swept trees downstream into a vast swamp that once covered this area. Groundwater transported silica dioxide into downed timber, eventually turning it into the quartz stone logs seen today, which can be as small as pebbles and as large as full-size downed trees. Visitors are free to touch the wood but it is forbidden to take any piece of it.

Manganese results in a blue hue

Wood turns to near-solid quartz

↑ Painted Desert Inn, a National Historic Landmark, sitting atop the colored buttes

The short loop is only 1 mile (1.6 km), but it's unmissable. The park's namesake petrified wood is also the star of the 0.4-mile (0.6-km) Giant Logs Trail, which is located behind the Rainbow Forest Museum at the park's south entrance. Here, a paved walkway travels among all sizes of petrified wood including the largest piece in the park, "Old Faithful," measuring 10 ft (3m) in diameter.

Another highlight is the Longs Logs Trail, a 1.6-mile (2.6-km) loop encircling an area that houses the largest concentration of petrified wood in the park. The first half-mile is accessible for mobility equipment and strollers. It's worth combining this trail with Crystal Forest (0.75 miles/1.2 km) to explore a collection of petrified logs, and Agate House (2 miles/ 3.2 km) to see a pueblo.

The wonders you can spot on hikes go far beyond what Mother Nature created. The first people here 10,000 years ago were nomadic hunter-gatherers who left behind petroglyphs, pottery, and dwellings. Take the short Parco Pueblo loop trail among the remains of a large pueblo to see petroglyphs carved by ancestral Puebloans.

## Painted Desert

For many, the park's undisputed highlight is the Painted Desert, a swath of badlands on a high plateau stretching 150 miles (241 km) across northern Arizona between the Grand Canyon to Petrified Forest. It was named El Desierto Pintado (The Painted Desert) in the 1540s by Spanish explorer Francisco Vazquez de Coronado, who thought the pigmented colors and dramatic contoured buttes looked like a painting.

It's visible in the north of the park via the Painted Desert Rim Trail, which travels an unpaved path for 1 mile (1.6 km). The hike offers sweeping views of the Painted Desert, not to mention opportunities to see species of desert plants and animals.

## Overnight stays

The more intrepid will want to explore the backcountry of the Petrified Forest National Wilderness Area, which has one unit in the north and one in the south. It's possible to hike, take a guided tour, or backpack overnight in this area. With the area being an International Dark Sky Park, an overnight stay is perfect for after-hours stargazing and great astrophotography.

# EAT

Beyond one option in the park, find more dining spots in the nearby city of Holbrook.

### Painted Desert Diner

Enjoy casual food such as tacos and burgers as well as good vegetarian options.

🏠 Painted Desert Visitor Center 🌐 petrified foresttrading.com

### Mesa Italiana Restaurant

A relaxing Italian spot serving pizza, pasta, and American favorites.

🏠 Holbrook
📞 (928) 524 6696

$ $ $

# STAY

Aside from overnighting in the wilderness (permits can be picked up at the park's visitor centers), there are no lodgings in Petrified Forest. Holbrook and other nearby towns have good overnight options.

### Wigwam Motel

Simple but charming tepees are your room for the night at this beloved motel, located on Historic Route 66. It's full of nostalgia, with a vintage car display in the parking lot.

🏠 Holbrook 🌐 sleep inawigwam.com

Best for *Photographing kaleidoscopic canyons*

# ZION

📍 Utah   🔁 $35 per vehicle, valid for seven days   🌐 nps.gov/zion

The first of Utah's "Mighty 5" national parks to be established, Zion delivers big on beauty and grandeur. At the heart of this mystical landscape are the towering Navajo sandstone formations, formed over millennia by wind, rain, continental uplift, and the powerful Virgin River. Everywhere you turn, you'll find narrow slot canyons, bulwarklike towers of sandstone, deep emerald pools, and canyons the color of fire – all, as the name suggests, in biblical proportions. Get ready for a wealth of adventures, both great and small, in Utah's most iconic park.

The Virgin River Valley has been inhabited for more than 8,000 years. Nomadic families hunted, fished, and foraged, Pueblo communities later brought crop cultivation, and Paiute and Ute peoples migrated here seasonally, cultivating the land for hundreds of years. Then, in the 1860s, Mormon settlers moved to the canyon, naming it Zion after an ancient Hebrew word meaning "sanctuary" or "refuge." Farming continued on the canyon floor until 1909, when it was declared a national monument. Zion became Utah's first national park in 1919; fast-forward to today, it's one of the most visited parks in the system.

Aside from being downright beautiful, the natural balance of the desert ecosystem here is delicate, intricate, and marvelously complex. In the "low" elevations of around 3,700 ft (1,127 m) up to the heady heights of 8,700 ft (2,651 m) lives a remarkable array of plant and animal life. Along the riverbanks of the Virgin River, hanging gardens of ferns, carpets of humble mosses, and fields of wildflowers grow, with names like western wallflower, showy stoneseed, and shooting star. Giant cottonwoods stand tall amid lush wetlands, and above the valley floor, yucca, cactus, juniper, and desert grasses run riot.

## GETTING AROUND

Zion is located in the southwest corner of Utah near the Arizona and Nevada state lines. The closest airports are in Las Vegas (170 miles/ 274 km southwest) and Salt Lake City (313 miles/504 km north). Most people arrive via the south entrance, closest to Zion Canyon, from the town of Springdale. A free shuttle service runs from this entrance April through October, and is a great way to protect roadside vegetation and minimize congestion on roads and in trailhead parking lots. Another popular entrance is on the east side on Zion-Mt. Carmel Road, via the city of Kanab. To enter Kolob Canyons - a separate area of the park - drive to I-15 on the west. There's a final entrance on Kolob Terrace Road, which is a good option for those setting off on backcountry hikes. It's also possible to cycle through the park.

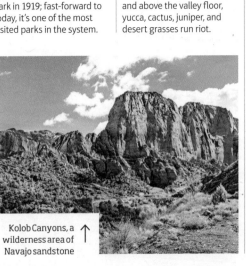

Kolob Canyons, a wilderness area of Navajo sandstone ↑

↑ The 1,000-ft (300-m), neck-craning views of The Narrows

→

The Emerald Pools trail, its lower pools lined with lush vegetation

# EAT

Zion is home to two great dining options within Zion Lodge, but your best bet is to try towns surrounding the park, including Springdale and Hurricane.

### Red Rock Grill Dining Room

Enjoy breakfast, lunch, and dinner with views of the canyon and rising stone walls. Options are wide ranging, such as soups, burgers, and vegetarian options. Reserve ahead from spring through fall.

⌂ Zion Lodge
ⓦ zionlodge.com

$$($)($)$$

### Castle Dome Cafe

Seasonal snack bar offering quick bites, from cinnamon buns for breakfast to french fries and hot dogs for lunch. Serves great coffee and microbrews on the patio, too.

⌂ Zion Lodge
ⓦ zionlodge.com

$$($)($)$$

### Spotted Dog

Casual bistro serving up fresh local produce, including Rocky Mountain red trout and Ahi tuna steak.

⌂ Springdale
ⓦ flanigans.com/dine

$$($)($)$$

## Exploring the park

At the heart of the park lies Zion Canyon, one of the most popular of Utah's natural wonders and arguably the park's main draw. The 6-mile (10-km) Zion Canyon Scenic Drive follows the Virgin River into the ever-narrowing canyon, but from April to October, the free park shuttle from the visitor center is the only way into the area. Most people choose to visit during these months for ease, and to take advantage of the weather to embark on hikes.

Zion's hiking trails are world-class, but what makes hiking so special here is the unique environment; some trails take you to waterfalls, others traverse the spine of monoliths rising high above the valley. Trailheads can be found all over the park, but the main hikes start up and down the main thoroughfare in Zion Canyon, and along the main roads in Kolob Canyons.

## Hiking Zion Canyon

From Zion Canyon, hikes match every ability and taste, and offer some of the best canyoneering in the world. Most popular is the celebrated Narrows, a tough 16-mile (26-km) hike above the amphitheater called Temple of Sinawava. Wading through knee- to waist-deep waters in the Virgin River (long parts of the hike lead down the route of the river, so you'll get your feet wet), with skyscraping 1,000-ft (300-m) walls on each side, you head deep into canyon country. Wilderness permits are required and must be obtained in-person at the Zion Canyon Visitor Center or the Kolob Canyons Visitor Center. To get outfitted for a dry suit and appropriate footwear, head to the nearby town of Springdale. Always check with the park visitor centers about weather and current conditions including potential flash flood warnings, which render this hike impossible.

Zion Canyon's geology is remarkable, with majestic walls rising up to 2,000 ft (600 m) on both sides. For the best detailed views of jagged peaks and formations in shades of red, pink, and white,

◷ IF YOU HAVE
**A day**
Spend four hours hiking to and back from Angels Landing, admiring the views at the top, then see the sun set against the canyon walls.

walk the 2.5-mile (4-km) Hidden Canyon Trail nestled inside the canyon. If you fear heights, give this a miss; you can expect exposure and sheer drops up to 1,000-ft (300-m), with lead chains bolted to the walls for support. From the end of this hike you can continue on an 8-mile (12-km) round-trip hike adventure along the East Rim Trail leading to Observation Point for epic views of Zion Canyon and Angels Landing.

Angels Landing is one of the most famous hikes in the world, and if you only have time for one hike during your visit, this is it. The 5.4-mile (8.7-km) out-and-back trail is strenuous, but the first 4 miles (6 km) provide incredible views on the way to Scout's Lookout. There you can rest and take it all in while deciding whether to forge the last mile, with the aid of support chains, along the narrow canyon spine to Angels Landing. The landing is perched at 4,500 ft (1,500 m) with views of the whole valley. Part of the beauty of this trail is that you can pause or turn back whenever you choose.

For something a bit gentler, try the Pa'rus Trail, a 3.5-mile (5.6-km) round trip that follows the banks of the Virgin River and is accessible to strollers, wheelchairs, bicycles, and leashed pets. The Emerald Pools trail also offers a mix of ease and adventure, and leads to a series of pools and waterfalls. Note that swimming is off-limits in the pools. The park's shortest trail, the Weeping Rock at a 0.4-mile (0.6-km) round trip, is also one of the most enchanting thanks to the lush hanging gardens. Pathways are paved though the incline is steep, so be sure to take plenty of breaks to catch your breath and admire your surrounds.

## Did You Know?

Zion Canyon is home to more than 1,000 plant species, from cacti to ponderosa pines.

Hiking Angels Landing, a steep trail that climbs several switchbacks ↑

# STAY

The park has lodgings and campsites, which are a great way to make the most of your time here. Nearby towns such as Springdale also offer overnight and camping options surrounding the park.

### Zion Lodge

Choose from historic cabins, comfortable suites, and motel rooms, all with easy access to park trails. A gift shop, post office, and on-site parking are a bonus.

🏠 Zion Canyon
🌐 zionlodge.com

### Watchman Campground

Located next to the Zion Canyon Visitor Center, offering tent and electric RV camping with views of the famous "Watchman" spires nearby.

🏠 N of Springdale
🌐 nps.gov/zion/planyourvisit

↑ Taking in the Subway, with walls that round up on all sides

## Kolob Canyons trails

In the park's more remote northwest corner, Kolob Canyons – accessed through a separate entrance – also harbors impressive trails, many of them promising solitude. Indeed, at 40 miles (60 km) north of Zion Canyon, Kolob's trails are serenely set back from the main canyon crowds. Here, hiking trails lead to waterfalls, old homestead cabins, and beautiful rock formations.

A popular choice is the Northgate Peaks Trail, a 4.2-mile (6.8-km) round trip on a flat, single-track dirt trail with minimal elevation gain at just 100 ft (30 m). This section of the park is 3,000 ft

IF YOU HAVE
**A weekend**
Spend your first day exploring Zion Canyon, taking the shuttle bus to various trails and overlooks. Stargaze from camp overnight, then rise early to explore Kolob Canyons.

(914 m) higher than Zion Canyon, with the air much cooler up here, so bring layers that you can shed along your outing.

Though challenging and technical, the Subway trail is true bliss for experienced wilderness hikers who want

↑ The winding road to the Zion Canyon Overlook, near Springdale

to blaze a trail. Across 9 miles (14.5 km) you will be route finding, crossing riverbeds, and bouldering across steep rock faces while trekking to the main feature: the Subway. The trail namesake is an aptly named geological feature, whose canyon walls round up on all sides and feel like they were inspired by sub-terranean subway systems like those in New York City. Another route to the Subway, and a favorite with climbers and canyoneers, involves repelling from the top down. Free wilderness permits are required for this trail and run on a lottery; only a few are distributed each day, so ensure you plan ahead.

## Scenic drives

Those who are bringing their own vehicle to the park will be rewarded with scenic routes offering captivating views. The Zion-Mt. Carmel Highway and Tunnel drive is particularly stunning, with 6 miles (10 km) of paved road that carries you through dramatic landscapes to viewpoints and trailheads where you can wander off and explore the beauty of Zion. Halfway along the route you pass through the Mt. Carmel Tunnel – a carved-out passageway completed in 1930 leading vehicles through a huge rock face before emerging into daylight on the other side. There are height restrictions in place here so

check in advance if traveling in an RV. The tunnel is closed to cyclists and pedestrians at all times, though an exception was made in 2016 when 300 people walked through the tunnel in celebration of the centennial anniversary of the National Park Service.

A lesser-known but no less scenic drive traverses 5 miles (8 km) along Kolob Canyons Road. This area provides a more intimate driving experience as you travel off onto picturesque trails enfolded by narrow red- rock box canyons. Since it takes a little more effort to get to, there will be fewer crowds and better chances for wildlife sightings.

→
Starry skies
seen above
Angels Landing

## Wildlife

Zion's landscapes provide habitats for all kinds of wildlife, including mountain lions, bighorn sheep, mule deer, and foxes. For many, birding is the highlight, with some 291 species catalogued in the park's boundaries. With a pair of binoculars and a keen eye on the horizon, you can spot a huge variety of birds in just a few short hours. The iconic species to be on the watch for are some of the most remarkable predators of the sky: the peregrine falcon, bald eagle, California condor, and Mexican spotted owl. Along with the California condor, the peregrine falcon nests in the park, both birds having found a safe haven to recover their numbers after nearly being wiped out across the region. The desert wildflowers and riparian habitats make this a good spot to see hummingbirds, too, including the black-chinned varieties.

Spring is often cited as the best birding season, when temperatures are mild. Easy nature walks abound, providing opportunities to spot and photograph such birds and plantlife – and the surrounding natural wonders.

## Photography

With its sweeping landscapes and incredibly diverse wildlife, Zion is the perfect place to go shutter happy. One of the best shots can be taken from Observation Point, where you'll find a glorious panorama including nearly all of the park's attractions; you can reach this via the East Rim Trail, which begins at the Weeping Rock shuttle stop. If you're into the finer detail, Checkerboard Mesa is a fun area to play with the intricacies of Navajo sandstone and the color and texture unearthed by its crisscrossed natural lines. This unique rock formation can be found southwest of the park's east entrance. Sunrise and sunset are also

> The iconic species to be on the watch for are some of the top predators of the sky: the peregrine falcon, bald eagle, California condor, and Mexican spotted owl.

truly bewitching hours for photographers, and those with ambitions to capture the dizzying vastness of the night sky are in for a treat at Zion. At dusk, find a spot to yourself and watch as the canyon walls ignite in bursts of pink and orange. After the sun sets, when the moon rises and the stars come out, many head to the Pa'rus Trail for a night walk to see the Milky Way in all its glory. That said, you can go almost anywhere in the park and spot sandstone cliffs cradling twinkling stars. Check out astronomical viewing forecasts for celestial events and optimal days for skygazing.

↑ Zion's sandstone formations towering over the landscape

# A LONG WALK
# WEST RIM TRAIL

**Length** 14.5 miles (23.3 km) one-way **Stopping-off points** There are various backcountry campsites en route **Terrain** Rocky

A great pick for a long day hike or a two-day backpacking trip (permit required), the West Rim Trail showcases Zion's unique geology and sweeping views. The moderate trail descends from the north, so many hikers go south for an easier trek; less experienced hikers can pick either trailhead for a shorter out-and-back route.

**Locator Map**

**Key**

-- Walk Route

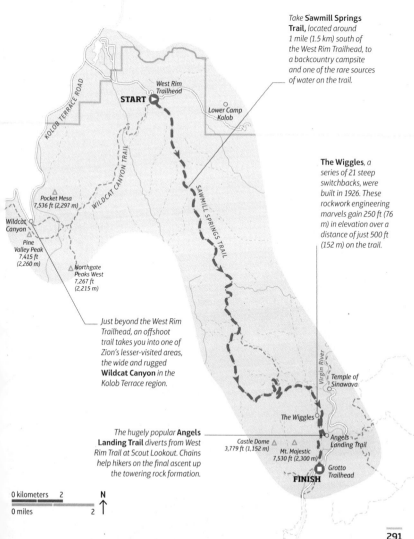

Take **Sawmill Springs Trail,** *located around 1 mile (1.5 km) south of the West Rim Trailhead, to a backcountry campsite and one of the rare sources of water on the trail.*

**The Wiggles,** *a series of 21 steep switchbacks, were built in 1926. These rockwork engineering marvels gain 250 ft (76 m) in elevation over a distance of just 500 ft (152 m) on the trail.*

*Just beyond the West Rim Trailhead, an offshoot trail takes you into one of Zion's lesser-visited areas, the wide and rugged* **Wildcat Canyon** *in the Kolob Terrace region.*

*The hugely popular* **Angels Landing Trail** *diverts from West Rim Trail at Scout Lookout. Chains help hikers on the final ascent up the towering rock formation.*

West Rim Trailhead

**START**

Lower Camp Kolob

Pocket Mesa 7,536 ft (2,297 m)

Wildcat Canyon

Pine Valley Peak 7,415 ft (2,260 m)

Northgate Peaks West 7,267 ft (2,215 m)

KOLOB TERRACE ROAD

WILDCAT CANYON TRAIL

SAWMILL SPRINGS TRAIL

Virgin River

Temple of Sinawava

The Wiggles

Castle Dome 3,779 ft (1,152 m)

Mt. Majestic 7,530 ft (2,300 m)

Angels Landing Trail

Grotto Trailhead

**FINISH**

0 kilometers   2

0 miles   2

N

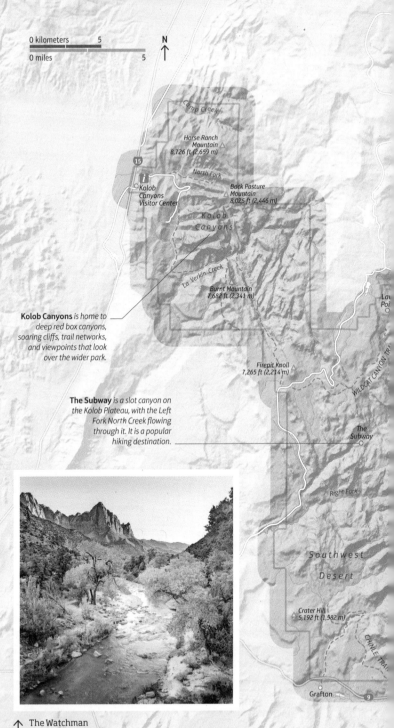

0 kilometers 5

0 miles 5

N

*Camp Creek*

Horse Ranch
Mountain
8,726 ft (2,659 m)

15

*North Fork*

i

Kolob
Canyons
Visitor Center

Back Pasture
Mountain
8,025 ft (2,446 m)

*Kolob
Canyons*

*La Verkin Creek*

Burnt Mountain
7,682 ft (2,341 m)

**Kolob Canyons** *is home to
deep red box canyons,
soaring cliffs, trail networks,
and viewpoints that look
over the wider park.*

La
Poi

WILDCAT CANYON TR.

Firepit Knoll
7,265 ft (2,214 m)

**The Subway** *is a slot canyon on
the Kolob Plateau, with the Left
Fork North Creek flowing
through it. It is a popular
hiking destination.*

The
Subway

*Right Fork*

*Southwest
Desert*

Crater Hill
5,192 ft (1,582 m)

CHINLE TRAIL

Grafton

9

↑ The Watchman
starkly illuminated
by the setting sun

# EXPLORING ZION

Zion National Park straddles three major ecosystems in southern Utah – the Mojave Desert, the Colorado Plateau, and the Great Basin – near the town of Springdale. The park covers almost 150,000 acres (60,700 ha) of remarkable sandstone towers and canyons.

↑ A tricky ascent on Angels Landing Trail

**The Narrows** *is a slot canyon and the narrowest section of Zion Canyon. It is a popular place to hike and explore the Virgin River when conditions allow.*

**Angels Landing** *is located at the top of a tall rock formation, reached by a popular hiking trail of the same name, with panoramic views of Zion Canyon.*

*North Fork Virgin River*

WEST RIM TRAIL

The Narrows

*Observation Point*

*Angel's Landing*

The Great White Throne

*Hidden Canyon Trail*

*East Rim Trail*

ZION CANYON SCENIC DRIVE

Court of the Patriarchs

*East Entrance*

rold oofs

*Checkerboard Mesa 6,670 ft (2,033 m)*

Zion Canyon Visitor Center

*Mt. Carmel Tunnel*

The Watchman

*Virgin River*

**The Watchman** *is a picturesque sandstone mountain formation sitting at 6,545 ft (1,980 m) on the south edge of Zion Canyon and was named for its guard-like appearance.*

*The* **Virgin River** *is a tributary of the Colorado River that has carved the landscape of Zion for 13 million years. It is a designated Wild and Scenic River.*

# BRYCE CANYON

⚲ Utah  🔁 $20-35 for a standard entrance pass
🌐 nps.gov/brca

Bryce Canyon's motley assortment of sandstone spires, rocky hoodoos, and steep fins seems plucked straight from a Norse myth. In fact, one of the park's most iconic features is the vast hoodoo known as Thor's Hammer, a towering rock formation jutting from the arid basin. Exploring the park's huge horseshoe-shaped amphitheaters, towering pink cliffs, and sublime viewing platforms makes for one of Utah's most unforgettable outdoor adventures.

Despite its name, Bryce Canyon is not in fact a canyon, but a series of surreal natural amphitheaters. The largest of these and the most famous is Bryce Amphitheater, filled with flame-colored pinnacle rock formations called hoo-doos, the striking hallmark of this park. Hoodoos are found on every continent but nowhere is a collection as spectacular as it is here. Hoodoos are slowly formed by pounding rain, howling wind, and centuries of ice that erode "fins" of harder rock to form columns and eventually, unique vertical forms.

Bryce's hoodoos are part of the Claron Formation, made up of limestone deposits and iron oxide mineral compounds that give the formations their

Best for *Backcountry camping and landscape photography*

← The sublime amphitheaters of Bryce Canyon

vibrant red, pink, and amber color. They might have been formed over the course of 65 million years, but they are the youngest geological feature to be found on the Colorado Plateau.

## Exploring the park

Bryce is located at a high altitude, reaching elevations of around 8,000–9,000 ft (2,400 m–2,700 m). The winds are stronger and the temperature cooler than in other Utah parks, so bring layers and warm clothing, especially during off-season.

Las Vegas or Salt Lake City are the closest airports, and both are about a four-hour drive to Bryce Canyon. Driving is by far the most popular means of getting around the park, with few public transportation options.

Many visitors combine their trip to the park with a visit to Zion National Park *(p284)* which sits a little over 75 miles (120 km) to the southwest. This part of Utah is rich in spectacular landscapes, so a longer road trip through the state is highly recommended.

Once inside the park, the vistor center should be your first stop. Sitting about one mile (1.6 km) from the park's entrance, here you can obtain accurate driving and hiking directions, weather forecasts, schedules of the wide range of park ranger guided programs, and information on area services including

lodging and dining. It's also recommended that you take a break at the center to watch the short film *A Song of Seasons* which plays throughout the day. The 24-minute film does a fantastic job of putting the park in its ecological and social context. The visitor center also has a bookstore.

 IF YOU HAVE
**A day**

Travel the main park road by car or bike and stop at viewpoints. From the road, you'll be able to look out over the park's assortment of spectacular hoodoos.

Looking out over the park from Sunset Point ↑

# EAT

For a sit-down meal, head to the Bryce Canyon Lodge *(p298)* for breakfast, lunch, or dinner from April through October.

**Valhalla Pizzeria & Coffee Shop**
Simple pizza spot serving lunch, dinner, coffee, and beers.

🏠 Bryce Canyon Lodge
🌐 visitbrycecanyon.com

$$$

---

**Ruby's Inn**
This lodging has three restaurants: Cowboy's Buffet & Steak Room, Canyon Diner, and Ebenezer's Barn and Grill.

🏠 Bryce Canyon City
🌐 rubysinn.com

$$$

---

**Bryce Canyon Pines**
A rustic lodge serving hearty American fare.

🏠 Bryce Canyon City
🌐 bcpines.com

$$$

## Scenic drives

The Bryce Canyon National Park Rim Road runs for 18 miles (29 km) along the rim of Paunsaugunt Plateau, from the park's only entrance in the north to its highest elevation in the south. The first 3 miles (5 km) of the drive provide views of the Bryce Amphitheater. Farther along the length of the road there are 13 viewpoints offering views of formations like the Natural Bridge and Thor's Hammer. The most popular viewpoints, all accessible from the road, are Bryce Point, Inspiration Point, Sunset Point, and Sunrise Point.

Traveling the full length of the main road to the Southern Scenic Drive area leads to Rainbow Point, where you can see the bristlecone pine tree, among the oldest living non-clonal organisms. The road was built by the Civilian Conservation Corps (CCC) to make the beauty of Bryce accessible for visitors, and more marketable for the park service.

## Viewpoints

Sunset Point is one of the park's most popular view-points. It's located just steps from a large parking lot, making it easily accessible, and just a mile (1.6 km) from the visitor center. In addition to a sprawling view of the cradle of hoodoos, you will see birds catching the air that thrusts up from the basin.

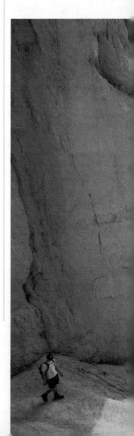

Hiking down the rocky slopes of Queen's Garden →

Thor's Hammer – an isolated balanced rock and iconic landmark in the park – is perched just below. This iconic hoodoo, shaped like the weapon of the Norse god of thunder, was formed as a result of the rock's thicker and thinner layers eroding at different rates, creating the unique leveled effect.

Bryce Point is just a short drive away from Sunset Point and is a prime spot to catch the first light on the canyons during sunrise (as such, Sunset Point is a particularly popular spot for landscape photographers). There is a chain fence on the edge of the viewpoint with a sheer drop falling from it, which may trouble those with a fear of heights.

Inspiration Point provides one of the most complete views of the main amphi-theater, set against the backdrop of Boat Mesa. This

### GETTING AROUND

Bryce Canyon is located 75 miles (120 km) northeast of Zion National Park, and 270 miles (430 km) from Salt Lake City and Las Vegas international airports to the north and southeast, respectively. There is no public transportation servicing the park but privately run tour operators offer bus trips into the park and to its main points of interest. If driving in a private vehicle, you will be traveling the park's one main road, stretching 18 miles (29 km) between the north and south edge of the park boundary. During the summer, there are free shuttles operating around the Bryce Canyon Amphitheater from the visitor center to the four main viewpoints at Sunrise, Sunset, Bryce, and Inspiration Points.

viewpoint is as challenging as it is beautiful, with an outlook taking in sheer drops, crumbling red rock, and plummeting valleys.

### Hiking

Offering a great way to see the park, most hiking trails start along the canyon rim. The 1.4-mile (2-km) round-trip Navajo Loop Trail zigzags sharply down the cliff face for 500 ft (150 m) to finish in a slow meander among slot canyons and rock stands. Note that the climb back up the trail is strenuous.

You can add to your Navajo Loop Trail adventure by connecting it with the nearby Queens Garden Trail (3 miles/5 km total) for a longer, moderately difficult

trip into the interior canyon. Along this route you will see a 700-year-old Douglas fir tree rising between a slot canyon and into the sky.

Queens Garden is a great place to rest, fuel up, and take pictures. Nearby, there are options to venture along various intersecting trail networks where you can chart your own course through the park's rocky landscapes. There is a short hike on a gentle paved road between Sunset Point and Sunrise Point that provides panoramic views of the large amphitheater.

Three popular trails that require more time and commitment are the Peekaboo Trail (5.5 miles/8.8 km), Riggs Spring Loop Trail (8.8 miles/14 km), and the longer 22-mile (35-km) Under-the-Rim Trail near Rainbow Point. All offer opportunities to venture into Bryce's backcountry. Stop at the visitor center for tips and to get more information about backcountry hiking conditions in Bryce.

## Park wildlife

The park crosses three so-called life or climatic zones, each home to different forests. In the lower elevations you'll see juniper, pinyon pine, and aspen trees, with ponderosa pine, spruce, and Douglas fir higher up. These forests create a perfect habitat for more than 175 bird species, including migratory birds. Violet-green swallows are frequently seen along the Rim Trail, while osprey nests are also sometimes found along the scenic drive. You may also be lucky enough to see peregrine falcons, eagles, and even the rare California condor at Bryce Point. If you do spot a California condor while in the park, it's advised that you report your sighting and the location of the encounter to a park ranger.

Bryce Canyon's mammal population includes the Utah prairie dog and the mule

→ Hiking the park's higher grounds in winter

# STAY

There is one lodge in the national park and two campgrounds: the North Campground and the Sunset Campground.

**Bryce Canyon Lodge**
A lodge built from timber and stone in 1923, with lodge suites, motel rooms, and cabins. Reservations are encouraged.

 Bryce Canyon
W nationalpark reservations.com

$$$

**Bryce Canyon Grand**
A historic rest stop with everything you need to power a park tour.

Bryce Canyon City
W brycecanyon grand.com

$$$

**Stone Canyon Inn**
Low-key bungalows set in a resort, with a sauna.

Bryce Canyon City
W stonecanyoninn.com

$$$

→ Rangers provide talks on the wonders of the Milky Way

deer, which you're likely to see cavorting in the park's lower elevations during the winter months, along with mountain lions, bobcats, and coyotes. Elk, fox, ground squirrels, and pronghorn antelope can also be found within the park's boundaries. Very rarely, you may spot the furtive black bear in the park's forested high country.

With a higher altitude and significantly cooler temperatures than other spots in the state, Bryce Canyon is also home to rare reptiles and amphibians such as the short-horned lizard, striped whip-snake, and salamander.

### Horseback riding

Exploring the park on horseback is a traditional way to travel in Bryce Canyon, with centuries of settlers and adventurers forging riding trails. Guided trips operated by the park's concessioner, Canyon Trail Rides, run for about three hours on dedicated horse trails, including the Peekaboo Loop Trail. Rides run from April through October (weather permitting) and advance reservations are required.

### Cycling

To truly experience the park's winding roads and back-country trails, two wheels are often best. Bikers must stay on paved surfaces on the vehicle-free Shared Use Path which runs for 5 miles (8 km) from the park's entrance, passing Sunrise, Sunset, and Inspiration Points. For a longer ride and to see more of the park's glorious landscapes, hit the full stretch of the main park road at its southern end.

 IF YOU HAVE
**A weekend**
Head out on foot into Bryce Canyon's backcountry, first taking in Thor's Hammer, then joining a serene horseback ride.

Be aware that the road is shared with cars, though the road is mostly wide enough for comfortable riding.

### Ranger programs

The park service provides special programs that allow guests to enjoy activities focused on specific attributes of the park, from astronomy to geology to bird-watching. Particular highlights include the Astronomy Festival (usually in June), the Geology Festival (usually in July), and the annual Christmas Bird Count. All events are seasonal and reservations are often required. Check the park website for more information about upcoming programs and event dates.

> **The park service provides special programs that allow guests to enjoy activities focused on specific attributes of the park, from astronomy to geology.**

# EXPLORING BRYCE CANYON

Bryce Canyon National Park is located in southern Utah, not far from the city of Bryce and only roughly 75 miles (120 km) northeast of Zion National Park. The park covers 35,835 acres (14,502 ha) surrounding its namesake natural amphitheater.

## Did You Know?

The park is designated as a Class I air quality area, the highest level of protection under the Clean Air Act.

← The park's spectacular Natural Bridge

**The Natural Bridge** is officially a natural arch and not a bridge, formed by the same natural forces which created the park's hoodoos.

**Ponderosa Canyon** is named after the huge ponderosa pines rising from the canyon floor.

Paunsau

6

BRYCE CANYON ROAD

63

Natural Bridge

Agua Canyon

Ponderosa Canyon

63

Black Birch Canyon

Rainbow Point 9,115 ft (2,778 m)

Yovimpa Point

0 kilometers 3
0 miles 3

N ↑

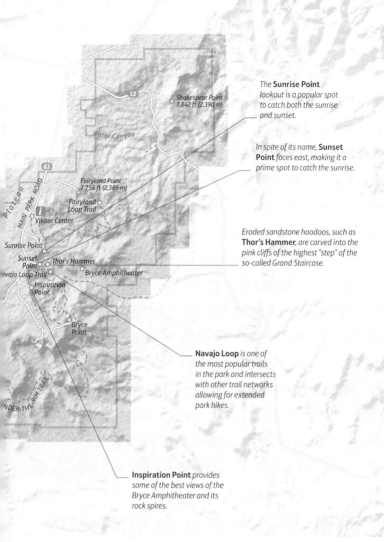

Shakespear Point
7,842 ft (2,390 m)

Water Canyon

12

63

Plateau

MAIN PARK ROAD

Fairyland Point
7,758 ft (2,365 m)

Fairyland
Loop Trail

i Visitor Center

Sunrise Point

Sunset
Point

Thor's Hammer

Navajo Loop Trail

Bryce Amphitheater

Inspiration
Point

Bryce
Point

UNDER-THE-RIM TRAIL

The **Sunrise Point**
lookout is a popular spot
to catch both the sunrise
and sunset.

In spite of its name, **Sunset
Point** faces east, making it a
prime spot to catch the sunrise.

Eroded sandstone hoodoos, such as
**Thor's Hammer**, are carved into the
pink cliffs of the highest "step" of the
so-called Grand Staircase.

**Navajo Loop** is one of
the most popular trails
in the park and intersects
with other trail networks
allowing for extended
park hikes.

**Inspiration Point** provides
some of the best views of the
Bryce Amphitheater and its
rock spires.

↑ Superb views over the
sandstone from Sunset Point

Orange and yellow aspen trees making a splash against Wheeler Peak

# GREAT BASIN

**⊙ Nevada  ⊘ Free (fee for cave tours)  ⊡ nps.gov/grba**

Sat on the eastern state line, Great Basin presents a Nevada that most wouldn't recognize, worlds away from the bright lights of Las Vegas. The park has an almost savage beauty, and, despite having some of the tallest mountains in Nevada, one of the longest cave systems in the western U.S., and the oldest trees on the planet, its remoteness means it manages to fly under the radar. The result? This is one national park to escape the crowds.

Great Basin is named for the area between the Sierra Nevada and the Wasatch Range, where the Continental Divide diverges and no water flows in nor out. This is one of the most mountainous areas in the contiguous United States, as old as the Ice Age, and the national park is centered on soaring Wheeler Peak and other peaks in the Snake Range. It's on Wheeler Peak that you'll find the park's prized feature: bristlecone pines, with their thick, twisted trunks rooted in the harsh land. The range has a number of caves (another prized feature), including the 2-mile (3.2-km) Lehman Caves, their grand marble caverns filled with limestone stalactites and stalagmites, drapes, cave popcorn, and a collection of

↑ Looking out toward Wheeler Peak over bristlecone pine trees

rare "shields." Known as limestone solution caverns, they began forming around 600 million years ago when shallow seas covered what is now Nevada. Tucked inside the Snake Range, the caves were discovered in the mid-1880s by a miner-turned-rancher named Absalom Lehman. He became a passionate advocate for the park and inspired the first set of laws protecting the cave system in 1922.

## Exploring the park

Given its location far from Nevada's big cities, only about

---

 **IF YOU HAVE**
**A day**

Wind up the Wheeler Peak Scenic Drive and take a hike among the bristlecones, before descending for a tour of the Lehman Caves.

→

The so-called "sectored architecture" of the long-living bristlecone pine

# EAT

Dining options are limited in the park so bring provisions or stop in Ely or Baker.

### Great Basin Café

The park's only option, inside the Lehman Caves Visitor Center.

 Great Basin ℂ (775) 234 7200

$ $ $

### Ridley's Family Markets

Nearest supermarket to the park, good for camping supplies.

 Ely ⓦ shop ridleys.com

$ $ $

# STAY

Aside from camping, there are no lodgings in the park.

### Stargazer Inn

Cheerful place offering rooms, RV sites, and a general store.

 Baker ⓦ star gazernevada.com

$ $ $

### Hidden Canyon Retreat

Named well, this lodge enjoys a natural setting near the park.

 Baker ⓦ hidden canyonretreat.com

$ $ $

↑ The limestone formations of the Lehman Caves

140,000 people enter the park in an average year, meaning it gets less than 10 percent of the traffic of parks like Yellowstone and Yosemite.

The park's main visitor center sits outside of the park proper, not far from Baker; at the Lehman Caves is another visitor center, where you can purchase cave tour tickets. The caves are an obvious draw for visitors, but the park also provides plenty of opportunity to hike or take a scenic drive.

## Lehman Caves

Visitors can only enter the caves on ranger-guided 90-minute tours; a fee is charged and reservations must be made months in advance. The cave is around 52°F (11°C) year-round, so warm clothes are advised.

## Hiking

You will want to see bristle-cone pines, the longest-living trees on Earth, while you're here. The most accessible bristlecones are on the moderate Bristlecone and Glacier Trail, a 4.6-mile (7.4-km) round-trip hike from Wheeler Peak Campground; the grove is about 1.5 miles (2.5 km) from the parking area. Living atop glacial moraines at subalpine altitudes, and exposed to little oxygen, bristlecones grow at a snail's pace. Their density and twisted shape shields them from infection and rot, aiding longevity. In 1964, a geographer named Donald R. Currey took samples from a bristlecone he believed to be over 4,000 years old; the tree was cut down and after examination was estimated to be 4,900 years old, the oldest known tree at the time.

The easy 2.7-mile (4.3-km) Alpine Lakes Loop passes through alpine meadows and woodlands on its way to a pair of backcountry lakes. There are great views of Wheeler Peak and good opportunities to see wildlife like mule deer, bighorn sheep, and golden eagles. The trail connects to another, more difficult trail to the summit.

 IF YOU HAVE
**A weekend**

Explore the caves and then set off for a two-day backcountry hike, camping overnight and gazing at the stars once night falls.

At 75 ft (23 m) tall, Lexington Arch is an impressive landmark in the southern reaches of the park, about 25 miles (40 km) of paved and dirt roads south of Baker. A 4WD vehicle is required to reach the trailhead to the 5.4-mile (8.7-km) hike to the arch.

## Camping

The park has a number of campgrounds, both developed and basic. Backcountry camping is allowed; permits are required at only Baker and Johnson lakes, but voluntary registration is recommended.

### GETTING AROUND

Straddling the Nevada-Utah state line, Great Basin is one of the most isolated national parks in the country. Las Vegas, Nevada, is about 300 miles (483 km) to the south via U.S. 93, and Salt Lake City, Utah, is about 200 miles (322 km) northeast via I-15, U.S. 6, and U.S. 50. Ely, Nevada, is about 60 miles northwest via U.S. 50. The main park entrance and visitor center are located 5 miles (8 km) west of Baker, Nevada, on Nev. Hwy. 488. Near the entrance, Wheeler Peak Scenic Drive ascends more than 3,000 ft (914 m) in 12 miles (19 km) to the base of Wheeler Peak, near one of the park's bristlecone pine groves. Great Basin runs a number of astronomy programs and moonlight hikes in summer; rangers also lead tours aboard the Nevada Northern Railway's *Star Train*, which runs from Ely on selected Friday nights in summer.

# EXPLORING GREAT BASIN

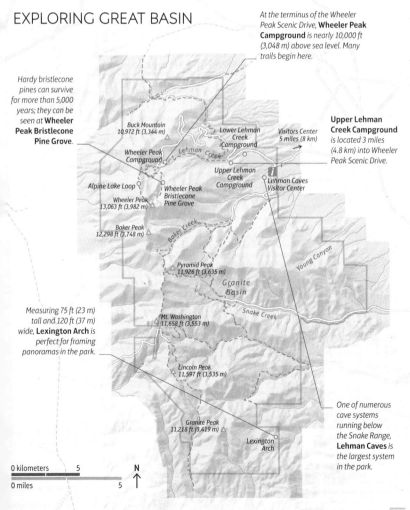

At the terminus of the Wheeler Peak Scenic Drive, **Wheeler Peak Campground** is nearly 10,000 ft (3,048 m) above sea level. Many trails begin here.

Hardy bristlecone pines can survive for more than 5,000 years; they can be seen at **Wheeler Peak Bristlecone Pine Grove**.

**Upper Lehman Creek Campground** is located 3 miles (4.8 km) into Wheeler Peak Scenic Drive.

Buck Mountain
10,972 ft (3,344 m)

Lower Lehman Creek Campground

Visitors Center
5 miles (8 km)

Wheeler Peak Campground

Lehman Creek

Upper Lehman Creek Campground

Lehman Caves Visitor Center

Alpine Lake Loop

Wheeler Peak Bristlecone Pine Grove

Wheeler Peak
13,063 ft (3,982 m)

Baker Peak
12,298 ft (3,748 m)

Baker Creek

Young Canyon

Pyramid Peak
11,926 ft (3,635 m)

Granite Basin

Snake Creek

Measuring 75 ft (23 m) tall and 120 ft (37 m) wide, **Lexington Arch** is perfect for framing panoramas in the park.

Mt. Washington
11,658 ft (3,553 m)

Lincoln Peak
11,597 ft (3,535 m)

One of numerous cave systems running below the Snake Range, **Lehman Caves** is the largest system in the park.

Granite Peak
11,218 ft (3,419 m)

Lexington Arch

0 kilometers 5

0 miles 5

N ↑

# CAPITOL REEF

📍 Utah 🚗 $20 per vehicle, valid for seven days
🌐 nps.gov/care

A wonderland of sculpted spires, imposing monoliths, and winding canyons, this remote park in the heart of Utah offers blissful backcountry in bucketloads. Imagine having miles upon miles of open gravel roads mostly to yourself, or hitting unspoiled trails with only impressive rock formations for company, all the while colorful sandstone cliffs turn fiery red and gold in the setting sun. At Capitol Reef National Park, desert solitude is a promise.

Over the course of 280 million years, Mother Nature has been hard at work in Utah's red rock country. Erosion chiseled away at the region's rock layers, creating awe-inspiring arches and denting the sandstone with potholes, or "pockets," which capture seasonal rains and help desert creatures survive in the arid climate. While the park may seem untouched, it has a human footprint that stretches back centuries, too. Petroglyphs by the Fremont Indigenous peoples, who inhabited the area in 300–1300 CE, adorn the cliffsides.

At the turn of the 20th century, prospectors coming across the desert were forced to stop at the Waterpocket Fold, a vast wall of rock that runs north-south through the desert. They likened this geologic wrinkle in the Earth and its layered ridges to an ocean reef, with its

⊙ IF YOU HAVE
**A day**
Enter at the Fruita Rural Historic District and take a scenic drive here, exploring orchards and soaking up the views at Panorama Point.

round white domes resembling the nation's Capitol Building, giving Capitol Reef its unique park name. Indeed, as the light changes through the day, the multicolored cliffs, buttes, and rock formations resemble a tropical reef.

## Exploring the park
Most of Capitol Reef is made of sedimentary strata rock, which is best viewed on scenic drives and along hundreds of miles of backcountry trails. The park is divided into three distinct areas: the popular

A lone car winding its way north past colossal red rocks ↑

Fruita Rural Historic District in the center, the rugged Cathedral Valley area to the north, and the Waterpocket Fold in the south, which is a prime spot for hardy explorers heading out on foot.

Scenic drives are an excellent way to see the endless beauty Capitol Reef has to offer, though roads may become impassable when flash floods are present so always check the forecast

> **Most of Capitol Reef is made of sedimentary strata rock, which is best viewed on scenic drives and along hundreds of miles of backcountry trails.**

before heading into remote areas. Cell phone reception is either nonexistent or unreliable, too; if you need help, support may be days away, so it is essential that you equip yourself with food, water, gas, and emergency supplies before setting off.

## Fruita Rural Historic District

The main visitor center is located in the village of Fruita, which is the preferred entry point for many and the most visited area of the park.

In the 1880s, Mormon settlers moved into the isolated area of the Fremont River valley, where Fruita is now located. They planted expansive fruit and nut orchards along irrigation lines, which were dug along the river long ago by the Fremont people, and founded a village here. The orchards still bear fruit, and from June to October you can pick apples, peaches, and apricots – a great way to fuel up before setting off on hikes. Also found in Fruita are the blacksmith shop, Gifford Homestead Store and Museum, and the historic remains of the Fruita schoolhouse. The district's historical importance doesn't stop there. During the early 20th century, the Fruita valley was a popular mining area where

### GETTING AROUND

Salt Lake City international airport, 230 miles (370 km) north of the park, is the closest access point if flying in from out of state. This park is isolated (the nearest traffic light to the park is 78 miles/126 km away) with only one road, Ut. Hwy. 24, leading to its main entry point in the Fruita Historic District at the park's center. It is highly recommended that you use a map for directional guidance rather than relying on GPS. Once within the park's perimeters, each of the three park sections have scenic drives with varying levels of accessibility. Scenic Drive in Fruita at the center is paved and accessible, as is the Loop-the-Fold drive in the southern Waterpocket Fold. The rugged Cathedral Valley in the north has a mix of paved and off-road sections. Weather events could impede travel so check at the visitor center for information first.

heavy deposits of limestone and uranium in the desert rock were quarried; spot the names of historic miners and settlers at the Pioneer Register site. Another popular point of interest in Fruita are the Fremont Petroglyphs and Panorama Point. These petroglyphs were carved in sandstone and depict animals, people, and scenes of daily life from centuries ago. Bring a pair of binoculars to get a closer view and take your time – there are often more petroglyphs to see than immediately strikes the eye.

## Cathedral Valley

North of Fruita Rural Historic District is this rugged section, which protects impressive desert landscapes and numerous rock formations. Here you're guaranteed to find solitude amid one of Utah's most enchanting and best-kept wilderness secrets.

To explore this area, drive the Cathedral Valley Loop Road, an adventurous, off-road loop 58 miles (93 km) long that's popular with mountain bikers and those in a 4WD. Note that there are possible river crossings along

the loop, so a high-clearance vehicle may be required.

While driving along primitive roads and getting out to hike along unmarked trails, you'll come across curious scenery such as the 400-ft- (122-m-) high Temple of the Sun and Temple of the Moon cathedral-shaped formations, which gave the

→

Cathedral Valley, its rock formations resembling Gothic cathedrals

←
Halls Creek Narrows, a scenic backpack route best done as a three- to four-day trip

area its name. While these features tower high, the Gypsum Sinkhole falls deep into a 200-ft (60-m) chasm that plunges beneath the surface. Under the bold desert sun, exposed gypsum made of selenite crystals sparkles on Glass Mountain, a small formation near the Temple of the Moon. Another highlight in this area is the Morrell Cabin, built in the 1930s and once used as a waypoint for cattle ranchers.

With so much to see, it's worth spending a night at one of the six sites at the Cathedral Valley campground, halfway along the Cathedral Valley Loop Road.

### Waterpocket Fold

The park's south harbors the most exciting and main geologic feature in the park: a 100-mile- (160-km-) long wall of rock. Surprisingly, this is the least visited part of Capitol Reef, and is open year-round (though weather conditions might limit access). The sedimentary strata rock spans from Thousand Lake Mountain to Lake Powell, and a popular way to explore it is along the 124-mile (200-km) Loop-the-Fold driving tour. That said, it's a wonderful area to hike, so stop to take in sections along the way.

A hotspot for backpackers, Waterpocket Fold has few marked trails. Two of the most popular backpacker routes include the remote 21-mile (34-km) Halls Creek Narrows and the strenuous 17-mile (27-km) Lower Muley Twist Canyon, which traverses a desolate canyon. Hikes through the backcountry have unearthed ancient finds; if you come across an artifact, take a picture, and share it with the NPS to identify it.

## EAT

Food options in the park are limited, but there are dining spots in the nearby town of Torrey.

**The Pioneer Kitchen**
Chef-created casual comfort food with views of the Colorado Plateau.

🏠 Torrey [W] capitolreefresort.com

$$$

**Capitol Burger**
A burger joint with vegetarian options for a quick casual bite.

🏠 Torrey
☎ (435) 491 0742

$$$

## STAY

There are no lodges within the national park but there are several spots in adjacent towns.

**Capitol Reef Resort**
Offering rooms, suites, and cabins with modern amenities and sweeping views of the red rock landscape.

🏠 Torrey area [W] capitolreefresort.com

$$$

**Cathedral Valley Inn**
A comfortable motel, closest to the Cathedral Valley section on the north side of the park.

🏠 Hanksville area
[W] cathedralvalleyinn.com

$$$

The **Cathedral Valley Loop Scenic Roadway** leads to towering rock formations and the Bentonite Hills.

The **Fremont River**, a tributary of the Colorado River, runs through the southern section of the park.

**Panorama Point** has some of the best views of Capitol Reef's sandstone cliffs just a short walk from the parking area.

**Sunset Point** is a popular viewpoint reached by a short trail overlooking panoramic views onto Waterpocket Fold, the Fremont River, and the Henry Mountains.

The **Capitol Reef Visitor Center** is in the heart of the Fruita Rural Historic District, with park rangers on hand to offer trip guidance, other information, and park memorabilia.

Visitors can tour the **Gifford Homestead**, built in 1908 and now serving as a museum dedicated to the 1880s Mormon settlement that once flourished here.

**Waterpocket Fold** was formed 65 million years ago as the Earth's crust buckled upward revealing multicolored ripples of rock that continue to be shaped by erosion.

# EXPLORING CAPITOL REEF

Capitol Reef National Park is located west of the town of Torrey in the center of southern Utah. The remote and rugged park spans 240,000 acres (97,000 ha), a vast wilderness of gargantuan red rocks.

### Did You Know?

Capitol Reef was originally going to be named "Wayne Wonderland."

↑ The long and strange wrinkle in the Earth known as the Waterpocket Fold

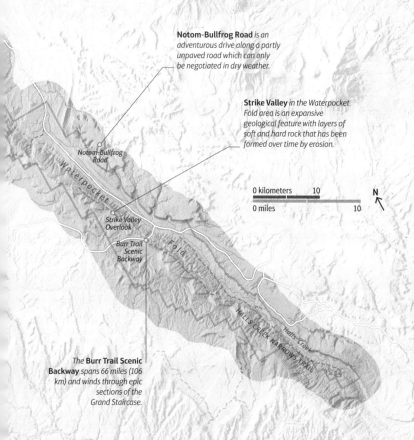

**Notom-Bullfrog Road** is an adventurous drive along a partly unpaved road which can only be negotiated in dry weather.

**Strike Valley** in the Waterpocket Fold area is an expansive geological feature with layers of soft and hard rock that has been formed over time by erosion.

0 kilometers 10
0 miles 10

N

The **Burr Trail Scenic Backway** spans 66 miles (106 km) and winds through epic sections of the Grand Staircase.

Best for *Backpacking and canyoneering*

# ARCHES

⚲ Utah 🚗 $30 per vehicle, valid for seven days; reservations and timed-entry permit required Apr–Oct 🌐 nps.gov/arch

Arches National Park holds the largest collection of sandstone arch formations on Earth, with more than 2,000 catalogued within the park boundary. These remarkable structures have been carved out over hundreds of millions of years, their surreal shapes protected by delicate layers of cryptobiotic crust. The iconic red rocks are among the most popular sights in the U.S., but the park's wonders are myriad: desert trails provide superb hiking, rock markings testify to Indigenous history, and low light pollution reveals the night sky in its dizzying immensity.

Natural arch formations come in many shapes and sizes, but to be classified as an arch a rock must have an opening measuring at least 3 ft (0.9 m) wide or high. While arches are the theme and namesake of Arches National Park, there are many other curious rock formations within the park's boundaries, including pinnacles, towers, and balanced rocks that cradle the deep-blue desert sky. Looking out across these otherworldly formations is a unique joy.

The beauty of the rocks is often heightened by the region's weather patterns: summer storms turn up magical skies at sunrise and sunset, to the delight of photographers. As the day grows dark, planets, galaxies, and more than 2,500 visible stars twinkle in the night sky.

There are cultural discoveries to be made here, too: rock art, quartzite tools, and other artefacts carved by Ancestral Puebloan, Ute, Shoshone, and Paiute cultures reveal a human history spanning more than 10,000 years. These petroglyphs etched into the red rock tell fascinating stories of hunter-gatherer existence.

## Exploring the park

The park is in south-east Utah, 5 miles (8 km) north of Moab on U.S. Hwy. 191.

### GETTING AROUND

There is only one entrance to Arches, north of Moab on U.S. Hwy. 191. At the entrance is the park's only visitor center. If traveling from April to October, you will likely have plenty of time to stop there, as the park operates on a system of timed pre-book entry. Lines of passenger vehicles frequently stretch along the highway waiting to bypass the entrance gate and get onto the sole park road (a webcam displays current activity at the entrance station which you can check out in advance). If you find yourself waiting outside the park entrance, check out the Courthouse Wash Rock Art Panel located just south of the park entrance on U.S. Hwy. 191. Note that points of interest and trailheads are often congested, and arriving early is recommended. There are no shuttles.

The tripartite rock formation known as the Three Gossips ↑

↑ Delicate Arch, one of the more famous of the park's many formations

The vast majority of visitors to Arches arrive at the park's one entrance by car.

Arches Scenic Drive, the main vein of the park, runs for 36 miles (58 km), starting at the visitor center just off Hwy. 191. The visitor center provides an excellent introduction to the geology of this beautiful but fragile land.

When driving the road, you should allow at least 4 to 5 hours, or longer if you're keen to go off piste and explore the paved offshoot roads. During the peak summer season, expect heavy congestion at the entrance. Bring water and snacks, and ensure you fuel up your gas tank, as there are no services inside the park.

When exploring the park, note that there are a number of rules to preserve the integrity of the landscape. Pets are not allowed, and taking a dip in Ephemeral Pools is forbidden as the water supports organisms and wildlife. Carving, marking, scratching, or removing any piece of the sandstone and red rock is punishable by law. To ensure a safe and enjoyable trip, equip yourself with water, multiple layers, and sturdy outdoor gear.

## Car-accessible arches and formations

With more than 2,000 documented arches in the park and many more rock formations, it can be hard to know where to focus your time. Thankfully, many of the best features can be enjoyed from the park's 36-mile (58-km) Scenic Drive.

The first attraction you'll see when taking the road from the visitor center is Park

← Hiking up to the huge North Window formation

IF YOU HAVE
**A day**
Drive the paved Scenic Drive, stopping at the designated viewpoints and wandering the short trails on the road's perimeter.

Avenue, a 2-mile (3-km) paved trail leading past sky-high spires and rock walls. The route is wheelchair accessible and a shuttle bus runs from the visitor center. Down a short staircase on the route is the Courthouse Towers Viewpoint overlooking a series of gigantic monoliths.

Balanced Rock is a massive boulder perched atop a mudstone base standing 128 ft (39 m) tall and visible from Park Avenue. There is a short, partly paved trail surrounding it that is suitable for children and wheelchairs.

The Windows Section contains some of the park's largest arches; there is easy hiking from the road to the infamous Double Arch and North Window. From the window, you can frame Turret Arch as a perfect backdrop through the rocky opening.

Nearby, and easily accessible from the road, are the Wolfe Ranch petro-

## Timeline

**20 BCE**
▽ Ancestral Puebloans establish agricultural villages in and near Arches, where they cultivate plants and create rock art panels.

**1200s**
Indigenous peoples like the nomadic Shoshoneans, Utes, and Paiutes arrive, leaving petroglyphs at Wolfe Ranch.

**1844**
French-American fur trapper Denis Julien chisels his name and June 9, 1844, into the rock, an early marker of European contact.

**1880s–90s**
▲ White farmers and ranchers, including John Wolfe of the Wolfe Ranch, found permanent settlements in the area.

→ Balanced Rock with snow on the distant La Sal Range

glyphs, carved by nomadic Shoshonean, Ute, and Paiute peoples. The works depict riders on horseback alongside bighorn sheep.

### Hiking

The most famous arch in the park is Delicate Arch, which has become a recognizable symbol of the state (it's depicted on both the Utah state license plate and Utah's commemorative "America the Beautiful" quarter issued by the U.S. Mint). Olympians even passed the torch beneath it during the 2002 Winter Games in Salt Lake.

There are a few options when it comes to hiking Delicate Arch. The lower viewpoint is easily accessible. The walk to the upper viewpoint, however, is moderately strenuous, with some uphill sections over 1 mile (0.5 km). The most popular hike to the arch brings you right up to its base: the terrain is smooth but steep and there is no shade along the 3-mile (5-km) out-and-back trail, so be sure to bring plenty of water. Many visitors undertake the walk in the evening to see the setting sun framed by the rock (expect large crowds).

The 2-mile (3-km) Broken Arch trail on the north side of the park is a popular spot during spring wildflower

*1910s*

Moab newspaper editor Loren Taylor spearheads efforts to preserve the landscape by designating it as a national park.

*1929*

On April 12, 1929, President Herbert Hoover sets aside land in Windows and Devils Garden for Arches National Monument.

*1973*

△ Geography professor Dale Stevens devises a scientific method for cataloguing the natural arches; about 2,000 have been identified so far.

## EAT

There are no restaurants in Arches, but there are plenty of places to eat in Moab.

**Milt's Stop & Eat**
A cult classic established in 1954, serving burgers, fries, onion rings, and milkshakes.

🏠 Moab
🌐 miltsstopandeat.com

$

**Antica Forma**
Wood-fired pizza, pasta, and salads on Main Street in the heart of Moab.

🏠 Moab
🌐 anticaforma.com

$$

**The Broken Oar**
A decent restaurant offering burgers and other comforting hits.

🏠 Moab
🌐 thebrokenoarmoab.com

$$

# STAY

There is one established campground at Devils Garden, and a handful of designated back-country camping spots. There are no lodges in the national park, but Moab has a number of great options.

### Devils Garden Campground

The only established campground in the park, surrounded by striking rock formations. Reserve your spot in advance for the peak season between March and October.

🏕 Arches
🌐 recreation.gov

### Red Cliffs Lodge

This rustic lodge perched on the Colorado River is the ideal base from which to explore the surrounding wilds.

🏕 Moab
🌐 redcliffslodge.com

Taking in the massive North Window arch ↑

season. The arch itself is not actually broken, just thinning due to gradual erosion.

Devils Garden is one of the most popular hiking areas in the park, with a vast network of trails for all abilities. A popular 2-mile (3-km) hike leads to Landscape Arch – the largest in the park spanning 300 ft (90 m) – before passing Pine Tree Arch and Tunnel Arch. From there, the trail leads 4 miles (6.6 km) farther toward Double O Arch; after Landscape Arch the route

gets more difficult, with some climbing and rock scrambling involved. Dark Angel is a 150-ft (45-m) sandstone tower just 0.5 miles (0.8 km) beyond Double O Arch.

The Fiery Furnace is another of the most dramatic areas of the park for hiking, with a maze of canyons, fins, and spires. The terrain in the area is steep and rugged, and only experienced hikers should attempt the routes leading through this part of the park. Ranger-led hikes require tickets and solo adventures require permits, both of which must be purchased in advance through the visitor center or through the website.

←
Climbing the park's tall rock formations

↑ Dark skies framed by the infamous red rock

IF YOU HAVE
**A weekend**

Camp in Devils Garden and start your days watching the sunrise. Hike on the first day, reserving the second for the Scenic Drive.

climbers who want to catch views of arches, sprawling canyons, and the famed La Sal Mountains in the distance. While rock climbing and bouldering are popular activities in the park, BASE jumping, and slack-lining are forbidden, as is climbing delicate arch formations.

## Rock climbing

The park's iconic soft Entrada sandstone is ideal for rock climbing, canyoneering, and bouldering. Elephant Butte, the park's highest point, is particularly popular. Multi- and single-pitch routes rising 300 ft (90 m) from the landscape entice technical

## Stargazing

Arches has some of the darkest skies in the Lower 48 states and is certified as an official International Dark Sky Park. Some of the best places for stargazing include the Balanced Rock Picnic Area, the easily accessible Windows Section, the Garden of Eden

Viewpoint, and Panorama Point. Park rangers lead regular stargazing outings which can be joined from the visitor center; check out the park website for upcoming events. It's also advisable to bring a star chart to spot constellations and galaxies.

# EXPLORING ARCHES

Arches National Park lies north of Moab in the state of Utah. Bordered by the Colorado River to the southeast, the park's almost 80,000 acres (32,000 ha) are home to more than 2,000 natural sandstone arches, including the famous Delicate Arch in the east of the park.

↑ The narrow columns known as Courthouse Towers

Eagle Park
Dark Angel
Private Arch
Double O Arch
Navajo Arch
Landscape Arch
Devils Garden Trailhead
Tower Arch
Marching Men
Salt Valley
Salt Valley Wash
Herdina Park
Willow Flat
Courthouse Wash
Three Gossips
Arches Visitor Center
191
0 kilometers 4
0 miles 4
N

**Courthouse Towers** *are a collection of statuesque columns located near the park entrance.*

*The 350-ft (106-m) tall* **Three Gossips** *formation resembles a trio of people talking.*

*The* **Arches Visitor Center** *is the gateway to the park where you can load up on information and memorabilia, and receive permits for outings in the park.*

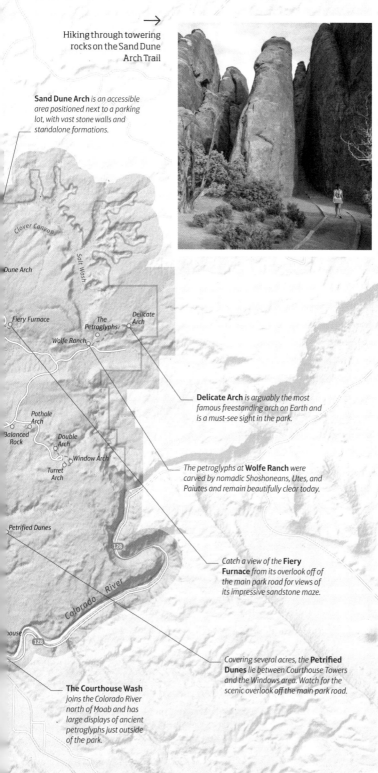

→ Hiking through towering rocks on the Sand Dune Arch Trail

**Sand Dune Arch** is an accessible area positioned next to a parking lot, with vast stone walls and standalone formations.

Clover Canyon

Salt Wash

Dune Arch

Fiery Furnace

The Petroglyphs

Delicate Arch

Wolfe Ranch

**Delicate Arch** is arguably the most famous freestanding arch on Earth and is a must-see sight in the park.

Pothole Arch

Balanced Rock

Double Arch

Window Arch

Turret Arch

The petroglyphs at **Wolfe Ranch** were carved by nomadic Shoshoneans, Utes, and Paiutes and remain beautifully clear today.

Petrified Dunes

128

Catch a view of the **Fiery Furnace** from its overlook off of the main park road for views of its impressive sandstone maze.

Colorado River

house

128

Covering several acres, the **Petrified Dunes** lie between Courthouse Towers and the Windows area. Watch for the scenic overlook off the main park road.

**The Courthouse Wash** joins the Colorado River north of Moab and has large displays of ancient petroglyphs just outside of the park.

Best for *Winding drives and rock climbing*

# CANYONLANDS

📍Utah  💲$15–30 for a standard day pass  🌐nps.gov/cany

Utah's Canyonlands National Park is a sprawling dreamscape of red rock, formed as the Colorado and Green rivers carved a passage through the Colorado Plateau over millions of years. Here, picture-perfect desert sunsets and magical starry night skies play out above glimmering canyons, rocky mesas, and towering buttes. The national park is separated into four districts: Island in the Sky, the Needles, the Maze, and the Colorado and Green Rivers. Each one offers a distinct array of landscapes and geological features, as well as lasting imprints of the area's historic communities and outdoor adventures aplenty.

The park's scenic drive leading into the canyon ↑

The first evidence of human activity in the area around what is now Canyonlands dates back approximately 10,000 years. Projectiles used by early hunter-gatherers have been uncovered within the park, and highly distinctive rock art found around Barrier Canyon speaks of the area's early communities. Comprised of remarkable pictographs and evocative petroglyphs, this rock art (generally demonstrating the "Barrier Canyon Style") was painted between 1,500 and 4,000 years ago. The area's hunter-gatherers were followed by Ancestral Puebloans, Utes, Navajos,

and Paiutes, who each used the region's distinctive geological features to facilitate their innovative agricultural methods. The first Europeans to permanently settle in the region were ranchers. From the late 19th century until 1975, vast swaths of the area that is now within the park's boundaries was used for ranching. Today, features in each district of the park bear the names of many of the park's early ranchers.

> **Later in the 20th century, it was discovered that some of the rock in Canyonlands contained uranium, and a wave of prospectors built new roads.**

Later in the 20th century, it was discovered that some of the rock in Canyonlands contained uranium, and a wave of prospectors built a new network of roads on public land. Many of these routes, including the White Rim Road at the Island in the Sky, remain in use today.

The park was signed into law by President Lyndon B. Johnson in 1964.

### Exploring the park

The Green and Colorado rivers (which jointly comprise one of the park's four districts), trisect the 337,598-acre (136, 621-ha) national park into three additional areas – the Island in the Sky, the Needles, and the Maze – that are all distinct and draw visitors for different reasons.

Canyonlands is located 6 miles (10 km) north of Arches National Park *(p312)* and near the La Sal Mountains, a popular place for mountain biking on the slickrock landscape. Given the park's size and complex terrain, it can be difficult to navigate, and there are a number of restrictions to be aware of. Pets are only allowed in designated campgrounds and in private vehicles on scenic driving roads, but they are prohibited on trails and in the backcountry. Hot summers can make extended outdoor experiences challenging, while winter brings ice.

> IF YOU HAVE
> **A day**
>
> Explore the Island in the Sky section by car, stopping at viewpoints and hiking a handful of the park's incredible mesa-top trails.

> As day turns to night, viewpoints become gathering places, with crowds enjoying the sublime sunset panoramas over the canyons, giving way to night skies.

## Island in the Sky

This popular district sits on a level mesa rising 2,000 ft (610 m) above the Colorado and Green rivers, earning it its name. The district is popular for scenic drives, motorcycle rides, stops at intriguing archeological sites, and day hikes that lead into the vast wilderness.

Park rangers lead guided walks and evening talks, sharing stories about the area's history. As day turns to night, viewpoints become gathering places, with crowds enjoying the sublime sunset panoramas over the canyons, giving way to dusky night skies. The park is one of Utah's nine incredible designated International Dark Sky Parks, so if you have the energy to stay into the night, you'll be in for a cosmic treat.

The 34-mile (54-km) paved scenic driving road is an engineering feat and the simplest way to see Island in the Sky in a short amount of time, meandering through the mesa with views of the canyon wilderness descending as low as 1,000 ft (300 m) below the road. There are stops at several archeological sites that preserve Indigenous paintings and artefacts dating back 10,000 years. The drive's crown jewel is the view from the highest point at Grand View Point which many believe to be the most spectacular view across the whole park.

Admiring the sunrise at Mesa Arch, a pothole arch ↑

## Hiking and biking in Island in the Sky

There are a number of hikes in Island in the Sky, ranging from easy to moderate to strenuous. Mesa Arch is perhaps the most iconic site at Canyonlands and is an easy hike at just 0.5 miles (0.8 km). Note that parking at the trailhead is limited. Each morning at sunrise, photographers line up to see the day's first ray of sun pierce through the arch formation with a view of the Colorado River, Monument Basin, and La Sal Mountains pictured in the arch window.

White Rim Road is 100 miles (160 km) long, encompassing the mesa top of Island in the Sky. Multi-day trips by 4WD or by mountain bike take a few days to complete. Steep sections on Shafer Trail, Lathrop Canyon

### GETTING AROUND

Salt Lake City is the nearest commercial airport, and there are two smaller airports nearby: Grand Junction Regional and Green River Municipal. There is no public transportation that services Canyonlands. Most visitors access the two most visited areas of the park – Island in the Sky and the Needles – from U.S. Hwy. 191. Once in the park, plan to get around by car – whether it be a standard 2WD passenger vehicle along established paved roadways or with a 4WD vehicle in the more rugged areas of the park. Colorado and Green river experiences by boat begin along the many drop-in points along the shores.

↑ Rock formations on the Chesler Park Loop trail

# EAT

There are no food outlets in the park but restaurants can be found in towns near each section of the park. Moab is nearest to Island in the Sky and Monticello is nearest to the Needles.

### The Broken Oar
Casual eats in a lodge-like atmosphere with steaks, seafood, pasta, and barbecue.

 Moab
W thebroken oarmoab.com

$$$

### Doug's BBQ
Hearty American menu with a focus on ribs, burgers, and meats.

 Monticello
W orderdougsbbqut.com

$$$

---

### IF YOU HAVE
**A weekend**

Take a backpacking trip through the Needles to hit a multitude of trails, before ending each day camped out under starry night skies.

---

Road, Murphy Hogback, Hardscrabble Hill, and the Mineral Bottom make for challenging backcountry mountain biking routes; they are considered world class in the biking circuit. Whether traveling by foot, car, or bike, you'll want to check for current conditions before your expedition.

## The Needles
The rock formations in the Needles area were named for the colorful red and white layered pinnacles that dominate the desert landscape. There are more than 100 hikes in this area of the park, and the wild backcountry is perfect for hikers, campers, mountain bikers, and photographers. Pothole Point and Cave Springs are favorites, and the park service offers tours of lesser known networks that are equally impressive, starting at the visitor center. The 10.7-mile (17-km) Chesler Park Loop trail makes for a standout walk, leading to a small number of campsites (reservation only) that allow you to set up base before traveling farther to iconic areas such as the Joint Trail. Nearby is a slot canyon where you can slither through tight canyon walls.

When in the Needles section, factor in time for a stop at the Newspaper Rock Petroglyphs. Created on rock faces along the Puerco River up to 2,000 years ago, some 650 visually arresting depictions of hunting and fishing practices were etched by the Ancestral Puebloans. The works are beautiful to behold.

## The Maze
Located west of the Green and Colorado rivers, the Maze is the wildest and most remote area of the park, offering a backcountry haven for those with an adventurous spirit and skill in navigating difficult terrain. On average, only 3 percent of the park's total visitors will venture into the Maze, making it the least-visited district.

You are unlikely to see other adventurers here so it's essential that you have advanced plans (which you should try to communicate to the park service). A print map is also essential as GPS and cell phone service cannot be counted on in the Maze. Hans Flat Ranger Station is located on the boundary of the Maze, offering emergency services, but note that it's only open for limited hours. Though 2WD vehicles can access the first part of the unpaved roadway, to get farther into the backcountry, you will need either a 4WD vehicle, a mountain bike, or sturdy hiking boots.

## Horseshoe Canyon

Horseshoe Canyon is a notable, albeit remote, landmark within the Maze. Located between the nearby towns of Green River and Hanksville, most visitors access Horseshoe Canyon from the Hanksville side. The canyon has some of the most well-preserved rock art

### Did You Know?

Spring through fall, park rangers present talks on the unique geology of the canyons.

in North America on display. The works at the so-called Great Gallery date back as early as 9000–7000 BCE and comprise both pictographs (paintings of more than one color decorated onto sandstone surfaces) and petroglyphs (images chiseled and pecked onto rock surfaces). The vast panel features around 80 life-sized figures depicted in shades of red, white, and brown. The

human figures are accompanied by depictions of a range of animals, birds, and other more abstract objects. Ethnographers have long puzzled over the intention behind these works. Some believe the murals were created for purposes such as hunting rituals or to aid shamanistic magic, while others hold that the works were a form of highly skilled recreation. Either way, they are a visually stunning reminder of humans past.

## The Green and Colorado rivers

The Colorado River is a major waterway running through the western U.S. It flows for 1,450 miles (2,300 km) passing through five states, with the Green River its primary tributary. The watershed of

the Green River is known as the Green River Basin, and the river runs from the Wind River Mountains in Wyoming and finally meets the Colorado in Canyonlands. The Colorado River and its tributaries are popular places for boat trips, either by canoe on packrafting trips or exhilarating whitewater rafting expeditions. Cataract Canyon is one of the most popular spots, with around 15 miles (20 km) of rapids to negotiate, ranging in difficulty up to the very hardest waters. Note that the canyon is a particularly hazardous and fast-flowing section of the Colorado River and is subject to extreme water level fluctuations, meaning all sections can pose a challenge. Check online or at the visitor center before taking to the

↑ Canoeing down the Colorado River in summer

waters in this area. You must have a river permit for all trips through Cataract Canyon. Make a trip to the visitor centers in either the Needles, Islands in the Sky, or the Hans Flat Ranger Station for more information.

# STAY

There are only two designated camp-grounds, one in the Needles area (single and group sites) and one in Island in the Sky. Lodgings can be found in nearby towns including Moab, Monticello, and Hanksville.

**Whispering Sands**
Centrally located for easy access to Utah's national parks, this motel offers simple, homely rooms.
🏠 Moab
🌐 dukesslickrock.com

**Muddy Creek Mining Company**
Comfy log cabins near the parks, a short walk from local amenities.
🏠 Hanksville
🌐 muddycreekmining company.com

← Surveying the scene from the raised mesa near Green River

# EXPLORING CANYONLANDS

Canyonlands National Park is located in southeastern Utah near the town of Moab. The park's more than 330,000 acres (130,000 ha) are divided into three regions: the Needles, Island in the Sky, and the Maze, each offering superb back-country hiking and incredible views.

0 kilometers    6

0 miles    6

N

*Horseshoe Canyon*

**Horseshoe Canyon** *has a large display of rock art dating back around 9,000 years.*

**The Maze** *overlook is the starting point for a strenuous trail in the least-frequented area of the park.*

*WHITE RIM RO*

*Hans Flat 3 miles(5 km)*

*Maze Over*

T H E
M A Z E

*Colorado River*

*Cate Can*

**Cataract Canyon** *is a long canyon of the Colorado River with fast-flowing rapids.*

↑ Pictographs found on the Great Gallery in Horseshoe Canyon

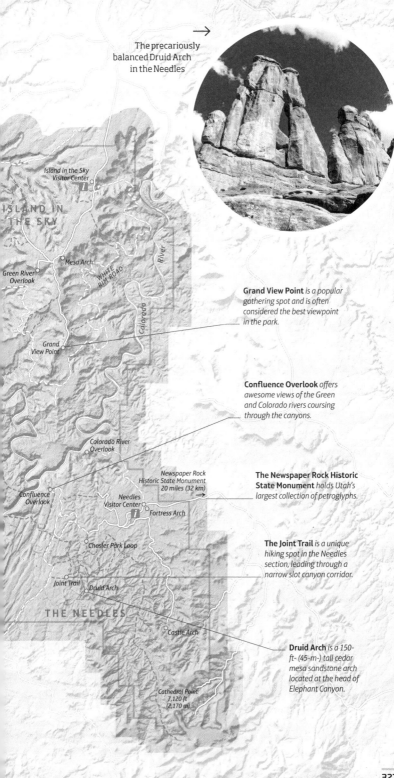

The precariously balanced Druid Arch in the Needles

**Island in the Sky Visitor Center**

**ISLAND IN THE SKY**

Mesa Arch

Green River Overlook

WHITE RIM ROAD

Colorado River

River

Grand View Point

**Grand View Point** *is a popular gathering spot and is often considered the best viewpoint in the park.*

Colorado River Overlook

**Confluence Overlook** *offers awesome views of the Green and Colorado rivers coursing through the canyons.*

Confluence Overlook

Newspaper Rock Historic State Monument 20 miles (32 km)

Needles Visitor Center

Fortress Arch

**The Newspaper Rock Historic State Monument** *holds Utah's largest collection of petroglyphs.*

Chesler Park Loop

**The Joint Trail** *is a unique hiking spot in the Needles section, leading through a narrow slot canyon corridor.*

Joint Trail

Druid Arch

**THE NEEDLES**

Castle Arch

**Druid Arch** *is a 150-ft- (45-m-) tall cedar mesa sandstone arch located at the head of Elephant Canyon.*

Cathedral Point 7,120 ft (2,170 m)

The beautiful heights of Balcony House cliff dwelling ↑

# MESA VERDE

📍 Colorado 🚗 $30 per vehicle, valid for seven days ($20 late
Oct-Apr) 🌐 nps.gov/meve

There's no better place to discover the 750-year history of the
Ancestral Puebloan peoples than Mesa Verde. More than 4,000
archeological sites are spread across the park's cliffs – including
beautifully preserved pueblos, towers, and agricultural structures –
yielding insights into one of North America's oldest cultures. But
the park is famed for more than its human history: this protected
wilderness provides a wildly diverse ecosystem, home to bobcats,
coyotes, owls, snakes, and rare wildflowers.

The Indigenous Ancestral
Puebloan people (also known
by their Navajo name, the
Anasazi) dwelt within the
Mesa Verde (Spanish for
"green table") region between
550 and 1300 CE, building
increasingly elaborate cliff
dwellings across the mesa
tops. The Puebloans, whose
descendants include the
Acoma, Hopi, and Zuni people,
were expert builders, and
Mesa Verde is their master-
piece. At once fertile and
defensible, the flat-topped
mountain provided a perfect
location for these communities to pivot from nomadic
hunting and gathering to
agriculture. For around 750
years, the Ancestral
Puebloans honed their construction skills and built a
series of dwellings that were
abruptly abandoned over just
two generations.

The structures were largely
forgotten until their re-
discovery by white settlers
in the late 1800s. Thieves
began looting the dwellings,
leading to the establishment
of the national park in 1906.
Mesa Verde is the only
national park dedicated to
protecting humanmade works.

The archeological sites
are fascinating, with many
more still to be uncovered,
and there is an array of
archeological mysteries and
conundrums surrounding the
park's complex structures.

### GETTING AROUND

Roughly a seven-hour
drive from Denver,
Mesa Verde National
Park is 35 miles (56 km)
west of Durango,
Colorado, on U.S. Hwy.
160. The closest towns
to the park are Mancos,
8 miles (13 km) east of
the park on U.S. Hwy.
160, and Cortez, 10
miles (16 km) to the
west. Mesa Top Ruins
Rd. enters the park's
north side from the
highway, passing the
campground, several
striking overlooks, and
Far View Lodge en
route to Chapin Mesa.
At Chapin Mesa, the
Cliff Palace Loop, a
6-mile (10-km) drive,
has overlooks of cliff
dwellings and trail
access, and the 6-mile
(10-km) Mesa Top Loop
Rd. has 12 stops with
short walks to some of
the best archeological
sites. Wetherill Mesa
Rd. ends at an infor-
mation kiosk where
you can catch a tram to
the park's archeological
sites in summer or hike
out from numerous
trailheads year-round.

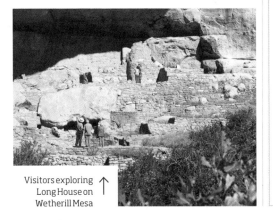

Visitors exploring
Long House on
Wetherill Mesa ↑

→
The site of Cliff Palace, the largest cliff dwelling in the U.S.

# EAT

There are four places to eat in the park, and Mancos and Cortez have a variety of restaurants.

### Metate Room
Continental dishes with a Southwestern twist, served in a spot with sweeping park views.

🏠 Far View Lodge
🅦 visitmesaverde/
dining.com

$$$ $$ $$

### Far View Terrace Café
Breakfast buffet or à la carte dishes, along with soups and sandwiches.

🏠 Far View Lodge
🅦 visitmesaverde/
dining.com

$$$ $$ $$

### Spruce Tree Terrace Café
Cafeteria-style café serving comforting American favorites.

🏠 Wetherill Mesa
☎ (970) 529 4465

$$$ $$ $$

## Exploring the park

Many visitors base themselves in the town of Cortez, an hour's drive from the park, which offers an array of accommodations and dining options. The visitor center is located near the park entrance on Hwy. 160. The Mesa Verde Museum, park headquarters, and Spruce Tree House are 21 miles (34 km) from the park entrance. Note that the road into the park is a winding mountain trail which can be treacherous even in seemingly fair conditions; watch for wildlife and for rocks that may have fallen onto the road. The drive is scenic, with a number of overlooks and panoramas that provide great views.

From Mesa Verde visitor center, you can pick up maps and brochures and purchase tickets for the park's many guided tours (only two of Mesa Verde's cliff sites are open for self-guided tours). The Cliff Palace is particularly popular so visitors are advised to book early to avoid missing out on a tour.

From the visitor center, you can also browse the Chapin Mesa Archeological Museum, which shows a short film on Ancestral Puebloan culture and has numerous exhibits. To get a brief overview of the park's landscapes, the Mesa Top Loop Road is a 6-mile (10-km) loop that offers an excellent overview of the entire park.

## Cliff tours

The Ancestral Puebloans used three primary construction materials – sandstone, mortar, and wooden beams –

to build the cliff dwellings. They used flat stones from nearby riverbeds to shape sandstone blocks, then cemented them in place with mortar made from soil, water, and ash. Finally, workers would use pebbles to fill gaps in the mortar and stabilize the walls. The method has proven especially resilient over the centuries, and archeologists today

←

One of the namesake petroglyphs along the Petroglyph Point Loop

puzzle over the strength required to transport these blocks high into the cliffs. The largest cliff dwelling in North America, Cliff Palace is open to visitors via 60-minute guided tours from mid-May to late October. The tour takes you through the structure that once housed a small population of about 100 people. Cliff Palace is significantly bigger than most cliff dwellings, with 150 rooms and 23 circular *kivas*, partly or wholly underground rooms used in religious rites. As most of the cliff dwellings in the park have five or fewer rooms and a lower percentage of *kivas*, archeologists believe Cliff Palace had important ceremonial and administrative uses. The park service restored the tower, which was left to fall into ruins in the 1800s. The tour involves about 100 ft (30 m) of elevation change on stairs and ladders while walking about 0.25 miles (0.4 km).

Just east of Cliff Palace, Balcony House is likewise only accessible via a guided tour from late May to late October. It's not for everyone: the tour involves scaling several tall ladders and crawling through a narrow tunnel to get in and out of the two-story dwelling, which is perched about 700 ft (213 m) above the canyon floor. Aside from the adventure of getting around, the tour demonstrates how the Ancestral Puebloans' construction methods evolved over time. The 38-room structure was once home to a group of about 30 people.

 IF YOU HAVE
**A day**

Tour the incredible Cliff Palace dwelling. Once finished, hike the Spruce Canyon Trail to look for wildlife, including coyote.

Rangers also offer guided tours of Square Tower House in the park's backcountry from early June to late October. The difficult 1-mile (1.6-km) round-trip route navigates a 20-ft (6-m) ladder and rough trails to the tallest standing structure, Square Tower House. Once part of an even larger complex, the four-story, 27-ft (8-m) house has been stabilized by archeologists, and includes painted murals and rock art. From the overlook on Mesa Top Loop, you can see original roof beams and intact plastered walls.

On Wetherill Mesa, Long House is open to visitors, with two-hour guided tours that

**A tour of Balcony House, once home to about 30 people, demonstrates how the Ancient Puebloans' construction methods evolved over time.**

involve hiking about 2 miles (3.5 km), and climbing two 15-ft (4.6-m) ladders. The structure may once have been home to up to 175 people, with architectural studies suggesting it was likely a gathering place where people from all over the mesa held community events. The large plaza in the center of the site has been of particular archeological interest. It is considered the second-largest dwelling in the park.

Also on Wetherill Mesa, you can take the tram from the kiosk nearby or bicycle or hike the 5-mile (8-km) Long House Loop to Badger House Community. This easy 2.4-mile (3.9-km) round trip has interpretive signage detailing the history of several sites dating from Basketmaker culture (c. 600 CE) as well as Ancestral Puebloan

dwellings. Also on Wetherill Mesa is the moderate 0.8-mile (1.3-km) trail to Step House, with 27 rooms and three *kivas* that date to the 1200s. The site also includes older pit houses from the Basketmaker era.

Wetherill Mesa was closed in 2023 in order to rebuild facilities damaged by recent wildfires; work is ongoing and the closure is expected to extend into the 2024 season.

## Hiking

Because most visitors come here for the human history and ancient architecture, the park's trails are relatively crowd-free. While many of these trails are flat and gentle, the park's elevation is around 7,000 ft (2,134 m), resulting in thinner air which can cause symptoms of altitude sickness.

---

IF YOU HAVE
**A weekend**

Head to less-visited Wetherill Mesa to tour Long House, before hiking the park's gentle trails. The following day, hike to Step House and Badger House.

---

Overlooking Soda Canyon from atop the park's high mesa ↑

↑ A narrow gap between canyon walls in Mesa Verde

Spruce Canyon Trail takes you on a moderate 2.4-mile (3.9-km) round trip that descends from the Spruce Tree House (closed to the public) into a tributary of Spruce Canyon. The same trailhead also accesses the moderate 2.4-mile (3.9-km) Petroglyph Point Loop that will take you to some striking rock art in a side canyon and back up to the rim. Closer to the park entrance, Point Lookout Trail takes you on a 2.2-mile (3.5-km) round trip, with superb panoramas of the Montezuma Valley stretching below.

## Camping

With more than 350 individual campsites, Morefield Campground is one of the largest in any national park. Located near the entrance on the north side of the park, it has showers and an amphitheater. Reservations are recommended, as though the campground is large, it can get busy in the summer. Backcountry camping is not allowed in Mesa Verde.

## Nearby Ancestral Puebloan sites

Though the sites within the park are incredible, areas beyond the park's borders are home to numerous other examples of Ancient Puebloan culture.

Straddling the Colorado-Utah border, Hovenweep National Monument is located 50 miles (80 km) west of Mesa Verde. There are six separate sites and a number of impressive towers here; the Square Tower Group on the Utah side has the best-preserved Puebloan dwellings in the area.

Canyon of the Ancients National Monument protects several archeological sites in southwestern Colorado, including the roughly 1,000-year-old Lowry Pueblo, located 29 miles (47 km) west of Cortez, which has the remains of a massive *kiva*, one of the largest ever unearthed. The Canyon of the Ancients Visitor Center and Museum in the town of Dolores, 12 miles (19 km) north of Cortez, is the best place to start exploring the monument.

Just west of Mesa Verde on the land of the Ute Mountain Ute peoples, Ute Mountain Tribal Park protects a number of cliff dwellings that rival the complexity of those in Mesa Verde. The park can be accessed only on guided tours that begin at the Ute Mountain Visitor Center and Museum in Towaoc, about 15 miles (24 km) south of Cortez.

# STAY

The park's only lodging, Far View Lodge is between the park entrance and Cliff Palace. There is also a range of accomodations in Mancos and Cortez.

**Far View Lodge**
The only lodge in the heart of the park, this spot offers modern rooms with great views.
⌂ Mesa Verde
[W] visitmesaverde.com
$

**Mesa Verde Motel**
Restored roadside motel with a boutique feel, decorated with quirky art.
⌂ Mancos
[W] mesaverdemotel.com
$$

**Retro Inn at Mesa Verde**
Rooms and suites with a retro aesthetic but reliably modern amenities.
⌂ Cortez
[W] retroinnmesaverde.com
$$

EXPERIENCE The Southwest

# EXPLORING MESA VERDE

Mesa Verde National Park is in Montezuma County, southwest Colorado, with its entrance located between the towns of Cortez and Mancos. The park's incredible archeological features and vast cliff dwellings are spread across over 52,000 acres (21,000 ha).

## Did You Know?

The area's high cliff dwellings provided excellent protection against invading groups.

0 kilometers 3
0 miles 3

N

**Step House** has ruins originally built by two separate cultures 600 years apart: the Basketmakers (c. 600 CE) and the Ancestral Puebloans (c. 1200 CE).

Accessible by trail, the **Badger House Community** includes four separate archeological sites that preserve structures from different eras.

Nearly as large as Cliff Palace with around 150 rooms, **Long House** is considered the second-largest cliff dwelling at Mesa Verde.

Set in a deep alcove, **Spruce Tree House** is one of the most pristine cliff dwellings in the park.

With 150 rooms over 4 levels, **Cliff Palace** is not only the largest cliff dwelling in the park, it is the largest one in North America.

Representative of a mid-sized Ancestral Puebloan dwelling, **Balcony House** probably housed about 30 people. It's accessible by a guided tour.

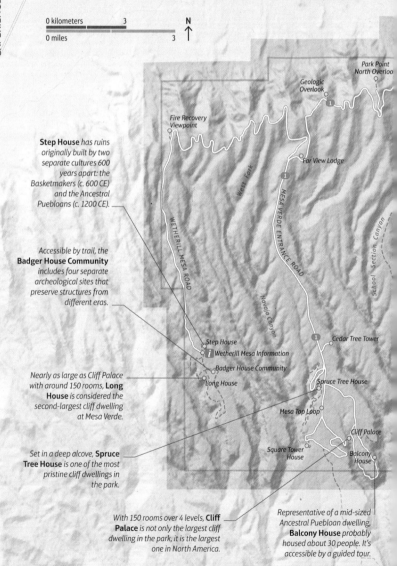

Park Point North Overloo

Geologic Overlook

Fire Recovery Viewpoint

Far View Lodge

West Fork

WETHERILL MESA ROAD

MESA VERDE ENTRANCE ROAD

School Section Canyon

Navajo Canyon

Step House
Wetherill Mesa Information
Badger House Community
Long House

Cedar Tree Tower

Spruce Tree House

Mesa Top Loop

Cliff Palace

Square Tower House

Balcony House

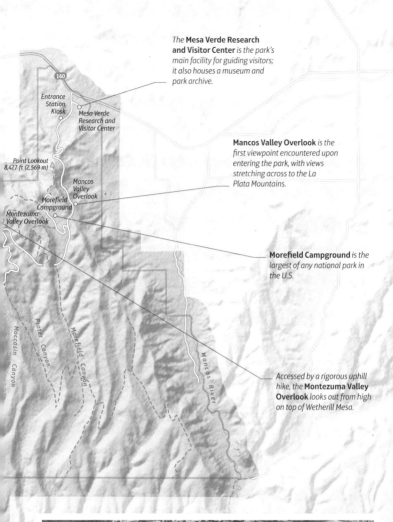

The **Mesa Verde Research and Visitor Center** *is the park's main facility for guiding visitors; it also houses a museum and park archive.*

160

*Entrance Station Kiosk*

*Mesa Verde Research and Visitor Center*

*Point Lookout 8,427 ft (2,569 m)*

*Mancos Valley Overlook*

*Morefield Campground*

*Montezuma Valley Overlook*

*Moccasin Canyon*

*Prater Canyon*

*Morefield Canyon*

*Mancos River*

**Mancos Valley Overlook** *is the first viewpoint encountered upon entering the park, with views stretching across to the La Plata Mountains.*

**Morefield Campground** *is the largest of any national park in the U.S.*

*Accessed by a rigorous uphill hike, the* **Montezuma Valley Overlook** *looks out from high on top of Wetherill Mesa.*

↑ Climbing a ladder to reach the Long House cliff dwelling

# WHITE SANDS

📍 New Mexico  🚗 $25 per vehicle, valid for seven days  🌐 nps.gov/whsa

The spectacular White Sands is formed of glistening gypsum sand dunes rising from the Tularosa Basin in southern-central New Mexico. This is the largest gypsum dune field in the world, covering 145,000 acres (59,000 ha) of the vast Chihuahuan Desert. The effect of the landscape is truly dazzling, with the glowing sand forming wave-like drifts as it catches the wind, and an assortment of hardy plants and animals punctuating the otherwise uniform expanse.

---

**IF YOU HAVE**
**A day**

Take a scenic tour of Dunes Drive, which leads to lookout points and trailheads along the base of expansive rolling sand dunes.

---

White Sands is known for its pure white gypsum sands, formed of decomposing limestone. Gypsum is a water-soluble mineral, rarely found in the form of sand due to its propensity to quickly evaporate. These rolling dunes are a rare exception, with the landscape uniquely situated to allow gypsum to form. With no drainage outlet to the sea, the sediment washed by the rain into the basin becomes trapped. As the rain evaporates, dry lakes form, and strong winds blow the gypsum up into the vast fields of rippling dunes the area is now famed for.

←

A hiker traversing the undulating white sand dunes

Today, White Sands is a favorite for landscape and nature photographers seeking serene shots of the desert succulents and yucca plants that bloom from May through June, spotting the pure white landscape.

In 2021, a scientific discovery made in the park rewrote a chapter of the continent's history. Sixty-one fossilized human footprints were found in the Tularosa Basin beside an ancient lakebed. The find lengthened the timeframe of human existence in North America: it was previously thought that humans arrived on the continent around 16,000 years ago, but the footprints date back 23,000 years. Visits to the research area are not possible, but you can learn more about the findings from ever helpful park rangers in the visitor center.

## Exploring the park

White Sands is nestled in the Tularosa Basin between the Sacramento and San Andres Mountain ranges in the Chihuahuan Desert. The park protects around 145,000 acres (59,000 ha) of white gypsum sand dunes, surrounded on all sides by the White Sands Missile Range. In the southwest corner of the park is Lake Lucero, accessed by a trail passing abstract gullies. Most visitors explore by driving Dunes Drive.

### GETTING AROUND

Texas's El Paso airport is located 85 miles (136 km) from the visitor center which can be reached from U.S. Hwy. 70. You can rent cars there or in the cities nearest the park: Alamogordo, 15 miles (24 km) away, and Las Cruces, 54 miles (86 km) away. Dunes Drive is the only road through the park; the only other way to enter is on foot, walking directly onto the dunes and wandering park trails. White Sands doesn't offer public transportation. There is one sizable parking lot at the front entrance that accommodates RVs and travel trailers as well as buses. There is a second parking area at the end of Dunes Drive.

### White Sand visitor center

Begin your experience at White Sands at the historic visitor center. You can't get into the park without traveling right by it, so a stop there is easy enough.

The complex in which the center sits was completed in 1938 and was constructed in Spanish Pueblo-style adobe architecture using local materials. Today, it offers a park store, daily programs, a small museum, and a native plant garden outside the center's back doors. From here, you can join guided tours, get information from park rangers, and pick up Junior Ranger books.

### Dunes Drive

This popular 8-mile (12-km) scenic loop drive starts at the visitor center and travels alongside the gypsum dune fields. While the drive is relatively short, allow plenty of time to explore: along the route you can learn about natural features and cultural history at wayside exhibits, and capture photographs.

Beyond the roadway, desert scrublands give way to billowing heaps of snow-like sand, commonly under a rich blue sky and puffy white clouds. The first half of the road is paved and the second half is hard-packed sand which can be traversed by cars, motorcycles, RVs and buses, and bicycles. This is the only area of the park where bikes are allowed and there is little (if any) shoulder, so plan on sharing the roadway with other travelers. There is sand maintenance throughout the year and the drive is swept by road-plows on a daily basis, clearing the road of sand blown in by strong desert winds.

### Sand sledding

If you are looking for an exhilarating adventure, wax up a sandboard or plastic saucer purchased from the visitor center and sled down the powdery white dunes. This activity is available all year long in designated areas along Dunes Drive, as long as you are careful not to disturb sensitive vegetation. There are simple techniques you can learn online or from park rangers that can help you have a safe adventure without injury. One of the great things about this activity is that sledding doesn't damage the ever-moving landscape so you can fly across the gypsum to your heart's content.

### Wildlife tracking

While many of the park's wild animals are nocturnal and hard to spot, they leave compelling tracks across the white sands. Discovering and learning about wild animal tracks is a great activity when

---

There are no restaurants or hotels in the park; head to Alamogordo or Las Cruces.

# EAT

### CJ's Si Señor
A classic Mexican eatery offering tacos and enchiladas.

🏠 Alamogordo
🌐 chisosmountain lodge.com

$$$

---

### Asian Garden
This locally popular spot offers an extensive menu of Thai staples.

🏠 Alamogordo
🌐 asiangarden.com

$$$

# STAY

### The Classic Desert Aire
Hotel offering a range of suites and a pool.

🏠 Alamogordo
🌐 theclassic desertairehotel.com

$$$

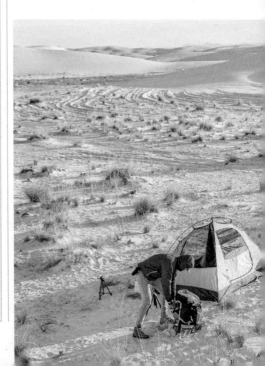

**IF YOU HAVE**
**A weekend**

Begin with a walk around the Interdune Boardwalk before tackling the Alkali Flat Trail. Stay in Alamogordo, before returning to cruise Dunes Drive.

exploring the park. Early in the mornings, look out for coyote, desert cottontail, or porcupine prints spread across the dune fields.

Spotting birds is unlikely in the heart of the dunes, but around the peripheral scrubland you may spot barn swallows in spring, black-chinned humming-birds, and even great horned owls and barn owls.

### Hiking

There are five established trails in the park's front-country on sandy slopes, leveled ground, and an elevated boardwalk. The Interdune Boardwalk is accessible along a wooden platform where you can

↑ Sledding down the sand dunes, a popular family activity in the park

see vegetation and dunes before ending at a view-point that looks onto the Sacramento Mountains in the distance. The 0.5-mile (800-m) Playa Trail is easy and short, but the route still reveals desert wildflowers and vegetation. The 1-mile (0.5-km) loop on the Dunes Life Nature Trail is a family favorite; look out for yucca sprouting on the horizon.

The 5-mile (8-km) Alkali Flat Trail leads across the dune fields for a more strenuous adventure – despite the name, the trail features steep climbs.

Note that if the temp-erature is above 85°F (29°C), the park service recommends that you do not begin a hike. Trails are marked with colors and symbols to help you orient your location.

### White Sands Missile Range

The White Sands Missile Range surrounds the park. The site was chosen by J. Robert Oppenheimer for his nuclear bomb tests in 1944; today, missile tests are still conducted throughout the year which may disrupt your time there. When testing occurs, Dunes Drive and other areas of the park close as a precautionary measure, with closures lasting for several hours. The visitor center is equipped for these closures and offers activities.

←

Preparing to camp in the backcountry of White Sands

# EXPLORING WHITE SANDS

White Sands National Park is found in southern New Mexico, around 15 miles (24 km) southwest of the city of Alamogordo. The park's roughly 145,000 acres (60,000 ha) are surrounded on all sides by the vast White Sands Missile Range.

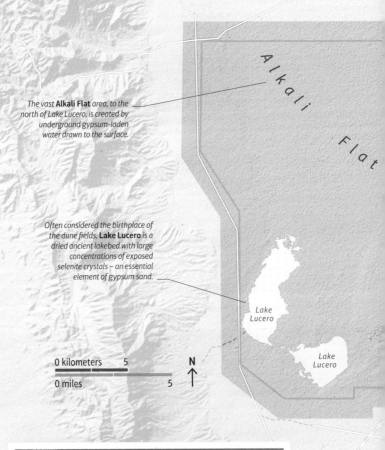

*The vast* **Alkali Flat** *area, to the north of Lake Lucero, is created by underground gypsum-laden water drawn to the surface.*

A l k a l i   F l a t

*Often considered the birthplace of the dune fields,* **Lake Lucero** *is a dried ancient lakebed with large concentrations of exposed selenite crystals – an essential element of gypsum sand.*

Lake Lucero

Lake Lucero

0 kilometers 5
0 miles 5

N ↑

← Rangers leading a tour through the sand to the banks of Lake Lucero

The **Alkali Flat Trail** is a strenuous hiking route heading into the dunes toward the San Andres Mountain range. The salt-infused area was once home to an ancient lake.

The **Interdune Boardwalk** is a great place for group hiking; it's accessible to strollers and wheelchairs, and reveals dunes and vegetation across the elevated boardwalk.

The **Playa Trail** travels along a shallow lakebed that is most often dry but occasionally fills with rainwater during summer monsoon season. The water feature is a draw for animals and sustains plantlife throughout the year.

**Dunes Drive** starts after the national park entrance gate off of U.S. Hwy. 70. It is the only established road in the park and the starting point for your White Sands adventure.

Alkali Flat Trail

Amphitheater

Playa Trail

DUNES DRIVE

Interdune Boardwalk

Dune Life Nature Trail

70

Visitor Center

**Dune Life Nature Trail** is a great place to look for animals that are attracted to the convergence of desert scrubland and gypsum sand.

70

White Sands Missile Range
35 miles (56 km)

The **White Sands Missile Range Museum,** located outside and east of the park, displays missiles tested on the range and is an interesting stop for history buffs.

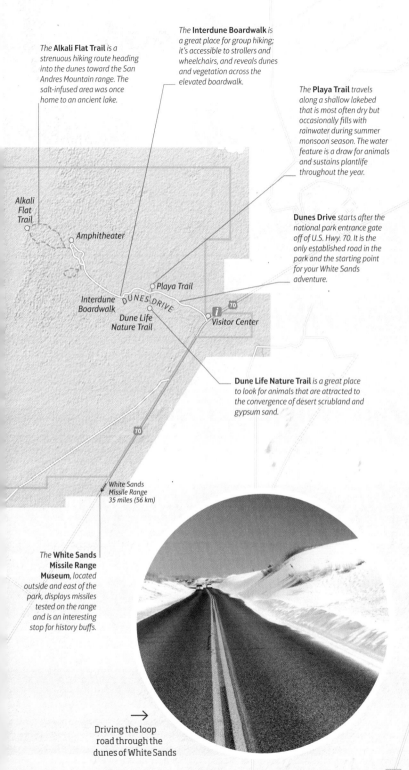

→
Driving the loop road through the dunes of White Sands

The paved route through the Big Room, the largest cave in North America ↑

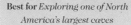
# CARLSBAD CAVERNS

⚲ New Mexico 🚗 $15 per person; reservations required for Carlsbad Cavern Ⓦ nps.gov/cave

Located in the heart of the Chihuahuan Desert, Carlsbad Caverns protects one of the largest cave systems on the planet. There are more than 100 known caves roughly carved out of limestone below the peaks of the Guadalupe Mountains, including the park's namesake cavern. Most striking of all, perhaps, is the huge chamber known as the Big Room, which at nearly 4,000 ft (1,220 m) long and 255 ft (78 m) high is the largest single cave in North America.

Pictographs near Carlsbad Cavern's Natural Entrance imply that Indigenous peoples once visited the caves. But this magical world remained largely hidden until Jim White, a 16-year-old cowboy, rediscovered the caves in 1898 while tending cattle. Using only a kerosene lantern and homemade ladder, he explored the caverns over several years and gave many of the formations their whimsical names. Ever since, visitors have marveled at White's "sticky uppers" (stalagmites) and "hangy downers" (stalactites), the Witch's Finger, Bottomless Pit, and Rock of Ages.

The caves are also known for their prodigious bat populations. From spring to fall at sunset, visitors take in the spectacle of hundreds of thousands of Mexican free-tailed bats taking flight to hunt the night skies.

## Exploring the park

With only the Carlsbad Caverns Highway leading through the park, exploring

↑ Overlooking the vast expanse of Rattlesnake Canyon just after sunset

by car is simple. This 7-mile (11-km) route heads through the Chihuahuan Desert, offering special views of the desert, canyons, and valleys, before arriving at the visitor center. From here, you can book guided tours through the caves and learn more about their geology and the fascinating history of their exploration.

Above ground, more than 50 miles (80 km) of trails, including the Chihuahuan Desert Nature Trail, lead through the canyons.

→

Swarms of Mexican free-tailed bats exiting the caves at nightfall

# EAT

There are two basic eateries in the park, and more in Carlsbad.

### Underground Lunch Room

Infamous snack bar located 750 ft (230 m) below ground.

Carlsbad Cavern 🌐carlsbadcaverns tradingco.com

$\text{\textcircled{\$}}\text{\textcircled{\$}}\text{\textcircled{\$}}$

### Carlsbad Caverns Trading Company

Southwestern specialties, grab-and-go sandwiches, and salads.

Visitor Center 🌐carlsbadcaverns tradingco.com

$\text{\textcircled{\$}}\text{\textcircled{\$}}\text{\textcircled{\$}}$

### The Flume

American and Mexican dishes, served all day.

Carlsbad 🌐stevens inncarlsbad.com

$\text{\textcircled{\$}}\text{\textcircled{\$}}\text{\textcircled{\$}}$

# STAY

The closest place to stay is in Whites City or nearby Van Horn.

### Hotel El Capitan

Historic hotel with Mission architecture.

Van Horn 🌐thehotel elcapitan.com

$\text{\textcircled{\$}}\text{\textcircled{\$}}\text{\textcircled{\$}}$

↑ A cluster of flowering barrel cacti, endemic to the Chihuahuan Desert

## Cave tours

Of 120 known caves in the park, just two are currently open for visitors to tour: Carlsbad Cavern (p346) and Slaughter Canyon Cave.

In Carlsbad Cavern, the Big Room and Natural Entrance are open to self-guided tours; pick up audio guides at the visitor center. You can either take the elevator directly to the well-lit Big Room, or follow the Natural Entrance Trail. This moderate but steep route descends 750 ft (229 m), passing such formations as the Boneyard, Devil's Den, and Iceberg Rock. It connects to the Big Room Trail, a relatively flat, 1.25-mile (2-km) pathway leading to the Big Room, the largest under-ground cave chamber in the country, with such massive rock formations as the Rock of Ages and the excellent Twin Domes.

Several ranger-led tours are also available: the King's Palace Tour takes you to the deepest part of the cave open to the public, while more strenuous tours run to other areas of Carlsbad Cavern as well as other caves for the more intrepid spelunkers.

## Above ground

The park's great plethora of subterranean wonders means you might just get the surface hiking trails all to yourself. An easy 1-mile (1.6-km) loop that starts at the visitor center, the Nature Trail offers a primer on desert ecology, but if you want to delve deeper into the dazzling backcountry, try the moderate 6-mile (9.7-km) round trip on the Rattlesnake Canyon Trail. Backpackers favor the Guadalupe Ridge Trail, which covers 100 miles (160 km) through Carlsbad Caverns National Park and Guadalupe Mountains National Park (p348). Over 20 miles (32 km) of this epic trail is within the borders of Carlsbad Caverns, showcasing a wide array of the park's greatest features.

> 🕐 IF YOU HAVE
> **A day**
>
> Take the Natural Entrance Trail and explore the geological wonders in the caves. Upon returning above ground, hike Rattle-snake Canyon to see the best of the park's landscapes, before watching the bats take flight at sunset.

## Wildlife watching

Located in front of Natural Entrance, Bat Flight Amphitheater is the best place to see hundreds of thousands of Mexican free-tailed bats make their nightly exodus from Carlsbad Cavern. The free Bat Flight Program, which runs from late May through to early October, sees a ranger talk about bat behavior and ecology prior to their flight in the evening. No reservations are required for this program. The bats typically return to the cave between 4–6am.

### GETTING AROUND

Carlsbad Caverns National Park is located 30 miles (48 km) southwest of the city of Carlsbad, New Mexico, via U.S. Hwy. 62/180. El Paso, Texas, located 150 miles (241 km) east, is the nearest major city. From U.S. Hwy. 62/180, Carlsbad Caverns Hwy. (N.M. Hwy. 7) takes you directly to the visitor center, from which you can gain direct access to the caves. You can access trails on Reef Top Cir. and experience the broader Chihuahuan Desert on the unpaved Walnut Canyon Dr.; the latter is permanently closed to RVs and trailers to prevent visitors staying overnight (which is forbidden throughout the park). Visitors often combine their trip to Carlsbad Caverns with a visit to the nearby Guadalupe Mountains National Park (p348), 35 miles (56 km) southwest of Carlsbad Caverns on U.S. Hwy. 62/180.

# EXPLORING CARLSBAD CAVERNS

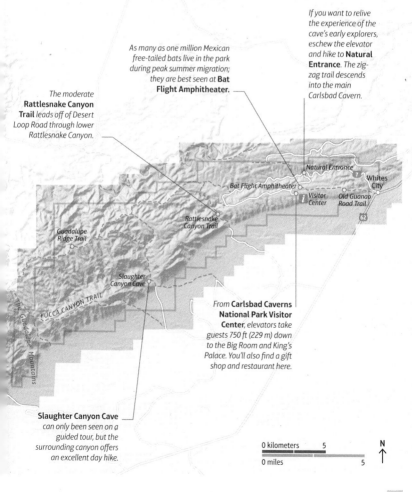

If you want to relive the experience of the cave's early explorers, eschew the elevator and hike to **Natural Entrance**. The zig-zag trail descends into the main Carlsbad Cavern.

As many as one million Mexican free-tailed bats live in the park during peak summer migration; they are best seen at **Bat Flight Amphitheater.**

The moderate **Rattlesnake Canyon Trail** leads off of Desert Loop Road through lower Rattlesnake Canyon.

From **Carlsbad Caverns National Park Visitor Center**, elevators take guests 750 ft (229 m) down to the Big Room and King's Palace. You'll also find a gift shop and restaurant here.

**Slaughter Canyon Cave** can only been seen on a guided tour, but the surrounding canyon offers an excellent day hike.

Natural Entrance

Whites City

Bat Flight Amphitheater

Visitor Center

Old Guanao Road Trail

62

Rattlesnake Canyon Trail

Guadalupe Ridge Trail

Slaughter Canyon Cave

YUCCA CANYON TRAIL

The Guadalupe Mountains

0 kilometers 5

0 miles 5

N

## GOING UNDERGROUND

The caves of Carlsbad Caverns began forming more than 200 million years ago when rainwater seeped through limestone in the Guadalupe Mountains. Water from below created sulfuric acid, accelerating the creation of the caverns; when the water dripped into the hollows, it slowly fashioned rock formations such as stalactites and stalagmites. The process has created some of the deepest and largest caverns in North America.

Cross section of Carlsbad Caverns, showing trails through the main caves ↓

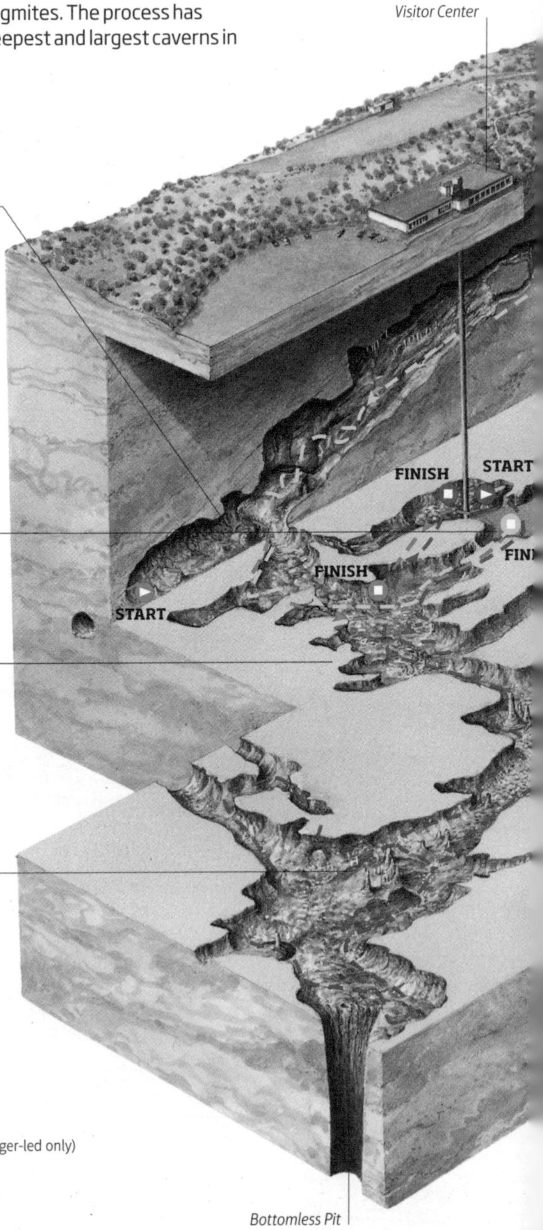

*Visitor Center*

*King's Palace Tour takes in the deepest cave open to the public, 830 ft (250 m) below ground.*

*A paved section of the cavern is home to a popular underground snack bar, and restrooms.*

*The Boneyard is a complex maze of dissolved limestone rock.*

*A self-guided tour takes in the 14-acre (5.6-ha) Big Room and passes features such as the Bottomless Pit.*

FINISH  START

START  FINI

FINISH

START

### Key
— Big Room Trail
— King's Palace Tour (ranger-led only)
— Natural Entrance Trail

*Bottomless Pit*

*Most summer evenings at dusk, clouds of free-tailed bats emerge from the Bat Cave to cross the desert in search of food.*

RT

## SPELEOTHEMS

Known as speleothems, the spectacular cave formations found in Carlsbad Caverns were created drop by drop as rain filtered through the limestone. As the water evaporated, it left deposits of crystallized calcite. Slow drips leave ceiling deposits, making stalactites, soda straws, and drapery formations. Faster drips hit the floor and build upward, as stalagmites, flowstone, and totem pole formations. The process has happened over the past million years or so though few speleothems today are actively growing.

*Rock of Ages*

*The small Doll's Theater cave is named for its size and is filled with fine, luminous soda-straw formations.*

→

The atmospheric zig-zag path leading to the entrance of Carlsbad Caverns

Best for *Mountain walks and striking geological features*

# GUADALUPE MOUNTAINS

📍 Texas 🎫 $10 per person, valid for seven days
🌐 nps.gov/gumo

Long before the arid Chihuahuan Desert formed, a vast inland sea covered this corner of West Texas. The sea left behind a fossilized reef buried in sediment until tectonic forces forced it up in the startling form of the Guadalupe Mountains. The national park designated around these peaks is now a geological wonder, with fossilized sponge reef rising through ponderosa pine forests to reach Guadalupe Peak, the highest point in Texas.

One of the least-visited parks, Guadalupe Mountains National Park rewards visitors with epic mountain views, untouched wilderness, and plenty of solitude on its numerous hiking trails. The park's relative lack of visitors makes for a quieter experience than some of the bigger names nearby, with a welcome lack of traffic on the roads.

The escarpment at the heart of the park is the exposed portion of a huge fossilized reef that runs for 350 miles (563 km) through Texas and New Mexico; the same ancient limestone is found underground in nearby Carlsbad Caverns National Park (*p342*). The imposing and iconic El Capitan is the reef's southernmost feature. The Capitan is a massive, fine-grained limestone reef that formed from the slow accumulation of algae, sponges, and

**IF YOU HAVE A day**

Ascend Guadalupe Peak to enjoy views from the peak, and then hike to one of the park's few green oases on the Smith Spring Loop.

other small animals' skeletons over millions of years.

To the north of the park, the 8,751-ft (2,667-m) Guadalupe Peak is the highest point in Texas. Forested McKittrick Canyon, meanwhile, offers a shaded break from the rugged desert wilderness that surrounds the mountain range; the canyon is especially beautiful when draped in fall colors.

## Exploring the park

Guadalupe Mountains National Park is found in West Texas. When planning your visit, note that there are no gas stations for 35 miles (56 km) in any direction.

If you're planning a visit in winter, be aware temperatures can vary greatly, particularly at higher elevations. Some of the park's best views can also be obscured by thick fog. Spring and fall are arguably the best seasons to visit the park, when temperatures are mild and there is a lower chance of rain or snow.

> **The Capitan is a massive, fine-grained limestone reef that formed from the slow accumulation of algae, sponges, and other small animals' skeletons.**

← The steep facade
of El Capitan in the
Guadalupe Mountains

## Guadalupe Peak

Many visitors are keen to
climb the state's highest peak.
The Guadalupe Peak Trail is
a very difficult 8.4-mile (13.5-
km) round trip, starting at
Pine Springs and leading to
the highest point in the state.
It gains about 3,000 ft (914 m)
on the way, from arid desert
through lush pine forest
to the rocky summit, which
offers grand views of the
surrounding desert and
mountains. The route usually

### GETTING AROUND

Guadalupe Mountains National Park is located 65 miles
(105 km) north of the city of Van Horn, Texas, via Tex.
Hwy. 54 and U.S. Hwy. 62/180. El Paso, Texas, located 115
miles (185 km) east, is the nearest major city. The main
visitor center is located at Pine Springs, just off U.S.
62/180, and there's another visitor center at McKittrick
Canyon, 10 miles (16 km) to the northeast. There's also
an entrance at Dog Canyon at the north side of the park,
about 70 miles (113 km) west of the city of Carlsbad, New
Mexico, but no roads traverse the interior. Visitors often
combine a visit with Carlsbad Caverns National Park
(p342), 35 miles (56 km) northeast on U.S. Hwy. 62/180.

# EXPLORING GUADALUPE MOUNTAINS

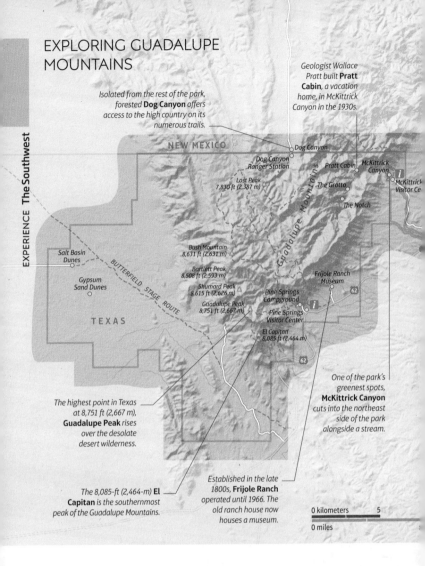

Isolated from the rest of the park, forested **Dog Canyon** offers access to the high country on its numerous trails.

Geologist Wallace Pratt built **Pratt Cabin**, a vacation home, in McKittrick Canyon in the 1930s.

NEW MEXICO

Dog Canyon

Dog Canyon Ranger Station

Pratt Cabin

McKittrick Canyon

The Grotto

McKittrick Visitor Ce

Lost Peak
7,830 ft (2,387 m)

The Notch

Guadalupe Mountains

Bush Mountain
8,631 ft (2,631 m)

Salt Basin Dunes

BUTTERFIELD STAGE ROUTE

Bartlett Peak
8,508 ft (2,593 m)

Gypsum Sand Dunes

Shumard Peak
8,615 ft (2,626 m)

Guadalupe Peak
8,751 ft (2,667 m)

Pine Springs Campground

Frijole Ranch Museum

62

Pine Springs Visitor Center

TEXAS

El Capitan
8,085 ft (2,464 m)

62

One of the park's greenest spots, **McKittrick Canyon** cuts into the northeast side of the park alongside a stream.

The highest point in Texas at 8,751 ft (2,667 m), **Guadalupe Peak** rises over the desolate desert wilderness.

Established in the late 1800s, **Frijole Ranch** operated until 1966. The old ranch house now houses a museum.

The 8,085-ft (2,464-m) **El Capitan** is the southernmost peak of the Guadalupe Mountains.

0 kilometers 5

0 miles

takes between six to eight hours to complete.

## Frijole Ranch

The Frijole Ranch Museum occupies the former head-

**IF YOU HAVE
A weekend**

Explore McKittrick Canyon by hiking to Pratt Lodge and the Grotto. The following day, make a slow ascent of Guadalupe Peak.

quarters of a ranch, and features exhibits and displays documenting the human history of the Guadalupes, from Indigenous communities through early ranching to the establishment of the park. Though the building is no longer a functioning ranch, it retains the architectural features characteristic of the park's ranching communities.

The Frijole Ranch Museum is open seasonally and is run largely by volunteers. The grounds around the museum are open all year; they provide

a good spot to observe birds. From a trailhead at Frijole Ranch Museum, the moderate 2.3-mile (3.7-km) Smith Spring Loop explores one of the park's greenest spots at the mountain's base.

## McKittrick Canyon

In the northeastern corner of the park, McKittrick Canyon is famous for its sublime landscapes, especially in fall when the leaves change color. The area can be explored by day only; the entry gate is locked at night.

←

Ascending the Hiker's Staircase, a three-tier natural rock formation

> **In the northeastern corner of the park, McKittrick Canyon is famous for its sublime landscapes, especially in fall when the leaves change color.**

A 10-mile (16-km) round-trip hike will take you to the Notch, a narrow cut in the cliffside; the first 3.4 miles (5.5 km) are moderate and the last 1.6 miles (2.6 km) up to the Notch are steeper and more difficult. You can hike 2.4 miles (3.9 km) to historic Pratt Cabin, or add another mile to get to the alcove cave known as the Grotto.

### Hiking and backpacking

A short walking trail from the main visitor center at Pine Springs leads to the remains of a stone wall and foundations of a former frontier stagecoach station. This was built as part of the Butterfield Trail, which linked St. Louis and California in 1858. Another easy walk in the Pine Springs area is Devil's Hall Trail, a 4-mile (6-km) route into Pine Spring Canyon. The trail passes the Hiker's Staircase, a three-tiered rock form. If you have time to get to Dog Canyon on the north side of the park, the moderate 6.4-mile (10.3-km) round-trip hike up Lost Peak is a good place to see mule deer, wild turkey, and other wildlife.

For a multiday backpacking trip, the difficult but rewarding 100-mile (160-km) Guadalupe Ridge Trail connects Guadalupe Mountains National Park and Carlsbad Caverns National Park, starting at the base of Guadalupe Peak. The Bowl is another difficult 13-mile (20.9-km) loop that rises to the top of an escarpment before entering a pine forest.

### Camping

The park has two campgrounds at Pine Springs and Dog Canyon as well as 10 backcountry campgrounds. Reservations are not accepted for the former; a permit is always required for backcountry camping.

## EAT

There is a good range of places to eat and stay in the nearby towns of Van Horn and Carlsbad.

**Chuy's**

Tasty Mexican dishes served in a lively restaurant, with great cocktails.

**🏠 Van Horn [W] chuys.com**

$$$

## STAY

**Stevens Inn**

Full-service lodging, with a pool and restaurant, the Flume *(p346)*.

**🏠 Carlsbad [W] stevensinncarlsbad.com**

$$$

# BIG BEND

**Texas** **$30 per vehicle, valid for seven days**
**nps.gov/bibe**

One of the Lower 48's wildest frontiers, this desert wilderness is named for the wide curve of the Rio Grande along the U.S.-Mexico border. The stark, yucca-speckled lowlands give way to the forested Chisos Mountains, rising high above the river on the South Rim. With three sheer canyons, the Rio Grande is a major rafting destination, while the desert and mountain trails make for sublime hiking.

> **IF YOU HAVE**
> **A day**
>
> Hike the Chisos Basin Loop Trail in the park's mountains, and summit Emory Peak if you have the time and energy. The highest point of the Chisos Mountains, it affords superb views.

Early Spanish explorers nicknamed the Chihuahuan Desert west of the Pecos River in Texas "El Despoblado," or the depopulated zone, despite the fact that Indigenous people had lived here for thousands of years. More recently, this beguiling borderland has seen ranchers, miners, and pioneers, drawn to the bounty of the rugged land. Snaking along the south side of the park (and the country, as this is the U.S.-Mexico border), the Rio Grande has cut three majestic canyons in the area over the eons: Santa Elena, Mariscal, and Boquillas. The lowland wilderness gives way to the Chisos Mountains in the heart of Big Bend National Park, where a cooler climate allows

←
A view of the Rio Grande
river from Castolon
in Big Bend

pine and oak forests to thrive above the arid desert below.

## Exploring the park

Big Bend is a large park with few roads, but they access some of the best scenery within its boundaries. Ross Maxwell Scenic Drive takes you to the southwestern corner, passing a number of overlooks with panoramas of the desert and the Chisos Mountains. At the end of the road, the Rio Grande flows into Santa Elena Canyon, the western-most of the canyons.

There are 200 miles (320 km) of excellent hiking trails throughout the park,

and hiking is the preferred mode of travel for visitors.

## Basins and canyons

Chisos Basin is the park's center of activity and a hub for hiking and backpacking. The road rises sharply to the basin's floor, which sits at an impressive 5,400 ft (1,646 m) above sea level.

### Did You Know?

Big Bend is home to more species of bird than any other U.S. park, with 450 species found here.

→
The aptly named
Balanced Rock, in the
heart of Big Bend

← Carrying a kayak into the shallows of the Rio Grande

can continue on the moderate 5.6-mile (9-km) Window Trail into a forested canyon to the base of the gap. The Window offers excellent opportunities to frame perfect landscape photographs

The easy 1.6-mile (2.6-km) Chisos Basin Loop connects with the difficult Emory Peak Trail for a 10.5-mile (16.9-km) hike to the top of the park's highest point and back. Many backpackers continue from the loop on routes into the park's backcountry, including the South Rim, where you can see deep into Mexico.

On Panther Pass north of Chisos Basin, the moderate 4.8-mile (7.7-km) Lost Mine Trail climbs through forests with numerous desert and mountain views. Off Ross Maxwell Scenic Drive, Mule Ears Spring Trail is a moderate 3.8-mile (6.1-km) hike through the desert below the Chisos to its namesake natural spring and rock formations.

### GETTING AROUND

Big Bend National Park is located about 80 miles (129 km) south of Alpine, Texas, via Tex. Hwy. 118, which enters the park at the west entrance. From there, the highway becomes Panther Junction Rd. and continues 22 miles (35 km) to the main visitor center. On the way, Ross Maxwell Scenic Dr. runs south to Santa Elena Canyon, Chisos Basin Dr. takes you to Chisos Basin, and Park Rte. 12 leads to Rio Grande Village and the crossing to Boquillas, Mexico.

El Paso is the nearest major city, located about 300 miles (483 km) to the west via U.S. 90. The gateway towns of Terlingua and Study Butte are located outside the park's west entrance on Twx. Hwy. 118, and Marathon is 42 miles (68 km) north of the north entrance on U.S. 385.

The views of the changing ecology as you rise from desert to mountain forest are worth the trip, but visitors can also explore the nearby Castolon Historic District, a "ghost town" with the ruins of various structures from the early 1900s.

Boquillas Canyon is also a popular hiking spot; you can drive to the canyon on the southwest side of the park, where a pretty riverside trail leads through the canyon. After exploring Boquillas, Hot Springs is a ruin of a resort on the bank of the Rio Grande, where a spring fills the remnants of a bathhouse with 105°F (41°C) water. Bathing is permitted.

### Hiking

Chisos Basin is the point of origin for numerous trails and backpacking routes. An easy 0.3-mile (0.5-km) round trip will get you to a sunset view through a gap in the rock called the Window, and you

→ Hiking into the high country at Big Bend

## Rafting

The park's 118-mile (190-km) stretch of the Rio Grande is a popular destination for rafting excursions, with relatively calm water and a dramatic desert landscape. There are numerous rafting outfitters in Study Butte and Terlingua outside the park's western entrance. Trips run from a single day to 10 days. While on the water, look out for beavers and kingfishers.

## Wildlife watching

The park has a unique and diverse wildlife population, including bats, bears, tarantulas, pig-like javelinas, and 450 species of birds. Chisos Basin and Hot Springs are particularly popular for birdwatching, with many visiting at sunrise.

## Visiting Mexico

There is an official border crossing into Mexico near the small village of Boquillas del Carmen, just south of the Rio Grande on the southeastern boundary of the park.

Boatmen charge a small fee to row visitors across the river, and you can either walk 0.5 miles (0.8 km) into the village or pay for transportation on horse, burro, or car. There are a few restaurants and a bar, and local artisans selling their wares. A passport or other documentation is required; U.S. currency is accepted.

## Camping

There are three developed campgrounds in Big Bend at Chisos Basin, Rio Grande Village, and Cottonwood near Santa Elena Canyon, as well as a popular RV park at Rio Grande Village. Reservations are recommended. Backcountry camping is permitted, but permits, available from the visitor center, are required.

**The park has a unique and diverse wildlife population, including bats, bears, tarantulas, pig-like javelinas, and 450 species of birds.**

There is one lodging in the park, and places to eat in the Terlingua area.

## EAT

**Starlight Theatre**
A movie house-turned-restaurant, serving burgers and steaks.

🏠 Terlingua
[W] thestarlighttheatre.com

$$$

## STAY

**Chisos Mountain Lodge**
This dining room offers Southwestern classics.

🏠 Chisos Basin
[W] chisosmountainlodge.com

$$$

# EXPLORING BIG BEND

Big Bend National Park is located in remote southwest Texas, close to the border with Mexico. The park's over 800,000 acres (300,000 ha) include the entire Chisos mountain range and a vast swath of the Chihuahan Desert.

*The high country above the Chihuahuan Desert can be accessed from a bowl-shaped area in the **Chisos Basin**. The park's only lodging and dining is located here.*

*The highest mountain in Big Bend, the 7,825-ft (2,385-m) **Emory Peak** is accessible from trails in Chisos Basin. The views from the summit span the mountains and desert below.*

*With 1,500-foot (457-m) walls looming above the Rio Grande, **Santa Elena Canyon** is the most popular rafting destination in the park due to easy access to put-ins near the road.*

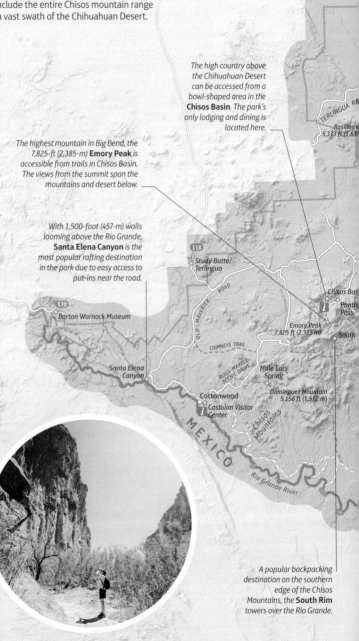

TERLINGUA R.

Rosillos
5,373 ft (1,63

118

Study Butte/
Terlingua

Chisos Bas

Panth
Pass

170

Barton Warnock Museum

OLD MAVERICK ROAD

CHIMNEYS TRAIL

ROSS MAXELL SCENIC DRIVE

Emory Peak
7,825 ft (2,385 m)

South

Santa Elena
Canyon

Mule Ears
Spring

Dominguez Mountain
5,156 ft (1,572 m)

Cottonwood

Castolon Visitor
Center

Chisos
Mountains

MEXICO

Rio Grande River

*A popular backpacking destination on the southern edge of the Chisos Mountains, the **South Rim** towers over the Rio Grande.*

↑ Looking up at the towering walls of Santa Elena Canyon

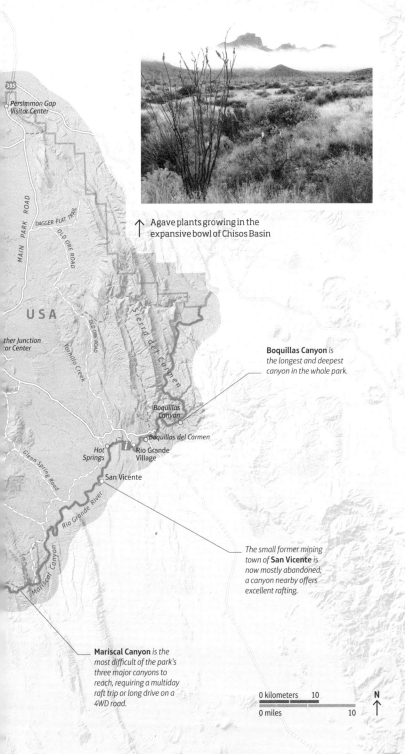

Agave plants growing in the expansive bowl of Chisos Basin

385
Persimmon Gap
Visitor Center

MAIN PARK ROAD

DAGGER FLAT TRAIL

OLD ORE ROAD

Sierra del Carmen

USA

...ther Junction
...or Center

OLD ORE ROAD

Tornillo Creek

Boquillas
Canyon

Boquillas del Carmen

Hot
Springs

Rio Grande
Village

Glenn Spring Road

San Vicente

Rio Grande River

Mariscal Canyon

**Boquillas Canyon** *is the longest and deepest canyon in the whole park.*

*The small former mining town of* **San Vicente** *is now mostly abandoned; a canyon nearby offers excellent rafting.*

**Mariscal Canyon** *is the most difficult of the park's three major canyons to reach, requiring a multiday raft trip or long drive on a 4WD road.*

0 kilometers 10
0 miles 10

N

VOYAGEURS
*p362*

ISLE ROYALE
*p366*

MINNESOTA

MICHIGAN

WISCONSIN

MAINE

ACADIA
*p390*

VT

NH

NEW
YORK

CT

MA  RI

INDIANA
DUNES
*p376*

CUYAHOGA
VALLEY
*p382*

IOWA

NJ

PENNSYLVANIA

ILLINOIS  INDIANA

OHIO

MISSOURI

GATEWAY
ARCH
*p372*

# GREAT LAKES AND THE NORTHEAST

The chain of five freshwater lakes that straddles the U.S.–Canada border – Superior, Michigan, Huron, Erie, and Ontario – is one of the greatest natural features on Earth. It's little surprise, then, that the parks in this region offer beauty in abundance. Nestled on the lakeshores or situated on verdant islands, the parks are havens of biodiversity and magnets for outdoor adventurers. Almost peeking into Canada, in the northern reaches of Minnesota, Voyageurs is home to huge beaver ponds, large packs of eastern wolves, and splendid fishing lakes. The feather-streaked archipelago of Isle Royale sits amid Lake Superior, offering rugged hiking or tranquil sailing. Farther to the northeast, Acadia is home to Cadillac Mountain, the highest point on the East Coast. Whether floating on the water or trekking on land, epic adventures await in the northeast.

1 Ohio and Erie Canal towpath.

2 The Gateway Arch.

3 Abraham Lincoln's tomb in Springfield.

4 The golden sands of Mount Baldy Beach.

# 5 DAYS
## *in the Mid-West*

## Day 1

Welcome to St. Louis, Missouri, once the gateway to the Western frontier. Dominating the Mississippi riverfront, Eero Saarinen's Gateway Arch is the centerpiece of America's smallest national park *(p372)*. Start your visit at the museum, before taking a "tram" ride to the top of the arch (in elevator-like capsules) for dazzling views of the surrounding city. Later you can pop inside the 19th-century Old Cathedral and the handsome Old Courthouse, a short walk away, best known for the Dred Scott trial that opened here in 1847. Spend the evening in Laclede's Landing, a section of warehouses converted into bars and restaurants, just north of the Arch.

## Day 2

Rise early for the drive to Indiana Dunes *(p376)* – it's about five hours straight, but you'll want to make a few stops on the way (it's worth visiting Springfield, the Illinois state capital, where you can see Abraham Lincoln's tomb). You'll arrive at the shore of Lake Michigan by late afternoon, and can get your first taster of the park at West Beach, hemmed in by a range of sandy, scrub-covered foothills. Several trails run through giant dunes and around tranquil Long Lake. There's a collection of motels in Portage, off I-94.

## Day 3

Start at the Indiana Dunes Visitor Center this morning before driving over to Kemil Beach. Hike the Dunes Ridge Trail for superb views of the Great Marsh (a popular feeding area for migrating wetland birds), then stroll along Lake Front Drive to view the unique "Century of Progress Homes" from the 1933 Chicago World's Fair. Enjoy a waterside lunch at Lake View Beach Picnic Shelters. In the afternoon, visit Mount Baldy Beach to see the tallest moving sand dune in the park. Finally, tour the historic Bailly Homestead and Chellberg Farm to learn about the pioneer history of the area. Drive back to Kenil Beach as the sun sets to enjoy some unpolluted stargazing.

## Day 4

It's another early start today for the five-hour drive to Cuyahoga Valley *(p382)*. There are plenty of places to break the journey, with Toledo boasting an excellent museum of art. Assuming you arrive at the Valley by late afternoon, you can get an introduction to the park by exploring the Lock 29 area in the village of Peninsula. Try to reserve rooms at the luxurious Inn at Brandywine Falls for the evening *(www. brandywinefallsinn.com)*.

## Day 5

The best way to explore Cuyahoga Valley is to rent a bike in Peninsula *(www. centurycycles.com)* and cycle the Ohio and Erie Canal Towpath Trail. You can ride north to Lock 39, from where you can visit the enlightening Canal Exploration Center, or south to Akron, from where you can take the Cuyahoga Valley Scenic Railroad *(www.cvsr.org)* back to Peninsula. You can then tackle the longer Brandywine Gorge Loop, which circles the park's biggest attraction, the 60-ft (18-m) Brandywine Falls. End your journey with a meal at Lock Keepers *(www.lockkeepers. com)*, overlooking the Cuyahoga River.

Best for *Restorative time on the water*

# VOYAGEURS

◉ Minnesota   🎫 Free   ⓦ nps.gov/voya

Abutting the Canadian border, Voyageurs National Park seems to float on the country's edge. More than one-third of its 218,000 acres (88,220 ha) is water. Its four major lakes – Rainy, Kabetogama, Sand Point, and Namakan – are joined by 26 inland lakes, more than 500 islands, and 655 miles (1,054 km) of untouched shoreline. The only way to get around this floating wonderland is by boat, but the park's waterways provide access to secluded campsites, dark skies, and the natural beauty of the remote north. The park's remote northerly location makes it a perfect place to take in the splendors of the northern lights.

Voyageurs takes its name from the French-Canadian fur traders who traveled the region in the 18th and 19th centuries in search of beaver pelts. They traversed the lakes and rivers in *canot de nord*, workhorse 25-ft (7.5-m) "north canoes" built from birch bark and cedar by the Ojibwe people, who'd lived here since at least the early 1700s. After the demise of the fur trade, this remote region became an escape for wealthy tourists, who became known as the "Rainy Lake Aristocracy," a center of caviar production, and a trafficking corridor for bootleggers running

> **IF YOU HAVE**
> **A day**
>
> Spend time learning about traditional Ojibwe medicine at the Rainy Lake Ethno-botanical Garden, then explore Rainy Lake in a boat or kayak.

Canadian booze during the Prohibition era.

In the modern day, Voyageurs' inaccessibility remains a large part of its appeal, and while it may not have as many headline attractions as some other parks, it compensates in its endless opportunities for exploration. After all, as the fur traders could have told you, it's about *le voyage*, not the destination.

### Exploring the park

Voyageurs has three visitor centers – Rainy Lake, Kabeto-gama Lake, and Ash River – where you can get infor-mation and launch your boat to explore the park's interior. All three close for part of the year, so be sure to check their schedule before visiting.

↑ Enjoying a family hike through a forest of pine trees

↑ Stand-up paddleboarding
on the serene waters of
Kabetogama Lake

→ Waterside views; about 40 percent of Voyageurs National Park is water

# EAT

Stock up on groceries or factor in meals outside the park.

### Arrowhead Lodge

Tuck into a walleye dinner or some cheese curds as you gaze out over Kabetogama Lake.

🏠Kabetogama 🌐arrowheadlodgeresort.com

$ $ $

# STAY

Voyageurs has a hotel and a number of campsites. Houseboats are the draw, though. Several companies provide rentals; the service listed here is just one example.

### Kettle Falls Hotel

At the far end of the Kabetogama Peninsula, this easy-to-like hotel gives new meaning to the phrase "getting away from it all."

🏠Voyageurs 🌐kettlefallshotel.com

$ $ $

### Rainy Lake Houseboats

Boats for 2 to 12 people; some with waterslides.

🏠International Falls 🌐rainylakehouseboats.com

$ $ $

↑ White-tailed doe and her fawn, beside Kabetogama Lake

From the visitor centers, the only way to journey farther into the park is by watercraft. A classic Voyageurs experience is to travel by houseboat, which lets you access the park's most remote areas and take your bed with you. Several companies in Ash River, International Falls, and Crane Lake rent houseboats. Note that a houseboat permit (available from *www.recreation.gov*) is required for the dates of your visit.

## Camping

The lack of development on Voyageurs makes it an ideal place to paddle and pitch, and that's one of the joys of visiting this park. Front-country sites can be found on lakeshores, while backcountry sites are located on interior lakes, meaning you'll have to tie up your vessel and then hike in. Backcountry campsite reservations either include or provide the option of renting a canoe for use on interior lakes. To protect the water from the spread of invasive species, you're not allowed to portage your own canoe or kayak.

## Fishing

All that water of course makes for great fishing. You'll need a Minnesota fishing license before you cast, but with that in hand you'll have access to waters that abound in smallmouth bass, perch, walleye, and northern pike, which can reach lengths of 4 ft (1.2 m).

## Stargazing

After dark, be sure to look up. A near total absence of artificial light makes the park one of the best places in the country for stargazing. In summer, you'll be treated to the sparkling Milky Way, while winter brings the occasional ethereal aurora borealis, or northern lights.

## In winter

The fact that Voyageurs must be navigated by boat makes it a summertime destination, but there's also plenty to do

 IF YOU HAVE
**A weekend**

Rent a houseboat and travel the park's remote eastern reaches to sites like the Ellsworth Rock Gardens and historic Kettle Falls Hotel, fishing and stargazing as you go.

in winter. The Rainy Lake Visitor Center rents cross-country skis and traditional Ojibwe- and Huron-style snowshoes for use on park trails, and you can go sledding on Sphunge Island. Winter sees boats replaced by snowmobiles, which can travel along 110 miles (177 km) of groomed trails, and – no joke – cars. After the lakes freeze over, you can drive the Rainy Lake Ice Road and the Kabetogama Lake Ice Road, which runs between the Kabetogama Lake and Ash River visitor centers.

## GETTING AROUND

The park's three visitor centers (Rainy Lake, Ash River, and Kabetogama Lake) can be reached by car. To get to Rainy Lake Visitor Center, take Hwy. 11 east from International Falls to Park Rd. For Kabetogama Lake Visitor Center, take U.S. Hwy. 53 south from International Falls and then head north on Salmi Rd/Gamma Rd. For Ash River Visitor Center, take U.S. Hwy. 53 to County Hwy. 129/Ash River Trail, and then head north on Mead Wood Rd. Once in the park, the only ways to get around are by boat or on foot - here, there are no roads, and no public transportation. Rentals are available at gateway towns (including Crane Lake, outside of the park in the southeast). If you cross into Canadian waters, international travel regulations and Canadian boating requirements apply.

# EXPLORING VOYAGEURS

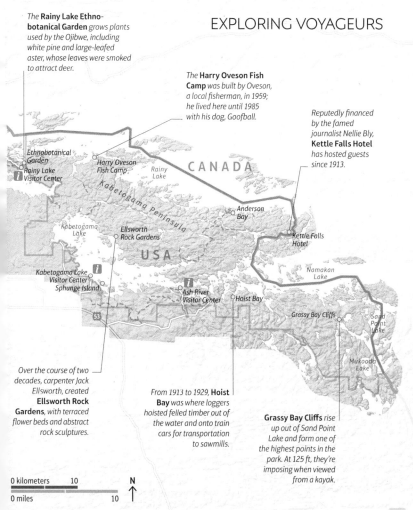

The **Rainy Lake Ethnobotanical Garden** grows plants used by the Ojibwe, including white pine and large-leafed aster, whose leaves were smoked to attract deer.

The **Harry Oveson Fish Camp** was built by Oveson, a local fisherman, in 1959; he lived here until 1985 with his dog, Goofball.

Reputedly financed by the famed journalist Nellie Bly, **Kettle Falls Hotel** has hosted guests since 1913.

Over the course of two decades, carpenter Jack Ellsworth, created **Ellsworth Rock Gardens**, with terraced flower beds and abstract rock sculptures.

From 1913 to 1929, **Hoist Bay** was where loggers hoisted felled timber out of the water and onto train cars for transportation to sawmills.

**Grassy Bay Cliffs** rise up out of Sand Point Lake and form one of the highest points in the park. At 125 ft, they're imposing when viewed from a kayak.

0 kilometers   10
0 miles   10

N

Best for *Remote walks in untouched wilderness*

# ISLE ROYALE

📍 Michigan  🚗 $7 per person, per day to enter or remain in the park  🌐 nps.gov/isro

Isle Royale consists of the titular island and more than 450 other islands and islets adrift in Lake Superior, the world's largest lake by surface area. Its isolation makes it an important center of scientific research, gives it some of the most pristine waters in North America, and leaves it the least-visited national park in the contiguous U.S. Curiously, though, it's also one of the most revisited. Clearly, this hard-to-get-to place is worth coming back for.

Isle Royale looks as if an artist has painted a rapid brush-stroke across Lake Superior's surface. A solid expanse of forest in the southwest, the island is striated with countless bays, coves, and inland lakes in the northeast. For hikers, campers, backpackers, boaters, and lovers of nature, it truly is a work of art.

Long before the island became a tourist destination in the 1890s, Minong (as it was then known) was the land of the Ojibwe people, who hunted and fished here. Later, it supported mining and logging industries. Today, Isle Royale is a leading center of ecological research, home to the world's longest predator-prey study (documenting the island's wolf-moose relationship) and, with 99 percent of its terrain protected wilderness, one of the most pristine places left in the U.S.

 IF YOU HAVE
**A day**
Take the Grand Portage ferry to Windigo, hike the Windigo Nature Trail, and kayak up Washington Creek before catching the ferry back to the mainland.

## Exploring the park

There's no doubt about it: Isle Royale can be a challenging destination and making the most of it requires a degree of self-sufficiency. Though the park is open April 16 to October 31 (it completely shuts down in the winter), the visitor centers and many services are only available from May to mid-September. There's no Wi-Fi, cell service is unreliable, and winter stays late and arrives early. If you've got the gumption (or just come in the summer), however, Isle Royale is endlessly rewarding.

## Hiking

Around 165 miles (265 km) of trails thread across the island's little-touched wilderness, taking visitors through hardwood forests of sugar maples and yellow birch in the interior, and boreal forests of spruce, aspen, and balsam fir draped in scraggly old man's beard lichen along the shore. Given the island's remoteness, plus lower visitor numbers, hikes here are solitary affairs – a

> There's no doubt about it: Isle Royale can be a challenging destination and making the most of it requires a degree of self-sufficiency.

←

The pristine waters
of Lake Superior
around Isle Royale

walker could spend all day hiking and not see a fellow explorer. But there's wildlife. Snack on wild strawberries and thimbleberries as you hike, and watch for red foxes and wolves. The latter seek to avoid humans but are sometimes seen along lakeshores and in open areas. You're more likely to spot their main prey, moose, especially in and around Washington Creek and Ojibway Lake. To find out more about the island's moose and wolf populations, visit the Bangsund Cabin.

### GETTING AROUND

Reach the island by ferry or seaplane from either Minnesota or Michigan's Upper Peninsula. There are two points of entry: Windigo, in the southwest, and Rock Harbor, in the northeast. From Minnesota, ferries depart Grand Portage for Windigo; seaplanes depart Grand Marais for Windigo and Rock Harbor. From Michigan, ferries depart Houghton and Copper Harbor for Rock Harbor; seaplanes depart Houghton for Rock Harbor and Windigo. Ferries and seaplanes operate from mid-May to September. The park website provides links to each ferry and seaplane booking site; book well in advance. You can also travel by private boat, though overnight stays require a permit purchased in advance from the Houghton Visitor Center. On the island, all transportation is by foot, boat, or seaplane. No vehicles are allowed.

# EXPLORING ISLE ROYALE

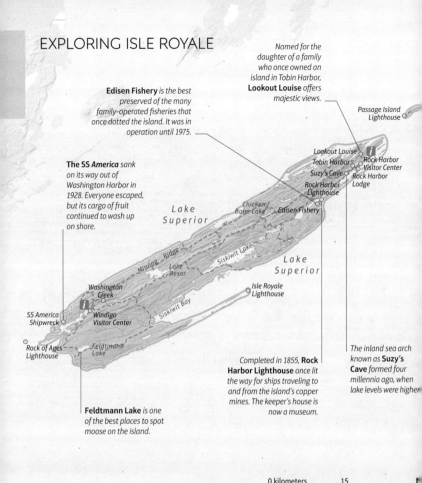

Named for the daughter of a family who once owned an island in Tobin Harbor, **Lookout Louise** offers majestic views.

**Edisen Fishery** is the best preserved of the many family-operated fisheries that once dotted the island. It was in operation until 1975.

**The SS America** sank on its way out of Washington Harbor in 1928. Everyone escaped, but its cargo of fruit continued to wash up on shore.

Passage Island Lighthouse

Lookout Louise
Tobin Harbor
Suzy's Cave
Rock Harbor
Lighthouse

Rock Harbor
Visitor Center
Rock Harbor
Lodge

Lake Superior

Chicken Bone Lake

Edisen Fishery

Minong Ridge

Lake Desor

Siskiwit Lake

Lake Superior

Washington Creek

Isle Royale Lighthouse

SS America Shipwreck

Windigo Visitor Center

Siskiwit Bay

Rock of Ages Lighthouse

Feldtmann Lake

The inland sea arch known as **Suzy's Cave** formed four millennia ago, when lake levels were higher

Completed in 1855, **Rock Harbor Lighthouse** once lit the way for ships traveling to and from the island's copper mines. The keeper's house is now a museum.

**Feldtmann Lake** is one of the best places to spot moose on the island.

0 kilometers        15
0 miles                    15

---

If you come ashore at Rock Harbor, good hikes include the 4.2-mile (6.8-km) Stoll Memorial Trail to Scoville Point, which combines woods and rocky Lake Superior shoreline, and the 3.8-mile (6.1-km) walk from the visitor center to Suzy's Cave, a sea arch formed by the waves. In Windigo, stroll the simple and short Windigo Nature Trail (1 mile/1.6 km) or test your mettle on the 28-mile (45-km) Minong Ridge Overlook Trail. The island's toughest trail, it takes ramblers through forests, over dams, and up onto a ridge. The rewards are views that stretch to Canada. On extended hikes, make use of the island's 36 campgrounds; campsite reservations are only required for groups of seven or more.

## On the water

As expected, time on the water here is time well spent. Visitors can rent boats, canoes, and kayaks at both the Rock Harbor and Windigo marinas (note that motorized craft are not permitted in inland lakes and streams). Northeast Isle Royale offers

**IF YOU HAVE**
**A weekend**

While Isle Royale can be visited in a day, it's far better to spend longer here. From Rock Harbor, explore the area's many bays and inlets by boat and hike campsite to campsite along the park's trails.

particularly enchanting days on the water. Spend a day or two paddling up and down Tobin Harbor, where you're sure to hear the ethereal calls of loons. Other winged natives you may notice include sandhill cranes, merganser ducks, and, as the joke goes, Michigan's state bird: the mosquito, of which there are 64 species on the island.

For something more relaxing, join one of the sightseeing tours aboard the MV *Sandy*. Tours depart from Rock Harbor beginning in June, and travel variously to the Passage Island Lighthouse, Hidden Lake, Bangsund Cabin moose and wolf research station, and other destinations.

## Diving and fishing

Naturally, many boaters come to the park to fish for trout, pike, and walleye. A fishing license is required to fish Lake Superior but not Isle Royale's

↑ A moose in the lake water at sunset

inland lakes. And you might not expect it this far north, but Isle Royale is also an esteemed scuba-diving destination. It has the most intact collection of shipwrecks of any national park, and with a permit you can explore 10 sunken vessels in the surrounding waters, from side-paddle steamers to steel freighters.

Numerous private companies can arrange diving or fishing charters (and many will also provide guided hiking, backpacking, and kayaking trips).

→ Rock Harbor Lighthouse, built in 1855

# EAT

Most visitors bring their own provisions, but there are a few options on the island.

**Windigo Store**
Groceries and camping supplies like freeze-dried meals, bagged ice, fuel, and fishing tackle.

🏠 Windigo
🌐 rockharborlodge.com

$

**Greenstone Grill**
Pizza, burgers, and beer from Houghton's Keweenaw Brewing Company.

🏠 Rock Harbor
🌐 rockharborlodge.com

$$

# STAY

The island has a hotel, cabins and campgrounds; more options on the mainland.

**Rock Harbor Lodge**
Well-appointed rooms and suites near Rock Harbor's port; secluded cabins for large groups.

🏠 Rock Harbor 🌐 rockharborlodge.com

$$$

**Windigo Camper Cabins**
A pair of cabins with bunk beds, electrical outlets, and grills but no indoor plumbing.

🌐 Windigo
🌐 rockharborlodge.com

$

## THE SHIPWRECKS OF ISLE ROYALE

Sailing on the Great Lakes has always been fraught with danger. Powerful storms, high winds, and the lakes' sheer size make them a challenging, and often deadly, place to navigate. Since 1679, more than 6,000 shipwrecks have been recorded on the five lakes, claiming some 30,000 lives. The waters of Isle Royale present their own challenges, and not all have managed them. Ten ships have gone down here, from passenger steamers to giant freighters. Here are four of the most noteworthy.

### SS ALGOMA

Built in 1883, the passenger steamer SS *Algoma* was one of the first steel-hulled vessels to ply the Great Lakes, leading the Thunder Bay Sentinel to crow about its "superiority over all other Lake craft." On November 6, 1885, en route from Owen Sound, Ontario, to Thunder Bay, the ship ran into heavy snow and hurricane-force winds. The next morning, it ran aground near Mott Island, off Isle Royale's northeast coast, soon splitting in half. While 14 lived, 45–47 people (the exact total is unknown) perished, making the *Algoma* the deadliest wreck in Lake Superior's history.

↑ The SS *Algoma*, which ran aground in 1885

### SS KAMLOOPS

The SS *Kamloops* is a mysterious tale. The package freighter was sailing west at the end of the 1927 shipping season when it was caught in a blizzard. The ship went down – but no one knew exactly when, or where. The following spring, Isle Royale fishers began finding bodies. The corpses wore life preservers with "Kamloops" written on them, but the wreck itself remained lost. It would stay that way for half a century, until sport diver Ken Engelbrecht found it in 1977, near Twelve O'Clock Point, on Isle Royale's north shore.

### SS AMERICA

The excursion vessel SS *America* had just dropped passengers off at their hotel and was on its way out of Washington Harbor, when Captain Edward Smith turned command over to first mate John Wick and retired to his cabin. Wick, a newcomer to both the crew and Isle Royale, promptly

### November 7, 1885

The *SS Algoma* passenger steamer runs aground near Mott Island. As many as 47 people die, making it Isle Royale's deadliest wreck.

### December 7 or 8, 1927

▽ The *SS Kamloops* sinks in a blizzard. Some sailors may make it to shore, but all eventually perish.

*Notable wrecks*

### July 25, 1877

△ Isle Royale's first major wreck, the *SS Cumberland* strikes the Rock of Ages reef.

### November 6, 1918

The *SS Chester A. Congdon* sinks. Loss of ship and cargo is estimated at more than $1.5 million (equal to $28 million today).

Exploring the wrecked
SS *Emperor*, still
remarkably intact ↑

clipped a reef. Smith managed to ground the vessel, and all passengers made it to land safely. For several weeks afterward, fruit from the cargo hold washed up on shore; as local resident Stanley Sivertson noted, the islanders "ate fruit all summer." It's now Isle Royale's most popular dive site.

### SS EMPEROR

The bulk carrier SS *Emperor* was the last large ship to wreck on Isle Royale. In 1947, it pulled out of Port Arthur (now Thunder Bay), bound for Ashtabula, Ohio. Though the weather and visibility were good, the ship was understaffed, and the first mate had had to forego his break in port to oversee the loading of tons of bulk iron ore. He likely fell asleep while on watch, and just after 4am the next morning, the *Emperor* struck Canoe Rocks, off Isle Royale's northeastern tip. Lifeboats were launched, but the sinking ship created a suction that pulled the port lifeboat and several sailors down. Twelve were lost. Survivors were brought back to Thunder Bay, where the ship's owner, Canada Steamship Lines, Ltd., gave them $100 for new clothes and essentials.

### WRECK DIVING

Experienced divers can visit most of Isle Royale's shipwrecks. Register for a permit at a park visitor center and come prepared: diving is remote and cold; surface water temperatures rarely hit 55°F (13°C). Isle Royale Charters (*www.isleroyalecharters.com*) runs multiday trips on a custom-built boat from June to mid-September.

---

**June 7, 1928**

△ The SS *America*, which carried passengers between Duluth, Isle Royale, and Thunder Bay, sinks in Washington Harbor.

**May 27, 1933**

The SS *George M. Cox's* first voyage is also its last. It runs aground off western Isle Royale as its passengers are having dinner.

**June 4, 1947**

The SS *Emperor* sinks near the Canoe Rocks, claiming the lives of 12 sailors. It's Isle Royale's last major shipwreck.

**August 21, 1977**

▽ Diver Ken Engelbrecht, together with Randy Saulter and Ken Merryman, discovers the wreck of the SS *Kamloops*, nearly 50 years after it mysteriously went down.

Gateway Arch, once known as the Jefferson Memorial, soaring above the river ↑

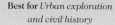

# GATEWAY ARCH

📍 Missouri 🎟 Free 🌐 nps.gov/jeff

Gateway Arch is the U.S.'s smallest and only urban national park, and everything that most national parks are not. Located in downtown St. Louis, soaring high on the banks of the Mississippi River, the diminutive 91-acre (37-ha) park and its famed monument – the silver-steel Gateway Arch –were built to commemorate the Louisiana Purchase and the central role the city played in the country's 19th-century western expansion.

Gateway Arch National Park occupies the strip of land where, in 1764, French explorers set up the trading post that would grow to be today's St. Louis. The park was originally called the Jefferson National Expansion Memorial, in honor of the president who made the Louisiana Purchase and spurred America's westward expansion, but was renamed and redesignated in 2018. The decision was met with controversy, as the park's size, setting, and landscaped grounds were so out of step with other national parks. Even the National Park Service's acting deputy director opposed the choice, recommending that it be designated a national

↑ The manicured grounds around Gateway Arch National Park

monument instead. But a new national park never did anyone any harm, and Gateway Arch adds a unique urban experience to the park system.

## Exploring the park

Given its small size, this park is easily toured on a day trip. The visitor center is a good starting point and from here ranger tours are available.

## The arch

While there may be controversy about Gateway Arch's status as a national park, there's no such debate over the arch itself. It's one of the country's most beautiful

---

**IF YOU HAVE**
**A day**

Stroll the manicured grounds, visit the Old Courthouse, and ride the tram to the top of the Arch for great views over St. Louis and the Mississippi River.

→

Exhibitions exploring St. Louis' riverboat history in the Gateway Arch museum

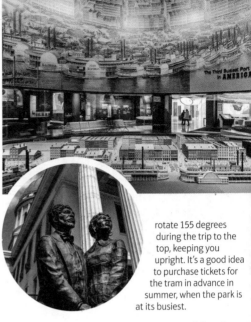

# EAT

The park has a café, but you're best taking advantage of St. Louis' culinary scene.

### Anthonino's Taverna
Try a St. Louis specialty: toasted ravioli (deep-fried, actually).

⌂ St. Louis
🌐 anthoninos.com

$$$

---

### Pappy's Smokehouse
Dry-rubbed ribs from one of the top BBQ joints in the country.

⌂ St. Louis 🌐 pappys smokehouse.com

$$$

# STAY

The park's downtown location means there are plenty of options.

### Hyatt Regency St. Louis at The Arch
Most rooms promise a view of the arch itself.

⌂ St. Louis 🌐 hyatt.com

$$$

---

### St. Louis Union Station Hotel
A former 19th-century train station, featuring an impressive barrel-vaulted ceiling.

⌂ St. Louis 🌐 hilton.com

$$$

↑ Statue of Dred and Harriet Scott, who sued for their freedom

structures and, at 630 ft (192 m), its tallest human-built monument. Designed by the Finnish-American architect Eero Saarinen and completed in 1965, it's a layer cake of carbon steel, concrete, and stainless steel. Photos usually depict it head-on and from a distance, its graceful inverted horseshoe framing either the St. Louis skyline or open sky, but as you walk around the grounds and view it from different angles, it seems to twist and become a different form entirely.

## Take the tram
After you've craned your neck up at the arch from the outside, ride the interior tram up to its viewing platform. Opened in the late 1960s, the ingenious contraptions were designed by elevator manufacturer Dick Bowser in just two weeks (Bowser notably never finished college). Somewhere between an elevator and a Ferris wheel, the trams consist of eight barrel-shaped capsules that rotate 155 degrees during the trip to the top, keeping you upright. It's a good idea to purchase tickets for the tram in advance in summer, when the park is at its busiest.

## Museum and theater
Beneath the arch is a museum with exhibits on the structure and the city's history, and a theater (tickets required) that shows a documentary about the arch's construction. Both the museum and theater are fully accessible and provide the likes of touch stations and assistive listening devices.

## The Old Courthouse
The park's other main feature is the Old Courthouse. Built from 1839 to 1862, it's one of St. Louis' oldest buildings and was the setting for two of the country's most consequential trials. In 1847, Dred and Harriet Scott, both enslaved, sued for their freedom, and in 1873, Virginia Minor sued for her right to vote as a woman. Both cases eventually came before the U.S. Supreme Court, and both plaintiffs lost, but the cases served as catalysts to emancipation and women's suffrage.

At the time of publication, the Old Courthouse is closed for renovations. It will likely reopen in 2025. When renovation is completed, visitors will be able to view exhibits on the Scotts and the U.S. court system.

## Around the arch

The terrain surrounding the arch is best described by the park's own website: "From an ecological perspective, the lands within the park's boundaries are highly unnatural." Instead of mountains and rivers, you'll find reflecting ponds, walking paths, a native grass meadow, and tiny zen gardens. As for the diversity of fauna, the park has seen fit to note the recorded presence of two domestic cats. There is avian life aplenty, however, including year-round residents like cardinals, blue jays, and Peregrine falcons.

### GETTING AROUND

Given its urban location, getting to Gateway Arch is very simple. The easiest way to reach the park is to take St. Louis' MetroLink light rail to 8th & Pine Station or Laclede's Landing Station. From 8th & Pine, walk five blocks east to the park. Laclede's Landing Station is located on the park's northern edge. You can also take MetroBus #40 to the 4th Street and Locust stop. From there, walk south on 4th Street to the Old Courthouse. Bike lanes on Chestnut Street and Leonor K. Sullivan Boulevard also provide access to the park. If you're driving, the park is immediately northeast of the I-44/55–I-64/55 interchange. The park offers discounted parking rates for visitors at the Stadium East Parking Garage. Once at the park, its small size means it's easily toured on foot or by bicycle. St. Louis has numerous bicycle rental stores, if you haven't brought your own wheels.

# EXPLORING GATEWAY ARCH

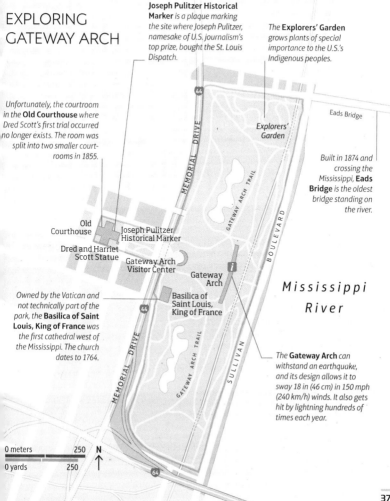

**Joseph Pulitzer Historical Marker** is a plaque marking the site where Joseph Pulitzer, namesake of U.S. journalism's top prize, bought the St. Louis Dispatch.

The **Explorers' Garden** grows plants of special importance to the U.S.'s Indigenous peoples.

Unfortunately, the courtroom in the **Old Courthouse** where Dred Scott's first trial occurred no longer exists. The room was split into two smaller courtrooms in 1855.

Built in 1874 and crossing the Mississippi, **Eads Bridge** is the oldest bridge standing on the river.

Owned by the Vatican and not technically part of the park, the **Basilica of Saint Louis, King of France** was the first cathedral west of the Mississippi. The church dates to 1764.

The **Gateway Arch** can withstand an earthquake, and its design allows it to sway 18 in (46 cm) in 150 mph (240 km/h) winds. It also gets hit by lightning hundreds of times each year.

Eads Bridge

Explorers' Garden

Old Courthouse
Joseph Pulitzer Historical Marker
Dred and Harriet Scott Statue
Gateway Arch Visitor Center
Gateway Arch
Basilica of Saint Louis, King of France

*Mississippi River*

MEMORIAL DRIVE
GATEWAY ARCH TRAIL
BOULEVARD
SULLIVAN

0 meters 250
0 yards 250
N

# INDIANA DUNES

⬛ Indiana ⬛ $25 per vehicle, valid for seven days (not valid for Indiana Dunes State Park) ⬛ nps.gov/indu

Set along the shore of Lake Michigan, Indiana Dunes is something of an oddity among national parks. Instead of a vast expanse of wilderness, it's a patchwork of protected dunes, forests, and wetlands separated by suburbs, industrial complexes, and the related but distinct Indiana Dunes State Park. Despite its lack of cohesion and small size, it's the fourth-most biologically diverse national park, and a melting pot of habitats and species.

### Did You Know?

The park's dunes are an example of "singing sands," because of the sounds they emit.

Nature and industry have long been in tension in northwestern Indiana. By the 1910s, the dunes here were a popular retreat for Chicagoans, but steel mills and power plants had started to encroach. Even as naturalists agitated for the dunes' protection, the largest, the 200-ft (61-m) Indiana Slide, was being carted away, a boxcar at a time, to make Ball jars and plate glass. Part of the region was finally declared a national lakeshore in 1966, but even today, the national park is a compromise with development, skirting steel yards, industrial ports, and residential tracts. Their proximity, however, makes

← Walking through the dunes, with lake views up ahead

the park that much more important, and that much more wondrous. Even on a brief visit you can hike through half a dozen different ecosystems, spot some of the 350 species that call at one of the country's best birding locales, or laze on beaches that you'll scarcely believe are in Indiana.

## Exploring the park

Its extensive beaches and proximity to Chicago make Indiana Dunes a prime destination for families and casual national parks visitors. It's open every day, though some sections keep different hours. In Gary, in the west of the park, is the Paul H. Douglas Center for Environmental Education, a venue for hands-on exhibits, crafts, and a Nature Play Zone that's especially good for kids.

## Hiking

Indiana Dunes has fascinating terrain, and the best way to discover it is to walk it. The park has more than 50 miles (80 km) of trails and 14 trail systems. One of the top routes is the Paul H. Douglas (Miller Woods) Trail. From the Center for Environmental Education, it runs north to the beach through wetlands, interdunal ponds, black oak savanna, and immense dunes.

→ Hitting the beach, a shoreside playground in the summer months

A particular highlight is the savanna, a mix of hardwood forest and tallgrass prairie. Land like this once covered 50 million acres (20 million ha) between Michigan and Nebraska; today, only several thousand acres remain.

The trail also runs forward through time. Lake Michigan formed some 11,000 years ago, when the Ice Age's Wisconsin Glacier began to melt. As it did so, lake levels fluctuated. When levels were low, the wind swept exposed sand into dunes. Over time, these migrated inland and were forested over, only to be replaced by new dunes along the lakeshore. So as you walk the trail toward the beach, you're traveling from the park's oldest dunes to its youngest.

In the park's eastern reaches, the Great Marsh Trail runs through the largest wetland complex in the Lake Michigan watershed, often providing glimpses of beavers, kingfishers, and green herons. Just outside Porter, the Bailly Homestead, Chellberg Farm, Little Calumet River, and Mnoké Prairie trails system cuts through maple, beech, and basswood forest, and gives an idea of what the region's primeval grasslands looked like at the restored Mnoké Prairie.

Goal-oriented ramblers will find that Indiana Dunes is also a good spot for geocaching, with both traditional geocaches and EarthCaches, which provide information about a natural feature.

### The beaches

With 15 miles (24 km) of beaches that would seem more at home in Florida than in a state known for cornfields and hog farms, the park is most popular in summer. Simple pleasures include swimming, bodysurfing, kiteboarding, or merely lazing on the sand catching the Lake Michigan breeze. Indiana Dunes has eight separate beaches. The easternmost, Mount Baldy, sits in front of the eponymous dune, a 126-ft (38-m) giant. (The tallest dunes are actually in the state park.) At the park's opposite end is the popular West Beach. Here you'll find a short trail honoring Alice Gray, a free spirit from Chicago who, on

Halloween 1915, packed up a blanket and two pistols, boarded a train, and proceeded to spend the rest of her life in makeshift shacks on the dunes.

### Bird-watching

Spring and fall are for the birds, when dozens of migrating species pass through, drawn by the dunes, beaches, wetlands, and open water. Serious twitchers follow them in, but even if you're a complete amateur, you won't have any trouble

↑ An eastern bluebird nestled on a branch

---

### GETTING AROUND

The disjointed make-up of the park means you'll probably find driving the easiest way to get around, especially if you want to visit multiple places. Nearly all of the park is within a couple of miles (3 km) of Hwy. 12, which runs parallel to the lakeshore. You can also reach the park by train from as far away as downtown Chicago via the South Shore Line, which has five stops in or near the park. From Gary, bus route L2 will take you to the Paul H. Douglas Center for Environmental Education and West Beach at the park's western end. Cyclists can bike across the park's expanse via a 37-mile (60-km) system of trails. Bike rentals are available near the visitor center.

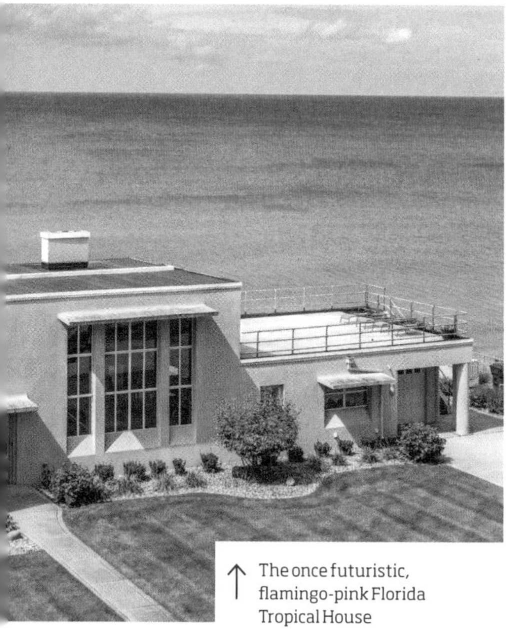

↑ The once futuristic, flamingo-pink Florida Tropical House

> IF YOU HAVE
> **A weekend**
> Explore the park's biodiversity on a walk or geocaching adventure, check out the 1933 Chicago World's Fair Century of Progress Homes, and indulge in a beach day.

spotting species like yellow warblers, red-winged blackbirds, and cardinals.

### In winter

The park is quieter but no less beautiful in winter, when you can snowshoe or cross-country ski on many of its trails. The Glenwood Dunes and Tolleston Dunes trails are especially well suited to snowy excursions.

### Historic future homes

The park's quirkiest attraction, by far, is a collection of five suburban houses. The dwellings were originally built to demonstrate modern architectural design and new technologies like dishwashers and air conditioning at the 1933 Chicago World's Fair. In a very American display of salesmanship and showmanship, the developer Robert Bartlett had them shipped by barge and truck to Beverly Shores, a resort community he was developing, in the hope that they'd spur sales in the neighborhood.

Amazingly, the homes still look modern nearly a century on. (Well, four do. One was designed to resemble a rustic log cabin.) The flamingo-pink Florida Tropical House looks like it's visiting from Miami Beach, while the Armco-Ferro House is made out of bolted corrugated steel panels. Meanwhile, the House of Tomorrow's first floor has an airplane hangar, as it was assumed that eventually every family would have its own plane. The homes are private residences and can only be visited on an annual tour, but you can view them from the road and contemplate their residential prophesies anytime.

## EAT

The park's layout means you're never far from a place to eat in the surrounding towns.

**Leeds Public House**
Gastropub in a 1903 building with a large patio and an emphasis on local ingredients.

**⌂ Michigan City [W] leedspublichouse.com**

$$$

**Wagner's**
Family joint serving award-winning BBQ ribs.

**⌂ Porter [W] wagnerribs.com**

$$

## STAY

The park has three campgrounds, and hotels are clustered in nearby Portage and Michigan City.

**Dunewood Campground**
66 campsites (four wheelchair accessible; 53 RV accessible) with modern restrooms and hot showers.

**⌂ Beverly Shores [W] nps.gov/indu**

$

**4411 Inn & Suites**
A sleek boutique take on the classic roadside motel.

**⌂ Michigan City [W] 4411innandsuites.com**

$

A glimmering pond
nestled beneath the
park's namesake dunes ↑

# EXPLORING INDIANA DUNES

Stretching along 15 miles (24 km) of Lake
Michigan shoreline from Gary to Michigan
City, Indiana Dunes is home to over 2,000
acres (800 ha) of dunes, wetlands,
prairies, and old-growth forest.

**Did You Know?**

More than 60 species
of butterfly have been
identified within the
park boundaries.

**The Paul H. Douglas Center for
Environmental Education** *offers a
host of programs and classes on local
ecology and sustainability.*

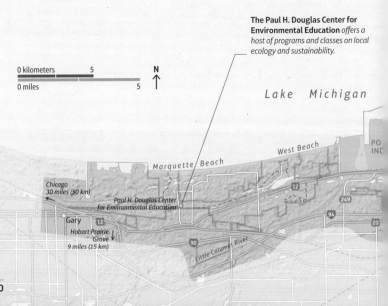

0 kilometers       5

0 miles            5

N ↑

Lake    Michigan

West Beach

PO
IN

Marquette Beach

Chicago
30 miles (50 km)

Paul H. Douglas Center
for Environmental Education

12

249

Gary

Hobart Prairie
Grove
9 miles (15 km)

90

94

20

Little Calumet River

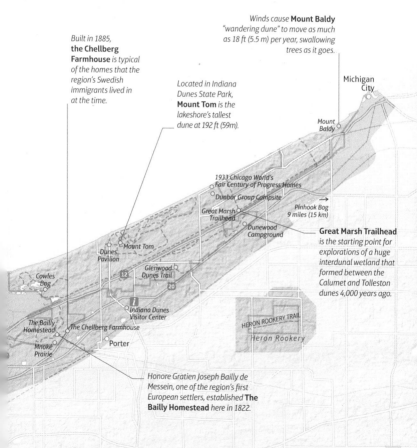

Winds cause **Mount Baldy** "wandering dune" to move as much as 18 ft (5.5 m) per year, swallowing trees as it goes.

Built in 1885, **the Chellberg Farmhouse** is typical of the homes that the region's Swedish immigrants lived in at the time.

Located in Indiana Dunes State Park, **Mount Tom** is the lakeshore's tallest dune at 192 ft (59m).

Michigan City

Mount Baldy

1933 Chicago World's Fair Century of Progress Homes

Dunbar Group Campsite

Pinhook Bog
9 miles (15 km)

Great Marsh Trailhead

Dunewood Campground

**Great Marsh Trailhead** is the starting point for explorations of a huge interdunal wetland that formed between the Calumet and Tolleston dunes 4,000 years ago.

Mount Tom

Dunes Pavilion

Cowles Bog

Glenwood Dunes Trail

12

20

i Indiana Dunes Visitor Center

HERON ROOKERY TRAIL

Heron Rookery

The Bailly Homestead

The Chellberg Farmhouse

Porter

Mnoke Prairie

Honore Gratien Joseph Bailly de Messein, one of the region's first European settlers, established **The Bailly Homestead** here in 1822.

**Best for** *Cycling along a stretch of history*

# CUYAHOGA VALLEY

 Ohio  Free  nps.gov/cuva

Squeezed between Cleveland and Akron, in Ohio's northeast corner, Cuyahoga Valley National Park follows two waterways: the Cuyahoga River and the Ohio and Erie Canal. One natural and one humanmade, the pair reflects the competing impulses that have defined the valley since the early 1800s. More than a century of industrial despoilment has been greatly rectified in recent decades, and today the 33,000-acre (13,400-ha) refuge is one of the country's most popular national parks, with some 2.2 million people coming here each year to hike, cycle, ride the rails, attend concerts, and learn about the valley's fascinating history.

Called the Ka-ih-ogh-ha, or "Crooked" River by Indigenous Americans, the Cuyahoga is short, only 100 miles (161 km) long, but it holds an outsized place in the national imagination. The river's water fed the Ohio and Erie Canal, which, when completed in 1832, linked the Ohio River with Lake Erie and, via the Erie Canal, the East Coast. The connection launched the valley's economy. Villages, mills, and brickyards sprouted. Iron ore and coal were shipped east. Business magnate John D. Rockefeller founded Standard Oil in Cleveland, and industrialist B. F. Goodrich established his rubber company in Akron. The growth took a toll. Filled with industrial waste and urban sewage, the Cuyahoga caught

**Though restoration remains a work in progress, the valley is now a beautiful retreat and a testament to nature's resilience, if only given a chance**

on fire 10 times between 1868 and 1969. The last conflagration added a sense of urgency to local cleanup efforts, however, and helped lead to the creation of the national park in 1974. Though restoration remains a work in progress, the valley is now a beautiful retreat and a testament to nature's resilience, if only given a chance.

### Exploring the park

You're never too far from the river in the park. The Boston Mill Visitor Center (open daily) sits on its west bank in a

handsome building that was once the company store of a firm that made paper sacks during the region's industrial heyday. Stop by for information, souvenirs, and, in winter, snowshoe and ski rentals. In summer, you might instead start your visit at the Canal Exploration Center, near the park's northern end. Formerly a tavern and general store, it offers detailed exhibits on the Ohio and Erie Canal. On weekends, volunteers in period costumes demonstrate how the adjacent canal lock worked.

### The Ohio and Erie Canal Towpath Trail

Running alongside the canal through the length of the park is 20 miles (32 km) of the 100-mile (161-km) Ohio and Erie Canal Towpath Trail, which mules once trod as they pulled boats along the waterway. You can walk, jog, and even travel it by horse-back, but the best way to experience the whole thing is on a bike – and that's exactly what many visitors to this park do. (If you don't have your own wheels, you can rent some from Century Cycles in Peninsula.)

 IF YOU HAVE
**A day**

Take your time cycling along the Ohio and Erie Canal Towpath Trail one way, and catch the Cuyahoga Valley Scenic Railroad back.

←

The Cuyahoga Valley Scenic Railroad, and the Station Road Bridge

# EAT

Find options in mid-park Peninsula, or Cleveland and Akron at the park's north and south.

### Pierogi Palace
Cleveland institution making local faves pierogies and "Polish Boys" in the historic West Side Market.

 Cleveland
clepierogi.com

$$$

### Fisher's
Third-generation and family-owned, serving wings and burgers.

 Peninsula
fisherscafe.com

$$$

# STAY

The park doesn't have any camping, but it offers two historic stays. You'll find hotels aplenty in Cleveland.

### Stanford House
An 1843 Greek Revival home for rent just off the Towpath Trail.

 Cuyahoga
conservancyfor cvnp.org.

$$$

### The Inn at Brandywine Falls
Charming six-room B&B in a home listed on the National Register of Historic Places.

 Cuyahoga brandy winefallsin.com

$$$

↑ Cycling along the Ohio and Erie Canal Towpath, a must-do at Cuyahoga National Park

Flat and compact, the trail makes for an easy ride and takes you past many of the park's highlights. Heading south from the Canal Exploration Center, you'll soon arrive at the Frazee House. Built with handmade bricks in the 1820s, it's one of two oldest homes in the valley. About 2.5 miles (4 km) farther on, pause at the Station Road Bridge for one of the park's signature photo ops: the arcs of the Brecksville-Northfield Bridge framing the river and the hills beyond.

Halfway through the ride, you can break your journey in either Boston or Peninsula, both charming villages that grew with the construction of the canal. Enjoy some of Cleveland's impossibly good Mitchell's ice cream in a rocking chair on Boston Store's wraparound porch, or grab lunch at a Peninsula restaurant and admire the town's well-preserved 19th-century buildings.

Four and a half miles (7 km) past Peninsula is the Beaver Marsh. In the 19th century, this was drained and replaced by a dairy farm and auto repair shop. When the park was established, the authorities' first inclination was to replace the farm and shop with an event site and, of all things, a parking lot. Fortunately, a colony of beavers had other ideas. Having just returned to Ohio for the first time in a century, they built dams that flooded the area and returned it to its original state. The marsh is now one of the best spots in the park for wildlife viewing. In addition to beavers, you may see muskrats, wood ducks, snapping turtles, otters, and water snakes among the lily pads.

Just before you reach the southern end of the park, turn east on Bath Road for another of the park's natural highlights, the Bath Road Heronry. From mid-February to early July, dozens of great blue herons nest in the trees here. May and June are especially fun, as parents make frequent delivery runs to feed their growing chicks.

> **IF YOU HAVE**
> **A weekend**
>
> As well as the cycle and railroad back-and-forth, hike to Brandywine Falls and the Ledges, and catch a concert in one of the park's performing arts venues.

## Cuyahoga Valley Scenic Railroad

If you don't want to bike back the way you came, just catch the train. The historic Cuyahoga Valley Scenic Railroad (CVSR), the only nonprofit heritage railroad operating within a national park, runs alongside the Towpath Trail between Akron and Independence. Its Explorer program lets hikers, bikers, and kayakers on the trail hail the train at any station and purchase a one-way ticket. Attendants will store any equipment you have in the luggage car.

The railroad also operates round-trip National Park Scenic Excursions, which provide a fun way to see the park, especially if you're traveling with kids. Several classes of ticket are available, including seats in a lounge car or a dome car with extra-large windows. CVSR periodically runs themed rides as well, including fine dining, wine-tasting, and Christmas excursions.

## Mountain biking

If you're looking for a more vigorous ride than the Towpath Trail, Cuyahoga

→

A stone staircase, found along the Ledges Trail, and (inset) a Canadian goose and goslings

### GETTING AROUND

Cuyahoga Valley National Park is a 30-minute drive from either Cleveland or Akron. From both cities, (I-77 runs along the park's western edge and Ohio State Route 8 runs along its eastern edge, connecting with roads that enter the park. Riverview Road runs north-south directly through the center of the park and passes the Boston Mill Visitor Center. There is no public transportation to the park, but the Cuyahoga Valley Scenic Railroad departs from Akron and the Cleveland suburb of Independence and makes several stops within the park from Wednesday to Sunday. You can also bike into Cuyahoga Valley from Cleveland or Akron on the Ohio and Erie Canal Towpath Trail. Within the park, driving, walking, and biking are the easiest ways to get around.

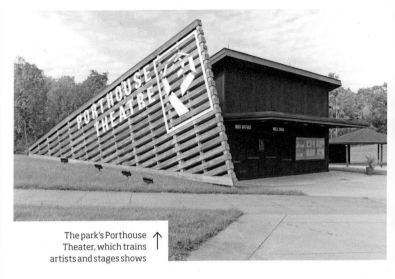

The park's Porthouse
Theater, which trains
artists and stages shows ↑

Valley is also a good mountain biking venue. Just northeast of Peninsula, the East Rim trail system provides 8 miles (13 km) of biking trails and a boulder field on either side of I-80.

## Hiking

There's plenty for those hiking rather than cycling. Within the park are more than 125 miles (200 km) of trails leading through forests, wetlands, and fields, including the Towpath Trail.

The 1.5-mile (2.4-km) Brandywine Gorge Loop takes walkers to the park's most popular site, the 60-ft (18-m) Brandywine Falls, whose changing appearance rewards repeat viewing. It's a rushing cascade in wet periods, a delicate veil that seems to slide down the rock when it's dry, and an abstract

sculpture of ice in winter. If you're hiking the trail in spring, keep an eye out for salamanders breeding in seasonal pools.

Pick up the Buckeye Trail (a state-wide trail that loops around every corner of Ohio) from Boston Mill Visitor Center to reach Blue Hen Falls. The falls are smaller than Brandywine but equally pretty, with thin streams pouring over a ledge into a pool at the base of a natural amphitheater. The hike is a 3-mile (4.8-km) round trip.

Another good hike in the park's center is the Ledges Trail, a 1.8-mile (2.9-km) loop that circles a fascinating rock outcrop and provides impressive views over the valley – it's perhaps one of the most scenic overlooks. The walk can be made longer by adding a loop around Kendall Lake.

### In winter

You'll find just as much to do at Cuyahoga Valley in winter. You can snowshoe and go

cross-country skiing on park trails or go sledding down Kendall Hills, just off Quick Road, southeast of Peninsula. There's even the Boston Mills/Brandywine ski resort, which is split into two venues. The Boston Mills half lies just west of Boston village

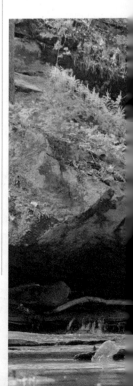

→

The waters of Blue Hen Falls, reached by walking the Buckeye Trail

## Did You Know?

Cuyahoga Valley is the only park that originated as a national recreation area.

> **Music and theater might not spring to mind when you think of national parks, but the performing arts are an integral part of Cuyahoga Valley**

and offers seven runs, while the Brandywine half, just northwest of the falls, has 11 runs and a tubing park.

## Performing Arts

Music and theater might not spring to mind when you think of national parks, but the performing arts are an integral part of Cuyahoga Valley.

At the park's southern end, the Blossom Music Center is the summer home of the Cleveland Orchestra. Purchase a ticket for a seat in the open-air amphitheater in advance, or pack a picnic and buy a ticket for a spot on the lawn upon arrival. The venue also hosts nationally touring rock, hip-hop, and country acts (Alanis Morisette, The Cure, The Chicks, and 50 Cent have all played here in previous years).

Next door to the music center is the Porthouse Theater, an outdoor playhouse operated by Kent State University. Since its opening in 1968, it's staged such plays and musicals as *Death of a Salesman*, *Chicago*, and *Fiddler on the Roof*.

Across the river you'll find Howe Meadow, where the Conservancy for Cuyahoga Valley National Park sponsors free jazz, reggae, and R&B performances one Sunday per month as part of its Rhythm on the River summer concert series. In winter, concerts are held at Happy Days Lodge, east of Peninsula. If you're a fan of Americana, be sure to also check out Voices in the Valley, a showcase of traditional roots music that's held in the appropriately old-timey G.A.R. Hall in Peninsula.

### FIRST LADIES NATIONAL HISTORIC SITE

A worthwhile side trip from the national park is the First Ladies National Historic Site in Canton, a 37-mile (60-km) drive from Peninsula. Here you can tour the grand home of First Lady Ida Saxton McKinley and learn about the legacies of First Ladies through history in the site's education center, housed in the 1895 City National Bank Building.

Staircase leading
past the charming ↑
Brandywine Falls

# EXPLORING CUYAHOGA VALLEY

Cuyahoga Valley preserves the beautiful
landscape on the banks of the Cuyahoga
River between Akron and Cleveland in
Northeast Ohio. The only park in the state,
it encompasses 30,000 acres (12,000 ha) of
forests, rivers, and wetlands.

0 kilometers    4

0 miles    4

N

The two-story
Federal-style **Frazee
House** is indicative of
the properties built by
early white settlers in
the valley.

Home of Cleveland Cavaliers
until 1994, **Richfield
Coliseum** was torn down in
1999. The site is now a
327-acre (132-ha) grassland
and wildflower meadow.

One of the valley's first
communities, Brandywine
village, grew around several
mills that were built here
beginning in 1814, when a
sawmill was built at the top
of the **Brandywine Falls**.

Built across Furnace
Run in the 1800s,
**Everett Covered
Bridge** is the only
covered bridge left in
the county.

After winter, beavers'
internal clocks are out
of sync with dusk, so
early spring visitors
should look for them in
the late afternoon at
the **Beaver Marsh**.

At **Cuyahoga Valley Farmers
Market**, local producers sell an
array of goods and crafts on
Saturday mornings from May
to October.

Great Falls of
Tinkers Creek

Canal
Exploration Center

Tinkers Creek

Cuyahoga River

Frazee
House

OHIO AND ERIE CANAL WAY AMERICA'S BWAY

Station
Road Bridge

BUCKEYE TRAIL

CUYAHOGA SCENIC RAIL ROAD

Brandywine
Falls

Brushwood Lake

Boston Mill
Visitor Center
Blue Hen
Falls

Boston
Boston
Store

Former Site of
Richfield Coliseum

G.A.R. Hall
Peninsula

Octagon
The Ledges
Trailhead

Oak Hill
964 ft (294 m)

Kendall Lake

First Ladies Historic Site
36 miles (58 km)

Everett
Covered
Bridge

Hale
Cuyahoga Valley
Farmers Market

Beaver
Marsh

Blossom
Music Center

BATH ROAD

BATH ROAD

Bath Road
Heronry

Best for *Scenic journeys, by car, by bike, or on foot*

# ACADIA

 Maine  $35 per vehicle; valid for seven days; $6 vehicle reservation to drive Cadillac Summit Road from late spring to late fall nps.gov/acad

Acadia National Park was established in 1919 (originally known as Lafayette National Park), becoming the first national park east of the Mississippi River. It encompasses parts of Mount Desert Island, the Schoodic Peninsula, Isle au Haut, and several outlying islands on Maine's Atlantic coast. It's one of the country's most popular national parks, each year welcoming some four million visitors who come for its inspiring sunrises, challenging mountain hikes, renowned bird-watching, historic carriage roads, and dramatic maritime scenery.

To the Indigenous Wabanaki, the "People of the Dawnland," what's now Acadia National Park is part of a homeland where generations hunted, picked berries, and harvested clams. To 17th-century French explorers, it was an arresting introduction to the continent, a place of U-shaped glacial valleys, towering rocky headlands, and 12-ft (3.7-m) tides. In the mid-1800s, paintings of that dramatic scenery by Thomas Cole and other members of the Hudson River School helped turn Mount Desert Island into a popular tourist destination for New Yorkers and Bostonians. Among the visitors was a who's who of America's rich and powerful, including the Rockefellers, Vanderbilts, Carnegies, and Astors. While the plutocrats' legacy lives on in the form of donated land and the park's system of carriage roads,

> **IF YOU HAVE**
> **A day**
> Spend your time driving Park Loop Road, stopping to picnic and admire the views at Jordan Pond, and hike the historic carriage roads.

today Acadia's riches are shared much more widely. All you need is a few bucks to enjoy some of the country's best hiking, birding, and coastal vistas.

## Exploring the park

Acadia National Park is sprawling, with the bulk on Mount Desert Island, which can be toured in a day (though allowing much more time is advised). Hulls Cove Visitor Center is conveniently located on Route 3, at the park's northern edge. Like many park facilities and local

> **Today Acadia's riches are shared much more widely. All you need is a few bucks to enjoy some of the country's best hiking, birding, and coastal vistas.**

↑ Bass Harbor Head
Light Station, an
iconic Acadia sight

## GETTING AROUND

There are regular flights from Boston to the Hancock County–Bar Harbor Airport, 10 miles (16 km) from the park. If you're traveling by car, take Route 1A southeast from Bangor to Ellsworth. For Mount Desert Island, continue straight onto Route 3. For the Schoodic Peninsula, veer east onto U.S. Route 1, exit south on Hwy. 186, and then turn onto Schoodic Loop Road. Alternatively, take a Concord Coach bus from Boston to Bangor, where a Downeast Transportation bus runs to Bar Harbor. Within the park, Island Explorer operates free buses from late June to early October. Buses make scheduled stops, but you can also flag them down at any point along its 13 routes. To reach Isle au Haut, take the passenger-only ferry from Stonington.

businesses, it's open only from late spring to late fall. Just 3 miles (4.8 km) down the road is the town of Bar Harbor, where you'll find lodgings, restaurants, groceries, and outfitters.

Given Acadia's popularity, summer sees huge crowds at the park; come in winter or during the week in fall for a (relatively) peaceful visit, or forgo the car and plan for a hike, cycle ride, or watery adventure, using public transportation and the Island Explorer to get to and around the park.

### Park Loop Road

The visitor center is the starting point for Acadia's supremely popular 27-mile (43-km) Park Loop Road, which circles the island's east and provides access to many of the park's most-visited sites. The road can get exceptionally crowded between June and September; to save yourself parking headaches (and do the environment a favor) consider using the free Island Explorer buses to get around. Route 4 travels the Park Loop Road, with departures every 30 minutes.

Traveling Park Loop Road clockwise (most of the road is one-way), you'll soon arrive at Sieur de Monts, an area known as the "Heart of Acadia." Visit the Sieur de Monts Nature Center (late May–early October) to learn about the work park scientists do; the Smithsonian-affiliated Abbe Museum for exhibits on Wabanaki history and culture; and the Wild Gardens of Acadia for more than 400 native plant species. The Great Meadow Wetland is also in the area.

Next up is Sand Beach. Yes, the name might be unoriginal

← Kayaking on Jordan Pond, and *(inset)* Bubble Rock, on the top of the South Bubble

Park Loop Road, weaving past fall foliage, as seen from the Bubbles

# EAT

You're in Maine, so fill up on local lobster and blueberries. Bar Harbor has a robust dining scene, but many places in the area close between late fall and late spring.

### Jordan Pond House Restaurant
Tea and popovers on the lawn is a summer tradition at the only eatery within the park. Feast on lobster stew or locally made ice cream.

🏠 Seal Harbor 🌐 jordan pondhouse.com

$$$

### Gateway Lunt's Lobster Pound
Three generations serve up Maine lobsters, lobster rolls, and clam chowder at this really excellent joint just over the bridge from Mount Desert Island.

🏠 Trenton 🌐 gateway luntslobster.com

$$$

### Jeannie's Great Maine Breakfast
Start the day with homemade oatmeal bread, enormous blueberry pancakes, or lobster omelets before heading into the park.

🏠 Bar Harbor 🌐 jeannies breakfast.com

$$$

but, in fairness, it is the only sand beach on Acadia's coast; most others are formed of smooth, round cobblestones. The wide expanse of khaki sand here wouldn't be out of place in Florida, but the water certainly would. Even at the height of summer in August, it doesn't get much warmer than 60°F (16°C).

Less than a mile south of Sand Beach is Thunder Hole, a narrow inlet on the rocky coast. When there's a storm or when the tide sends waves in at the right angle, spray shoots up to 40 ft (12 m) and the channel's air exits with a cacophonous roar. From Thunder Hole, Park Loop Road curves around Otter Point, where the Otter Cliffs provide views of the Cranberry Isles.

After tracing the coast for a couple more miles, the road turns inland and skirts Jordan Pond, one of Acadia's best places for kayaking and canoeing. Just before, you'll pass Jordan Pond Gatehouse, a handsome structure that John D. Rockefeller, Jr. had built in the early 1930s to control access to his carriage roads. On the lake's south shore is Jordan Pond House,

> **When there's a storm or when the tide sends waves in at the right angle, spray shoots up to 40 ft (12 m) and the channel's air exits with a cacophonous roar.**

Strolling along a
carriage road in the
east of the park ↑

a park restaurant famed for its popovers and picnic-perfect lawn, which looks across the water to the lumpy green forms of the Bubbles, twin glacier-smoothed summits.

Near the end of Park Loop is a 3-mile (4.8-km) road that leads to the top of Cadillac Mountain, a popular place to watch the sun come up. At 1,530 ft (466 m), it's the park's highest peak, and its position means that from October 7 to March 6, it's the first place in the country to witness the sunrise. The mountain is named for Antoine de la Mothe Cadillac, a 17th-century French adventurer, trader, and man of exceptionally

suspect character. Born Antoine Laumet, he created the more elaborate name to pass himself off as a noble. It worked, and in 1688 he was granted land on Mount Desert Island. A decade later, he founded the fort that would became the city of Detroit, birthplace of the car that still bears his fabricated name. Note that to drive up Cadillac Mountain between late May and late October, you'll need to make a vehicle reservation online at *www. recreation.gov*. Reservations provide a timed entry.

Almost all of Park Loop Road closes to traffic from roughly December 1 to April 15, but you can travel it by snowmobile in winter.

## Carriage roads

Forty-five miles (72 km) of historic carriage roads thread through the eastern half of Mount Desert Island. Constructed by Rockefeller, Jr. between 1913 and 1940, they

were designed to follow the contours of the land and provide travelers with scenic vistas. The roads wind past streams, cliffs, waterfalls, and mountains, and are a great way to explore the island's interior by foot, bicycle, or horseback – cars have never been allowed on them. As you travel them, notice the granite stones used as guardrails, playfully known as "Rockefeller's teeth."

If you want to step back in time a century, Carriages of Acadia, in Seal Harbor, offers three different carriage tours. It also has a wheelchair-accessible carriage.

In winter, the carriage roads are perfect for snowshoeing and cross-country skiing. If you don't have your own equipment, plenty of places in nearby towns have rentals.

## Bass Harbor Head Light Station

The western half of Mount Desert Island is quieter, with fewer visitors. The one exception is the 1858 Bass Harbor Head Light Station. Perched atop a rocky promontory at the island's southern-most point and backed by dark green pines, the white lighthouse and keeper's abode form an iconic Maine image. Unsurprisingly, this is one of the park's most famous and photographed locales. It gets especially busy around sunset.

→

Resting atop Otter
Cliffs, a popular
climbing spot

> **IF YOU HAVE**
> **A weekend**
>
> For a packed couple of days, watch the sun come up on Cadillac Mountain, hike the Ocean Path, visit Bass Harbor Head Light Station, go tidepooling at Wonderland, and bike on the carriage roads.

Other sites of note on this side of the island include Echo Lake, which has a pleasant beach and is home to nesting loons in summer, and the Carroll Homestead, which dates to 1825 and serves as a vivid example of typical 19th-century life in the region.

## Hiking

Hikers have over 150 miles (241 km) of trails to ramble down in Acadia. Paths traverse everything from forests to ridgelines to seashores. A simple out-and-back is the 2.2-mile (3.5-km) Ocean Path Trail, which runs along granite cliffs from Sand Beach to Otter Point, gifting you with salty sea breezes and Atlantic views. Here and there short detours run down to beaches where you can look for barnacles, crabs, seals, and harbor porpoises.

For a bigger challenge, set off on the 4-mile (6.4-km) Pemetic Mountain Loop. Running through forested lakesides, granite ledges, and ravines, and climbing to Pemetic's summit, it gives you a bit of everything Acadia has to offer. From the top, you can take in views of Jordan Pond and Penobscot Mountain.

## Bird-watching

Acadia is also one of the country's great birding destinations, with more than 300 species found here. No less than James Bond, the renowned ornithologist and secret agent namesake, said that it was Mount Desert

Island that inspired his studies. In the island's east, head to Otter Point to look for seabirds and migrating songbirds that rest in the spruce and fir forest; to Sieur de Monts, where the diverse habitats attract marsh birds, warblers, and flycatchers; and to the Precipice Trail area to spot peregrine falcons. On the west side of the island, the fir and boreal forests of the Western Mountains are home to white-winged crossbills, Swainson's thrush, and various species of warblers, while Seawall in late summer and early fall is a magnet for grebes, sandpipers, and terns.

> **Running through forested lakesides, granite ledges, and ravines, and climbing to Pemetic's summit, it gives you a bit of everything Acadia has to offer.**

→
A spectacular scene at
sunset, enjoyed on the
Schoodic Peninsula

# STAY

There are campsites in
the park and reserva-
tions must be made in
advance. Nearby hotels,
B&Bs, and glamping
sites abound, though
many close from late
fall to late spring.

### The Claremont Hotel
This grande dame has
been open since 1884.
Recent renovations
have produced breezily
stylish rooms that
maintain historic
details.

⌂ Southwest Harbor
ⓦ theclaremont
hotel.com

$ $ $

### Terramor Outdoor
Resort
Luxe tents with ceiling
fans and walk-in
steamer showers.

⌂ Bar Harbor
ⓦ terramor
outdoorresort.com

$ $ $

### Queen Anne's
Revenge
This downtown Bar
Harbor property leans
into the area's seafaring
heritage, but its
nautical decor never
goes overboard.

⌂ Bar Harbor
ⓦ queenannes
revengemaine.com

$ $ $

## Tidepooling
Yet another way to discover
Acadia's nature is to go
tidepooling in the shallows
when the tide goes out. On
Mount Desert Island, hike the
Wonderland or Ship Harbor
trail to the coast to look for
marine snails, sea urchins,
and crabs. On the Schoodic
Peninsula, head to Frazer
Point or Blueberry Hill.

## Schoodic Peninsula
If you're looking to escape
the crowds, make sure you
venture beyond Mount Desert
Island to the other pockets
that make up the park.
    Across Mount Desert
Narrows is the Schoodic
Peninsula, a rugged finger

### Did You Know?

The Schoodic
Peninsula is the
only part of Acadia
National Park on
the mainland.

of wave-battered granite
headlands. Fewer visitors is
an obvious draw but this part
of the park offers much more
besides. Take in views of
lighthouses, lobster boats,
and forested islands from
the Schoodic Loop Road or
explore this sliver of the
mainland on one of its hiking

trails or bike paths. Also here is the Schoodic Institute Welcome Center at Rockefeller Hall, part of a former naval base. Open daily year-round, it has park information and educational exhibits on naval history and Schoodic ecology, and offers some talks and events.

## Isle au Haut

Even more remote is Isle au Haut (High Island), some 15 miles (24 km) southwest of Mount Desert Island. Most of the island's southern half is national park land, providing access to 18 miles (29 km) of primitive trails that twist through and along bogs, wooded uplands, and rocky shorelines. From mid-May to early October, you can camp in one of the five basic lean-tos at Duck Harbor Campground with an advance reservation. There's potable water and a composting toilet but no electricity.

## Island tours

More than a dozen islands sit off Acadia National Park. Most are inaccessible, but you can visit two on ranger-led tours. Trips to Little Cranberry Island (not actually part of the national park) include a visit to the Isleford Historical Museum to learn about the islanders' lives, while tours to Baker Island make stops at an early 19th-century homestead and the still-active Baker Island Light Station, built in 1828.

→
An entrance way leading into Duck Harbor

# EXPLORING ACADIA

Acadia National Park encompasses nearly 50,000 acres (20,000 ha) along the Atlantic coastline of Maine. The park includes Mount Desert Island, Schoodic Peninsula, Isle au Haut, and the other outer islands.

↑ Carroll Homestead, built in 19th-century style

*John Carroll built the humble* **Carroll Homestead** *farmhouse in 1825, and three generations of his family would go on to live here, growing crops and working as masons.*

Tremont
17 miles (27 km) ↗

← Stonington

Sawyer Mountain
485 ft (148 m)

Isle au Haut

Moores Harbor

PARK ROAD

Long Pond

Duck Harbor Campground

0 km    2
0 miles  2

N ↑

Mt Desert Narrows

BAR HARBO

Mount Desert Island

Oak Hill
177 ft (54 m)

Somesville

Mount Desert

Somes Sound

Long Pond

Echo Lake

Acadia Mountain
682 ft (208 m)

PRETTY MARSH ROAD

Carroll Homestead

Seal Cove Pond

Bernard Mountain
1,069 ft (326 m)

Northe Har

SEAL COVE ROAD

Southwest Harbor

TREMONT RD

Tremont

Bass Harbor

Seawall

Bass Harbor Head Light Station

**Bass Harbor Head Light Station** *appears on some U.S. quarters minted in 2012 as part of the America the Beautiful coin series.*

Hike up South Bubble and you'll come across the lonely, hulking boulder known as **Bubble Rock**, dropped here by glaciers 15,000 years ago.

OAD

*Hulls Cove Visitor Center*

Bar Harbor

233

*Eagle Lake*

PARK LOOP ROAD

Sieur de Monts Nature Center

*he Bubbles 2 ft (266 m)*

Cadillac MoOuntain 1,530 ft (466 m)

Precipice Trail

Bubble Rock

*Jordan Pond*

Jordan Pond Gatehouse

*Jordan nd House*

Carriages of Acadia

PEABODY DRIVE

*Sand Beach*

*Thunder Hole*

Otter Point Overlook

186

*Schoodic Peninsala*

*Schoodic Head 433 ft (132 m)*

Rockefeller Hall

*Schoodic Island*

The thunderous boom you hear at **Thunder Hole** is air being forced out of a cave in the ledge as water rushes in.

A century ago, **Otter Point** was the first place in the country to learn of the end of WWI, when a U.S. Navy radio station on the cliffs received a bulletin announcing the armistice.

*Atlantic Ocean*

*Sutton Island*

Islesford Historical Museum

Islesford

*Little Cranberry Island*

*Great anberry sland*

Baker Island Light Station

*Baker Island*

**Baker Island Light Station** guides ships through the shallow shoals that have caused at least nine shipwrecks on Baker Island.

Waves crashing at Thunder Hole at high tide ↑

WEST
VIRGINIA

NEW RIVER
GORGE
*p404*
SHENANDOAH
*p404*

KENTUCKY
*p418*
VIRGINIA

MAMMOTH CAVE
*p412*

TENNESSEE

NORTH
CAROLINA

GREAT SMOKY
MOUNTAINS
*p432*

SOUTH
CAROLINA

ARKANSAS

HOT
SPRINGS
*p426*

CONGAREE
*p442*

GEORGIA

ALABAMA

MISSISSIPPI

LOUISIANA

FLORIDA

EVERGLADES
*p450*
BISCAYNE
*p446*

DRY TORTUGAS
*p460*

# THE
# SOUTHEAST

Stretching south of the Ohio River, the southeast of the
U.S. is comprised of extreme highlands and storm-fed
lowlands, mangrove forests and jewelbox islands, with
a whole gamut of climates running from subtropical to
stormy. This gloriously diverse terrain means the
region's parks seem to occupy different worlds entirely.
The harsh rapids of West Virginia's New River Gorge slice
through the Appalachian Mountains, making whitewater
rafting the ultimate adrenaline adventure. These waterways bear little resemblance to the swamps, marshes,
and sawgrass prairies of the Everglades at Florida's
southernmost tip. Topping most visitors' lists, however,
is Great Smoky Mountains, the country's most visited
park, which rolls from eastern Tennessee into western
North Carolina. While these parks attract wildlife lovers
and hardy explorers, the ancient thermal springs of Hot
Springs instead offer the original wellness break, with
thermal waters the perfect balm after outdoor pursuits.

# 6 DAYS
## *in Florida*

### Day 1

Start your southern Florida tour in the Shark Valley section of Everglades National Park *(p451)*. Leave your car at the visitor center and rent a bike *(www.sharkvalleytramtours.com)* to pedal the 15-mile (24-km) paved loop road through the "River of Grass" (you'll likely spot an alligator or two en route). Stop to take in the views from the Shark Valley Observation Tower halfway. When you've cycled back to the visitor center, book a serene trip with Miccosukee Airboat Rides *(www.miccosukee.com)*, during which you'll learn about Indigenous Miccosukee traditions (simple lunches are served at the nearby Miccosukee General Store). Later, spy more wildlife on the part-gravel Scenic Drive through Big Cypress National Preserve, before dinner at Joanie's Blue Crab Café *(39395 Tamiami Trail, Ochopee)*. Aim to spend the night in Everglades City.

### Day 2

Everglades City is the gateway to the Ten Thousand Islands section of Everglades. The Gulf Coast Visitor Center is the best place to get oriented, before you head out on the water to explore the largest mangrove forest in North America. Take a boat tour *(www.evergladesflorida-adventures.com)*, or rent canoes or kayaks to explore independently. After lunch at the Diving Pelican *(901 Copeland Ave., Everglades City)* visit the Museum of the Everglades then zip over the causeway to Chokoloskee Island, where the creaky Smallwood Store is redolent of early 20th-century pioneer life. From here it's around 80 miles (130 km) to Homestead, where there's plenty of accommodations and places to eat; we recommend Chefs on the Run *(10 E Mowry Dr.)*.

### Day 3

Today it's time for the southern part of Everglades, beginning with the Ernest F. Coe Visitor Center. Your first destination is Flamingo, reached via the park road. Stop for a stroll along the Anhinga or Gumbo Limbo trails through the hardwood jungle hammocks on the way. Aim to arrive at Flamingo for lunch and get your bearings at the Guy Bradley Visitor Center. This

[1] Kayaking in Everglades. ↑

[2] Alligator in Big Cypress.

[3] Downtown Key West.

[4] The Anhinga Trail.

[5] Snorkeling on the coast near Fort Jefferson.

afternoon, hike (or bike) the trails that run through tropical hardwood hammocks along the coast, or take a Backcountry Boat Tour *(www.flamingoeverglades.com)*. Spend the night in a houseboat, "Eco-Tent", or the eco-conscious Flamingo Lodge (constructed from old shipping containers).

## Day 4

After a final stroll through the Everglades to the Pa-hay-okee Lookout, drive to the Dante Fascell Visitor Center, the main hub for Biscayne National Park *(p446)*. From here, you can take a 3.5-hour boat tour to Boca Chita Key (where there's a small beach and historic lighthouse), Elliott Key, or Adams Key. Even better, join a six-hour snorkel and paddle eco-adventure *(www.biscaynenationalparkinstitute.org)* to really get a feel for Biscayne Bay's rich marine life. Spend the night back in Homestead.

## Day 5

It's around 3 hours nonstop to Key West from Homestead, with the Overseas Highway across the Florida Keys one of America's most spectacular routes, its giant causeways and bridges flying over channels patrolled by sharks, giant rays, and all sorts of marine life. There are plenty of seafood shacks, beaches, and attractions to visit on the way, and Key West is worth a day or two in itself. Spend tonight in this celebrated fishing capital and party town before your early drive to the Dry Tortugas.

## Day 6

Almost 70 miles (110 km) west of Key West, the remote Dry Tortugas National Park *(p460)* is best approached by high-speed catamaran *(www.drytortugas.com)*. Boats dock at Garden Key, the main island in the chain – you'll see redbrick Fort Jefferson rising from the ocean like a mirage long before you arrive. Explore the 19th-century fort, snorkel the pristine waters off the key, or take a well-deserved break by lounging on the island's small, golden beaches. Boats normally depart at 3pm for the ride back to Key West, where you can take in a final Florida sunset.

Rolling valleys and dense
woods, making up
Shenandoah's landscape

# SHENANDOAH

📍 Virginia 🚗 $30 per vehicle, valid for seven days
🌐 nps.gov/shen

Shenandoah National Park balances atop the Blue Ridge Mountains, the easternmost spine of the region-defining Appalachians. Running for 105 miles (169 km) from north to south, the park is less than a mile (1.6 km) wide at some points, but within its narrow bounds lie rocky mountain peaks, historic resorts, and 75 scenic overlooks, each more dramatic than the last. Two routes run the length of the park, one for cars and one for feet: Skyline Drive and the Appalachian Trail.

Shenandoah National Park had an unusual genesis. By the 1920s, the government had determined to create a national park within reach of East Coast cities, and it was only after a kind of geographic talent-hunt that Shenandoah was selected. It was a good pick: just an hour and a half from the nation's capital, the area combines thick forest with meadows, wetlands, and rocky outcrops.

The park is named after the nearby Shenandoah River, which, by various accounts, means "silver water," or "great meadow," or "river of high mountains," or "daughter of the stars." Take your pick, because they're all true: this is a place of elegant waterfalls,

↑ Tranquil Doyles River Falls, reached on a trail near Loft Mountain

wildflower-flecked grasslands, soaring summits, and brilliant night skies. Skyline Drive, an integral part of the park, brings it all within reach and transports you to some of the mid-Atlantic's best hiking, camping, and bird-watching.

## Exploring the park

Almost everything of interest in the park is accessed from Skyline Drive. Mileposts run the 105-mile (169-km) length of the road, numbered from

---

🕐 IF YOU HAVE
**A day**

Cruise down Skyline Drive, pausing for the occasional hike into the woods and to marvel at mountain vistas from the scenic overlooks that are dotted along the road.

↑ Cruising along Skyline Drive; the road is especially scenic during the fall

north to south. There are entrance stations at Front Royal and Rockfish Gap, in the north and south, respectively, as well as part way along Skyline Drive at Thornton Gap and Swift Run Gap. Food and/or accommodations, including camping, is available at Mathews Arm, Elkwallow, Skyland, Big Meadows, Lewis Mountain, Loft Mountain Wayside, and Loft Mountain.

## Skyline Drive

To nature lovers, a road might feel like an unfortunate but necessary imposition on a national park at best, but to Shenandoah's planners, it was the main attraction. Reflecting the early 20th-century enthusiasm for the

still-new automobile, they declared that Shenandoah's "greatest single feature" should be a road that would allow motorists to drive the Blue Ridge Mountains and take in their magnificent views. In 1935, four years before the national park was even established, construction began on Skyline Drive. (Its final, southern, section was completed in 1939.)

Some 90 years later, Skyline remains central to Shenandoah. It provides access to the park's two main entrances and is the only real way of getting from one part to the other. And, just as the park's founders envisioned, it continues to be an attraction in itself, and a great way to experience Shenandoah, especially if you're visiting for the first time.

You don't need a special vehicle to drive Skyline. The road is paved and well maintained, although it is occasionally closed due to inclement weather. Gas is available at Big Meadows Wayside, and there are EV charging stations at Skyland and Harry F. Byrd, Sr. Visitor Center. Power outages can

make pumps and EV chargers unreliable, however, so it's a good idea to make sure that your tank/battery is full before entering the park. Drive with care, and keep an eye out for deer, turkeys, and other park residents that regularly cross the road. Driving the length of Skyline takes about three hours, though you'll inevitably require longer to account for stops at the 75 scenic overlooks along the way.

Mileage on Skyline Drive is counted from north to south, and if you tackle it that way, you'll quickly arrive at the Dickey Ridge Visitor Center, where you can get advice and information, view exhibits on the park, and pick up some souvenirs. From there, a 30-minute drive will bring you to the Overall Run Trailhead, which leads to Overall Run Falls. At 93 ft (28 m), they're the highest falls in the park, though if it hasn't rained recently there might not be too much to see.

→

A black bear cub, exploring its new environment

---

**IF YOU HAVE**
**A weekend**

Test yourself with a trek along the park's accessible 101-mile-(163-km-) long section of the Appalachian Trail, overnighting in rustic trailside cabins along the way.

# 500

The number of miles (800 km) of hiking trails in Shenandoah National Park.

Around 6.5 miles (10.5 km) after crossing U.S. Route 211 – the first of two highways that run through the park from east to west and provide access to its center – you'll arrive at a pull-off for the Corbin Cabin Cutoff Trail. The path leads to a rustic log cabin in bucolic Nicholson Hollow, which was once the home of moonshiner George Corbin and is now listed on the National Register of Historic Places.

At mile 41.7, you'll come to Skyland. The resort has hosted travelers since the end of the 19th century, when its then manager, George Freeman Pollock, woke guests and announced meals with a blast from his bugle. Today, you can stay in its hotel rooms, suites, and cabins; eat in its restaurant and taproom; attend a ranger program; or join one of Skyland Stables' guided horseback rides. In the grounds, you'll also find the 1911 Massanutten Lodge, the home of George's wife and Skyland co-owner Addie Nairn Pollock. It now houses an exhibit on the lives of women who visited the resort in the Roaring 20s.

Ten miles (16 km) on from Skyland is the Harry F. Byrd, Sr. Visitor Center. In the immediate vicinity you'll find two of the park's highlights: Dark Hollow Falls and Big Meadows. Contrary to its forbidding name, Dark Hollow Falls is much more Rivendell than Mordor, with gentle tiered streams flowing over mossy rocks in a sylvan glen. Set atop a mountain, Big Meadows is a great venue for wildlife spotting during the day – look for Shenandoah's famed black bears – and stargazing at night. From spring through late fall, you can spend the night at either Big Meadows Campground or nearby Big Meadows Lodge, which has rooms and cabins.

Immediately after the visitor center, take a detour along Rapidan Road to Camp Hoover Road and Rapidan Camp, a rustic retreat that President Herbert Hoover had built between 1929 and 1932. Three of the original 13 buildings remain. Tours are usually offered from spring through fall.

# EAT

You'll find waysides and eateries connected to park lodges along Skyline Drive and some truly exceptional fine dining in surrounding towns such as Staunton, Sperryville, and Washington.

### New Market Taproom
In the park's Big Meadows Lodge, the New Market taproom serves highly noshable items like pizza and pulled-pork nachos alongside local beers.

🏠 Shenandoah National Park
🌐 goshenandoah.com/dining/big-meadows-lodge/taproom-menu

### Patty O's Cafe & Bakery
Three-Michelin-star chef and James Beard Foundation Lifetime Achievement Award-winner Patrick O'Connell's take on a neighborhood café.

🏠 Washington
🌐 pattyoscafe.com

$$$

### Three Blacksmiths
Chef-owners Sara and Jake Addeo do prix-fixe tasting menus that show off the region's seasonal ingredients in dishes such as burnt wheat orecchiette and Southern vinegar pie.

🏠 Sperryville
🌐 threeblacksmiths.com

$$$

# STAY

Shenandoah has three park-affiliated accommodations, plus five campgrounds and backcountry camping. Other hotels, resorts, and B&Bs are just a short drive away.

### Skyland

Perched atop Skyline Drive's highest point, park-affiliated Skyland offers hotel rooms, suites, cabins, and pet-friendly accommodations.

**⌂ Shenandoah National Park**
**[W] goshenandoah.com/lodging/skyland**

$$$

### Hotel Laurance

This boutique property has been in operation since 1883 and features 12 suites decorated in cool gray tones, most of which come with kitchens.

**⌂ Luray**
**[W] hotellaurance.com**

$$$

### Massanutten Resort

An on-site waterpark, escape rooms, ski hill, and much more make this sprawling resort ideal for families.

**⌂ Massanutten**
**[W] massresort.com**

$$$

Back on Skyline Drive, around 15 minutes from the Harry F. Byrd, Sr. Visitor Center you'll find the Lewis Mountain Campground and Picnic Grounds. While seemingly unremarkable today, this was the only place in the park that Black visitors were allowed to picnic and camp until Shenandoah was officially desegregated in 1950.

After a couple of dozen or so scenic overlooks, Shenandoah's southern entrance marks the terminus of Skyline Drive, but you don't have to stop there. The road doesn't end; it just turns into the Blue Ridge Parkway, which you can follow south for 469 legendary miles (755 km) to the entrance of Great Smoky Mountains National Park.

### The Appalachian Trail

The Appalachian Trail (AT) runs in tandem with Skyline Drive, through almost the length of the park, and provides access to all of the above sites, save Dickey Ridge Visitor Center. The difference, of course, is that the trail provides a much more intimate encounter with Shenandoah's dramatic rock outcrops, cascading streams, and more than 850 species of wildflowers.

If you're new to the trail, the 101 miles (163 km) that

→

Making the tough hike up Old Rag Mountain and (*inset*) squeezing through a narrow gap in the mountain's edge

run through the park are a fine place to get introduced, as the path here is in good shape and climbs rarely exceed 1,000 ft (305 m). Throughout Shenandoah, the trail is maintained by the Potomac Appalachian Trail Club. If you're planning to hike the AT, the club's website *(www.patc.net)* is a valuable resource and the place to make reservations for cabins along the trail (including Corbin Cabin). In addition to the facilities at Skyland and Big Meadows, hikers can get basic meals and groceries at Elkwallow Wayside (mile 24.1) and Loft Mountain Wayside (mile 79.5) on Skyline Drive.

## Old Rag Mountain

Ironically, Shenandoah's most popular destination, Old Rag Mountain, is hard to access from Skyline Drive and the

### GETTING AROUND

Unless you're through-hiking the Appalachian Trail, you'll need a car or bike to get to and around Shenandoah National Park, as public transportation is not available. The nearest major city is Washington, D.C. To reach the park and Dickey Ridge Visitor Center from the capital, take I-66 west to the town of Fort Royal, where Route 522/340 South leads to Skyline Drive. I-64 runs west from Richmond and Charlottesville and east from Waynesboro to the park's southern end. Within the park, there's essentially one road, Skyline Drive, which provides access to Harry F. Byrd, Sr. Visitor Center and almost all the park's trailheads and points of interest.

Appalachian Trail, and most visitors approach it from towns outside the park's eastern boundary. Hikes up the mountain are tough, with rock scrambles and large changes in elevation, but the payoff is 360-degree views over the Blue Ridges and Shenandoah Valley. With a full day, consider tackling the 9.4-mile (15 km) Old Rag

Circuit. From the parking area, ascend the Ridge Trail to the 3,291-ft (3,003-m) summit before taking the Saddle Trail down to the Old Rag Shelter and making your way back to the parking lot via Weakley Hollow Fire Road. Note that for Old Rag you may need to purchase a day-use ticket in advance, in addition to your park entrance pass.

# EXPLORING SHENANDOAH

In beautiful northern Virginia, Shenandoah spans a whopping 199,040 acres (80,547 ha). The park's main draw, the Skyline Drive, is the best way to explore, stopping off to absorb the views, quietly witness the white-tailed deer or black bears going about their daily routine, or stretch your legs by following parts of the legendary Appalachian Trail. Start your adventure in the early evening, when fewer cars are on the road.

↑ Big Meadows Lodge, the perfect stopping-off point along Skyline Drive

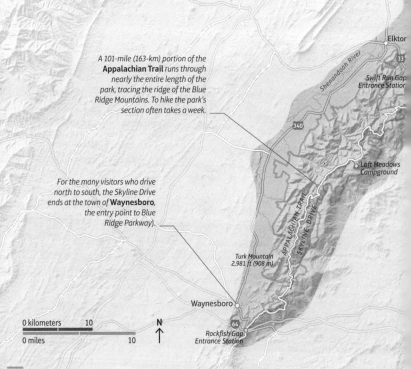

A 101-mile (163-km) portion of the **Appalachian Trail** runs through nearly the entire length of the park, tracing the ridge of the Blue Ridge Mountains. To hike the park's section often takes a week.

For the many visitors who drive north to south, the Skyline Drive ends at the town of **Waynesboro**, the entry point to Blue Ridge Parkway).

Elktor

Shenandoah River

Swift Run Gap Entrance Station

Loft Meadows Campground

APPALACHIAN TRAIL

SKYLINE DRIVE

Turk Mountain 2,981 ft (908 m)

Waynesboro

0 kilometers 10
0 miles 10

N

Rockfish Gap Entrance Station

## 75

The number of overlooks along Skyline Drive, with views of Shenandoah Valley and Piedmont.

Front Royal

Front Royal Entrance Station

Dickey Ridge Visitor Center

522

340

Overall Run Falls

APPALACHIAN TRAIL

SKYLINE DRIVE

Mathews Arm Campground

Three Sisters 2,085 ft (635 m)

211

Thornton Gap Entrance Station

211

The four-room **Corbin Cabin** on the Hughes River was restored in 2017 and has a dining area, a kitchen with a wood-burning stove, a living area with a fireplace, and a loft with bunk beds.

Massanutten Lodge

Skyland

Corbin Cabin

Hawksbill 4,051 ft (1,235m)

Old Rag Mountain 3,268 ft (996 m)

ig Meadows ampground

Harry F. Byrd, Sr. Visitor Center

Big Meadows Lodge

Dark Hollow Falls

**Skyland** sits at the park's highest elevation: 3,680 ft (1,122 m) above sea level. In addition to lodging and dining, the resort regularly hosts live music.

Lewis Mountain npground

Rapidan Camp

In addition to hiking, **Old Rag Mountain** provides a number of opportunities for bouldering and rock climbing. Climbing routes range in difficulty from 5.4 to 5.13a.

SKYLINE DRIVE

33

**Dark Hollow Falls** is accessible by a steep and rocky 1.4-mile (2.3-km) hike, one of the park's most trodden trails.

The remaining buildings at **Rapidan Camp** are the Brown House (like the White House, but with logs); the Prime Minister's Cabin, named for British Prime Minister Ramsay MacDonald's visit; and the Creel, where two of the president's aides stayed.

**Big Meadows Lodge** provides pet-friendly accommodations, and its Spottswood Dining Room has a Canine Cuisine Menu.

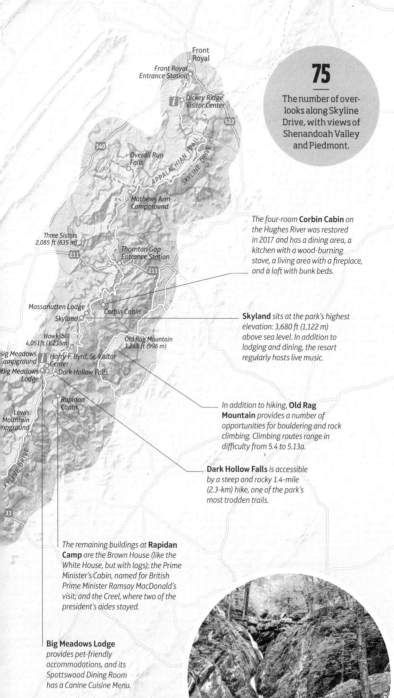

→ Dark Hollow Falls, where never-ending cascades flow amid dense greenery

# MAMMOTH CAVE

📍 Kentucky 🎫 Free 🌐 nps.gov/maca

Winding hundreds of miles beneath the bluegrass of Kentucky, the UNESCO World Heritage Site of Mammoth Cave is the largest cave in the world. Known for its expansive chambers, this mysterious labyrinth of passageways is lined with delicate blossoms of flower-like formations.

Stepping foot into Mammoth Cave transports you to a subterranean wonderworld where natural and cultural history converge. Millions of years ago, limestone dissolved to form the first passages of the cave, which have continued to grow and expand over time. Prehistoric peoples discovered the cave eons ago, while Indigenous hunter-gatherers used the cave as a quary for minerals such as gypsum, and for protection from harsh weather. In the 1800s, the cave was discovered by European explorers: legend has it that a hunter named John Houchins followed a bear into what is now the cave's main entry point. Word spread about the cave's curiosities, and tours, similar to the ones that still run today, began in earnest.

## Exploring the park

Most visitors to Mammoth Cave will spend all of their time in the park hundreds of feet below the surface: access to the cave's vast system of chambers is by tour only, which starts on the south side of the park, just up the hill from the visitor center, at the cave's historic entrance.

Above ground, the park is divided by the Green River, which flows east to west through its center; the Nolin River, an offshoot, runs to the northwest. These waters are a favorite destination with outdoor enthusiasts, who come to boat, fish, and take overnight camping trips along their 36 miles (58 km) of winding riverbanks. The park's northern section has more than 65 miles of rugged trails to entice hikers, bikers, and horseback riders.

## STAY

The park's one lodging is close to trails and cave tours. There are three campgrounds, too, as well as backcountry campsites, all of which must be reserved in advance. Nearby towns offer more options.

### Lodge at Mammoth Cave
A mix of modern rooms and historic cottages set among big oak woods in the heart of the national park.

🏠 Park City 🌐 mammoth
cavelodge.com

### Hampton Inn by Hilton
Offers all the necessities you need, five minutes from the park.

🏠 Cave City
🌐 hilton.com

The Green River, which cuts through Mammoth Cave National Park

↑ A park ranger lighting the way along a passage on the Historic Tour route

# EAT

There are a few sit-down dining and grab-and-go food options near Mammoth Cave Visitor Center. There's also a grocery store where you can pick up food and supplies to take to one of the park's picnic areas.

### Green River Grill

Fine dining featuring local farm-fresh foods and Kentucky favorites.

🏠 Lodge at Mammoth Cave
🌐 mammothcave lodge.com

$ $ $

---

### The Food Shack

Hot food options including burgers and pizza, beverages, ice cream, and a breakfast menu.

🏠 Next to Mammoth Cave Visitor Center
🌐 nps.gov/maca

$ $ $

⬅
Broken flowstone formations known as Frozen Niagara

→
A video walking visitors through Mammoth Cave's geology

## Park history

Tours of Mammoth Cave have been going strong for more than 200 years. In the early days, wealthy visitors from across North America came to marvel at this "new" attraction, drawn by the enthusiastic marketing of Franklin Goring, one of the first cave owners. Goring, who went on to become a U.S. Congressman in 1874, was a slaveowner from Kentucky, who sent enslaved people into the cave to mine for natural resources such as potassium nitrate, used in the creation of gunpowder. One of them was 17-year-old Stephen Bishop, who had a keen interest in the caverns and learned the layout of their passageways so thoroughly that he became a guide for the others. When he was eventually freed from slavery, he guided tours in Mammoth Cave for the remainder of his life. His gravesite is located on park grounds at the Old Guide's Cemetery.

## Cave tours

There are many different types of cave tour available at Mammoth Cave, from short taster tours that are ideal for families to more in-depth discoveries of this magical underground world. All of them give a memorable insight into the makeup of Mammoth Cave and its variety of passages: canyon passages, formed by streams of water; tube passages; large canyon composite passages, where several different passages have eroded together; and keyhole

📅 IF YOU HAVE
**A day**

Join one of the many tours on offer: opt for the Domes and Dripstones Tour for a great introduction to the world's largest cave.

passages. A few tours are seasonal, but there will always be some kind of tour on offer, no matter what time of the year you visit.

The most accessible tour of Mammoth Cave, and the shortest, lasting around an hour in total, is the Frozen Niagara. Named after the dramatic flowstone that is said to resemble a calcium-carbonate version of the famous waterfall, this tour was designed to offer a taste of the cave's vast network of interlinking passages without a huge time commitment and is perfect for children, elderly visitors, travelers with

mobility issues, and those who don't enjoy tight spaces but want to step out of their comfort zone a little bit.

For a classic Mammoth Cave experience, try the intermediate Domes and Dripstones Tour. It begins at a plunging sinkhole before passing through several domes to the Frozen Niagara flowstone. This tour is a great option for visitors wanting to learn more about the science of caves while viewing impressive collections of stalagmites and stalactites. It follows a route that's been used by guides for more than a century, and has hundreds of stairs and steep inclines.

The popular Historic Tour ventures into some of the huge chambers that helped give Mammoth Cave its name, including a vertical shaft known as "Mammoth Dome," which reaches up over 190 ft (58 m). The tour is also a good route for learning more about the cave system's keyhole

passages, which chart how water levels in Mammoth Cave changed over time; the tour squeezes through the aptly named keyhole passage of Fat Man's Misery.

If you want to get down and dirty, sign up for the 6-hour Wild Cave Tour, on which you'll be crawling and climbing your way through some of the cavern's narrowest passages. The tour is seasonal, so check with park rangers in adavnce.

Lantern Tours reveal historical relics such as abstract drawings and scrawled names that were painted with candle soot by early explorers. Look closely and you'll spot cave crickets scuttling along the walls and bats hanging from the craggy ceilings.

In addition to the regular tours, every year the park's rangers host a handful of special events, including an annual Christmas "Cave Sing."

### GETTING AROUND

The nearest airports to Mammoth Cave are in Louisville, Kentucky, and Nashville, Tennessee. Most of the visitor services are on the south side of the park, accessible from I-65. The park stretches across 53,000 acres (21,500 ha) and is bisected by the Green River. No bridges cross the river, but the free Green River Ferry operates year-round and will save you from driving around the park's perimeter when trying to get from south to north (or vice versa). The scenic 9-mile (14.5-km) Mammoth Cave Railroad Hike and Bike Trail connects the park with the nearby town of Park City, Kentucky, and runs along a forested portion of the old railroad.

# EXPLORING MAMMOTH CAVE

Winding hundreds of miles beneath Kentucky, Mammoth Cave is currently mapped at 426 miles (686 km). Exploring the national park's underbelly is only possible on a tour, but there's plenty to do above ground, too, from riding cycling paths to hitting hiking trails.

*The **First Creek Trail** winds through old-growth Kentucky forest for 6.7 miles (10.8 km), with a mighty drop down to First Creek Lake.*

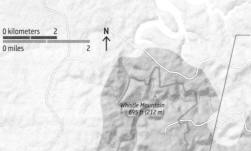

0 kilometers 2
0 miles 2
N ↑

OLLIE ROAD

Whistle Mountain
695 ft (212 m)

FIRST CREEK TRAIL

First Creek Lake

HOUCHIN FERRY ROAD

MCCOY HOLLOW TRAIL

COLLIEE RIDGE TRAIL

Nolin River

Green River

HOUCHIN

Houchin Ferry

Houchin Ferry
Campground

70

Good Spring
Church

Buffalo
Miles-Davis
Cemetery

Creek

Green River

SAL HOLLOW TRAIL

MAMMOTH CAVE ROAD

Turnhole
Bend

The Ceda
Sink Trail

↑ The Green River Ferry transporting visitors across the park

*The **Cedar Sink Trail**, a 1-mile (1.6-km) hike, is home to a large sinkhole and beautiful spring and summer wildflowers.*

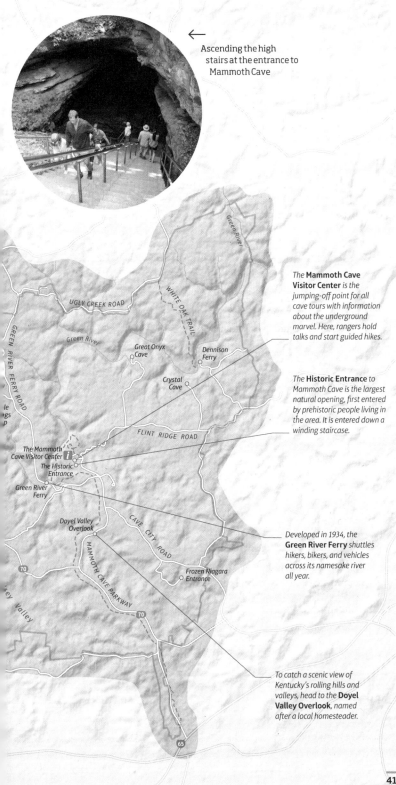

Ascending the high stairs at the entrance to Mammoth Cave

The **Mammoth Cave Visitor Center** is the jumping-off point for all cave tours with information about the underground marvel. Here, rangers hold talks and start guided hikes.

The **Historic Entrance** to Mammoth Cave is the largest natural opening, first entered by prehistoric people living in the area. It is entered down a winding staircase.

Developed in 1934, the **Green River Ferry** shuttles hikers, bikers, and vehicles across its namesake river all year.

To catch a scenic view of Kentucky's rolling hills and valleys, head to the **Doyel Valley Overlook**, named after a local homesteader.

GREEN RIVER FERRY ROAD

UGLY CREEK ROAD

Green River

WHITE OAK TRAIL

Green River

Great Onyx Cave

Dennison Ferry

Crystal Cave

FLINT RIDGE ROAD

The Mammoth Cave Visitor Center

The Historic Entrance

Green River Ferry

Doyel Valley Overlook

CAVE CITY ROAD

70

MAMMOTH CAVE PARKWAY

Frozen Niagara Entrance

70

65

Fall foliage coloring the landscape at the Endless Wall, a cliff beside the river ↑

# NEW RIVER GORGE

📍 West Virginia 🏷 Free 🌐 nps.gov/neri

This might be the U.S.'s newest national park, only established in 1978, but that's the only thing young about it. The misleadingly named New River is in fact one of the oldest rivers on Earth, having first cut a path through the heart of the Appalachian Mountains as many as 360 million years ago. The erosion brought about by the fast-flowing river has sculpted huge rocks into an array of abstract shapes, which today provide the park with some world renowned rock climbing, while the water itself offers some of the country's best whitewater rafting.

## Did You Know?

Every October, Bridge Day™ is held to commemorate the completion of the New River Gorge Bridge.

Flowing through the center of this national park, the New River has authored every chapter of this region's history. Its erosive power defined the landscape, shaping the Appalachians and carving out dramatic sandstone cliffs. As a passage through the rugged terrain, it has provided a conduit for migrating animals and drifting seeds, resulting in an area of exceptional biodiversity. And it wrote the prelude to West Virginia's modern history, exposing veins of coal in the earth and setting in motion the industrialization that defined the state's 19th and 20th centuries. Today, the river and

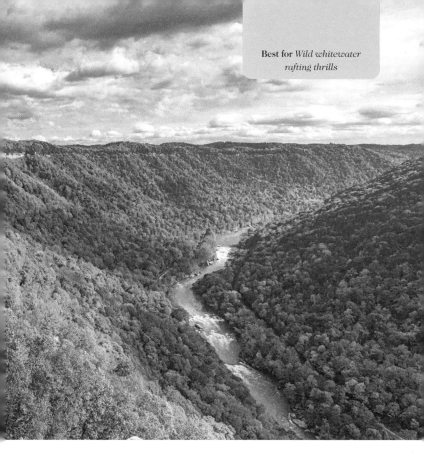

Best for *Wild whitewater rafting thrills*

its creations provide endless opportunities for adventure, whether you're coming to ride its whitewater, climb its rock walls, seek out wildlife, or dig into the lives of those who dug in the park's now-abandoned mining towns.

## Exploring the park

New River Gorge National Park covers 70,000-plus acres (over 28,300 ha) on either side of a 53-mile (85-km) stretch of the New River. Its shape and mountainous terrain mean you often have little choice except to drive from A to B – the park has no public transportation, and biking around is a challenge.

There are several access points, but most visitors focus their time in the area around the Canyon Rim Visitor Center, adjacent to the iconic New River Gorge Bridge at the park's north end. There are three other visitor centers – Sandstone in the south, and Grandview and Thurmond in the middle of the park – but opening months vary.

**IF YOU HAVE**
**A day**

Start with a splash on a whitewater rafting trip down the New River, passing under the New River Gorge Bridge. End the day hiking the Grandview Rim Trail for epic views.

$\rightarrow$
The park's Canyon Rim Visitor Center

# EAT

There are no restaurants in the park, but you'll find places to eat and grocery stores in Beckley, Beaver, Fayetteville, Hinton, and other towns close by.

### Tamarack Marketplace
This marketplace is home to both an art gallery and a fast-casual style restaurant. Tuck into Appalachian-inspired dishes like fried green tomatoes and chicken pot pie before checking out works from West Virginian artists. Note that it's closed on Tuesdays.

Beckley
tamarackwv.com

$$$

### Cathedral Cafe
Tuck into pancakes or paninis at this soulful café, housed in a former church.

Fayetteville
thecathedralcafe.com

$$$

### The Char
This old-school fine-dining steak house has a 50-year pedigree, serving up steaks, of course, as well as the likes of shrimp cocktail and fettuccine alfredo. Great wine and cocktail list, too.

Beckley
the-char.com

$$$

↑ Starting a whitewater rafting adventure below the New River Gorge Bridge

## Whitewater rafting
Naturally, the New River is the main pull to this park, and offers some of the country's best whitewater rafting. It also has a bit of a Jekyll and Hyde thing going on: the upper river, in the park's south, is ideal for families and beginners, with extended pools and rapids that don't exceed Class III, meaning you'll get a good rush while feeling safe and sound on the water. In the lower river, to the north, things get serious. This is where you'll find big water: Class IV and V rapids, mean crosscurrents, and menacing boulders. If you're an experienced paddler, it's adrenaline-pumping bliss.

The park's rafting season lasts from roughly April to October, though you can run the river outside that window, too. Numerous companies offer guided whitewater trips that can last anywhere from a few hours to a few days. They'll transport you to and from the river and provide you with instruction, equipment, and trained guides. Outfitters licensed by the West Virginia Department

> In the lower river, to the north, things get serious. This is where you'll find big water: Class IV and V rapids, mean crosscurrents, and menacing boulders.

of Natural Resources include West Virginia Adventures (www.trywva.com), Cantrell Ultimate Rafting (www.cantrellultimaterafting.com), and ACE Adventure Resort (www.aceraft.com).

## Rock climbing
For those who get their thrills from heights, New River Gorge is also the eastern U.S.'s best climbing destination, thanks to its more than 1,400 established rock climbs and Nuttall sandstone, which is both grippy and easy on fingers. Cliffs in the park range from 30 to 120 ft (10 to 40 m). Sport climbing, a discipline that makes use of preplaced bolts, is especially good here.

The bulk of the park's climbs are graded between

5.9 and 5.12, meaning expert and advanced climbers will have the most fun here. If you don't have loads of climbing experience, good routes to try include Jumping Jack Flash (5.7) at the Junkyard Wall and Mrs. Field's Follies (5.8). If you're a seasoned pro, be sure to tackle the raved-about Porter for the Recorder (5.11) and Legacy (5.11a), the latter of which is part of the Endless Wall, a 3-mile (5-km) cliff that overlooks the New River.

As with whitewater rafting, you'll find plenty of local companies that offer rock climbing lessons and guided excursions, including Appalachian Mountain Guides (www.appalachianmountain guides.com) and New River Climbing School (www.new riverclimbingschool.com). Spring and fall provide the best weather for climbing, so plan accordingly to scale the rocks.

## Hiking

If you're perfectly happy keeping both feet on the ground, you'll be glad to find more than 40 hiking trails within the park. Better yet, routes provide remarkable diversity in terms of difficulty, environment, and attractions. The moderate Grandview Rim Trail is a favorite, and runs 1.6 miles (2.6 km) between the Turkey Spur Overlook and the Grandview Overlook, where you're blessed with vistas of a sweeping horseshoe bend in the river and views straight down the gorge from 1,400 ft (427 m) up. Note that there are small, steep hills on this route. The gentle 1.2-mile (1.9-km) Burnwood Trail loop, meanwhile, takes you through copses of old-growth forest where some trees are more than 300 years old.

→
Spidering up the sandstone cliffs on one of more than 1,400 rock climbs in the park

The ghost town of Thurmond and its rail tracks, once a busy depot ↑

Ramblers seeking a longer adventure should set off on the Kaymoor Trail, which runs 8.6 miles (13.8 km) alongside the gorge and leads past beautiful views, waterfalls, and historic sites. One such site, the Kaymoor coal mine, was once one of the most successful mines in the area. As you hike the route, look out for some of the park's varied wildlife, including deer, black bears, and bobcats in the forest, and river cooters and giant hellbender salamanders in the New River and its tributaries.

Hellbender salamanders are especially interesting inhabitants, also known as snot otters, devil dogs, and lasagna lizards; they live along the rocky streambeds of cool, clear rivers in the park, and can grow to more than 2 ft (0.6 m) long.

## Driving

Since you're more than likely going to be getting between trailheads in the car, you might as well take advantage of the park's terrific drives. If you're short on time, cruise the Fayette Station Road, which packs a bit of everything into just 7.5 miles (12 km). From the New River Gorge Bridge, the century-old roadway twists down the gorge and back up the other side, letting you experience the dramatic terrain, giving you up-close looks at the New River and hardwood forests, and taking you through the remnants of coal-mining towns.

### GETTING AROUND

Amtrak's New York to Chicago Cardinal route makes stops in Hinton, at the park's south end; Prince, in its middle; and Thurmond, in its north. There's no public transportation within the park, so it's most convenient to get around by car. Canyon Rim Visitor Center is just off U.S. Hwy. 19, at the eastern end of the New River Gorge Bridge (if you approach from the west, you'll drive across it). At the opposite end of the park, Sandstone Visitor Center is located next to an exit on I-64, which runs east from the city of Beckley. To get to Grandview Visitor Center, take I-64 from Beckley and exit north onto Grandview Road. Thurmond Depot Visitor Center is reached via Thurmond Road from the town of Glen Jean.

Another brilliant option is to follow the African American Heritage Auto Tour. Available on the National Park Service app, the audio tour delves into the history of Black Americans in the region, particularly that of the men and women who came here to work in the coal mines and on the railroad. It makes stops both in the national park – including Nuttallburg and the Quinnimont Missionary Baptist Church – and the surrounding counties.

## Historic sites

New River Gorge's natural blessings are many, of course, but the region's human history is just as profound, and remnants of the past don't shy away here. Following the completion of a railroad in 1872, mining towns sprouted up throughout the gorge, as entrepreneurs sought to take advantage of the local coal deposits. During this time, miners endured harsh conditions to power the country's Industrial Revolution. By the mid-20th century, most of these boomtowns had gone bust and disappeared, but you can explore their remains in places like Kaymoor and Quinnimont. The most vivid such ghost town is Nuttallburg, where old mining equipment, coke ovens, and a tipple that loaded coal onto train cars recall a very different era in the gorge.

And then there's the park's incredible industrial history. Its signature image is the New River Gorge Bridge, a marvel of engineering that crosses the New River near the park's northern end. Completed in 1977, and costing a whopping $37 million, it towers 876 ft (267 m) above the valley and offers the western hemisphere's longest steel span, at 1,700 ft (518 m). To get an engineer's-eye view of the structure, sign up for a leisurely 2–3 hour tour along the catwalk with Bridge Walk (www.bridgewalk.com).

←
Admiring the verdant landscape from the Grandview Overlook

# STAY

You won't find any lodgings at New River Gorge, but there are family-friendly hotels and comfy B&Bs in the nearby towns. There are eight campgrounds scattered around the park, though they don't have any facilities or take reservations.

### Glen Ferris Inn

Almost 200 years old, the handsome Glen Ferris has hosted four U.S. presidents.

⌂ Glen Ferris ⓦ glenferrisinn.com

 $ $ $

### Adventures on the Gorge

AOTG has glamping tents, cabins, and lodges that sleep 2–20 people. It also operates whitewater rafting trips and zipline tours.

⌂ Lansing ⓦ adventuresonthegorge.com

 $ $ $

### The Historic Morris Harvey House

Time seems to have stopped in the 19th century at this gorgeous five-room B&B near the New River Gorge Bridge.

⌂ Fayetteville ⓦ morrisharveyhouse.com

 $ $ $

# EXPLORING NEW RIVER GORGE

New River Gorge National Park is as wild a land as you'll find in the eastern U.S. The New River flows through it, winding beneath broad slopes covered with oaks, maples, white pines and sycamores.

**Cotton Hill** provides great access to the river and activities that range from swimming to fishing. It's also a perfect place for rock climbing endeavors.

The Fayette County Chamber of Commerce hosts Bridge Day™ on the third Saturday of October. The **New River Gorge Bridge** is closed to traffic and opened to pedestrians who can watch BASE jumpers launch themselves into the gorge.

Now abandoned, **Nuttallburg** was an important coal-mining town that sprung up in 1873.

Founded in 1870, the town of Prince flourished as one of the area's first railroad towns. Amtrak trains still stop at the **Prince Depot** that dates to 1946

Cotton Hill
60
Hawks Nest Dam
16
Ames Heights
19
New River Gorge Bridge
Canyon Rim Visitor Center
Fayette Station Road
Endless Wall Trail
Nuttallbur Mine Site
Fayetteville
New River
Cunard
Thurmond
Thurmond Depot Visitor Center
25
MCKENDREE ROAD
New River
Terry
Prince Depot
Quinnimont Missionary Baptist Chur
41
Grandview Visitor Center
Turkey Spur Overlook
Grandview Overlook
Glade Creek
64

A coal conveyor still standing in Nuttallburg ↑

The sky-high **Grandview Overlook** offers some of the park's most dramatic scenery, including a horseshoe bend in the river.

↑ Sandstone Falls, spanning the river
where it's 1,500 ft (457 m) wide

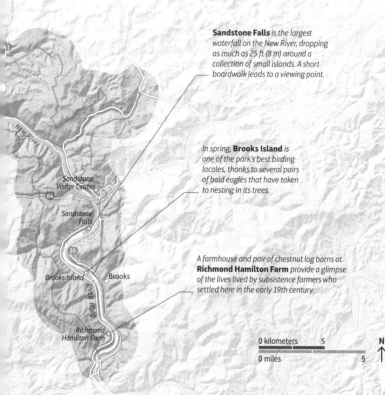

**Sandstone Falls** *is the largest
waterfall on the New River, dropping
as much as 25 ft (8 m) around a
collection of small islands. A short
boardwalk leads to a viewing point.*

*In spring,* **Brooks Island** *is
one of the park's best birding
locales, thanks to several pairs
of bald eagles that have taken
to nesting in its trees.*

*A farmhouse and pair of chestnut log barns at*
**Richmond Hamilton Farm** *provide a glimpse
of the lives lived by subsistence farmers who
settled here in the early 19th century.*

Best for *Some rest and relaxation*

# HOT SPRINGS

📍Arkansas 💲Free 🌐nps.gov/hosp

With a burst of steam, the concept of American wellness was born in this tiny pocket of Arkansas. Tucked into the Zig-Zag Mountains and surrounding the center of the town of Hot Springs, this is a park like no other, its thermal springs having attracted visitors for two centuries. Mountain views and forested hikes are naturally on offer here, but you don't visit this park for epic adventures; rest, rejuvenate, and relax.

### IF YOU HAVE
**A day**

Work up a sweat on a hike around Hot Springs Mountain, then recover with a soak at Buckstaff Bathhouse, finishing up with a much-needed Swedish massage.

For centuries, central Arkansas' thermal springs were known only to the region's Indigenous people. Then, in 1804, the explorers William Dunbar and George Hunter stumbled upon them, and word quickly got out. Settlers flocked to the area, and almost as soon as there was anything resembling a town here, there was a tourist town. Entrepreneurs hawked the waters as a "cure all" (despite the fact they cured nothing), and the sick and the tired journeyed here to bathe, drink the spring water, exercise, and hike. Recognizing the springs' popularity and the need to preserve them, President

**Did You Know?**

At 5,550 acres (2,200 ha), Hot Springs could fit inside Wrangell-St. Elias National Park almost 2,400 times.

→

A stunning stained-glass ceiling adorning the Fordyce Bathhouse

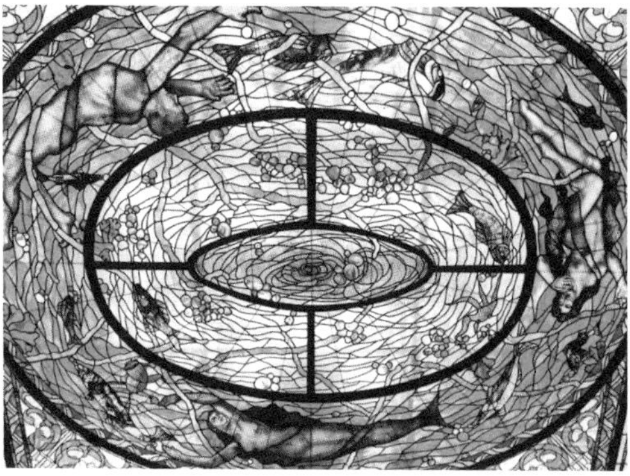

Andrew Jackson signed legislation setting aside some of the land for public use in 1832, in effect creating a park for the nation four decades before Yellowstone was established. In time, tumble-down bathing shacks gave way to sturdier wooden bathhouses, which were in turn replaced by the grand structures that today line the park's famed Bathhouse Row.

## Exploring the park

Much of the action at one of the U.S.'s smallest national parks is focused on Bathhouse Row, a strip of handsome early 20th-century structures built to accommodate the visitors who came here for some R&R. To get to the hiking trails and scenic overlooks beyond the baths, it's easy to get around by car or bike; the latter is the perfect way to work your muscles before a rewarding soak.

## Bathhouse Row

You'll inevitably begin your visit at Bathhouse Row, which serves as the park's entrance, the site of the visitor center, and the only place in the park that you can bathe in the waters. The park's hot springs are the product not of volcanic

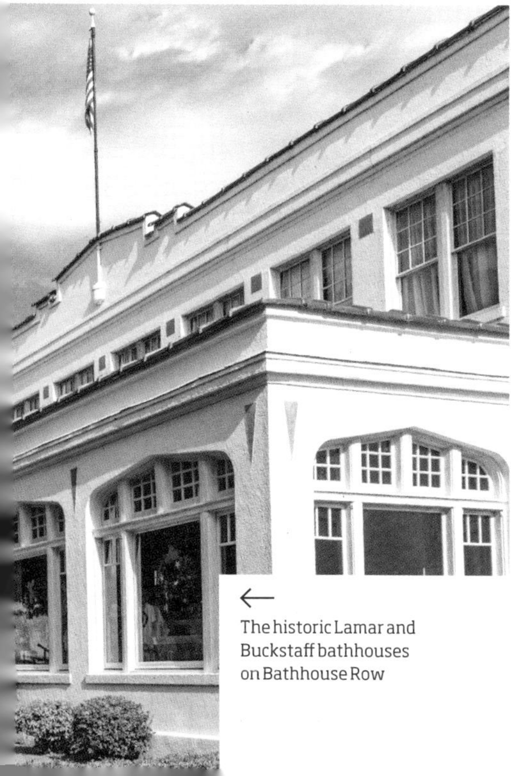

←

The historic Lamar and Buckstaff bathhouses on Bathhouse Row

# STAY

The park has good on-site lodgings, as does the surrounding city of Hot Springs.

**Gulpha Gorge**

The park's only campground offers electricity but no showers.

**⌂ Hot Springs National Park [W] recreation.gov/camping/campgrounds/247559**

$

**Hotel Hale**

Bathhouse Row's oldest structure, this boutique hotel has nine suites with spring water soaking tubs.

**⌂ Hot Springs National Park [W] hotelhale.com**

$$$

**Hilltop Manor**

Charming bed-and-breakfast on the park's quiet northeastern edge.

**⌂ Hot Springs [W] hilltopmanorhotsprings.com**

$$

↑ One of the park's hot springs, rich in silica and surrounded by lush vegetation

> When you treat yourself to a mineral bath here, the water in your tub is rain that fell not long after the Pyramids at Giza were built.

# EAT

The park has one brewery and two dining spots, with Hot Springs city offering plenty more options.

### Eden

Hotel Hale's restaurant does weekend brunch and fine dining.

 Hot Springs National Park Ⓦ hotelhale.com

$$$

---

### Superior Bathhouse Brewery

Wash down a burger with the world's only beer brewed with thermal spring water.

 Hot Springs National Park Ⓦ superior bathhouse.com

$$$

---

### Mr. Whiskers

A top place for catfish, a regional specialty.

Ⓐ Hot Springs Ⓦ greatcatfish.com

$$$

activity, but of gravity. After water seeps into the earth, the force pulls it down, and the deeper it goes, the hotter it gets. At a depth of 8,000 ft (2.4 km), the water hits a fault line, and pressure sends it back to the surface, where it emerges from springs near Bathhouse Row. The entire trip takes 4,400 years, so when you treat yourself to a mineral bath here, the water in your tub is rain that fell not long after the Pyramids at Giza were built.

There are eight bathhouses on the Bathhouse Row strip, only two of which still function as such. Going north from the park's entrance, the first is Lamar Bathhouse, named for the former Supreme Court justice, Lucius Quintus Cincinnatus Lamar. This bathhouse now houses the park store, offices, and a research library. Up next is Buckstaff Bathhouse, the only one to have operated continuously since it opened in 1912. It offers whirlpool mineral baths, Swedish massages, and manicures. Ozark Bathhouse, which closed in 1977, now houses

the Hot Springs National Park Cultural Center, which displays work from the Artist-in-Residence Program. Then there's Quapaw Bathhouse. This Spanish Colonial Revival-style building with its lovely chevroned dome is the park's other active bathhouse. It was named after a local Indigenous tribe and offers public thermal pools, a steam cave, and private baths for singles or couples.

Then you come to the park's visitor center and historical exhibits, housed in the Fordyce Bathhouse. This was once the row's standout bathhouse, with a lobby fountain, two-lane bowling alley, gymnasium, grand piano, and a stunning stained-glass ceiling – still here – depicting fish, bathers, and a mermaid. Now vacant, the Maurice Bathhouse was the only one with a pool. It also held staterooms, a gymnasium, two elevators, and a roof garden. Next up is the oldest structure on the strip, Hale Bathhouse, which was erected in 1892, though the stucco facade and Mission Revival-style redesign date to

1939. It's now home to the luxury boutique Hotel Hale.

Finally, you reach Superior Bathhouse: the row's smallest and cheapest bathhouse, despite its name. It provided hydrotherapy, massage, and mercury services, and today houses the Superior Bathhouse Brewery.

You can't bathe in the thermal waters anywhere outdoors at the park, but you can dip your hand in them at the Display Spring behind Maurice Bathhouse or the Hot Water Cascade at Arlington Lawn, where the water flows down a cliff into two pools. There are also nine fountains in and around that dispense spring water – seven thermal and two cold – where you can have a drink or bottle some to take home.

## Hiking

Of course, the other part of the traditional Hot Springs treatment was physical exertion, and the park provides good hiking opportunities. Most of the trails begin in the immediate vicinity of Bathhouse Row. The Hot Springs Mountain and North Mountain trails climb the hills immediately behind Bathhouse Row, while, just across Central Avenue, the West Mountain trails wind around the

→

The Hot Springs Mountain Tower, a wooden observation deck built in 1982

⊞ IF YOU HAVE
**A weekend**

Make the scenic drive up Hot Springs Mountain to hike the Sunset Trail, then bed down at Hotel Hale. After brunch here, compare the waters in the Buckstaff and Quapaw bathhouses.

### GETTING AROUND

Driving is the most straightforward way to reach Hot Springs. From the city of Little Rock, take I-30 west to U.S. Hwy. 70 and follow that into town. From Dallas or Texarkana, take I-30 east to Arkansas Hwy. 7 (AR 7), which runs north to the park. Hot Springs has a small airport that handles some regional flights, but if you don't have your own vehicle, you'll likely have to fly or take a train to Little Rock and then rent a car (the Greyhound bus service no longer stop at the city). In town, Intracity Transit Bus Route 3 runs from the Transportation Plaza past the visitor center and Bathhouse Row, though you can also walk to both from much of town. You'll need a car or bike to reach more remote sections of the park.

mountain. If you want your hike to be more than just an excuse to hit the spa, hit the Sunset Trail, which traverses the park's highest point and runs for 10 miles (16 km) through some of its most remote stretches.

## Scenic drives

The mountains offer good opportunities for scenic drives, too. The best follows the Hot Springs Mountain Drive loop and takes travelers along the route of an 1880s carriage road to Hot Springs Mountain Tower, a 216-ft (66-m) lookout that has both open and enclosed observation decks. Midway through the drive you can tack on a loop that leads to Goat Rock Overlook, which provides vistas of the mountain where Indigenous people once sourced novaculite stone to make arrowheads.

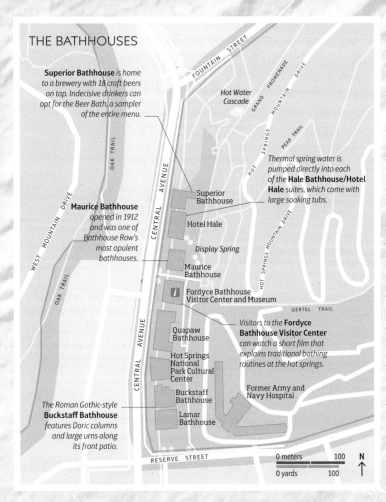

# THE BATHHOUSES

**Superior Bathhouse** is home to a brewery with 18 craft beers on tap. Indecisive drinkers can opt for the Beer Bath, a sampler of the entire menu.

*Hot Water Cascade*

Thermal spring water is pumped directly into each of the **Hale Bathhouse/Hotel Hale** suites, which come with large soaking tubs.

**Maurice Bathhouse** opened in 1912 and was one of Bathhouse Row's most opulent bathhouses.

Superior Bathhouse

Hotel Hale

*Display Spring*

Maurice Bathhouse

Fordyce Bathhouse Visitor Center and Museum

Visitors to the **Fordyce Bathhouse Visitor Center** can watch a short film that explains traditional bathing routines at the hot springs.

Quapaw Bathhouse

Hot Springs National Park Cultural Center

Buckstaff Bathhouse

Lamar Bathhouse

Former Army and Navy Hospital

The Roman Gothic-style **Buckstaff Bathhouse** features Doric columns and large urns along its front patio.

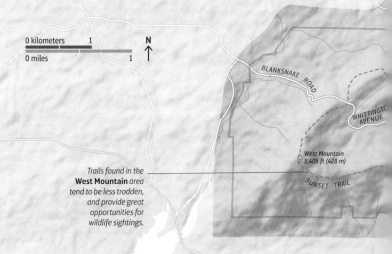

Trails found in the **West Mountain** area tend to be less trodden, and provide great opportunities for wildlife sightings.

*West Mountain 1,405 ft (428 m)*

# EXPLORING HOT SPRINGS

An entirely different park from those with sprawling landscapes, much of Hot Springs is contained within Bathhouse Row. The surrounding Ouachita Mountains, however, offer alternative forms of wellness along hiking trails through forests.

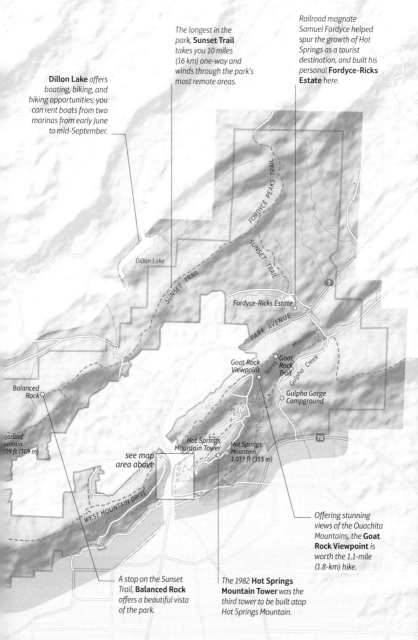

The longest in the park, **Sunset Trail** takes you 10 miles (16 km) one-way and winds through the park's most remote areas.

Railroad magnate Samuel Fordyce helped spur the growth of Hot Springs as a tourist destination, and built his personal **Fordyce-Ricks Estate** here.

**Dillon Lake** offers boating, biking, and hiking opportunities; you can rent boats from two marinas from early June to mid-September.

Balanced Rock

Sugarloaf Mountain 1,209 ft (369 m)

see map area above

Dillon Lake

FORDYCE PEAKS TRAIL

SUNSET TRAIL

SUNSET TRAIL

7

Fordyce-Ricks Estate

PARK AVENUE

Goat Rock Viewpoint

North Mountain

Goat Rock Trail

Gulpha Creek

Gulpha Gorge Campground

Hot Springs Mountain Tower

Hot Springs Mountain 1,033 ft (315 m)

70

WEST MOUNTAIN DRIVE

Offering stunning views of the Ouachita Mountains, the **Goat Rock Viewpoint** is worth the 1.1-mile (1.8-km) hike.

A stop on the Sunset Trail, **Balanced Rock** offers a beautiful vista of the park.

The 1982 **Hot Springs Mountain Tower** was the third tower to be built atop Hot Springs Mountain.

# GREAT SMOKY MOUNTAINS

**⊙ North Carolina, Tennessee  ⊘ Free  ⊞ nps.gov/grsm**

Great Smoky Mountains is the U.S.'s most popular national park. With over 12 million annual visitors, it sees more people pass through its gates than Grand Canyon, Yellowstone, and Yosemite combined. The park sprawls across 522,427 acres (211,415 ha) of mountains and hardwood forests, divvied up neatly between the states of North Carolina and Tennessee.

## Did You Know?

The park's mountains are estimated to be between 200 and 300 million years old.

The national parks are often described as "America's best idea." With Great Smoky Mountains, there's a literalness to the appellation. In 1925, Congress passed legislation establishing a national park here, but for years it existed only on paper, as the federal government didn't actually have any land

for it. The Tennessee and North Carolina state governments, aided by private donations, spent the next decade buying out thousands of timber companies, farmers, and landowners until, in 1934, the idea became reality.

Great Smoky Mountains were named by the Cherokee, the Indigenous Americans

←

Great Smoky Mountains, shrouded in the haze that gives them their name

who were the land's original inhabitants. The Cherokee called them Shaconage, "the place of blue smoke." An otherworldly blue mist often hovers in the valleys, giving the park a dreamlike appearance and inviting visitors to explore its haunting beauty.

## Exploring the park

Most people enter Great Smoky Mountains National Park from Gatlinburg in the northeast or Cherokee in the southeast and get oriented at the Sugarlands or Oconaluftee visitor centers. Both provide information on the park, like some of the best trails to take (the Cucumber Gap Trail being a favorite), and host ranger-led programs. The western Townsend entrance is the closest to Cades Cove and its visitor center. When you head into the Smokies, keep in mind that there's no Wi-Fi and little cell service, and that elevation within the park varies by nearly 6,000 ft

⊙ IF YOU HAVE
**A day**

Drive the Roaring Fork Motor Nature Trail, looping out and back from Gatlinburg and stopping along the way to explore forest creeks and to hike to 80-ft (24-m) Rainbow Falls.

→

Enjoying the fall colors on a walk along the Cucumber Gap Trail

Mountain Farm Museum, near Oconaluftee Visitor Center, north of Cherokee

(1,830 m), meaning weather can vary pretty drastically. Pack accordingly.

## Settler history

The lush valley of Cades Cove is one of the park's most popular destinations. For hundreds of years, the Cherokee hunted deer, elk, and bison here. European settlers arrived around 1820 and built log cabins, churches, and gristmills, many of which you can explore today. The cove's open terrain means it's one of the best places in the park to spot wildlife. Keep an eye out for deer, coyotes, and the Great Smoky Mountains' famous black bears.

A sibling destination in the park's east is Cataloochee, where you'll find 19th-century homes and churches dotting the valley beneath 6,000-ft (1,830-m) peaks. You might also spot elk here. After disappearing from the southern Appalachians in the early 1800s, they were reintroduced to the park

beginning in 2001 and are now once again thriving.

If you want a more in-depth look at how early European settlers eked out a living, the Mountain Farm Museum near Oconaluftee displays historic applehouses, smokehouses, and blacksmith shops, and demonstrates traditional agricultural practices.

## Clingman's Dome

Smack in the park's center is its highest point: Clingmans Dome. From April to November, you can drive most of the way up, leaving you with just a steep 0.5-mile (less than 1 km) hike to the summit, at 6,643 ft (2,025 m). Still not high enough? Head up to the observation deck, from where you can see 100 miles (160 km) on a clear day.

## Roaring Fork Motor Nature Trail

It's got an oxymoronic name, but the Roaring Fork Motor Nature Trail is a great way to experience the Smokies if you're pressed for time or aren't confident about heading into the backcountry. A one-way, 5.5-mile (9-km) loop, named after a mountain stream, departs Gatlinburg on Cherokee Orchard Road and returns to town on Roaring Fork Road. En route, you'll find yourself continuously pulling over

> European settlers arrived around 1820 and built log cabins, churches and gristmills, many of which you can explore today.

# EAT

There are no restaurants in the park, and visitor centers offer only limited drink and snack options. Restaurants and grocery stores are in nearby towns. If you don't mind the drive, Asheville is one of the South's best food cities.

**Applewood Farmhouse Restaurant**
Tasty homestyle meals served with complimentary apple fritters.

🏠 Sevierville, TN
🌐 applewoodfarm houserestaurant.com

**Rhubarb**
Partners with local farms to offer elevated Southern dining.

🏠 Asheville, NC
🌐 rhubarb asheville.com

$$$

# A DRIVING TOUR
# NEWFOUND GAP ROAD

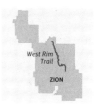

Locator Map

**Distance** 32 miles (50 km) one-way **Stopping-off points** Chimneys Picnic Area and Collins Creek Picnic Area are perfect for stretching the legs **Terrain** Paved road

Running from Gatlinburg, Tennessee, to Cherokee, North Carolina, this is the only fully paved road through the heart of Great Smoky Mountains National Park. The route accesses many of the park's natural and human-made attractions, and is a great way for newcomers to experience the park in a day.

**Key**

-- Drive Route

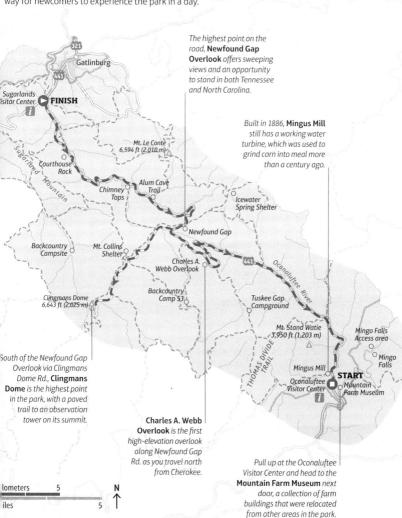

The highest point on the road, **Newfound Gap Overlook** offers sweeping views and an opportunity to stand in both Tennessee and North Carolina.

Built in 1886, **Mingus Mill** still has a working water turbine, which was used to grind corn into meal more than a century ago.

South of the Newfound Gap Overlook via Clingmans Dome Rd., **Clingmans Dome** is the highest point in the park, with a paved trail to an observation tower on its summit.

**Charles A. Webb Overlook** is the first high-elevation overlook along Newfound Gap Rd. as you travel north from Cherokee.

Pull up at the Oconaluftee Visitor Center and head to the **Mountain Farm Museum** next door, a collection of farm buildings that were relocated from other areas in the park.

kilometers 5

miles 5

N

← Taking in mountaintop panoramas from a viewpoint in the park

to explore old-growth forest and lively mountain creeks.

## The park's northeast and southwest

The most popular parts of America's most popular national park can get crowded. There are quieter corners in the Great Smoky Mountain's northeast. Head to Greenbriar for trout fishing and spring wildflowers, or to Cosby, a favorite with locals, for superb hiking. Short but rewarding trails lead to Hen Wallow Falls and the Sutton Ridge Overlook, or you can push yourself on the 10.6-mile (17-km) trek to the Mount Cammerer Lookout.

If you're an experienced backpacker and committed misanthrope, head to the park's vast, roadless south west, where hiking and horse trails provide the only way through the terrain and you're as likely to encounter Bigfoot as you are a crowd.

## Hiking

Great Smoky Mountains is one of the country's best hiking destinations. The marquee route here is the Appalachian Trail, and the park's section of the nearly 2,200-mile (3,540-km) epic runs for some 70 miles (113 km), more or less along the Tennessee–North Carolina border. The route takes you past several park highlights, such as Clingmans Dome; Newfound Gap, an important pass between mountain peaks that's covered in spruce and fir forest; and Charlies Bunion, a stone outcrop offering poetic views of rippling mountain ridges.

Of course, there's no need to commit to the entire Appalachian Trail. You can hike sections of it to both Clingmans Dome and Charlies Bunion from the Newfound

### GETTING AROUND

From the Tennessee side, drive south from Gatlinburg on U.S. 441 to the Sugarlands Visitor Center, or east from Townsend on TN-73. From the North Carolina side, drive north from Cherokee on U.S. 441 to the Oconaluftee Visitor Center. Within the park, 384 miles (618 km) of (mostly) paved roads will get you where you want to go (secondary roads close in winter). There's no public transportation to or within the park, but private companies offer shuttles to trailheads from your vehicle or nearby towns, usually between March and October; see the Shuttles page of the park website for more info. If you drive, you'll need to purchase a daily, weekly, or annual parking tag ($5/15/40).

→ Observation deck at Clingman's Dome, the highest point in the park

Gap parking lot, or simply set out on some of the other 800 miles (1,287 km) of trails within the park; almost all of the trails cross small streams (some should be avoided after heavy rainfall). The path to Chimney Tops starts conveniently right on U.S. 441 and, at only 3.5 miles (5.6 km) round-trip, offers a lot of bang for your buck. You'll cross rushing streams before making a steep ascent along Sugarland Mountain. The payoff is a stunning vista of Mount LeConte.

If you're driving the Roaring Fork Motor Nature Trail, take a break to stretch your legs on the challenging 2.7-mile (4.3-km) hike to Rainbow Falls. After rambling along LeConte Creek and past rhododendron and teaberry, you'll arrive at an 80-ft (24-m) cascade whose mist becomes a giant prism on sunny days.

## Cycling

Cycling is permitted on most roads within the park, but the steep terrain and often heavy traffic can make it difficult.

# STAY

The park has one lodge and 10 frontcountry campgrounds, plus lots of backcountry camping options (requires a permit and reservation).

### LeConte Lodge

Atmospheric, hand-built log cabins with a herd of pack llamas, near the summit of Mount LeConte. Accessible only by foot.

🅐 Mount LeConte
🅦 lecontelodge.com

### Gatlinburg Inn

Opened in 1937, this hotel lays on the Southern charm with rocking chairs on the porch and made-from-scratch biscuits.

🅐 Gatlinburg
🅦 gatlinburginn.com

### Cades Cove Campground

One of two park campsites open in winter, Cades Cove is dog-friendly and offers flush toilets and wheel-chair accessible restrooms.

🅐 Cades Cove
🅦 recreation.gov/camping

### Glenstone Lodge

Spacious rooms and brilliant pools make this lodge, only a few miles from the park and close to town amenities, an excellent place to stay.

🅐 Gatlinburg
🅦 glenstonelodge.com

The best option for a bike ride is Cades Cove Loop Road, particularly on Wednesdays from May to September, when the one-way, 11-mile (17.7-km) road is closed to traffic. Bikes are only allowed on three of the park's trails, including the Gatlinburg Trail. If you don't have your own wheels, you can rent a ride from the Cades Cove Campground store in summer and fall.

### Horseback riding

From spring to fall, you can sign up for a guided horseback ride at one of four stables: Cades Cove, Smokemont, Sugarlands, and Smoky Mountain. If you have your own steed, you can take it on some 550 miles (885 km) of the park's hiking trails.

### Fishing

To fish within Great Smoky Mountains National Park, you'll need either a Tennessee or North Carolina fishing license. The bad news is that neither is sold within the park; you'll need to buy one in a nearby town or online in advance. The good news is that both licenses are valid throughout the park, so you won't have to worry about which side of the state line you're on. Anglers come here mainly for trout and bass. Brook, rainbow, and brown trout can be found in remote headwater streams, while the best smallmouth-bass fishing is in the cool waters of Abrams Creek and the East Prong of Little River.

### Flora and fauna

No matter where you go and what you do in the park, take time to pay attention to the life around you. Great Smoky Mountains is the most biologically diverse national park in the country. More than 19,000 species have been documented here, but scientists believe that may only represent 15 percent of those that call the park home. The lowlands are home to plants and animals common to the South, while creatures of the North live at higher elevations, meaning that a hike up a mountain is a crash course in the ecology of the entire Eastern United States. Just keep in mind that this is remote learning – always give any wildlife you encounter plenty of distance and avoid disturbing the vegetation as much as possible.

The Smokies' most famous denizen is the black bear, of which there are roughly 1,500 in the park. That's a density of about two per square mile (2.5 sq km), so there's a decent chance you'll spot one

 IF YOU HAVE
**A weekend**

Hike one of the park's scenic sections of the Appalachian Trail, to Clingmans Dome or the rocky outcrop at Charlies Bunion, camp in wooded Cades Cove, and look for black bears and elk in the Cataloochee Valley.

A cool, clear mountain stream, bubbling over mossy rocks

while you're here. Some of the other 65 species of mammal in the park include raccoons, opossums, chipmunks, bats, and river otters, which were reintroduced in the 1990s. While you'll almost certainly see white-tailed deer and squirrels during your visit, the park's dense vegetation keeps most animals hidden. The best places to spot wildlife are in relatively open areas like Cades Cove and the Cataloochee Valley.

One of the Smokies' 1,500 or so black bears resting on a branch ↑

Birders here will hardly have a chance to put their binoculars down. More than 240 species of birds fill the air, half of which breed in the park. The area around Sparks Lane and Hyatt Lane in Cades Cove provides opportunities to spot kingbirds, sparrows, and northern harriers, a species of hawk nicknamed the "gray ghost." Distinctive long-eared owls sometimes make an appearance in this area in winter.

Great Smoky Mountains is often called the "Salamander Capital of the World," as its 30 different species give it one of the most diverse populations on Earth. All but six of those species are lungless, breathing instead through the walls of blood vessels in their skin. Keep your eyes peeled for the vivid black-chinned red salamander, which are fairly common throughout the park and resemble an elongated chili pepper.

Other ground-dwellers to look for include the slender glass lizard, which, despite not having legs, is not a snake, and the attractively patterned flamed tigersnail, which secretes a bubbly, bioluminescent orange mucus as an effective defense mechanism.

The park's most captivating natural display happens between late May and mid-June each year, during the firefly mating season. Firefly flashes aren't random. Each species has its own pattern, which enables males and females to identify each other. The males of one species in the park emit a burst of five to eight flashes, pause for eight seconds, and then light up again, but what makes this species' show especially magical is that they somehow synchronize their bursts. One moment the woods are pitch dark; the next they're lit up with thousands of sparkling lights. One of the best places to see this nighttime spectacle is in the woods around Elkmont, one and a half miles (2.5 km) off Little River Road, especially from the Little River and Jakes Creek trails.

Timeline

*2000 BCE*

▽ The Cherokee live for 4,000 years in the area that today makes up the national park, until they are forcibly relocated.

*1830*

▷ After President Jackson signs the Indian Removal Act, all tribes east of the Mississippi are made to walk to Oklahoma on the infamous Trail of Tears.

*1925*

The idea to make the area a national park is studied, including the ramifications for local people.

*1901*

Little River Railroad opens to export lumber from the Smokies (until 1939). Many oppose the park because of business interests.

*1976*

◁ The park is made an International Biosphere Reserve. The ecosystem is studied to ensure its sustainable development.

# EXPLORING GREAT SMOKY MOUNTAINS

Crossing the states of North Carolina and Tennessee, Great Smoky Mountains encompasses some of the best scenery the south has to offer: mysteriously misty mountains, verdant forests, and deep lakes.

Hiking trails crisscross the beautiful mountains, including part of the giant Appalachian Trail. No matter which U.S. state you're in, both share boundless vistas of streams, waterfalls, and forests.

*The **Sugarlands Visitor Center** is the perfect jumping-off point for exploring the park, home to exhibits, a free movie, and knowledgeable rangers.*

↑ Mingus Mill, which is home to a working cast-iron turbine

*The **Cades Cove Visitor Center** sells local grains ground at the historic mill next door. It's also a good starting point for wildlife watching in the area.*

0 kilometers 8
0 miles 8

N

Jumping over rocks along the Rainbow Falls trail, the most popular in the park

Reachable only via a difficult 4-mile (6.4-km) hike that climbs 2,000 ft (610 m), the gorgeous stepped **Ramsey Cascades** is the park's tallest waterfall, at 100 ft (30 m).

The 80-ft (24-m) **Rainbow Falls** is named after the rainbow produced by mist that's visible on sunny afternoons here.

Pittman Center

Greenbriar

Ramsey Cascades

Hen Wallows Falls

Mount Cammerer Lookout

321

32

40

APPALACHIAN TRAIL

Sutton Ridge

Big Creek

atlinburg

Roaring Fork Motor Nature Trail

Rainbow Falls

Mount LeConte 6,593 ft (2,009 m)

Mount Sterling

Charlies Bunion

Chimney Tops

Newfound Gap

441 NEWFOUND GAP ROAD

gmans Dome 3 ft (2,025 m)

Clingmans Dome Visitor Center

Cataloochee Creek

Cataloochee Valley

Mingus Mill

Oconaluftee Visitor Center

Mountain Farm Museum

Steep Creek

Bryson City

The **Cataloochee Valley** was the site of an early European settlement, divided into two communities: Big and Little Cataloochee. Several homes still stand here.

Demonstrations at **Mingus Mill**, an 1866 gristmill, show how it used a water-powered turbine to turn corn into cornmeal.

The **Mount Cammerer Lookout** was built by the Civilian Conservation Corps in the 1930s. The tower served as a fire lookout in the 1960s and still provides incredible views.

Standing sentinel over the Smokies, **Clingmans Dome** is a rounded mountain peak that's not just the highest point in the park but the highest on the Appalachian Trail.

Best for *Wildlife watching from the water*

# CONGAREE

📍 South Carolina 🎟 Free 🌐 nps.gov/cong

Located in the floodplain of the Congaree River, this national park is a watery realm of wetland forests, lakes, sloughs, and small creeks known as "guts." Its 26,000 acres (10,522 ha) protect the continent's largest intact expanse of old-growth bottomland hardwood forest, within which tiny birds whistle and chirp and leaves glisten in the hot summer humidity.

> **IF YOU HAVE**
> **A day**
>
> Admire loblolly pines and tupelo trees on the Boardwalk Loop Trail then hit the water on the Cedar Creek Canoe Trail, paddling for 15 miles (24 km).

A singing natural world unfolds at Congaree, nestled among a forest of bald cypress trees. The Indigenous Congaree, for whom the river and park are named, were its first people, inhabiting its floodplains for hundreds of years until Spanish conquistadors came through in 1541. European settlers arrived in the 18th century, followed by maroons – men and women escaping slavery, who used the wild land as a refuge. By the 19th century, the lumber industry came calling, but thanks to the park's remote location and lack of usable waterways, most of the trees were spared and operations

halted. But that wouldn't stop landowners trying to resume logging operations in the 20th century, which spurred local newspaper editor Harry Hampton – who spent a lot of time in the area – to advocate for its preservation. His campaign to protect the area from logging led to its designation as a national monument in 1976, and thanks to his efforts, this untameable realm survives as one of the last examples of the old-growth forests

## Did You Know?
Floodplains are covered by water only part of the year, while swamps are always covered with water.

and pine savannas that once blanketed the southeastern U.S. An official national park since 2003, Congaree is today a blissful haven for scores of wildlife and visitors alike.

### Exploring the park
Given that 80 percent of the park lies within the Congaree River's floodplain, the vast majority of the area is navigable only by canoe or kayak. While floods periodically render trails inaccessible, many people also opt to get around on foot. You'll find everything you need in the northwestern corner, where the entrance, visitor center, and majority of the hiking trails are bunched together. The visitor center hosts occasional ranger-led programs such as guided walks and yoga sessions, and is a good place to check in for weather and hazard updates before setting off.

### GETTING AROUND
Most visitors travel to Congaree by private vehicle. The park is easily accessed via a 19-mile (31-km) drive from the state capital Columbia: take Hwy. 48 southeast, turn right on Old Bluff Road, and then follow National Park Road to the Harry Hampton Visitor Center. You can also get to the park via the COMET, Columbia's bus system. Within the park, the only ways to get around are by foot, canoe, or kayak. There are 2.4 miles (3.9 km) of boardwalk, over 25 miles (40 km) of trails, and a 15-mile (24 km) canoe trail, plus other waterways to explore.

← Walking the Boardwalk Loop, which passes myriad tree species

# STAY

Reservations are required for Congaree's two campgrounds, and free permits are needed for backcountry camping. Columbia is the best option for hotels nearby.

### Longleaf Campground
Forest campground with group campsites and vault toilets but no running water.

🏕 Congaree National Park
🌐 recreation.gov/camping

---

### Bluff Campground
Six campsites with fire rings but no toilets or running water.

🏕 Congaree National Park
🌐 recreation.gov/camping

---

### Hotel Trundle
Independent boutique hotel with furniture made by local craftspeople.

🏕 Columbia
🌐 hoteltrundle.com

## On the water
Navigating the park's ancient floodplain is a rite of passage. Several outfitters in Columbia rent vessels and can organize guided tours, and the park can supply kayak adaptations to guests with specific requirements. For a leisurely adventure, paddle out on the ranger-guided Cedar Creek Canoe Trail, which follows the watercourse for 15 miles (24 km) from Bannister Bridge to its confluence with the Congaree River.

Water explorations don't start and end at canoeing and kayaking. Cast-fishers can drop a line anywhere (except for Westin Lake), and serene spots include Cedar Creek and oxbow lakes where bowfins, bluegill, and yellow perch are pulled up regularly.

## Hiking
It's no less an adventure to stay on dry land at Congaree. Upon entering the park, many visitors start their explorations by hiking the popular Boardwalk Loop Trail behind the visitor center. This fully accessible walk runs for 2.6 miles (4.2 km) between some of the park's most iconic species of tree, such as oak, tupelo, and towering loblolly pine. It also connects with the easy Firefly Trail where, for two weeks in late spring, synchronous fireflies turn the forest into a shimmering light show. The fireflies here are known as the Snappy Single Sync, and light up in a quick flash every 0.65 seconds. Those seeking a more challenging ramble can set out on the 11-mile (18-km) River Trail, which leads into the depths of the park all the way to the Congaree River. In

↑ Canoeing near Wise Lake, a great place to spot wading birds

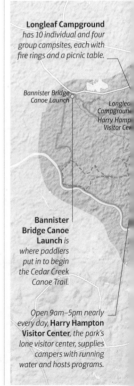

**Longleaf Campground** has 10 individual and four group campsites, each with fire rings and a picnic table.

Bannister Bridge Canoe Launch

Longleaf Campground
Harry Hampton Visitor Center

**Bannister Bridge Canoe Launch** is where paddlers put in to begin the Cedar Creek Canoe Trail.

Open 9am–5pm nearly every day, **Harry Hampton Visitor Center**, the park's lone visitor center, supplies campers with running water and hosts programs.

the park's southeast corner are two more short hiking routes, including the Bates Ferry Trail, which traces a road from the British colonial era.

## Flora and fauna

Whether you take to the trails or cruise the tannin-stained water, you're likely to spot deer, bobcats, wading birds, snapping turtles, and even alligators. Less elusive are the park's champion trees, behemoths judged the largest of their species based on height, circumference, and crown spread. Congaree's secret formula – long, warm growing seasons and moisture and nutrients from floods – results in loblolly pines as tall as 17-story buildings and bald cypresses that would take five people to encircle with their arms. Congaree is an ecologically fascinating environment.

# EAT

Food is not available in the park; pick up supplies or dine in the nearby town of Gadsden or the city of Columbia.

### Groucho's Deli
Columbia institution serving great sandwiches.

🅿Columbia Ⓦgrouchos.com

$Ⓢ$$$$

---

### Terra
Enjoy delectable dishes made using local, micro-seasonal ingredients.

🅿West Columbia Ⓦterrasc.com

$Ⓢ$$$$

### Blue Marlin Restaurant
Serves Southern favorites like seafood gumbo.

🅿Columbia Ⓦblue marlincolumbia.com

$Ⓢ$$$$

---

### Spotted Salamander
This lunchtime spot puts its own spin on classic Southern cooking.

🅿Columbia Ⓦspotted salamandercatering.com

$Ⓢ$$Ⓢ

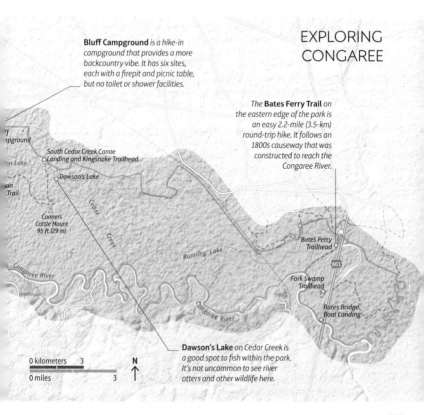

# EXPLORING CONGAREE

**Bluff Campground** is a hike-in campground that provides a more backcountry vibe. It has six sites, each with a firepit and picnic table, but no toilet or shower facilities.

The **Bates Ferry Trail** on the eastern edge of the park is an easy 2.2-mile (3.5-km) round-trip hike. It follows an 1800s causeway that was constructed to reach the Congaree River.

South Cedar Creek Canoe Landing and Kingsnake Trailhead

Dawson's Lake

Cooners Cattle Mount 95 ft (29 m)

Cedar Creek

Running Lake

Congaree River

Congaree River

Bates Ferry Trailhead

601

Fork Swamp Trailhead

Bates Bridge Boat Landing

**Dawson's Lake** on Cedar Creek is a good spot to fish within the park. It's not uncommon to see river otters and other wildlife here.

0 kilometers 3
0 miles 3

N ↑

*Best for Coral reefs and mangrove forests*

# BISCAYNE

🏴 Florida 🏷 Free 🌐 nps.gov/bisc

**Protected to safeguard a stretch of undeveloped shoreline on the east coast of Florida and its outlying keys, Biscayne's coral reefs and mangrove forests provide a varied home for over 600 species of fish, as well as manatees, American crocodiles, butterflies, and birds. Its carbon-trapping mangroves play a vital role in climate research.**

Despite its location just 15 miles (24 km) from the gleaming skyscrapers of Downtown Miami, Biscayne's position at the far northern tip of the Florida Keys – and at the end of one of the longest coral-reef systems in the world – bestows it with a biodiversity of animals that is greater than any other national park in the U.S.

**IF YOU HAVE**
**A day**

Rent a kayak or canoe and explore the mangrove creeks south of the Dante Fascell Visitor Center before paddling over to Elliott Key, where you can spot blown pelicans and roseatte spoonbills at Jones Lagoon.

Some 95 percent of the protected area is underwater, also making this one of the most unique parks in the U.S. Stony corals and seafans provide feeding grounds for angelfish, snappers, and wrasse (and the predators that hunt them), as well as rays, turtles, and manatees. Also known as "sea cows" due to their slow-moving gait, manatees are federally en-dangered, although sightings are common in Biscayne.

## Exploring the park

The Dante Fascell Visitor Center is a great first stop to get a lie of the land (and sea). The park's focus is 7-mile- (11-km-) long Elliott Key, reachable by boat, kayak or canoe. Once there, you can walk the Spite Highway Trail, and visit Boca Chita Lighthouse and birding hotspot of Jones Lagoon.

Boca Chita Lighthouse, at the northern end of Biscayne National Park

↑ Exploring Biscayne's
mangrove-lined creeks
by canoe

# EXPLORING BISCAYNE

On the northernmost point of the Florida Keys, this vibrant preserve nestles in the paradise waters of Biscayne Bay. Exploring by boat is the only way to go, starting at shoreside areas.

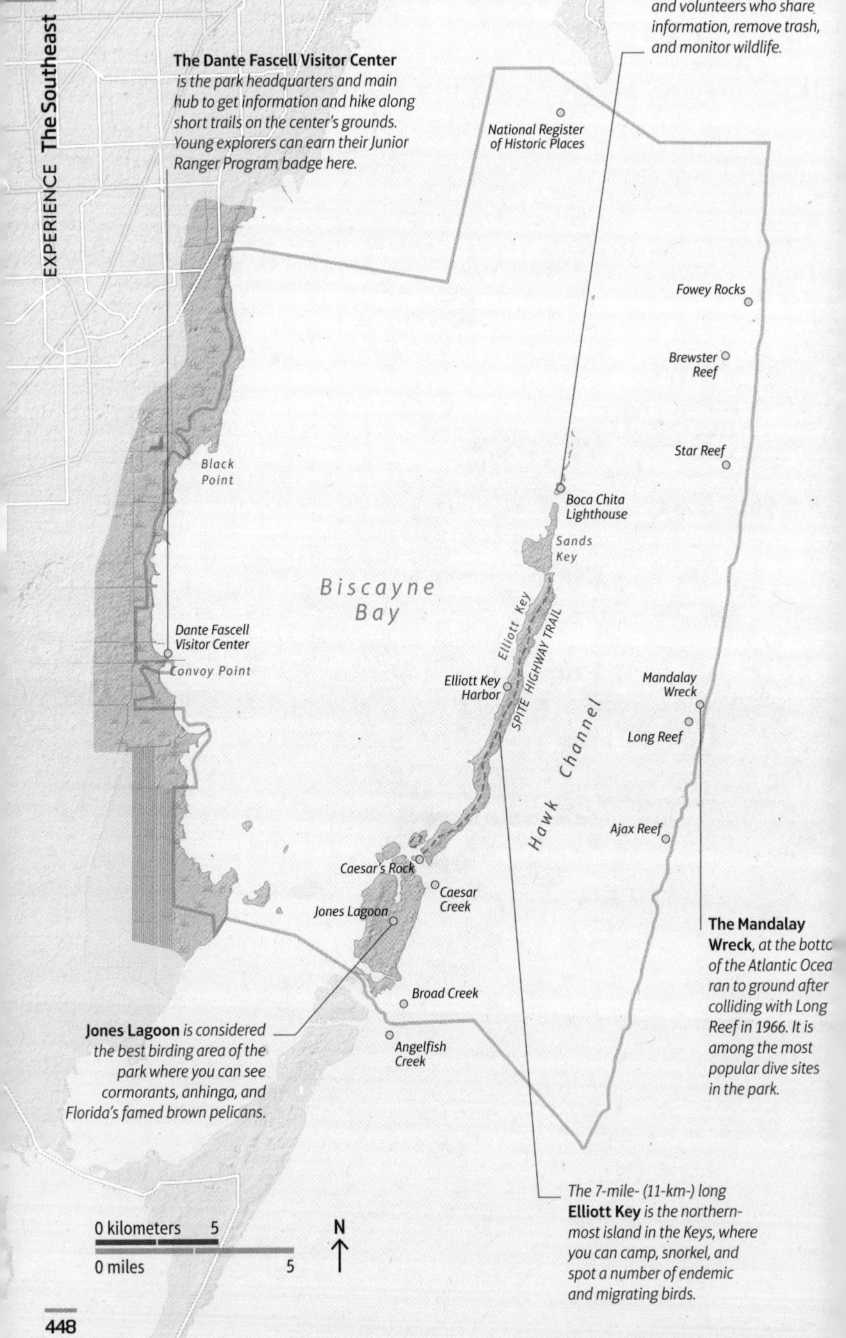

Open on weekends, the **Boca Chita Lighthouse** is serviced by park staff and volunteers who share information, remove trash, and monitor wildlife.

**The Dante Fascell Visitor Center** is the park headquarters and main hub to get information and hike along short trails on the center's grounds. Young explorers can earn their Junior Ranger Program badge here.

National Register of Historic Places

Fowey Rocks

Brewster Reef

Star Reef

Black Point

Boca Chita Lighthouse

Sands Key

*Biscayne Bay*

Elliott Key

SPITE HIGHWAY TRAIL

Dante Fascell Visitor Center

Convoy Point

Elliott Key Harbor

Mandalay Wreck

Long Reef

Hawk Channel

Ajax Reef

Caesar's Rock

Caesar Creek

Jones Lagoon

Broad Creek

Angelfish Creek

**The Mandalay Wreck**, at the botto of the Atlantic Ocea ran to ground after colliding with Long Reef in 1966. It is among the most popular dive sites in the park.

**Jones Lagoon** is considered the best birding area of the park where you can see cormorants, anhinga, and Florida's famed brown pelicans.

0 kilometers 5
0 miles 5

N

The 7-mile- (11-km-) long **Elliott Key** is the northern-most island in the Keys, where you can camp, snorkel, and spot a number of endemic and migrating birds.

# EAT

The closest restaurants are in the nearby town of Homestead, as well as in Miami and Key Biscayne.

**La Playa Grill**
American classics in a casual pub environment just a few minutes from the Biscayne National Park Institute.

Homestead laplaya grillseafoodbar.com

$$$$

**Lighthouse Cafe**
Open-air seafood restaurant with sweeping ocean views.

Key Biscayne lighthouse restaurants.com

$$$$

**Black Point Ocean Grill**
Burgers and seafood, served with bay views.

Homestead blackpoint oceangrill.com

$$$$

↑ A West Indian manatee; although endagered, they are a fairly common sight at Biscayne

## On the water

With a warm climate all year round, Biscayne is a reliable place for paddling along the coast, snorkeling, scuba diving, and boat tours. Self-guided kayaking adventures push off from Convoy Point near the visitor center. The park's Maritime Heritage Trail – known as the "Shipwreck Trail" – features six shipwrecks and is the only underwater archeological trail in America's national parks. Ranger-led ecotours are run by several outfits, including the Biscayne National Park Institute (BNPI), which also operates boat tours to Boca Chita Key.

## On land

Although only 5 percent of the park is above the water, there are still plenty of ways to enjoy your time on land, from birdwatching at Black Point and Jones Lagoon to ranger-led activities. Park rangers organize a Nature Journaling Club, inviting creatives to capture their observations through the written word and varied artwork. Groups meet twice a month at the Dante Fascell Visitor Center.

The most noted symbol in the park is on dry land, too, in the form of the 65-ft- (20-m-) high ornamental lighthouse at Boca Chita Key. The observation deck here provides wonderful views over the key, sea, and bay, and across to the Miami city skyline.

## Stiltsville

A harbor cruise to Stiltsville is one of the most interesting and rewarding experiences in Biscayne. Ocean Force Adventures operates pontoon boat rides from the Port of Miami. Stiltsville's colorful stilt houses here were built in the 1920s and rise up from the bay on the northern edge of the park boundary. For a time, it served as a stopover for the bootlegging of alcohol during the Prohibition era. The stilted houses were later a target for pirates, and in the 1950s they hosted exclusive parties at sea. Of the 27 houses that were built, only seven remain. It is a curious place, with plenty of local folklore that is eagerly regaled by the boat guides.

> **GETTING AROUND**
>
> Biscayne is around a 1.5-hour drive from both Miami and Fort Lauderdale. The Dante Fascell Visitor Center is accessed from the Florida Turnpike or from U.S. Hwy. 1. The Homestead National Parks Trolley runs from the town of the same name to the Dante Fascell Visitor Center, as well as the Homestead Bayfront Marina. It operates from late November to April, on weekends only. Boating access begins at Homestead Bayfront south of park head-quarters at Convoy Point. Other marinas include Black Point, Matheson Hammock, and Crandon on Key Biscayne, not far from Miami.

The vast wetlands of the Everglades, formed by sheet flow from Lake Okeechobee ↑

# EVERGLADES

Florida $35 per vehicle, valid for seven days
nps.gov/ever

Nicknamed "the River of Grass," the Everglades encompasses the largest subtropical wilderness in the U.S. This treasured but starkly threatened wetland landscape of mangrove forests, mud-flats, and sawgrass prairies has been forged out of the slow and complex interplay of land and water. The region's unique mixture of fresh and saltwater nurtures an array of rare aquatic habitats, while the network of waterways and humid swamps provides an abudance of opportunities for world-class kayaking, fishing, and birding. The park is best explored by boat, but there are some excellent hiking trails on dry land.

---

**IF YOU HAVE**
**A day**

Drive the eastern section of the park and stop for short walks along the boardwalks, keeping an eye out for alligators and manatees. In the afternoon, take a park-operated boat ride through the wetlands.

---

The Everglades is an awe-inspiring ecosystem that is as miraculous as it is fragile. Across more than 1.5 million sweeping acres (600,000 ha) of protected parkland, some of the planet's rarest and most endangered species find sanctuary, including the Florida panther, American crocodile, and alligator, and the West Indian manatee. There are nine plant and animal species that exist nowhere else on Earth.

Unlike most other wetland habitats which are directly fed by overflow from rivers or streams, the Everglades were formed over thousands of years from a slow process known as "sheet flow." During the rainy season, water overflows from the southern shorelines of nearby Lake Okeechobee, slowly trickling southward across sawgrass marshes, swamps, and forests. The incredibly slow-moving water (less than 2 inches per mile, 3 cm per km) is due to the gradual slope of the land, and the thick vegetation the water passes through. The region's varied aquatic habitats form at different elevations.

As civilization continues to expand on the banks of the Everglades, and temperatures

↑ The brightly feathered American purple gallinule

continue to rise in the region, the precarious natural order of these habitats hangs in the balance. As such, a range of innovative conservation efforts are underway in the park, many of which have been highly successful in restoring and protecting the ecosystem. Thanks to these untiring efforts, the Everglades continue to provide a truly restorative and majestic wilderness experience only an hour's drive from Miami.

## Exploring the park

At least one million people from around the world visit the park annually. It's easiest to navigate by splitting the park into two main areas: the southern section, accessible through the Ernest F. Coe Visitor Center, near Homestead and Florida City, and the northern section, accessible via Shark Valley and Everglades City. There are three main entry points to the park: the Gulf Coast Visitor Center, closest to Naples and south of Everglades City; the Shark Valley area that can be accessed by U.S. 41; and the Ernest F. Coe Visitor Center, the park's main headquarters.

The park experiences two distinct seasons which make for markedly different adventures. During the wet season, which runs from June through November, exploring can be a lot more challenging. Powerful afternoon thunderstorms can be expected daily with heavy but brief periods of rainfall. Always check the forecast and be prepared for sudden storms at any time. Also note that wet conditions and higher temperatures bring significant changes in the Everglades landscape: as the region's water levels rise, wild animals disperse, making viewing more challenging.

The dry season, on the other hand, runs from

# EAT

There are no restaurants in the park but you can buy snacks and drinks at each of the visitor centers.

### City Seafood
An outdoor seafood restaurant with stunning island views.
 Everglades City
🌐 cityseafood.com
$$$

### El Toro Taco Family Restaurant
Classic Tex Mex joint operating for more than 25 years.
 Homestead
🌐 eltorofamily.com
$$$

### Miccosukee Restaurant
Seafood, and authentic pumpkin and fry bread.
 Shark Valley entrance
🌐 miccosukee.com
$$$

## Did You Know?
The Everglades is home to the largest mangrove ecosystem in the western hemisphere.

→ An airboat whisking visitors through the park's swamps and marshes

December through May, and is by far the most popular time to visit. Travelers come to boat, camp, bike, paddle, and hike in one of the world's premier nature preserves.

## The south

The Main Park Road in Homestead connects with the park's south entrances, before meandering through shaded pineland forests and wooded areas. The Ernest F. Coe Visitor Center is located at the Homestead entrance of Everglades, considered the main entrance of the park on the southeast side closest to Miami. The visitor center is named after the so-called "father of the Everglades," who was instrumental in ensuring the region was legally protected by park status in 1947.

There are plenty of hiking, biking, and birding trails in the south of the park. The visitor center is also the terminus of a 99-mile (160-km) waterway where you can start boat tours and set off on kayak and canoe trips in the backcountry. Back-country trips can be short day-long excursions or can make up a challenging week-long adventure.

## Flamingo

Flamingo is the push-off point to Florida Bay, where mangrove-lined shores support fish, crustaceans, and other marine life. This area – just under 40 miles (64 km) from Homestead – has campgrounds, a marina where you can launch motorized and non-motorized boats, and excellent walking trails. Don't miss the Guy Bradley Visitor Center; here you can ask for information from trained wildlife guides, obtain essential backcountry wilderness permits, and get updates about local ranger-led activities. These include

## GETTING AROUND

There are four main regions in the park, each accessible by car and/or boat. The park has five visitor centers in separate regions with two major thoroughfares reaching all of them, driving east-to-west and west-to-southeast. There is one public transportation option provided by the Homestead Trolley that operates from December through April with stops at the Ernest F. Coe Visitor Center. The international airport in Miami is 80 miles (128 km) from Ernest F. Coe Visitor Center. There is a smaller airport in Naples, not far from Everglades City.

evening slideshows and talks, and daytime "slough-slogs" – walks through the swamp.

## Pa-hay-okee Overlook

The open expanse of saw-grass prairie known as the Pa-hay-okee Overlook is best viewed from an elevated boardwalk. The observation tower is a perfect spot from which to watch the sunlight play out over the slowly flowing waters, especially in the late afternoon. From the vie-point, you'll likely see wading birds, hawks, and snail

kites, whose only food – the apple snail – lives on the sawgrass. This prairie is also home to cattails and other rare wetland plants.

## Shark Valley

Named for two estuaries, Shark River and Little Shark River, Shark Valley is in the very heart of the park, about an hour's drive west of Miami along Tamiami Trail. A 15-mile (24-km) scenic road weaves through the valley; the road can be driven or cycled. Bikes are available to rent from Shark Valley Tram Tours (sharkvalleytramtours.com), who can also help you book valley tram trips.

Panoramic views await at the Shark Valley observation tower, where alligators and sea turtles swim below and aquatic birds fly overhead. There are two short walking trails starting at the Shark Valley Visitor Center, on the Bobcat Boardwalk and the unpaved Ottercave Trail.

## Gulf Coast

Farther north, the Everglades' Gulf Coast area is the gateway to the Ten Thousand Islands, a chain of small islets of which form part of the park. From here, you can hop on a tour boat to explore the sprawling mangrove forests that twist

The Anhinga Trail winding through sawgrass marsh ↑

their way into the waters, providing shelter for wildlife and birds. There are no hiking trails in this part of the park, but you can travel by self-propelled watercraft on the 99-mile (159-km) Wilderness Waterway that stretches from Everglades City to Flamingo.

↑ The American crocodile, generally a furtive species

Without a boat, there is very little to do in this section of the park.

Beachside camping is a great way to rest after a long day of paddling; Jewell Key is a popular camping spot. Here, freshwater and saltwater from the Gulf of Mexico finally converge. While the freshwater is known for large wading birds, you can also see dolphins and manta rays.

## Hiking

There are plenty of trail networks to explore on foot, with excellent trailheads leading into the park's diverse ecosystems. The Anhinga Trail is a short 1-mile (1.8-km) accessible trail crossing a boardwalk where alligators,

snakes, insects, birds, and fish thrive in the waters and hardwood forest.

The nearby Gumbo Limbo Trail is an easy walk across a paved path which meanders through a lush hardwood hammock. The popular – yet usually uncrowded – 0.5-mile (0.8-km) Mahogany Hammock Trail leads through one of the park's largest mangrove hammocks. The largest living mahogany tree in the U.S. can be found on the route.

## Bird-watching

Avian species in the Everglades are categorized into three groups: land birds, wading birds, and birds of prey. Head to West Lake to see a range of waterfowl

◷ IF YOU HAVE
**A weekend**

Rent a boat and head to the Ten Thousand Islands district, which offers a multiday canoe adventure to a number of small islands. Using the Wilderness Waterway, you'll be able to moor up and explore the chain of islets.

including ruddy, pintail, and shoveller. Many birders visit Mrazek Pond, near Flamingo, to spot and photograph a variety of avian life.

## Camping

Throughout the park you'll find "chickee" campsites – elevated wooden docks on stilts where you can pitch a tent above the freshwater. Reservations are required, and can be made through the park's website.

**Superb panoramic views await at the Shark Valley observation tower, where alligators and sea turtles swim below and aquatic birds fly overhead.**

# EXPLORING THE EVERGLADES

The vast network of wetlands and forests that comprise Florida's Everglades are fed by a river flowing 0.25 miles (0.4 km) per day out of Lake Okeechobee into Florida Bay. The park covers over 1.5 million acres (600,00 ha).

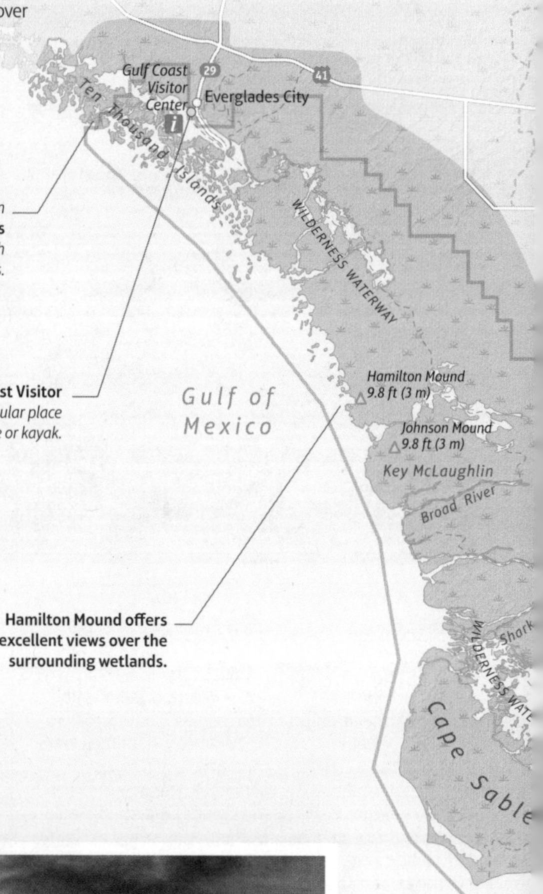

Gulf Coast Visitor Center

29

41

Everglades City

i

Ten Thousand Islands

The large island chain known as **Ten Thousand Islands** *protects small, mangrove-rich island habitats.*

WILDERNESS WATERWAY

Gulf of Mexico

The **Gulf Coast Visitor Center** *is a popular place to launch a canoe or kayak.*

Hamilton Mound
△ 9.8 ft (3 m)

Johnson Mound
△ 9.8 ft (3 m)

Key McLaughlin

Broad River

**Hamilton Mound offers excellent views over the surrounding wetlands.**

Shark

WILDERNESS WATE

Cape Sable

← Sunrise over the water at Long Pine Key

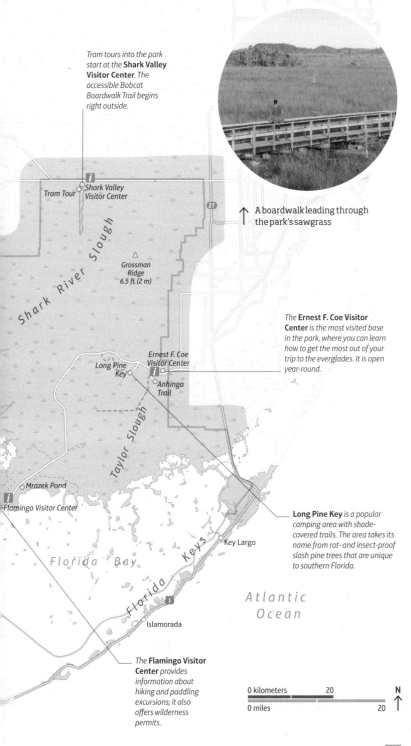

Tram tours into the park start at the **Shark Valley Visitor Center**. The accessible Bobcat Boardwalk Trail begins right outside.

↑ A boardwalk leading through the park's sawgrass

Tram Tour

Shark Valley Visitor Center

27

△ Grossman Ridge 6.5 ft (2 m)

Shark River Slough

The **Ernest F. Coe Visitor Center** is the most visited base in the park, where you can learn how to get the most out of your trip to the everglades. It is open year-round.

Long Pine Key

Ernest F. Coe Visitor Center

Anhinga Trail

Taylor Slough

Mrazek Pond

Flamingo Visitor Center

**Long Pine Key** is a popular camping area with shade-covered trails. The area takes its name from rot- and insect-proof slash pine trees that are unique to southern Florida.

Florida Bay

Florida Keys

Key Largo

Atlantic Ocean

1

Islamorada

The **Flamingo Visitor Center** provides information about hiking and paddling excursions; it also offers wilderness permits.

| 0 kilometers | 20 |
| 0 miles | 20 |

N ↑

# THE ECOSYSTEM OF THE EVERGLADES

The Everglades is a vast sheet river system – the overspill from Lake Okeechobee that moves across a flat bed of peat-covered limestone. Some 200 miles (322 km) long and up to 50 miles (80 km) wide, its depth rarely exceeds 3 ft (1 m). Tropical air and sea currents act on this temperate zone to create unique combinations of flora. Clumps of vegetation, such as cypress domes and bayheads, break the tract of sawgrass prairie. There are hundreds of animal species – some 350 species of birds, for which the area is particularly renowned.

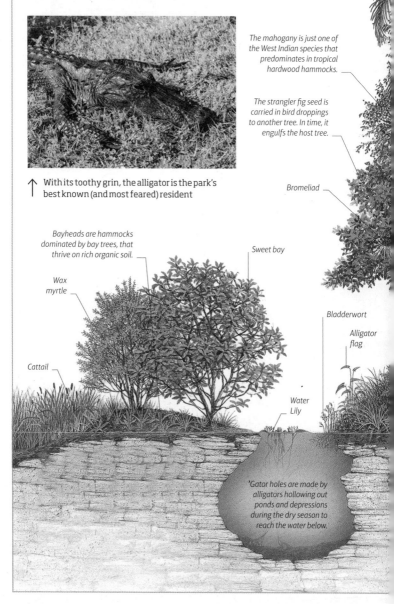

↑ With its toothy grin, the alligator is the park's best known (and most feared) resident

The mahogany is just one of the West Indian species that predominates in tropical hardwood hammocks.

The strangler fig seed is carried in bird droppings to another tree. In time, it engulfs the host tree.

Bromeliad

Bayheads are hammocks dominated by bay trees, that thrive on rich organic soil.

Sweet bay

Wax myrtle

Bladderwort

Alligator flag

Cattail

Water Lily

'Gator holes are made by alligators hollowing out ponds and depressions during the dry season to reach the water below.

→
A Great Blue
Heron perched
in the water

*Royal Palm*

←
Hammocks or tree islands are
areas of elevated land found
in freshwater prairies.

*The gumbo-limbo's bark
is red and peeling, hence its
nickname the "tourist tree."*

*Red mangrove trees
are recognized by their
distinctive roots.*

*Saw palmetto*

*Peat*

**Did You Know?**

In South Florida, some
Great Blue Herons have
plummage which is
completely white.

# DRY TORTUGAS

📍 Florida 💲 $15 per person, valid for seven days 🌐 nps.gov/drto

Dry Tortugas was named Las Tortugas ("The Turtles") by Spanish explorer Juan Ponce de León during a 1513 expedition. The change to "dry" came years later as a warning to other explorers that the once dense populations of sea turtles were disappearing without spring waters to sustain them. Today, this still beautiful park is a diver's paradise, with shipwrecks to explore and bountiful marine life to admire.

---

📅 IF YOU HAVE
**A day**

Fly in or boat across for a day trip to explore the Civil War-era Fort Jefferson and then don a snorkel and mask to try some of the various snorkeling sights around Garden Key.

---

Dry Tortugas National Park encompasses seven idyllic islands in the Gulf of Mexico, each fringed with white sandy beaches and surrounded by coral reefs. A visit here, either as a day trip or overnight camping, is all about getting off the beaten track and away from it all. With no Wi-Fi, no services to speak of, and remarkably few visitors, the Dry Tortugas offers a tranquility that's found in very few other parks in the U.S. Despite the name, over 99 percent of the park is water, home to over 30 species of coral and dozens of species of fish. Plus, of course, turtles: hawksbill, green, and loggerhead.

← Visitors crossing a moat into historic Fort Jefferson, Garden Key

## Exploring the park

Ferries and seaplanes arrive at Garden Key, the second-largest island in the Dry Tortugas, home to the park's visitor center, its campground, and historic Fort Jefferson. The vast majority of the park's visitors spend all of their time here, although in winter there is also the option of exploring Bush Key on ranger-led tours and with your own craft. Loggerhead Key, west of Garden Key, is open all year round but is only accessible to people with their own boats. Bush Key is closed from mid-January to mid-October, to protect nesting terns; East, Hospital, Long, and Middle keys are vital nesting sites for a variety of birds and sea turtles and are off-limits to the public.

Spring is the best time to visit. April and May have the calmest seas and the clearest waters and are the best months for snorkeling and diving. If you're camping overnight, note that rangers remain on-site and have accommodations inside Fort Jefferson; aside from composting toilets, there are no bathroom facilities available for campers after mid-afternoon.

### GETTING AROUND

Dry Tortugas is located 70 miles (113 km) west of Key West and is accessible only by boat or seaplane. The *Yankee Freedom* (*www. drytortugas.com*), a high-speed catamaran, departs daily from Key West, taking two and a half hours to reach the park. It's a fun way to travel, as the on-board naturalist provides background information on the park during the voyage there. Tickets include snorkeling equipment and a 45-minute narrated tour of Fort Jefferson. Once on land, you can explore the park on your own or join a number of ranger-led tours. You can also bring your own boat (permit required), or fly in by seaplane from Key West - the quickest way to get to the island, but also the most expensive. There are no facilities in the park: bring cash and any food with you.

# STAY

### Marquesa Hotel
The four buildings that comprise this boutique hotel date back to the 19th century. They're built around two pools, surrounded by foliage.

🏠 Key West
🌐 marquesa.com

$$$

### The Gardens Hotel
This was once a private estate with botanical gardens. Expect hardwood floors and four-poster beds.

🏠 Key West
🌐 gardenshotel.com

$$$

# EAT

### Blue Heaven
A local institution, serving Floridian-Caribbean cuisine. The dinner menu includes BBQ shrimp and Jamaican jerk chicken.

🏠 526 Angela St
🌐 gardenshotel.com

$$$

## Fort Jefferson

Historic Fort Jefferson is an engineering marvel and without doubt the park's main draw. The harbor at Garden Key was one of the most important deep-water anchorages in the Americas, located, as it was, along one of the world's busiest shipping lanes. Construction on the protective fort began in 1846 and work continued for nearly 30 years until it abruptly stopped in 1875; despite more than 16 million bricks being laid, the fort was never completed. Fort Jefferson was a spot for mariners to refuel, rest, and to seek safe refuge from violent storms at sea, and served as a prison during the American Civil War.

Today, visitors can enjoy expansive sea views from its roof and windows, and the fort, with its vivid greenery sprouting from the brickwork and through its 2,000-plus archways, has become a playground for keen photographers. Inquire about the after-dark ranger-led tours, where scorpions can be spotted scurrying along the fort's walls.

↑ A ruddy turnstone, foraging in the sand

## Loggerhead Key

Three miles (5 km) from Garden Key is Loggerhead Key, home to the colorful Little Africa snorkeling site, where stony and gorgonian coral reefs thrive, providing habitat for

# EXPLORING DRY TORTUGAS

*Gulf*

The **Windjammer** *wreck is located 1 mile (0.6 km) southwest of Loggerhead Key's southwest tip. At 20 ft (6 m) deep, it is a great spot for novice scuba divers.*

Dry Tortugas Lighthouse

*Loggerhead Key*

Windjammer Wreck

| 0 meters | 800 |
| 0 yards | 800 |

N ↑

*Southwest*

← Loggerhead Key lighthouse,
keeping watch over
Loggerhead Key

🗓 IF YOU HAVE
**A weekend**

Camp on Garden Key
and spend the days
walking the island and
the nights stargazing.
Take an after-dark tour
of Fort Jefferson, when
all of the day-trippers
have gone home.

more than a quarter of the area's tropical fish, as well as game fish and spiny lobster. Loggerhead is also home to the Windjammer Wreck, one of the most popular scuba-diving spots in the Dry Tortugas. The dive site consists of the bow and stern wreckage of the *Avanti*, a large Norwegian vessel that sank off Loggerhead Reef on its way to Uruguay in 1907.

For 35 years in the early 1900s, the Carnegie Research Institute operated tropical underwater research at the now defunct Tortugas Laboratory on Loggerhead. Still very much here, though, overlooking the 49-acre (20-ha) key from the center of the island as it has been since 1857, is the Logger-head lighthouse.

## Bush Key

If you're visiting the Dry Tortugas in the fall, don't miss the chance to take a trip to Bush Key. This upside-down "L"-shaped island, just east of Garden Key and facing Jefferson Fort across a deep channel, harbors a variety of flora and fauna that is found nowhere else in the continental U.S. Bush Key is only open from mid-October to mid-January, at which time you can access its western end by canoe, kayak, or dinghy (permit required), or on ranger-led tours from Garden Key. A 1-mile (1.5-km) trail loops around the top half of Bush Key (Long Key, tailing off the island's eastern end, is off-limits to the public throughout the year), from where you might spot the Dry Tortugas' prolific birdlife, including brown noddies, magnificent frigatebirds, and some of the island's colony of 750,000 sooty terns. The shallow waters off the key's southern end are a protected reserve for nurse sharks (closed Jun–Oct), while the pond at its eastern end is home to Bush Key's resident American crocodile.

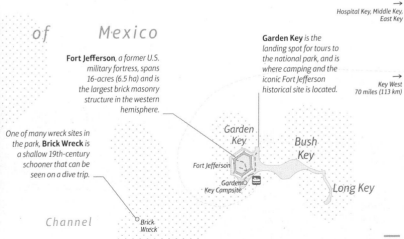

→
Hospital Key, Middle Key,
East Key

**Garden Key** *is the
landing spot for tours to
the national park, and is
where camping and the
iconic Fort Jefferson
historical site is located.*

→
Key West
70 miles (113 km)

**Fort Jefferson**, *a former U.S.
military fortress, spans
16-acres (6.5 ha) and is
the largest brick masonry
structure in the western
hemisphere.*

*of*     *Mexico*

*One of many wreck sites in
the park,* **Brick Wreck** *is
a shallow 19th-century
schooner that can be
seen on a dive trip.*

*Garden
Key*

*Bush
Key*

*Fort Jefferson*

*Garden
Key Campsite*

*Long Key*

*Channel*

*Brick
Wreck*

The golden sands of St. John

HALEAKALĀ
p478

Pacific
Ocean

HAWAI'I
VOLCANOES
Hawaii          p468

see Hawaii
inset map

Pacific
Ocean

Atlantic
Ocean

VIRGIN
ISLANDS
p490

NATIONAL PARK OF
• AMERICAN SAMOA
p486

# THE ISLANDS

Natural wonders of startling beauty await off the U.S.
mainland, with island parks of great biodiversity. Hawaii
is made up of six main isles in the Pacific Ocean, with
sweeping arcs of sand gently lapped by turquoise sea.
The islands are home to two national parks, both
defined by their volcanic landscapes: Hawai'i Volcanoes
has two majestic volcanoes within its borders, while
Haleakalā, on the island of Maui, is named after a
dormant shield volcano. The parks preserve some of
the world's rarest flora and fauna which thrives in this
unique island habitat. Virgin Islands National Park takes
up the majority of the U.S. Virgin Island of St. John; the
park is famed for its white-sand beaches fringed by
coral reefs. Even farther south of the mainland and the
only U.S. park found south of the equator, the National
Park of American Samoa is situated in the territory of
American Samoa. The park is distributed across four
islands: Tutuila, Ofu, Olosega, and Ta'ū, and is home
to some distinct lowland and montane rainforest
habitats, as well as waters rich in marine life, offering
some of the continent's best snorkeling.

1 The Pools of Ohe'o.

2 Hiking on cooled lava
at Mauna Loa.

3 Starlight above
the Kīlauea caldera.

4 Historic Makawao.

# 5 DAYS
## *in Hawaii*

## Day 1

Your awe-inspiring exploration of the volcanic parks of Hawaii starts at Haleakalā National Park *(p478)* in Maui, home to the world's largest dormant volcano. On your first day, take a tour of the park with Haleakalā Sunrise Tours *(www.haleakalaecotours.com);* they will pick you up bright and early for a magical sunrise viewed from Haleakalā's towering crater. After touring the Summit District, your tour will take you to the historic "paniolo" (cowboy) town of Makawao, the pineapple-growing center of Ha'iku, and the surfing hub of Pā'ia.

## Day 2

Today you'll be exploring the park independently – rent a car or book taxis in advance. The remote but enchanting Kīpahulu District can only be accessed by road; the safest route is via Hāna on the Hāna Highway. Come prepared with a packed lunch and plenty of water. Start at Kīpahulu Visitor Center before wandering down to the Hale Hālāwai, a replica Polynesian meeting house now used for cultural demonstrations. From here you can stroll the half-mile (0.8-km) Kūloa Point Trail for views of the Pools of Ohe'o and the Pacific, then hike the Pīpīwai Trail into the lush interior, passing Makahiku Falls in the hauntingly beautiful Bamboo Forest. Spend your last night on Maui bar-hopping and dancing in Pā'ia.

## Day 3

Hop on a flight to the Big Island; several airlines fly nonstop between Maui's Kahului Airport and Kona International Airport on the island of Hawai'i. Hawai'i Volcanoes National Park *(p469)* is around 80 miles (128 km) from the airport, so rent a car and drive to Volcano House *(p473)* where you can reserve dinner and a room. This afternoon get oriented at Kīlauea Visitor Center and visit the Volcano Art Center Gallery, before taking the Crater Rim Drive around the steaming Kīlauea Summit. The Kīlauea Overlook provides dramatic views of the caldera and the Halema'uma'u crater.

## Day 4

Start the day by completing the Crater Rim Drive to the south, stopping to hike the short Kīlauea Iki Trail, which cuts through a lush rainforest to the solidified lava lake on the floor of Kīlauea Iki crater. Continue on the Chain of Craters Road as it winds down to the sea through a blasted landscape of smoking cones and vents. Stop at Kealakomo, a sensational spot for a picnic. In the afternoon visit the Pu'uloa Petroglyphs and the Hōlei Sea Arch at the end of the road. If there's time on the way back to your base at Volcano House, climb Pu'uhuluhulu (hairy hill).

## Day 5

End your Hawai'i adventure at the Kahuku Unit of the park – it's about an hour's drive from Volcano along Rte. 11. Not far from the Kahuku entrance, take the trail to the top of grassy Pu'u o Lokuana cinder cone, before joining the strenuous Pit Crater Trail up to the Forested Pit Crater. Finish with a drive west along Māmalahoa Highway to see evidence of the lava flows that have poured off Mauna Loa. Toast the end of your trip by munching on tacos at local hotspot Tiki Mama's.

A stream of lava gushing into the sea, the heat and pressure causing a giant explosion

# HAWAI'I VOLCANOES

📍 Hawaii 💲$30 per vehicle, valid for seven days
🌐 nps.gov/havo

For 70 million years, volcanoes have erupted into the Pacific Ocean, forming a chain of islands that's still growing today. On Hawai'i (also known as the Big Island), two majestic volcanoes make up Hawai'i Volcanoes National Park: Mauna Loa and Kīlauea, two of the most active volcanoes in the world. To witness the Earth at its most elemental, look no further.

The goddess of volcanoes and fire, and the creator of the Hawaiian Islands, Pele looms large over Hawaiian culture, and perhaps nowhere more so than in Hawai'i Volcanoes National Park. Preserving a landscape that refuses to stand still, the park encompasses two restless volcanoes, Kīlauea and Mauna Loa. It's said that Pele made her home at the summit of Kīlauea, and that the volcano's rumbles, fumes, and fiery displays are all signs of the deity's explosive personality.

The domain of Pele it may be, but this remarkable park is one of Hawaii's most visited attractions. Inevitably the area has long been a magnet for scientists and naturalists, both expert and amateur alike, as well as travelers keen

↑ A park ranger describing the lay of the land at Kīlauea Visitor Center

to explore the effects of Mother Nature. The park offers the chance to see lava spew into an ocean, walk across a hardened lava lake, and watch steam rise from vents in the Earth. And while a volcanic eruption can cause devastation, there's life here too: old-growth koa and 'ōhi'a lehua rainforests, endemic birds such as the 'elepaio and 'apapane, and thousands of petroglyphs that speak of the island's earliest inhabitants.

### Did You Know?

Magma is the term for molten rock inside a volcano, and lava once it breaks the surface.

← Entering Nāhuku, or the Thurston Lava Tube, a popular short trail

**GETTING AROUND**

Visitors to the park typically fly into Kona on the west side of Hawai'i (also known as the Big Island) via commercial flights from the mainland. It's around a two-hour drive to the park via Hwy. 11. Alternatively, you can fly into Hilo on the east side of the island, arriving on inter-island flights from O'ahu. The 45-minute drive on Hwy. 11 leads through local villages and rainforests filled with tropical birds and vegetation. There are rental car agencies with large fleets at both airports. There is no shuttle bus or public transportation in the park.

## Exploring the park

Most of the park activity is based in the south of the park, around the Kīlauea caldera. Here you'll find the visitor center, an essential place to stop ahead of exploring the park. In addition to being a helpful planning resource, you can learn about island formation, ecosystems, invasive species, resource protection, and ranger-led activities. You'll also discover all-important information about rapidly changing trail and road access, and lava-viewing conditions, with lava flow, sulfur dioxide gas, and other hazards potentially restricting where you can go and what you can see. Note that there is sulfur in the air throughout most of the park, which might affect those who are sensitive to poor air quality.

Show your respect for the island and the beliefs of the Hawaiian people by leaving no trace and taking only that which you brought with you. Taking lava as a souvenir is forbidden and altering ahu (stacked rocks also known as "cairns") that mark trails is problematic for local guides and may be considered culturally offensive.

## Scenic drives

Those with only one day in the park will enjoy touring the park's sights on a scenic drive. Crater Rim Drive and Chain of Craters Road wind through the park, offering visitors the chance to explore the fiery landscape up close. The 11-mile (18-km) paved Crater Rim Drive skirts the edge of the Kīlauea caldera. It was once a full loop but sections have been closed indefinitely due to recent eruptions. The drive features scenery that the park is best known for: large craters, steam vents, volcanoes (of course), as well as wildlife, tropical birds, and plants. Some of the park's main attractions are found along the route, too, including the Thurston Lava Tube and the Kīlauea Overlook, which has views of the caldera and Halema'uma'u Crater (Kīlauea's main crater). The road can also be cycled.

To the south of Crater Rim Drive, the Chain of Craters Road veers off and heads toward the coast for 19 miles (30 km) from the Makaopuhi Crater to the Kalapana coast. As the road rapidly descends, you will experience a distinct change in landscape, from rainforest to barren lava

# EAT

Dining options are limited in the park, though Volcano House (p473) has a restaurant and lounge. Volcano Village is recommended for a bite to eat.

### Kilauea Lodge & Restaurant
Longtime favorite at a resort located just outside the park. Expect local ingredients and creative fare.

🏠 Volcano Village
🌐 kilauealodge.com

$$$

# A LONG WALK
# CRATER RIM TRAIL

**Length** 8.3 miles (13.4 km) one-way **Stopping-off points** Volcano House **Terrain** Rocky dirt trail

Following the edge of the Kīlauea summit caldera, this hike is the best way to get a look at one of the most active volcanoes in the world. There are several trailheads along Crater Rim Dr., which roughly parallels the trail around the caldera, for hikers of all abilities to explore shorter sections of the trail. Stay on the marked trail at all times; the volcano is active and many areas can be dangerous.

**Locator Map**

**Key**

-- Walk route

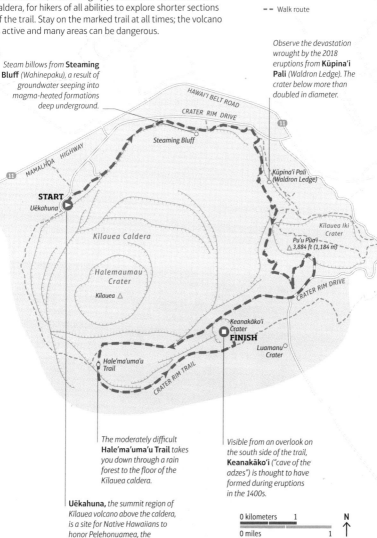

*Steam billows from **Steaming Bluff** (Wahinepaku), a result of groundwater seeping into magma-heated formations deep underground.*

*Observe the devastation wrought by the 2018 eruptions from **Kūpina'i Pali** (Waldron Ledge). The crater below more than doubled in diameter.*

HAWAI'I BELT ROAD

CRATER RIM DRIVE

MAMALHOA HIGHWAY

**START**
Uēkahuna

Steaming Bluff

Kūpina'i Pali
(Waldron Ledge)

Kīlauea Caldera

Halemaumau Crater

Kīlauea △

Kīlauea Iki Crater

Pu'u Pūa'i
△ 3,884 ft (1,184 m)

CRATER RIM DRIVE

Keanakāko'i Crater
**FINISH**

Luamanu Crater

Hale'ma'uma'u Trail

CRATER RIM TRAIL

*The moderately difficult **Hale'ma'uma'u Trail** takes you down through a rain forest to the floor of the Kīlauea caldera.*

**Uēkahuna,** the summit region of Kīlauea volcano above the caldera, is a site for Native Hawaiians to honor Pelehonuamea, the Hawaiian goddess of volcanoes.

*Visible from an overlook on the south side of the trail, **Keanakāko'i** ("cave of the adzes") is thought to have formed during eruptions in the 1400s.*

0 kilometers 1

0 miles 1

N↑

⊙ IF YOU HAVE
**A day**

A drive along either (or both) of the park's scenic roadways is an ideal way to see the best of the park. Before you set off, stop in at the visitor center to chat to park rangers and venture into the Thurston Lava Tube.

fields. The scenic views are studded with pit craters and recent lava flows. Stop at the Kealakomo Overlook to admire the amazing view of lava fields extending out to the Pacific Ocean; look out, too, for the 5,550-year-old basalt Hōlei Sea Arch on the coast. Several hiking trails are found along the road, including the trail to the Puʻu Loa Petroglyphs.

### Walking and hiking

Seeing the park from your vehicle has its merits but to really get a sense of this ever-changing landscape, you need to lace up your boots.

The Crater Rim Trail *(p471)* arcs around the Kīlauea caldera, with multiple trailheads giving walkers the chance to complete as much or as little of it as they like.

One of the park's most popular hikes is the Kīlauea Iki Trail. This 4-mile (6.5-km) loop passes through rainforest filled with native flora, colorful birds, and other wildlife before entering a lava-covered caldera formed when Kīlauea erupted in grand fashion in 1959. That event sent lava nearly 2,000 ft (610 m) skyward and eventually formed a hardened molten lake of lava.

The Puʻu Loa Petroglyphs hike is an easy 1.5-mile (2.5-km) round-trip hike to a collection of rock art etchings crafted by Hawaiian elders (kūpuna) depicting the lives of Native Hawaiian traditions and way of life. They are an immaculate presentation of cultural heritage and believed to be an offering to the gods.

An easy 1.2-mile (2-km) round-trip path, starting from the Kīlauea Visitor Center, leads to Haʻakulamanu, also known as the Sulfur Banks. The path follows an accessible boardwalk, which provides views of vibrant mineral deposits. This area is particularly known for attracting birds, probably because of the warmth emitting from the volcanic ground. Visitors with respiratory problems, pregnant women, and young children should avoid this walk due to the gases that seep from the landscape.

### Thurston Lava Tube

Near Kīlauea Iki is the Thurston Lava Tube, or Nāhuku. It can be accessed via an easy 15-minute trail that begins with a steep descent into the rainforest. The trail is dense with towering green ferns and leads into a pit crater and the entrance to the lava tube. Formed when the exterior of a lava flow cooled to a crust while the still-molten interior magma flowed out, the tube resembles a giant tunnel. The interiors are electrically lit, revealing glittering, multi-colored, mineral-rich walls and the thin roots of ʻōhiʻa trees which dangle through the ceiling. Tours of the tube are self-guided.

### Volcano Art Center

This center (open 9am–5pm daily) promotes Hawaii's rich culture through artworks, performances, exhibitions, and concerts. Its gallery features works by more than 300 local artists inspired by Hawaii's environmental and cultural heritage. On Mondays, the center has free guided rainforest tours where visitors

← 

The famed Hōlei Sea Arch, seen toward the end of the Chain of Craters Road

↑ Admiring the view of Mauna Loa, which rises over 13,600 ft (4,100 m) above sea level

← The bright red ōhiʻa lehua flower, native to the islands of Hawaii

can learn about Kīlauea's last old-growth koa and ʻōhiʻa lehua rainforests.

## Mauna Loa

This national park is not just about Kīlauea, of course. Covering the entire southern half of the island, Mauna Loa is the world's largest active volcano, at 60 miles (95 km) long and 30 miles (50 km) wide. Since its first documented eruption in 1843, it has erupted numerous times. The caldera at the summit, Mokuʻaweoweo (Hawaiian for "island of lurid burning"), is more than 3 miles (5 km) long and 1.5 miles (2.5 km) wide, with 600-ft (180-m) walls.

Two trails within the park lead up to the summit area, though both are impacted by recent eruptions. Beginning at the Mauna Loa Observatory, the 6.4-mile (10.3-km) out-and-back Observatory Trail is a tough day hike across a rugged, lunar-like landscape. The 19.1-mile (30.8-km) Mauna Loa Trail begins amid rainforest at the end of the unpaved Mauna Loa Road. There is a lookout here that offers excellent views of the volcano; it can be visited even if you're not planning to tackle the hike. The Mauna Loa Trail takes several days to complete; there are cabins on the route, the Puʻuʻulaʻula Cabin and Summit Cabin (permits required).

Both trails eventually intersect with the Summit Trail for the final approach to the peak. These trails are best left to experienced hikers, thanks to the high altitude and uneven terrain of rough lava rocks.

# STAY

The park has only one hotel and a couple of campgrounds, but there are several places to stay in Volcano Village, on the park boundary. Backcountry cabins can be found along the Mauna Loa Trail.

### Nāmakanipaio and Kulanaokuaiki Campgrounds

Basic cabins and space to pitch a tent at Nāmakanipaio; first-come, first-served sites at Kulanaokuaiki (no water at this location).

🏕 Hawaiʻi Volcanoes
🌐 hawaiivolcano house.com

### Volcano House

Country inn-style lodge with over 30 guest rooms. Expect stellar views of the park.

🏕 Hawaiʻi Volcanoes
🌐 hawaiivolcano house.com

Formed when the exterior of a lava flow cooled to a crust while the still-molten interior magma flowed out, the tube resembles a giant tunnel

# EXPLORING HAWAI'I VOLCANOES

The park stretches across a significant portion of Hawai'i. In the north, or the upper end, of the park, is Mauna Loa, while in the south is Kīlauea. Due to the park's volcanic landscape, expect areas to be closed at short notice.

↑ An example of the thousands of petroglyphs etched onto the surface

*One of the park's two massive volcanoes, **Mauna Loa** broke through the surface of the Pacific Ocean almost half a million years ago, and it's still growing today.*

*One of many pit craters in the park (formed when the Earth fractures as a volcano moves or expands), the **Forested Pit Crater** is found in the Kahuku Unit of the park.*

Mauna Loa

Mauna Loa

Pōhakuhanalei
12,772 ft (3,893 m)

Sulphur Cone
11,364 ft (3,464 m)

Red Cone
11,443 ft (3,488 m)

Ālika Cone
7,824 ft (2,388 m)

Keau
6,522 ft (1,988 m)

Ihuanu
5,295 ft (1,614 m)

Forested Pit Crater

Kahuku Visitor Station

11

## 1916

The year both Hawai'i Volcanoes National Park and the National Park Service were established.

0 kilometers  8
0 miles  8

N ↑

The **Kīlauea Visitor Center** provides information about things to do and see, as well as exhibits on historical, cultural, and environmental features of the park.

The **Kīlauea Iki Overlook** provides views onto a large crater that once held a lake of lava; walkers can descend into the crater on the Kīlauea Iki Trail.

Hawaii's rich culture is explored through hula performances, exhibitions, and concerts at the **Volcano Art Center**.

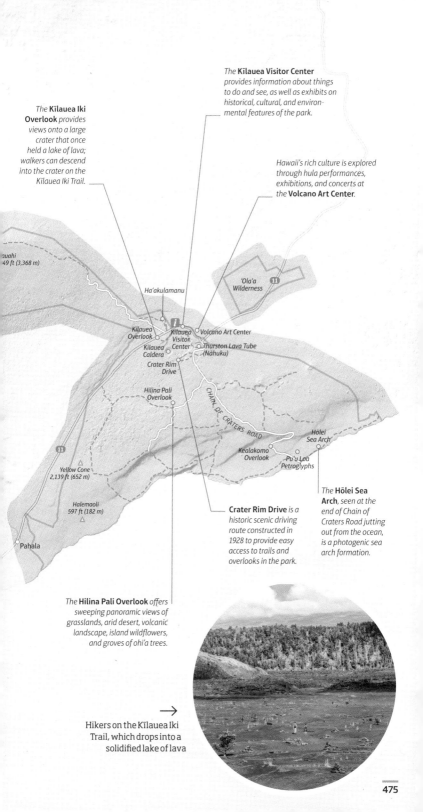

auahi
49 ft (3,368 m)

Ha'akulamanu

'Ola'a Wilderness

[11]

Kilauea Overlook

Kilauea Visitor Center

Volcano Art Center

Kilauea Caldera

Thurston Lava Tube (Nāhuku)

Crater Rim Drive

Hilina Pali Overlook

CHAIN OF CRATERS ROAD

Hōlei Sea Arch

[11]

Kealakomo Overlook

Pu'u Loa Petroglyphs

Yellow Cone 2,139 ft (652 m)

Halemaoli 597 ft (182 m)

Pahala

**Crater Rim Drive** is a historic scenic driving route constructed in 1928 to provide easy access to trails and overlooks in the park.

The **Hōlei Sea Arch**, seen at the end of Chain of Craters Road jutting out from the ocean, is a photogenic sea arch formation.

The **Hilina Pali Overlook** offers sweeping panoramic views of grasslands, arid desert, volcanic landscape, island wildflowers, and groves of ohi'a trees.

→ Hikers on the Kīlauea Iki Trail, which drops into a solidified lake of lava

# FORMATION OF THE HAWAIIAN ISLANDS

The Hawaiian Islands are the tips of a large chain of volcanoes stretching almost 3,100 miles (5,000 km) from Hawai'i Island to the Aleutian Trench in the north Pacific. Most are now underwater stumps, fringed by coral reefs, but many were once great shield (dome-shaped) volcanoes. Hawaii's oldest volcano is slowly disappearing into the Aleutian Trench, while its youngest volcano, Kīlauea, still spews out basaltic lava today, creating new land on Hawai'i Island. This cycle of destruction and creation, driven by the conveyor-belt movement of the Pacific Plate over a stationary hot spot of magma, has been occurring for millions of years and will continue to happen for many more.

*Stretching almost halfway along O'ahu, the **Nu'uanu Pali** (cliffs) formed when a large section of the Ko'olau shield volcano slumped into the sea.*

*O'ahu's **Hanauma Bay** is a late-stage volcanic crater, one of several forming a line of cones, craters, and vents caused by an eruption at least 10,000 years ago. The ash cones are the result of explosive interaction of rising magma with seawater.*

*Ni'ihau*

*Kaua'i's amazing **Waimea Canyon** is carved into the Wai'ale'ale shield volcano. The layers of lava flows that created the volcano are visible. Large canyons of this nature are typical of Hawaiian volcanoes in their late erosional stage.*

*The areas of undulating ocean floor are deposits of giant landslides. Little is known about them because they sit in deep water, and their precise age of formation is unknown.*

*Ocean floor*

*The Pacific Plate moves northwesterly at a rate of 2–3.5 in (5–9 cm) a year.*

Illustration showing the formation of the Hawaiian Islands ↑

← The striking Waimea Canyon, carved into a shield volcano

## CONVEYOR BELT

As it moves, the Pacific Plate – the huge slab of Earth's crust beneath the Pacific Ocean – rides over a stationary hot spot (mantle plume) that feeds heat and basaltic magma toward the surface. Mauna Loa, Kīlauea, and the "new" underwater volcano Lōʻihi are presently over the hot spot. As the plate moves to the north-west, volcanoes are gradually pulled off the hot spot while new volcanoes grow in their place.

Lānaʻi

**Molokaʻi's sea cliffs** *formed when half of the Wailau shield volcano slumped into the sea in a landslide. Marine erosion keeps the cliffs steep by undercutting their bases.*

*Hawaiʻi Island's pair of giant shield volcanoes,* **Mauna Kea** *and Mauna Loa, make up the Earth's largest single volcanic erosional depression – often misnamed a crater – formed where two large valleys merged.*

Kahoʻolawe

*Maui's* **Haleakalā** *(p478) is Hawaii's only active shield volcano outside of Hawaiʻi Island. It is last thought to have erupted around 500 years ago.*

Hawaiʻi Island

Vent

**Mauna Loa** *makes up over one-half of the volume of Hawaiʻi Island.*

Rift zone

**Kīlauea**, *located in Hawaiʻi Volcanoes National Park, has been erupting since 1983 and shows no sign of stopping.*

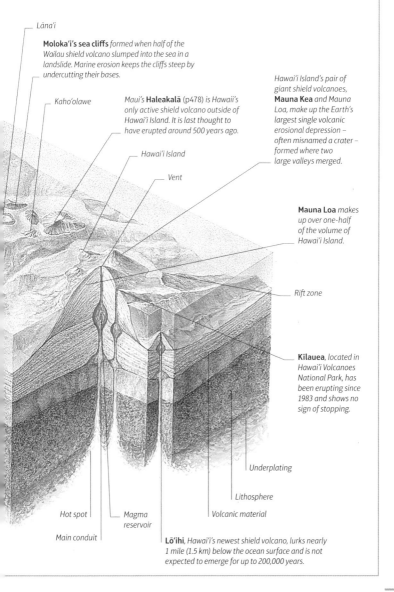

Underplating

Lithosphere

Volcanic material

Hot spot

Magma reservoir

Main conduit

**Lōʻihi**, *Hawaiʻi's newest shield volcano, lurks nearly 1 mile (1.5 km) below the ocean surface and is not expected to emerge for up to 200,000 years.*

# HALEAKALĀ

**⚲ Hawaii 🚗 $30 per vehicle, valid for three days 🌐 nps.gov/hale**

If there was only one park to watch the sun rise on a new day, it would have to be Haleakalā. The "House of the Sun" attracts visitors aplenty to its summit, all eager to see the sun emerge behind a practically primeval landscape. But to restrict a visit here to the early hours would be to miss out on so much more: rare endemic flora and fauna, night skies bursting with stars, and lush forest that tumbles down to rocky shores.

Stretching from craggy peaks to shimmering coastline, this magnificent national park covers the top of the vast Haleakalā shield volcano,

← Taking in the view from the Haleakalā Visitor Center

the crown of the island of Maui and its highest peak. Scientists estimate Haleakalā to be about one million years old. They believe that what's commonly referred to as the crater isn't the result of a volcanic eruption at all, but was caused by two valleys slowly merging on either

The rising sun peeking through the clouds over Haleakalā ↑

side of the peak. While thought to have last erupted more than 400 years ago, Haleakalā crater is still considered an active volcano. As you gaze into the 7-mile (11-km) crater, it's easy to imagine the rumble of molten rock under the surface and the dormant volcano coming to life again, like a mythic beast woken from its slumber.

The national park is a study in contrasts. The expansive and dusty Summit District, colored in tones of burned crimson and dark ash, is an otherworldly place, home to some of the world's rarest plants and animal species. In contrast, the Kīpahulu District on Haleakalā's coastal south-eastern slope is humid and deeply forested. Hiking trails here wind past gushing water-falls, freshwater streams, and shimmering pools, while over-looks provide views of the ocean, and the chance to see whales, dolphins, and seals.

# EAT

There are dining options and stores near the summit area (Pukalani, Makawao, and Kula), and in Hāna, not far from the Kīpahulu area.

### Kula Bistro
This lively joint cooks up homely fare: pasta, paninis, and the like. B.Y.O. beer and wine.

🏠 Kula   🌐 kulabistro.com

### Lumeria's Wooden Crate
Farm-to-table meals and a rotating seasonal menu.

🏠 Makawao
🌐 lumeriamaui.com

### Hāna Farms
Farm, roadside stand, bakery, and restaurant, all serving up fresh, local produce and dishes. The banana bread is a must-try.

🏠 Hāna   🌐 hanafarms.com

### Coconut Glen's
Delicious vegan and organic ice cream, made with Maui coconuts.

🏠 1200 Hāna Highway
🌐 coconutglens.com

# A LONG WALK
# KEONEHE'EHE'E TRAIL

**Length** 17.6 miles (28.3 km) **Stopping-off points** Kapalaoa Cabin, if you reserve ahead **Terrain** Rocky dirt trail makes this hike difficult

Marked by stunning mountain scenery, the Keonehe'ehe'e ("sliding sands" in Hawaiian) Trail traverses rugged backcountry through a volcanic crater. From the trailhead, the trail quickly descends into the crater before regaining some of that elevation near the end. The trail is best suited to experienced hikers.

**Locator Map**

**Key**

-- Walk Route

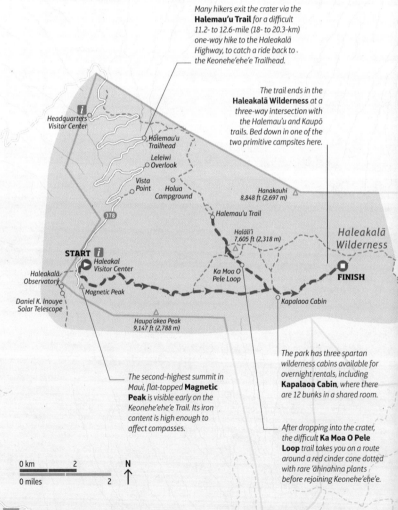

Many hikers exit the crater via the **Halemau'u Trail** for a difficult 11.2- to 12.6-mile (18- to 20.3-km) one-way hike to the Haleakalā Highway, to catch a ride back to the Keonehe'ehe'e Trailhead.

The trail ends in the **Haleakalā Wilderness** at a three-way intersection with the Halemau'u and Kaupō trails. Bed down in one of the two primitive campsites here.

Headquarters Visitor Center

Halemau'u Trailhead

Leleiwi Overlook

Vista Point

Holua Campground

Hanakauhi 8,848 ft (2,697 m)

Halemau'u Trail

Halāli'i 7,605 ft (2,318 m)

Haleakalā Wilderness

**START** Haleakalā Visitor Center

Haleakalā Observatory

Magnetic Peak

Daniel K. Inouye Solar Telescope

Ka Moa O Pele Loop

**FINISH**

Kapalaoa Cabin

Haupa'akea Peak 9,147 ft (2,788 m)

The second-highest summit in Maui, flat-topped **Magnetic Peak** is visible early on the Keonehe'ehe'e Trail. Its iron content is high enough to affect compasses.

The park has three spartan wilderness cabins available for overnight rentals, including **Kapalaoa Cabin**, where there are 12 bunks in a shared room.

After dropping into the crater, the difficult **Ka Moa O Pele Loop** trail takes you on a route around a red cinder cone dotted with rare 'āhinahina plants before rejoining Keonehe'ehe'e.

0 km 2
0 miles 2

N

## Exploring the park

Haleakalā National Park is almost two parks in one: the volcanic Summit District and the lush southeast coast of the Kīpahulu District. One isn't better than the other, and you'll want to spend time in both to say you've truly seen all of the park's delights.

There are three visitor centers in the park: the Park Headquarters Visitor Center, around a mile (1.5 km) past the Summit District entrance; Haleakalā Visitor Center, about 30 minutes from the Park Headquarters; and Kīpahulu Visitor Center, on the coast. Visit for exhibits, ranger talks, and to find out

about the weather and climate; temperatures and conditions can dramatically change from one part of the park to another.

### Sunrise and sunset

Legend has it that the first Hawaiians chose their island name after the demigod Māui, who climbed Haleakalā to lasso the sun as it rose in the morning sky. He released the sun only after it agreed to move more slowly through the sky to bestow more light on the island. With this folklore in mind, it is no surprise that the island's sunrises and sunsets are of legend, too.

One of the best places to view them is from the top of Haleakalā crater – but you won't be alone. Watching the sun emerge is one of the park's most popular activities and so advance reservations are required (not so for sunsets). Book via the park website well in advance (last-minute tickets are often released online a

few days ahead). Make sure to dress warm: the temperature at the summit can drop below freezing during the night.

### Stargazing

To see the sunset from the summit is a spectacular thrill, but as the park service says: "Half the park is after dark." Haleakalā offers great stargazing thanks to its high altitude and lack of light pollution. On a clear night, you can see constellations and planetary objects in all their glory. Stargazing is especially spectacular when the moon is phasing out; the lack of moonlight makes the stars brighter.

### Did You Know?

Something of a trickster, Māui is an important folk hero across Polynesia.

# STAY

The park has campgrounds (Hosmer Grove in the Summit District and Kīpahulu on the coast) and cabins. There is a maximum of three overnight stays for all park areas in a 30-day period. Outside of the park, stay in Kula or Hāna.

### Wilderness Cabins

The park has three rustic cabins, one each in Hōlua, Kapalaoa, and Palikū. The cabins accommodate 12 people each, and have woodburning stoves and outdoor pit toilets. Reserve up to six months in advance.

🏠 Summit District
🌐 recreation.gov

$ $ $

→

The Milky Way, photographed from Haleakalā National Park

If you prefer to admire the cosmos with other stargazers, the park offers plenty of organized, expert-led tours. If you're happy to go it alone, pack a scope, binoculars, or zoom lens, collect a stargazing map at one of the visitor centers, and prepare to enjoy the experience of stargazing from the middle of the Pacific Ocean.

## Hiking

Hiking the Summit District makes for a memorable adventure. There's a real variety here, from short trails that take less than 30 minutes to multiday backpacking trips. Note that conditions in the district aren't suited to everyone: the summit is highly exposed and the air is thinner; what's more, temperatures can drop below freezing. Pack sensibly: a first-aid kit, snacks, and plenty of water are recommended.

For experienced hikers, the Sliding Sands Trail, known in Hawaiian as Keonehe'ehe'e, is a park favorite (p480). Another popular trail is the moderate-to-difficult Supply Trail (4.6 miles / 7.4 km round-trip). On

this walk you'll experience Haleakalā's volcanic landscape, and spot local plants and wildlife.

The hiking trails in Kīpahulu wind past gushing waterfalls, freshwater streams, and shimmering pools, as well as to remnants of ancient taro farms and fishing villages. The half-mile (1-km) Kuloa Point Trail, starting at the visitor center, is a great way to get a taste of Kīpahulu in a short period of time. It loops the popular Pools of Ohe'o, also known as the Seven Sacred Pools, which are fed by waterfalls. Note

that the pools are sacred to Native Hawaiians and no swimming is allowed.

The 4-mile (6.5-km) Pīpīwai Trail winds through a forest to the base of the Waimoku Falls. At times the forest is thick with bamboo.

## Crater Road

Switchbacking its way up to the summit of Pu'u'ula'ula, the highest point on Maui, Crater Road (also known as Haleakalā Road) makes for an incredibly scenic drive or cycle. The paved, two-lane road is well maintained, and drivers and cyclists can expect to share the space. For those on two wheels, note that due to its high altitude and length, the route can be difficult and is perhaps best left to experienced cyclists. But this doesn't mean you have to miss out: Bike Maui (www.bikemaui.com) offers downhill bikes to rent, and will drive you up to the summit so you can whizz back down again.

## Flora and fauna

Haleakalā is home to some of the world's rarest plants and animal species. Among them are the endangered nēnē and the endemic Haleakalā silversword, whose honey-

Cycling along Crater Road, which leads to the summit of Haleakalā

scented blossoms can take up to 50 years to develop. More than 200 nēnē (Hawaiian geese) – the state bird of Hawaii – survive in Haleakalā, as does the Hawaiian petrel, which nests in colonies at the volcano's summit. You can also find tiny Hawaiian bats in the park, which are the only endemic Hawaiian land mammals in existence.

From the many overlooks in the Kīpahulu area of the park, you may spot humpback whales and dolphins out in the ocean, or green sea turtles and monk seals on Kīpahulu's rocky shores. Look out, too, for the bright red 'apapane bird and the 'i'iwi bird. Full-day bird-watching treks are offered by Explore Maui Nature (www.exploremauinature.com).

### ⊙ IF YOU HAVE
## A weekend

Prepare for an early start and watch the sunrise from the crater summit. After, explore the Summit District. The next day, drive the Road to Hāna to enjoy lush coastal scenery.

→

The pretty-as-a-picture Pools of Ohe'o, and (inset) hiking along the volcanic landscapes

# EXPLORING HALEAKALĀ

Located on the Hawaiian island of Maui, Haleakalā National Park is formed of two dramatically different sections: the currently dormant volcano of Haleakalā, the park's namesake, and the coastal Kīpahulu area.

The sheltered **Leleiwi Overlook** has views onto Haleakalā crater, the Kaupō Gap, and Maui's north shore. It was built under the Mission 66 program, aimed at creating more areas for visitors to enjoy.

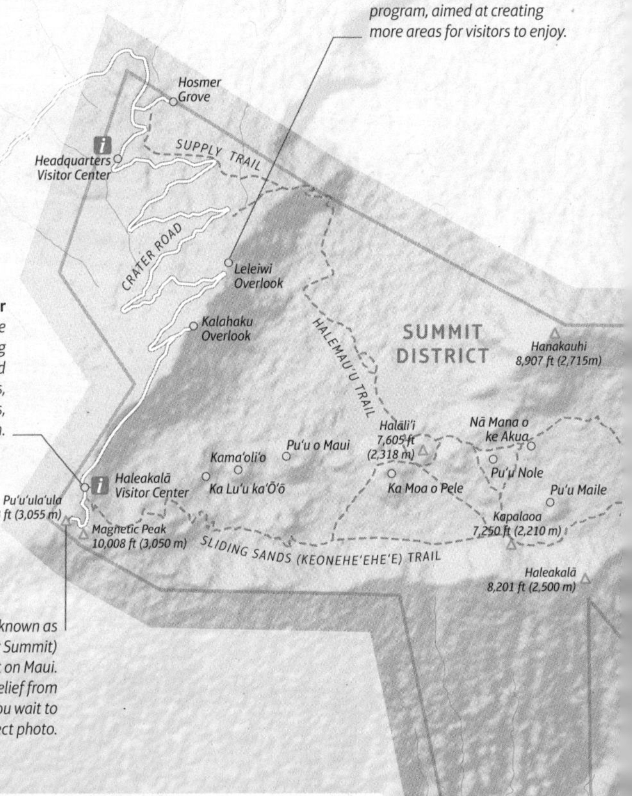

The **Haleakalā Visitor Center** stands atop the edge of a sweeping volcanic valley. Find interactive exhibits, helpful park rangers, and park information.

**Pu'u'ula'ula** (also known as "Red Hill" or Crater Summit) is the highest point on Maui. A shelter provides relief from the cold while you wait to take the perfect photo.

Hosmer Grove

Headquarters Visitor Center

SUPPLY TRAIL

CRATER ROAD

Leleiwi Overlook

Kalahaku Overlook

HALEMAU'U TRAIL

SUMMIT DISTRICT

Hanakauhi 8,907 ft (2,715m)

Haleakalā Visitor Center

Kama'oli'o

Pu'u o Maui

Halāli'i 7,605 ft (2,318 m)

Nā Mana o ke Akua

Ka Lu'u ka'Ō'ō

Ka Moa o Pele

Pu'u Nole

Pu'u Maile

Pu'u'ula'ula 10,023 ft (3,055 m)

Magnetic Peak 10,008 ft (3,050 m)

Kapalaoa 7,250 ft (2,210 m)

SLIDING SANDS (KEONEHE'EHE'E) TRAIL

Haleakalā 8,201 ft (2,500 m)

31

↑ The visitor center in the Kīpahulu area of the park, with beautiful ocean views

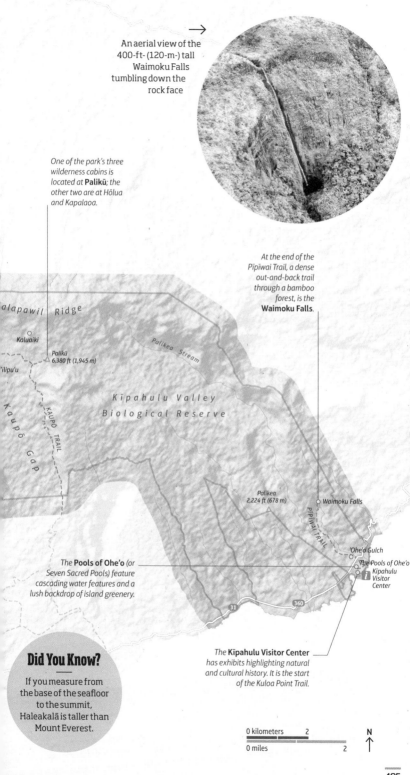

An aerial view of the 400-ft- (120-m-) tall Waimoku Falls tumbling down the rock face →

One of the park's three wilderness cabins is located at **Palikū**; the other two are at Hōlua and Kapalaoa.

At the end of the Pīpīwai Trail, a dense out-and-back trail through a bamboo forest, is the **Waimoku Falls**.

*alapawil* Ridge

Kaluaiki ○

Palikū
6,380 ft (1,945 m)

'ilipu'u

Palikea Stream

K ī p a h u l u  V a l l e y
B i o l o g i c a l  R e s e r v e

KAUPŌ TRAIL

K a u p ō  G a p

Palikea
2,224 ft (678 m)

○ Waimoku Falls

PĪPĪWAI TRAIL

'Ohe'o Gulch

The Pools of Ohe'o
Kīpahulu
Visitor
Center

The **Pools of Ohe'o** (or Seven Sacred Pools) feature cascading water features and a lush backdrop of island greenery.

31    360

**Did You Know?**

If you measure from the base of the seafloor to the summit, Haleakalā is taller than Mount Everest.

The **Kīpahulu Visitor Center** has exhibits highlighting natural and cultural history. It is the start of the Kuloa Point Trail.

0 kilometers    2
0 miles    2

N ↑

# NATIONAL PARK OF AMERICAN SAMOA

📍 American Samoa   🎟️ Free (passports valid for six months and a return plane ticket are required for entry to American Samoa)   🌐 nps.gov/npsa

In the heart of the South Pacific, Samoan culture and natural wonders converge, creating the most unusual park in the National Park Service's portfolio. This is the only U.S. national park in the southern hemisphere, located closer to New Zealand than it is to Hawaii and the rest of the U.S. But ticking this one off the list is more than worth it: here, you'll find a park steeped in traditional Samoan culture that dates back some 3,000 years.

### 🕐 IF YOU HAVE
**A week**

Aim to explore all three islands, starting with Tutuila. Stop by the visitor center, hike the Mount Alava Adventure Trail, and take a scenic drive. On Ofu enjoy snorkeling and on Ta'ū arrange a guided walk with the locals.

While the islands of American Samoa might look paradisical, if you're looking for beachside cabanas and vibrant nightlife, you aren't going to find them. What you will find is a unique national park steeped in traditional Samoan culture dating back 3,000 years. And that's what makes a trip to the National Park of American Samoa so special.

Protected park areas are located on three islands: Tutuila, home to the capital city of Pago Pago; and Ta'ū and Ofu, which are both part of the Manu'a Island chain. All three have raw, natural beauty in abundance, as well as plenty of native bird- and marine life. Fruit bats (also known as "flying foxes") glide from branch to branch like tree monkeys, while sharks and brightly colored fish weave through unbleached coral reefs.

← Typically lush rainforest and beautiful sea views, both common in the park

## Exploring the park

Tutuila is the largest of the islands and it's here you'll likely fly into and spend most of your time. Because the park takes some getting to, consider staying longer to ensure you see each of the islands (distances between each are not insignificant). Pago Pago (shortened to one word and pronounced "Pongo") has a visitor center, as does Ofu.

American Samoa has a conservative culture. Modest clothing is expected and weekly prayer quietens the island every Sunday evening. Tourists are expected to adjust to the Samoan way of life, so managing your expectations is crucial.

## Tutuila

Scenic drives and hikes are the main draw on Tutuila. The Mount Alava Adventure Trail is a can't miss for intrepid hikers. Crawling the ledges of jungle rainforest are rope ladders and over 780 steps, which climb around 1,600 ft (490 m). The overlook at the trail's apex provides views onto Pago Pago Bay, where boats nestle in the harbor, before stretching out into the deep blue Pacific seas. There is a shortened version of this trail where you can still see a variety of birds, insects, fruit

→ Pink cauliflower coral in the species-rich seas of American Samoa

# EXPLORING NATIONAL PARK OF AMERICAN SAMOA

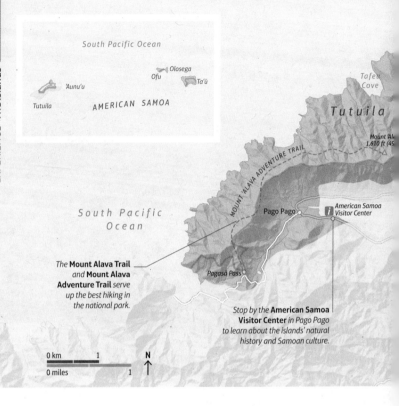

South Pacific Ocean

AMERICAN SAMOA

Olosega
Ofu
Ta'ū
'Aunu'u
Tutuila

Tafeu Cove

Tutuila

Mount 'Ala
1,610 ft (49

MOUNT 'ALAVA ADVENTURE TRAIL

Pago Pago

American Samoa Visitor Center

*The **Mount Alava Trail** and **Mount Alava Adventure Trail** serve up the best hiking in the national park.*

*Pagasā Pass*

*Stop by the **American Samoa Visitor Center** in Pago Pago to learn about the islands' natural history and Samoan culture.*

0 km — 1
0 miles — 1

N

## GETTING AROUND

To get to the park fly to the Tafuna International Airport in Pago Pago on the island of Tutuila. The most common route flies in from Honolulu, Hawaii. There are flights to Western Samoa from Australia and New Zealand. There is only one driving road in Tutuila, which you can travel by rental car or local bus. To visit Ofu or T'aū, travel by small plane or boat. Local transportation can be arranged by the park service, local tourism board, or by your hotel or lodge stay.

bats, and plant species. At the time of writing the trail was closed for maintenance.

Tutuila once served as a base for U.S. forces and a number of military sites from World War II are preserved on the island. To see them, set out on the 1.7-mile (2.7-km) World War II Heritage Trail.

### Ofu

Perhaps the most popular spot in the park, Ofu is a beacon to snorkelers and divers. Not only is Ofu beach regularly named one of the world's most beautiful beaches, but the waters that surround the island teem with over 950 species of fish and over 250 species of coral. Such diversity has earned it designation as a National Marine Sanctuary,

one of only 15 in the U.S. and its territories.

While snorkeling is stellar, you'll find that planning is essential to making it happen: there's not much in the way of diving infrastructure on American Samoa, so bring your own gear and expect to charter boats.

### T'aū

Ta'ū is considered the most traditional of the islands in American Samoa. A visit here offers the opportunity to explore untamed terrain with locals passionate about sharing their homeland. You might hike past ruins and through jungles, or watch from the rocky coastline as Pacific waters crash skyward. The moderate 5.7-mile (9.2-km) Si'u Point Trail follows an

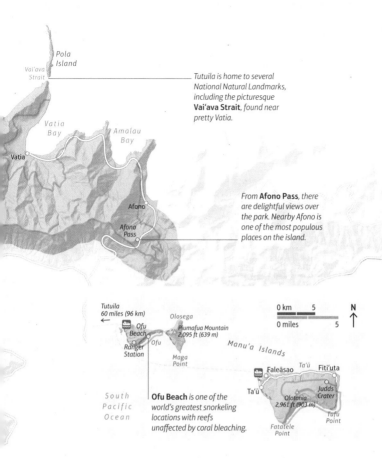

Tutuila is home to several National Natural Landmarks, including the picturesque **Vai'ava Strait**, found near pretty Vatia.

From **Afono Pass**, there are delightful views over the park. Nearby Afono is one of the most populous places on the island.

Tutuila 60 miles (96 km)

Pola Island

Vai'ava Strait

Vatia Bay

Amalau Bay

Vatia

Afono

Afono Pass

Olosega

Ofu Beach

Ranger Station

Ofu

Piumafua Mountain 2,095 ft (639 m)

Maga Point

Manu'a Islands

South Pacific Ocean

Faleāsao

Ta'ū

Ta'ū

Fiti'uta

Olotania 2,961 ft (903 m)

Judds Crater

Tufu Point

Fatatele Point

0 km 5
0 miles 5

N

**Ofu Beach** is one of the world's greatest snorkeling locations with reefs unaffected by coral bleaching.

old dirt road to a culturally important Samoan site.

Ta'ū is home to Lata Mountain, the highest peak in American Samoa at over 3,000 ft (900 m) above sea level, though it's often shrouded in cloud.

↑ The cardinal myzomela, a type of honeyeater often seen in American Samoa

# EAT

Finding places to eat on Tutuila, which has an array of options from fresh markets to local diners, is simple, but not so on the outer islands. Seek out opportunities to enjoy a traditional umu feast. An umu is an above-ground "earth oven" commonly used across Polynesia for special occasions. Freshly caught and gathered food is prepared laboriously by hand and then cooked.

# STAY

There are hotels on Tutuila and lodges on Ofu; camping in the park is not allowed. The NPS and local families have created a unique homestay program that places tourists with resident families, providing the opportunity to learn about local customs, traditional cuisine, and Samoan craft making. Accommodations and availability varies; contact the NPS.

Best for *Snorkeling, swimming, and sun-soaking*

# VIRGIN ISLANDS

📍U.S. Virgin Islands 🎟Free (Trunk Beach has a $5 day-use fee per person) 🌐nps.gov/viis

Out in the Caribbean Ocean, not far from Puerto Rico, lie the U.S. Virgin Islands, formed of the islands of St. Croix, St. John, and St. Thomas, and some 50 other islands and cays. Roughly two-thirds of St. John, plus a patch of the island's surrounding waters, make up Virgin Islands National Park, renowned for its teal-blue waters, vibrant coral reefs, and lush rainforests. In 2017 Hurricane Irma devastated many of the island's beautiful ecosystems as well as much of its infrastructure, an event St. John, and the national park, are still recovering from.

For thousands of years, the Indigenous Taino people lived on St. John, enjoying a way of life carefully cultivated – that is until the arrival of European seafarers in 1493. Christopher Columbus's tales of the fabled "emerald isles" sparked the interest of European colonizers, and the island passed between many nations for hundreds of years, all eager to profit from sugarcane and cotton, lucrative cash crops that grew readily on the island. Native vegetation was wiped out to make way for plantations, with enslaved Africans and their descendants forced to labor on the land. After emancipation, plantation farming waned, and was later replaced by the rise of tourism. The establishment of the park in 1956 protected the island from being overwhelmed with development, while crucial reforestation sought to recover the land from the plantation era.

Today, the park protects more than half of the island – as well as the surrounding waters. This is where most of the park's wildlife resides, with more than 300 fish

---

**IF YOU HAVE**
**A day**

If time is tight, take the North Shore Road for a scenic drive, then chill out on beautiful Trunk Bay, dipping into the sea and basking in the sun.

---

# EAT

The park has a few options, but you'll find more in Cruz Bay and Coral Bay.

**Trunk Bay Snack Shack**
Full bar and snacks on the beachfront.

🏠Trunk Beach

$$$

**Miss Lucy's**
Family-run place, serving Caribbean classics with a side of live music.

🏠South of Coral Bay
🌐misslucys restaurant.com

$$$

**Dolphin Market**
Grocery stores with a good selection.

🏠Cruz Bay and Coral Bay 🌐dolphinmarkets. com

$$$

↑ The Virgin Islands National Park visitor center

↑ Picture-perfect Trunk
Bay, a favorite of visitors
to the park

→ The remains of a windmill at the Annaberg Sugar Plantation

## STAY

There are two options within park boundaries, and a wide range of luxury resorts, vacation rentals, and other lodgings on the island.

**Cinnamon Bay Beach and Campground**
Stay in cottages or eco-tents, and dine in the on-site Rain Tree Cafe.
🏠 Cinnamon Bay
[W] cinnamonbayvi.com
$$$

**Concordia Eco Resort**
"Eco-cabanas" and villas on a forested hillside close to the beach.
🏠 Salt Pond Bay
[W] concordiaeco resort.com
$$$

**Hotel Cruz Bay**
Boutique hotel within walking distance of restaurants and the Cruz Bay ferry landing.
🏠 Cruz Bay
[W] hotelcruzbay.com
$$$

species and three of the world's seven species of sea turtles – green, hawksbill, and the massive leatherback – found here.

### Exploring the park

St. John is just 9 miles (14 km) long so visitors can quite easily explore the whole (on land) park on a single trip. Unsurprisingly, the park is a haven for mariners and island hoppers: basking in the sunshine, snorkeling, and swimming are everyday pastimes.

The visitor center is located in Cruz Bay, the park entrance.

↑ A green turtle, the most common of the sea turtles found in the park

### Beaches

The north shore attracts the most visitors, and little wonder: Trunk Beach is widely considered one of the most beautiful beaches on Earth. It also has the most facilities of any beach in the park, with a snack bar, rental shop, and showers. Offshore is an underwater snorkel trail with signage planted along about 400 ft (122 m) of seabed. Cinnamon Bay is home to the longest beach in the park (and the park's only lodging), while Maho Bay is one of the best places to see sea turtles and rays.

### Snorkeling

The park is a premiere snorkeling destination. Gear rentals are available at numerous businesses on the island, in particular in Cruz Bay and Coral Bay. The park offers a snorkeling guide highlighting the best areas; Hawksnest Bay and Watermelon Cay are two popular spots.

### Hiking

A number of hiking trails traverse the park, providing access to beaches or offering superlative viewpoints over the island. South of Coral Bay is Salt Pond Beach, from where you can hike the Ram Head Trail, around 2.5 miles (4 km).

To the south are Great and Little Lameshur bays; they require a 4WD vehicle to reach. From here, you can hike to Reef Bay Beach on a moderate 4-mile (6.5-km) trail that passes plantation ruins, ancient rock art, and some of the park's tallest trees. There's also the Reef Bay Trail, which runs across the island.

### Human history

South of Mary Point lie the ruins of Annaberg Sugar Plantation, the largest sugar-

IF YOU HAVE
**A weekend**
Base yourself in Coral Bay and explore the Lameshur area, hiking to Reef Bay. Spend the second day on a pre-booked sailing trip around the island, stopping to snorkel.

producing estate on the island. Visitors can learn about 18th- and 19th-century plantation life, taking in the remains of a windmill, animal mill, and the living quarters of enslaved people.

## Tours and day trips

Numerous businesses on St. John offer sailing excursions, kayak tours, and dive trips. Most depart from Cruz Bay. You can also catch ferries for day trips to St. Thomas in the U.S. Virgin Islands and Tortola and Jost Van Dyke in the British Virgin Islands.

### GETTING AROUND

Visitors to the park typically fly into Cyril E. King Airport on the island of St. Thomas. Hourly ferries circulate between Red Hook, St. Thomas, and Cruz Bay, St. John (3 miles/4.8 km), from morning to midnight; there is a limited schedule from Crown Bay, St. Thomas. Rent a jeep (from Cruz Bay or St. Thomas) if you plan to explore the island on a longer trip; you'll drive on the left side of the road with the steering wheel remaining on the left side of the car. Only two main roads cross the island: Route 10, or Centerline Rd., which runs through the mountainous interior and leads to Coral Bay and the Lameshur area, and Route 20, or North Shore Rd. Route 20, which passes Trunk and Maho bays before intersecting with Route 10 near Coral Bay, is a supremely scenic way of seeing the best of the island.

# EXPLORING THE VIRGIN ISLANDS

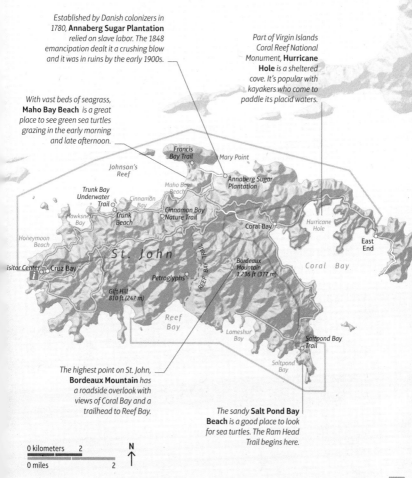

Established by Danish colonizers in 1780, **Annaberg Sugar Plantation** relied on slave labor. The 1848 emancipation dealt it a crushing blow and it was in ruins by the early 1900s.

Part of Virgin Islands Coral Reef National Monument, **Hurricane Hole** is a sheltered cove. It's popular with kayakers who come to paddle its placid waters.

With vast beds of seagrass, **Maho Bay Beach** is a great place to see green sea turtles grazing in the early morning and late afternoon.

The highest point on St. John, **Bordeaux Mountain** has a roadside overlook with views of Coral Bay and a trailhead to Reef Bay.

The sandy **Salt Pond Bay Beach** is a good place to look for sea turtles. The Ram Head Trail begins here.

0 kilometers  2
0 miles  2

N ↑

# NEED TO KNOW

Driving in North Cascades National Park

# BEFORE
# YOU GO

Whether you're a U.S. resident or visiting from overseas, plan ahead to make the most of your time in the national parks.

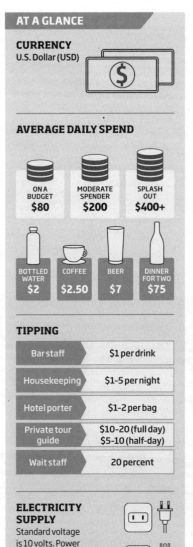

## AT A GLANCE

### CURRENCY
U.S. Dollar (USD)

### AVERAGE DAILY SPEND

| ON A BUDGET | MODERATE SPENDER | SPLASH OUT |
|---|---|---|
| $80 | $200 | $400+ |

| BOTTLED WATER | COFFEE | BEER | DINNER FOR TWO |
|---|---|---|---|
| $2 | $2.50 | $7 | $75 |

### TIPPING

| Bar staff | $1 per drink |
|---|---|
| Housekeeping | $1-5 per night |
| Hotel porter | $1-2 per bag |
| Private tour guide | $10-20 (full day) $5-10 (half-day) |
| Wait staff | 20 percent |

### ELECTRICITY SUPPLY
Standard voltage is 10 volts. Power sockets are type A and B, fitting two- or three-pronged plugs.

## Passports and visas

For those visiting the U.S. from overseas, check entry requirements with your nearest U.S. embassy or check the **U.S. Department of State** website. Canadians typically do not require visas to enter the U.S. Holders of a U.K., European Union, Australian, or New Zealand passport with a return ticket do not require visas if staying in the U.S. for 90 days or less, but must apply for an Electronic System for Travel Authorization (**ESTA**) at least 72 hours before travel. Visitors from all other countries must secure a visa before traveling.
**ESTA**
w esta.cbp.dhs.gov/esta
**U.S. Department of State**
w travel.state.gov

## Government Advice

It is important to consult both your and the U.S. government's advice before traveling to the U.S. The U.S. Department of State, the **U.K. Foreign, Commonwealth and Development Office**, and the **Australian Department of Foreign Affairs and Trade** offer the latest information on security, health, and local regulations.
**Australian Department of Foreign Affairs and Trade**
w smartraveller.gov.au
**U.K. Foreign, Commonwealth and Development Office**
w gov.uk/foreign-travel-advice

## Customs Information

Find information on the laws relating to goods and currency taken in or out of the U.S. on the **U.S. Customs and Border Protection** website.
**U.S. Customs and Border Protection**
w cbp.gov

## Insurance

We recommend taking out a comprehensive insurance policy covering theft, loss of belongings, medical care, cancellations,

and delays, and reading the small print carefully. The U.S. healthcare system is predominantly private – and costly – so appropriate medical cover is essential.

# Health

The U.S. has a private health care system that, though excellent, is extremely expensive. Medical travel insurance is virtually essential in order to cover some of the costs related to an accident or sudden illness.

### In the Parks

Most national parks are extremely remote and a long way from major hospitals. While most have their own medical centers, and all park rangers are trained in basic first aid, serious medical treatment will require long transfers over land, or more likely, by air – which you will have to pay for. If you do require medical care find a park ranger, or call 911 or the park phone number.

On hiking trails you are on your own: only the most popular (and generally short) day hikes are regularly maintained or patrolled: if you get injured or sick in the wilderness it can be hours or even days before help arrives, usually in the form of a "Search and Rescue" (SAR) operation, which is incredibly expensive for the parks. With that in mind, be prepared to deal with minor accidents or ailments on your own; learn the basics of first aid and pack a first-aid kit with all the essentials. Prevent dehydration and heat exhaustion by taking plenty of water.

# Vaccinations

No inoculations are required to visit the U.S.

# Accommodation

Accommodation within major national parks ranges from grand five-star lodges and reliable hotels, to simple cabins, "eco-tents", and back-country campgrounds, where you'll need your own equipment.

During the popular summer season (June through September), accommodations at parks like Grand Canyon, Yosemite, and Yellowstone tend to be completely booked up many months in advance, and prices are often extremely inflated. If possible, start planning six months

(or preferably a year) before your visit. Though cancellations can sometimes provide last-minute options they should not be relied upon.

### Reservations

For lodges, cabins, and hotels, check individual park pages on the **National Park Service** (NPS) website. Most parks partner with a private company (like Aramark or Xanterra), and you'll be directed to a separate website to make bookings. Most campgrounds, managed by the parks themselves, can be reserved through **Recreation.gov**. Some parks still maintain "first-come, first-served" camp-grounds, but these are rare in the summer.
**National Park Service**
Ⓦ nps.gov
**Recreation.gov**
Ⓦ recreation.gov

### Backcountry Camping

Check rules and regulations with individual parks on the National Park Service website before setting off into the backcountry. Wilderness permits, fees, and reservations will vary park to park.

### Outside of the Park

You don't have to stay within the park itself. Yellowstone, for example, is surrounded by small towns almost completely dedicated to supplying accommodation and services to park visitors – though this means a longer drive to start your day, you'll get much cheaper rates at hotels in these towns (and they rarely become completely full in the summer if you plan a last-minute trip).

# Food and Drink

Like accommodation, places to eat and drink within the national parks tend to be handled by private concessions, though park shops may sell basic snacks and drinks.

In general, where there are onsite lodges and hotels, there will usually be restaurants attached (and sometimes cheaper canteens or cafes). Major parks feature multiple places to eat and drink, but in most parks it's best to bring your own picnic. If you are bringing your own food, be sure to check and follow food storage regulations; some parks will require the use of bear cannisters, for example.

## Money

Major credit and debit cards are accepted almost everywhere within the national parks, while prepaid currency cards, contactless options, and American Express are accepted in many shops and restaurants. Many parks are increasingly going cashless, accepting electronic payments only for entry and services. In major parks that still accept cash you'll find ATMs in the major resort hubs (though most charge a fee of $3 per transaction). Despite the move toward a cashless system, it's still a good idea to bring extra cash, especially when visiting the smaller parks. Changing foreign currency is usually impossible within national parks so international visitors should plan accordingly.

### Tipping

Tipping for service is essential at park lodges and restaurants, with many in the service industry relying on tips to earn a living wage. Note, however, that park rangers, being employed by the federal government, will not accept tips.

## Travelers with Specific Requirements

Though the National Park Service is committed to making parks accessible to visitors with disabilities in general, in reality facilities, programs, and services vary park to park. Facilities at most parks were built long before the current Federal accessibility rules, and the wild nature of park terrain can be challenging. Each park has its own accessibility section on its website highlighting its facilities, as well as any specific issues.

Many outdoor park exhibits and visitor center exhibits are audio described on the free NPS app (p504), and most park videos are captioned. Most park shuttle buses are wheelchair accessible. In larger parks like Yellowstone, Yosemite, and Grand Canyon sign language interpreters are available for ranger programs with three weeks notice, assistive listening is provided at visitor centers, and there are large print and braille versions of official maps.

Most parks will have accessible restrooms, lodging options, and accessible roadside exhibits and viewpoints. All campgrounds will have at least one wheelchair-accessible site. Most walkways and self-guiding trails have at least one accessible route, and manual wheelchairs are available for loan at visitor centers and lodges (including beach wheelchairs).

U.S. citizens or U.S. permanent residents that have been medically determined to have a permanent disability qualify for a free Access Pass that provides free entry to all parks.

## Language

The official language of the U.S. is English, although more than a hundred languages are spoken across this multicultural country.

## Entrance Fees

While some parks are free to visit, others are not. Fees are paid per vehicle (up to $35) and last for seven days. Fees for visitors on motorbikes, bicycles, or on foot are slightly cheaper.

Parks that charge an entrance fee are open free of charge several times a year; check the National Park Service website.

## Reservations

Most parks require reservations for accommodation, but with visitor numbers rising year on year some highly visited parks also require timed-entry reservations, either seasonally or year-round, to enter altogether. It's important to check this in advance; if you show up without a reservation you'll be turned away. Some parks also require reservations to drive scenic highways or to hike popular trails, or, in the case of Haleakalā National Park, to view the sunrise from the top of the volcano. Make reservations on the Recreation.gov website (p497).

At the time of writing, the following parks require reservations in one form or another: Acadia, Arches, Glacier, Great Smoky Mountains, Haleakalā, Rocky Mountain, Shenandoah, Yosemite, and Zion.

Some permits are only available through seasonal lottery; instructions are provided on individual park websites.

### Permits

Individual parks will require permits for certain activities, like backcountry camping or fishing. Depending on what you plan to do in the park, check invididual park websites or visitor centers in advance to ensure you have the right permit.

## Passes

With major national parks now charging for entry, it's worth looking into discount cards and entrance passes before you visit, especially if you are planning to visit several parks.

The National Park Service's "America the Beautiful" passes cover the entrance fee for one private vehicle or four per person fees at all national parks. There are a variety of passes available, lasting a year or even a lifetime. Passes can be purchased at federal sites or online at Recreation.gov (p497).

The Annual Pass costs $80 for anyone 16 or older (those under 16 are always admitted free).

Note that many individual parks also offer their own annual pass, which provides access to that specific park for a year.

U.S. citizens or permanent residents who are 62 years or older qualify for a Lifetime Senior Pass ($80) or an Annual Senior Pass ($20); both passes incur a $10 processing fee.

Members of the U.S. military and dependents are eligible for an Annual Military Pass, while Gold Star Families and veterans can claim the Lifetime Military Pass.

The Access Pass, providing free entry to all parks, is available to those with a medically determined disability (p498).

The Senior, Military, and Access passes are all available via the **USGS** website. Each pass admits the pass-owner, plus three adults in a private vehicle (children under 16 always enter free of charge).

Lucky U.S. 4th graders are eligible for a free annual pass, which is valid for the duration of the 4th grade school year and following summer (September–August). The pass admits the pass-owner and any passengers in a vehicle, or the pass-owner and up to three adults at sites that charge per person. Go to the **Every Kid Outdoors** website to find out more.

Those who volunteer in the national parks or other federal lands are awarded an annual Volunteer Pass once they've accrued 250 service hours.

**Every Kid Outdoors**
ⓦ everykidoutdoors.gov
**USGS**
ⓦ store.usgs.gov/recreational-passes

## Opening Hours

All but one national park (Isle Royale, p366) are open 24 hours a day, every day of the year – though the same is not true for the services and roads or trails within them.

Visitor centers tend to open 8am to 5pm, with restricted hours in the off-season or during public holidays, when many close altogether. Tour companies, rental concessions (for kayaks, bicycles, and so on), restaurants, park lodges, and stores have their own operating hours and many close during major federal holidays.

Services (and major roads and trails) within parks that experience extreme seasonal conditions also close or run on very limited schedules in the off-season. In winter all mountain national parks (such as Glacier, Yellowstone, and Yosemite) and most parks in Alaska have closures, for example, while the Everglades often becomes waterlogged during the wet season May–November. These closures aren't necessarily a bad thing; snowshowing around a much quieter park out of season can be a magical experience.

## Park Closures

Situations can change quickly and unexpectedly. Always check the National Park Service website before visiting parks, and hospitality venues for up-to-date opening hours.

In addition to fairly predictable off-season or weather-related closures, parks can sometimes see temporary closures (certain areas, attractions, trails, or roads) for a number of other reasons.

Parts of the U.S. are increasingly prone to natural disasters, which can include earthquakes wildfires, floods, hurricanes, and even volcanic eruptions. Such events can have serious consequences at national parks, knocking out areas for one or two years, even. Access to Denali National Park, for example, is likely to be limited until summer 2026 because of the Pretty Rocks Landslide; the whole of Death Valley National Park was closed 2022–23 after heavy flooding; and Hawai'i Volcanoes National Park is often affected by eruptions.

Another reason an attraction or area of a park may be closed is for maintenance work. The Old Courthouse at Gateway Arch National Park is closed for renovations until 2024 or 2025, for instance.

Note also that while rare, U.S. "government shutdowns" (when federal government curtails all agency activity and services until funding legislation is passed and signed into law) will result in all national parks being closed, often at very short notice.

To ensure you're as prepared for your visit as possible, check individual park websites for alerts; alerts are displayed on the front page and there is also a dedicated alerts section. Alternatively, download the free National Park Service mobile app (p504).

| FEDERAL HOLIDAYS | |
| --- | --- |
| Jan 1 | New Year's Day |
| Third Mon in Jan | Martin Luther King, Jr. Day |
| Third Mon in Feb | Presidents' Day |
| Last Mon in May | Memorial Day |
| Jun 19 | Juneteenth |
| Jul 4 | Independence Day |
| First Mon in Sep | Labour Day |
| Second Mon in Oct | Columbus Day |
| Nov 11 | Veterans Day |
| Fourth Thu in Nov | Thanksgiving Day |
| Dec 25 | Christmas Day |

# GETTING AROUND

Whether you're visiting one park or planning a great American trip around several, discover how best to reach your destination and travel like a pro.

## Arriving by Air

Most national parks lie within 100 miles (160 km) of a domestic airport, typically served by one or two flights from a regional hub that offers international connections. While flying to one of these smaller airports can save you time, these flights tend to be expensive and the choice of rental cars can be limited on arrival. Many visitors fly to major international airports such as Atlanta, Chicago (O'Hare), Dallas-Fort Worth, Denver, Houston, Las Vegas, Los Angeles, Miami, New York (JFK and Newark), Orlando, Seattle, and San Francisco, and rent transportation from there. Without a rental car you'll usually be reliant on local taxis or shuttle buses (arranged in advance) to transfer from airports into the national park – public transportation is very limited beyond the major cities.

### Air-taxi

Some parks are remote (specifically most of those in Alaska) and can only be reached by air-taxi. Check individual parks for details.

## Arriving by Train

The use of passenger trains in the U.S. is dwindling, and the only park you might consider visiting by train in the Lower 48 is Glacier; the *Empire Builder* runs between Seattle/Portland and Chicago, stopping at East Glacier and West Glacier, both of which have shuttles that run the short distance into the park. While it is possible to travel to other national parks using trains, in practice you'll be taking fairly long bus and taxi rides from stations. In Alaska, it's possible to visit Denali National Park and Kenai Fjords National Park (via Seward) on trains from Anchorage.

**Alaska Railroad**
🆆 alaskarailroad.com
**Amtrak**
🆆 amtrak.com

## Arriving by Bus

Buses are typically the most economical way to get around the U.S., but often not the most

## TRAVEL PLANNER

| Park | City | Journey time by car |
| --- | --- | --- |
| Acadia | Boston (MA) | 4–5 hours |
| Glacier | Seattle (WA) | 9–10 hours |
| Grand Canyon | Phoenix (AZ) | 3–4 hours |
| Great Smoky Mountains | Atlanta (GA) | 3 hours |
| Joshua Tree | Los Angeles (CA) | 3 hours |
| Rocky Mountain | Denver (CO) | 1.5 hours |
| Yosemite | San Francisco (CA) | 4–5 hours |
| Yellowstone | Salt Lake City (UT) | 5.5–7 hours |
| Zion | Las Vegas (NV) | 3 hours |

convenient, especially over huge distances – long-distance lines generally do not serve national parks, and you'll have to transfer to local shuttles or book taxis to complete your journey. **Greyhound Lines** runs across the whole country, sometimes in conjunction with regional operators, while budget lines such as **FlixBus** and **Megabus** operate on the busy East Coast corridor and other primary routes. Greyhound also runs routes across the borders with Mexico and Canada; Megabus runs between New York and Toronto.

Only a handful of parks can be accessed by local bus operators that connect with the national Greyhound network: Yosemite Area Regional Transportation System (**Yarts**, for Yosemite) and **Salt Lake Express** (for Grand Teton and Yellowstone) are two examples. Discounts are available on Greyhound for children (aged 2–16), students, and seniors (aged 62 and older).

**FlixBus**
🅦 flixbus.com
**Greyhound Lines**
🅦 greyhound.com
**Megabus**
🅦 us.megabus.com
**Salt Lake Express**
🅦 saltlakeexpress.com
**Yarts**
🅦 yarts.com

## Arriving by Water

Cruises and guided boat trips on lakes and rivers within national parks are relatively common,

but it's generally not possible to travel between parks by boat. There are exceptions: the islands of Biscayne Bay National Park, Channel Islands National Park, and the Dry Tortugas National Park are only accessible by ferry; Isle Royale and much of Voyageurs National Park are also accessible primarily by boat.

The **Alaska Marine Highway System** links several Alaskan towns with Bellingham, in Washington state; it's possible to use this ferry service to visit several Alaskan national parks, including Glacier Bay, Wrangell–St. Elias, Kenai Fjords, and Katmai, albeit in conjunction with local transfers.

**Alaska Marine Highway System**
🅦 dot.alaska.gov/amhs

## Driving

Given the locations of the national parks, the best way to explore the majority is by car. The U.S.'s highway network is excellent and generally well maintained. Once you've arrived at your destination, however, it's often more rewarding (and sometimes mandatory) to leave your car and switch to national park shuttles, rental bikes, or hiking trails.

### Car rental

Most car rental companies have offices at airports across the country, and even smaller airports near national parks will have a choice of two or three renters. Arrange pick-ups online in advance as opening times may be limited.

You will need a credit card when checking out the car (debit cards may be refused). Most rental companies offer GPS (SatNav) for an additional daily fee, and child seats with advance notice. Free unlimited mileage is usually included (check ahead), but leaving the car in a different location to the one in which you rent it may incur a substantial drop-off fee. Most companies also charge a daily fee for additional drivers ($10+), but there are some exceptions, notably in California, where all additional drivers are free. In ten other states (including New York, Illinois, Texas, and Utah), the fee is waived if the additional driver is a spouse.

Non-U.S. residents may be asked to show a passport and return airline ticket when picking up. Note that standard rental cars in the U.S. have automatic transmission.

To rent a car you'll need a valid driving license and to have held it for at least one year; it's also a good idea to bring additional photo ID. Visitors under 25 may encounter restrictions when renting, and if you're under 21, you will usually not be able to rent a car at all. Foreign drivers' licenses are valid in the U.S., but if your license is not in English, you must get an International Driver's License.

## Insurance

If you are renting a car, you will be asked to add on a bewildering array of insurance extras. The insurance rules differ by state, but all require at least some type of liability insurance. Check to see if your own car insurance will cover rentals, or whether your credit card provides coverage for rental cars (you must use the card to pay, and the rental must be in the cardholder's name).

In brief, loss-damage waiver (LDW) or collision-damage waiver (CDW) means you can avoid paying for any damage to or theft of the car. However, there are sometimes "minimums" as opposed to "full" coverage, which can mean you are liable for the first $1,000 of damage, for example. Punctured tires and windshield damage are often not covered. Supplemental liability protection (SLP) will pay for damage you cause to other drivers' vehicles or property – again, check how much this actually covers. Personal accident insurance covers medical costs if the car is involved in an accident.

If you're a non-U.S. resident, it's generally safer to opt for some kind of insurance (even if you are covered at home, the rental company will make you pay for damages first and you'll have to claim the money back later). Take out at least LDW and SLP, as even a minor accident can result in astronomical costs.

## Rules of the road

Highway speed limits are set by each state; each park will have its own speed restrictions, too.

Distances throughout the country are measured in miles. Drive on the right-hand side and always wear a seatbelt. Right turns on red (unless otherwise indicated) are allowed after coming to a complete stop. All vehicles must give way to emergency service vehicles, and traffic in both directions must stop for a school bus when signals are flashing. Get information on U.S. traffic rules from your rental company or the **AAA** (American Automobile Association), which also provides maps.

Most states prohibit use of cell phones while driving, with the exception of a "hands-free" system. Speeding will usually result in a fine that should be paid in person if possible (rental companies are known to charge hefty additional admin fees). Driving under the influence (DUI) of alcohol is a very serious offense, likely leading to arrest.

**AAA**
w aaa.com

## Toll roads

There are a number of toll roads in the U.S. Most still have cash toll booths, but many states have introduced electronic systems. If you drive on one of these roads without an electronic pass, you face a hefty fine and admin fees from your rental company.

Your car may be fitted with an electronic pass, subject to a daily fee from the rental company (regardless of usage), plus tolls incurred. Make sure you understand the billing structure before you drive off. If you expect to drive on a high number of toll roads, it may be worth buying a transponder yourself (the **E-ZPass** system is the largest).

**E-ZPass**
w e-zpassiag.com

## Backcountry driving

For travel in remote parts of the U.S. and in some areas of the national parks, it is important to check your route to see if a 4WD vehicle is required. Motoring organizations and visitor centers can provide information.

There are basic safety points to be observed when driving in the backcountry. Plan your route in advance and carry up-to-date maps, a cell phone, and even a satellite device. When traveling between remote destinations, inform the police or park wardens of your departure and expected arrival times. Check road conditions before you start, and be aware of seasonal dangers such as flash floods. Carry plenty of food and water as an added precaution. If you run out of gas or break down, stay with your vehicle.

It is forbidden to remove or damage native flora and fauna. Do not drive off-road, unless in a designated area and especially not on reservation land. If driving an RV, you must stop overnight in designated campgrounds. Be aware that gas stations can be few and far between, so fill your tank before driving across remote areas.

### Parking

Once you've paid your entry fee, parking within national parks is usually free (Great Smoky Mountains National Park charges for parking tags instead of an entrance fee, but this is unusual). Only park in designated lots or areas – rangers will issue parking tickets for $100 or more if you're in the wrong place. In peak periods it can be hard to find spaces at popular sites; in that case you'll have to drive on and try again later, don't be tempted to park on the road or verge. Even at parks that have timed entry, don't assume there will be enough parking spots for everyone. It's worth preparing a plan "B" if the park is restricting access when you arrive (long waits at park entrances are not uncommon during peak season).

## Cycling

Cycling is a great way to get around national parks, especially during the warmer months, though some of the steeper roads in the mountains can be tough going for the inexperienced. Almost every park has bike trails or car-free roads (even Grand Teton National Park has a fairly level section to cycle), with private concessionaires that rent bikes (and sometimes e-bikes) inside or often just outside the park boundary. Most park shuttle buses will be able to carry a limited number of bikes, but always check if you're planning to hitch a ride in advance.

Note that park roads can become heavily congested with traffic in the summer, and in places like Yellowstone there are no bike paths along roadways.

## Walking

Hiking is by far the best way to experience America's land-based national parks, though most are far too big to visit entirely on foot (Death Valley National Park, for example, is the same size as Puerto Rico and bigger than the states of Delaware and Rhode Island combined). Trails range from easy jaunts near visitor centers to serious multiday treks through the wilderness. Check individual park websites or talk to a ranger on arrival to work out what trail would be best for your fitness level and available time. Day hikes are conveniently categorized by difficulty and distance, though park rangers will be better able to advise what each trail can offer in any given season.

While virtually no preparation is required for short day hikes, long treks require planning and a fair degree of fitness. Backcountry hiking and camping – beyond the clearly marked trails and roads in the busiest section of the parks – almost always require a permit (usually free, but increasingly awarded by seasonal lottery in busy parks like Yosemite). Always stay on marked trails and when walking in remote areas always tell someone where you're going and when you expect to be back (p504).

## On the Water

So many of the national parks are blessed with bodies of water: rivers, lakes, even the ocean. Exploring the parks by stand-up paddleboard, kayak, or canoe, or even by raft, is a real possibility. Some of the best places for kayaking and canoeing include the vast lakes of the Alaskan national parks, the tranquil wetlands and mangrove forests of the Everglades, along the Rio Grande in Big Bend, among the bays, lakes, and ponds of Acadia, and the reefs and islands of Biscayne Bay.

Private concessionaires within or just outside parks can rent equipment, though for some parks you will need to bring your own. Note that some of the remote Alaskan parks, like Lake Clark and Gates of the Arctic, are only accessed by a floatplane and so inflatable kayaks or canoes may be your only option.

## Getting Around in Winter

Road and trail closures are not uncommon during the winter season, but it's during this time that many parks take on a new life. As well as being much quieter, the parks offer opportunities for cross-country skiing, snowshoeing, snowmobiling, ice skating, and fat biking – getting around the parks becomes a truly unique experience.

### WEBSITES AND APPS

**AllTrails app**
Essential for hikers and mountain bikers, with thousands of trails mapped and described using your phone's GPS (so you don't need a signal).

**GasBuddy**
A must for U.S. road trips, this app locates nearby gas stations and notifies you about deals (www.gasbuddy.com).

**InciWeb**
This site offers instant updates on extreme weather (www.inciweb.nwcg.gov).

# PRACTICAL
# INFORMATION

A little know-how goes a long way. Here you will find more advice and information that'll help your visit to the national parks go smoothly.

## EMERGENCY NUMBERS

GENERAL
EMERGENCY

## 911

### TIME ZONE
The continental US spans four time zones: PST/MST/CST/EST. Most of Alaska uses AKST; Hawaii uses HST.

### TAP WATER
Unless stated otherwise, tap water should be safe to drink. Most parks provide water fountains.

## WEBSITES AND APPS

**National Park Service app**
Best source for real-time conditions within national parks, with updates on road closures, long entry lines, and weather advisories.

**Oh, Ranger! ParkFinder™**
Free app that allows you to find the nearest national park, monument or campground.

**Recreation.gov**
The main website for booking park campsites, as well as securing permits and timed-entry tickets.

**US National Park Service**
Full information on national parks (including individual pages for each park) can be found at *www.nps.gov*.

## Personal Security

The national parks are generally safe for visitors, but petty crime in busier areas can take place. Use your common sense, keep valuables in a safe place, and be alert to your surroundings. If you do have anything stolen, report the crime as soon as possible at the nearest ranger station and make sure to get a copy of the crime report in order to claim on your insurance. Contact your embassy or consulate immediately if your passport is stolen, or in the event of a serious crime or accident.

Since the introduction of the Civil Rights Act in 1964, the U.S. has been a country where the law treats everyone equally, regardless of their race, gender, or sexuality. However, in practice, systemic racism is still a major issue, and negative attitudes towards LGBTQ+ communities are not uncommon. The National Park Service works hard to foster diversity and inclusion; the parks are, after all, for everyone. Initiatives such as Black History Month cast a spotlight on Black history and heritage, while partnerships with Indigenous communities connect visitors with the parklands' rich culture and traditions.

## Natural Hazards

National parks can be affected by natural disasters; always check park websites for alerts (*p499*).

If setting off on a long-distance trail or similar, check in at visitor centers or ranger stations, and let someone know when you intend to return or arrive at your next destination. Park rangers can advise you of conditions and any challenges; some parks also have mandatory wilderness or wildlife safety talks. Always carry a first-aid kit (*p497*) and plenty of water, especially in the desert: dehydration, and heat and sun exposure are by far the most serious threats to hikers. Storms and flash floods can also be incredibly dangerous, so always check the latest weather forecast before setting off.

### Wildlife Safety
When hiking in forest or mountain national parks your biggest irritations are likely to be with

mosquitoes, flies, and blackflies, which are common in the early summer.

As part of bear-safety protocols (p172), visitors should always be highly aware of their surroundings when hiking, biking, or camping. Keep trash in secure receptacles, and never keep food or smelly items in a tent with you. Carry bear spray and a whistle, and if confronted, don't run, or make loud noises or sudden movements.

Cougar, mountain lion, and puma attacks are very rare, as are attacks by alligators. Snake bites are more common in some parts of the U.S. (rattlesnakes are abundant in the west), but only a handful are reported each year and fatalities are rare. Wear proper boots while hiking in the wild and if you do disturb a snake, back away so that it has room to move freely. Even the most venomous bites can be treated successfully with immediate medical attention.

To protect against giardiasis and other parasites and bacteria, boil, filter, or chemically treat all water found in the backcountry before drinking it.

## Responsible Travel

Visitor numbers to the national parks are higher than ever before. Do your bit to preserve these precious landscapes by "packing out what you pack in," and following "leave no trace" principles.

Do not remove anything – it is illegal to take plants and flowers, shed antlers, indigenous artifacts (like arrowheads), and even rocks. Do not mark or damage natural features (graffiti is strictly banned). Most importantly: do not approach, pet, or feed wildlife, and stay a reasonable distance at all times.

With forest fires increasingly common, carefully dispose of cigarette butts and flammable litter; starting a forest fire, even if accidental, is deemed a criminal offence. Smoking while traveling on trails is prohibited, though you can smoke while off-trail (except when specific fire restrictions are in effect).

Note that drones are banned in the parks.

## Smoking, Alcohol, and Drugs

You must be 21 to smoke, drink, or purchase alcohol; expect to show photo ID. Other rules differ from state to state and even from park to park, though it's usually permitted to drink

alcohol (as long as you're not driving), and smoke cigarettes off the trails. Most parks prohibit alcohol in park and concession buildings, and in parking lots and pullouts. Indoor restaurants, bars, and hotels generally ban smoking.

Federal law prohibits cannabis use in the U.S., which means that marijuana is illegal in all national parks even if the park is in a state where recreational use is permitted (many states have legalized limited amounts for recreational use for those over the age of 21). Taking cannabis across state lines or country borders is illegal, and being caught in possession of any other drug will likely result in jail time.

## ID

There is no requirement for visitors to carry ID in national parks, but you may be asked to show a picture ID when buying alcohol, confirming reservations, or purchasing a pass (p498).

## Cell Phones and Wi-Fi

In general, don't expect cell coverage in national parks, especially in the more remote areas – the further from the park entrance or the nearest settlement you are, the less likely you are to have a signal. The park service provides free Wi-Fi at some visitor centers but this will rarely extend beyond the immediate area. Many park lodges and restaurants also provide free Wi-Fi. It's unwise to rely on your device's roaming plan for navigation on park trails or even some roads. Always carry a paper map and compass; if traveling extensively, consider renting or purchasing a satellite device.

## Post

Some of the bigger parks have full-service post offices (generally open 9am–5pm Monday to Friday and Saturday 9am–noon); in smaller parks expect more limited facilities that run at reduced hours.

## Taxes and Refunds

Sales taxes vary from state to state. Since none of these taxes are levied at a national level, tourists cannot claim sales tax refunds.

# INDEX

# ACKNOWLEDGMENTS

The publisher would like to thank the following for their kind permission to reproduce their photographs:

(Key: a-above; b-below/bottom; c-center; f-far; l-left; r-right; t-top)

**123RF.com:** arinahabich 234, boydhendrikse 318, checubus 111tr, elec 284, f11photo 313t, haveseen 228b, kitleong 296-297br, lorcel 44-45tc, mathiasberlin 258, mkopka 196, veeterzy 485, volgariver 312

**4Corners:** Susanne Kremer 452-453, Udo Siebig 219

**Alamy Stock Photo:** Accent Alaska 173bl, Amanda Ahn 395, All Canada Photos / Peter Blahut 316bl, Art Collection 2 36tl, Associated Press / Carlos Avila Gonzalez 53b, B.A.E. Inc. 341, Ken Barber 221, Arpad Benedek 88, Russ Bishop 86-87t, Russ Bishop 278, Peter Blottman 114-115t, Bob Pardue - SC 22b, Dimitry Bobroff 260cra, Daniel Borzynski 388, Daniel Borzynski 414-415ts, Janice and Nolan Braud 10br, Don Breneman 364ca, Ramunas Bruzas 150-151, Robert Bush 478-479b, Cavan Images 214b, Cavan Images / Aurora Photos / Carol Barrington 226tl, Cavan Images / Ethan Welty 162, Cavan Images / Kennan Harvey / Aurora Open RF 225cr, Cavan Images / Menno Boermans 157, Mike Cavaroc 283, Mike Cavaroc 351, Engel Ching 96br, LOETSCHER CHLAUS 303cr, Serhii Chrucky 373, Ronnie Chua 202, Chuck Haney / DanitaDelimont 216-217br, Tim Clark 222, CSU Archives / Everett Collection 51b, Diego Cupolo 98, Colin D. Young 224-225, Ian Dagnall 69, Ian Dagnall 198, Ian Dagnall 242-243br, Ian Dagnall 260-261tc, Ian Dagnall 406, Ian Dagnall 458, Ian G Dagnall 251, Ian G Dagnall 426-427b, Danita Delimont 441, Danita Delimont / Adam Jones 414bl, Danita Delimont / Chuck Haney 190-191t, DanitaDelimont / Chuck Haney 260tl, DanitaDelimont / Larry Ditto 353br, DanitaDelimont.com / Chuck Haney 276-277bl, David R. Frazier Photolibrary, Inc. 195t, Danita Delimont 172-173, Danita Delimont 89, Design Pics / Radius Images 252-253t, Design Pics / Radius Images 253br, Design Pics Inc / Alaska Stock / Carl Johnson 175, Design Pics Inc / Alaska Stock / Kevin Smith 182-183t, Design Pics Inc / Alaska Stock / Michael Jones 158-159, Design Pics Inc / Alaska Stock / Scott Dickerson 171, Design Pics Inc / Alaska Stock RF / Michael Jones 142-143t, Design Pics Inc / Amber Johnson / Alaska Stock RM 164cla, 169bl, Design Pics Inc / Axiom / T. C. Knight 250, Design Pics Inc / Bill Brennan 462-463t, Design Pics Inc / Doug Lindstrand 173tr, Design Pics Inc / Joe Stock 160, Design Pics Inc / Karen Kasmauski 474, Design Pics Inc / Matt Hage 144t, Design Pics Inc / Nick Jans 184t, Design Pics Inc / Scott Dickerson 180, Design Pics Inc / Sunny Awazuhara- Reed / Alaska Stock 19t, Ian Dewar 31bl, Kate Diamond 52, Trent Dietsche 314bl, Douglas Peebles Photography 293, Cody Duncan 105br, Eagle Visions Photography / Craig Lovell 44cra, Richard Ellis 442-443b, Everett Collection Historical 26t, Everett Collection Inc 73bc, Hudson Fleece 67b, Zachary Frank 412, Zachary Frank 422tl, Dennis Frates 240, Bernard Friel / DanitaDelimont 228t, georgesanker.com 206cl, Joseph S. Giacalone 63t, GL Archive 34b, Tim Graham 19cl, GRANGER - Historical Picture Archive 72bl, 96bl, H. Mark Weidman Photography 156, ML Harris 153, Heritage Image Partnership Ltd 35tr, Janette Hill 206br, Dave G. Houser 469, Ian Dagnall Commercial Collection 201cr, Image Source Limited / Peter Amend 48bl, Image Source Limited / Seth K. Hughes 301ca, Image Source Limited / Victoria Zeffert 338-339b, imageBROKER.com GmbH & Co. KG / Ingo Schulz 315cb, imageBROKER.com GmbH & Co. KG / Konrad Wothe 92ca, imageBROKER.com GmbH & Co. KG / Michael Weber 38tl, Images By T.O.K. 275cr, incamerastock / ICP 466bl, Kerrick James 491, Jeffrey Isaac Greenberg 18+ 410, R. Patrick Jennings 46, Andre Jenny 482, Mark Kanning 386tl, Khairil Azhar Junos 417, Kingdom of Maps 34tl, Melissa Kopka 218, Dan Leeth 257, Dianne Leeth 248, Chon Kit Leong 188tr, Chon Kit Leong 429, Malgorzata Litkowska 125, Jon Lovette 436tl, Patrick Lynch 446, Dennis MacDonald 290bl, mauritius images GmbH 120tl, Jennifer McCallum 8cl, Media Drum World 290tr, Mint Images Limited 176br, Mira 140cr, Brad Mitchell 136, Raquel Mogado 216t, Jeff Mondragon 449, Juan Carlos Muoz 450-451, National Geographic Image Collection / Patrick Kelley 468, natthaphong janpum 272, Natural History Archive 11br, 236, Natural History Archive 38-39tc, Natural History Archive 82, Natural History Library 33br, Natural History Library 408-409b, Nature and Science 266b, Nature Picture Library / Jack Dykinga 344ca, Nature Picture Library / Kirkendall-Spring 212, 444, Niebrugge Images 140t, North Wind Picture Archives 53t, Boyd Norton 144ca, NPS Photo 24bl, Efrain Padro 239, Efrain Padro 347tr, Panther Media GmbH / Steve Prorak 378br, Panther Media GmbH / Steve Prorak 380-381t, Jim Parkin 25b, Pat & Chuck Blackley 360t, 385bl, Pat & Chuck Blackley 384, Pat & Chuck Blackley 385br, Pat & Chuck Blackley 392-393t, Pat & Chuck Blackley 433br, Douglas Peebles 473cla, Jamie Pham 483r, Ronald S Phillips 459, PHOTO.ZOOMMER.RU 267, PhotoAlto sas / Jerome Gorin 282, Pictorial Press Ltd 38br, Pictorial Press Ltd 80cl, J.K. Putnam 358, Lee Rentz 462cra, Whit Richardson 164t, robertharding / Christian Kober 478cla, robertharding / Marco Simoni 460-461, robertharding / Michael Nolan 173cra, Rocky Grimes 466t, Pep Roig 161, Pep Roig 173bc, RooM the Agency / DeepDesertPhoto 268c, Robin Runck 472, Maurice Savage 264bl, James Schwabel 244, 457, James Schwabel 419br, James Schwabel 422-423b, James Schwabel 424, James Schwabel 434, James Schwabel 454-455, James Schwabel 492tr, Science History Images 35bl, Carmen K. Sisson / Cloudybright 22-23t, Witold Skrypczak 13c, Michael Snell 427tr, Spring Images 64-65, Tom Stack 403tl, Stephen Saks Photography 91br, Stephen Saks Photography 428, C. Storz 477, Stray

Lens 206cb, Sundry Photography 83, SuperStock / Don Paulson Photography / Purestock 21cr, SuperStock / Max Seigal 230, SuperStock / Purestock / Don Paulson Photography 103tl, SuperStock / RGB Ventures / Ed Darack 70-71, Emanuel Tanjala 386-387b, Stan Tess 399, Tetra Images / Don Mason 421, Tetra Images, LLC 124, Tetra Images, LLC / Peathegee Inc 39tr, The History Collection 370cra, The History Emporium 35tl, The Print Collector 96cb, TMI 118, TMI 111tl, Turner Forte Photography 144-145b, Greg Vaughn 117, Greg Vaughn 100, Scott Warren 238, Jason O. Watson 256, Sally Weigand 416, Jim West 29cla, Zoonar / Cheri Alguire ImagesByCheri.com 484, Zoonar / ImgesByCheri.com 397br

**AWL Images:** J.Banks 288-289t, Walter Bibikow 464, Danita Delimont Stock 4-5, 6-7, Danita Delimont Stock 206bl, Danita Delimont Stock 242tl, Danita Delimont Stock 403tr, Danita Delimont Stock 411, Michele Falzone 12bl, Christian Heeb 108, Christian Heeb 324-325, J.Banks 207, Markus Lange 8-9br, Markus Lange 261cla, Markus Lange 265t, Jason Langley 436-437, Mark Sykes 264cr

**Depositphotos Inc:** hannator 27t, Justek16 134-135t, petersilvermanphoto 308tl, sepavone 418-419t, zrfphoto 246-247

**Dreamstime.com:** 51t, Cheri Alguire 254tr, Valentin M Armianu 466cr, Evan Austen 11c, Linda Bair 189tr, Patrick Barron 330bl, Francisco Blanco 402tl, Steve Blandino 110tl, Anastassiya Bornstein 301, Byelikova 101, Tristan Brynildsen 332, David Crane 302-303, Davidhoffmannphotography 60, Kenneth Donaldson 110tr, Anna Dudko 44tl, Christina Felschen 325tr, Sandra Foyt 447, Dominic Gentilcore 18bl, Gettysburg 248-249br, Henmand 440, Melanie Hobson 280-281tr, Indy2320 35br, Jon Lauriat 21bl, Leonardospencer 25c, Lhb Companies 348-349, Margaret619 330-331t, Billy Mc Donald 475, Cynthia Mccrary 304ca, Mudwalker 27cb, Mudwalker 27br, Svetlana Nikpnpva 266tl, Paulacobleigh 197, Sean Pavone 343, Ruth Peterkin 152, Jason P Ross 192ca, Pere Sanz 269tr, Spvvkr 74, Vadim Startsev 451br, Steveheap 476, Dimitrios Timpilis 402tr, Vacclav 483bl, Kelly Vandellen 38bl, Michael Vi 188tl, , Wirestock 420, Yailen26 67t, Colin Young 327, Zhukovsky 296tl

**Getty Images:** 500px / Charles Johnson 404, 500px / Stass Gricko 94-95tr, 62-63b, Peter Adams 200-201l, Peter Amend 59cr, Anchorage Daily News 174, Art Wager 372, Aurora Photos / Jerry Monkman 392bl, bauhaus1000 37tl, benedek 110-111ca, Bettmann 36bl, Bettmann 37tr, Bettmann 37bl, Bkamprath 492ca, Brandon Colbert Photography 3, Per Breiehagen 362-363, Antonio Busiello 86b, CampPhoto 333, Cavan Images 11t, Cavan Images 299, Yiming Chen 92t, Matteo Colombo 322-323, Corbis / Library of Congress 73clb, Diana Robinson Photography 315t, John Elk 254cra, Patrick J. Endres 40-41, Patrick J. Endres 178-179, ericfoltz 10bl, Erik Page Photography 235, Michele Falzone 285, Michele Falzone 481, Dean Fikar 262-263, Gallo Images 155br, Hulton Archive / Stringer 37br, Jeremy Cram Photography 316-317t, KingWu 126-127, Patrick Lienin 237, Lisa5201 186, LWA

344t, David Madison 150b, Alan Majchrowicz 163, Alan Majchrowicz 76-77t, Matt Anderson Photography 213, Juan Melli / 500px 1-2, Merrill Images 270t, Modoc Stories 127br, MPI / Stringer 36br, MPI / Stringer 38cla, Linka A Odom 220, Daniel Osterkamp 261tr, Andrew Peacock 176bl, Andrew Peacock 59, Photo by James Keith 456, Photography by Deb Snelson 352-352t, Posnov 304t, Federico Robertazzi 454, robertharding / David Tomlinson 306-307, George Rose 113, Jordan Siemens 131, Jordan Siemens 287br, The Washington Post 408cr, Peter Unger 8clb, Universal Images Group / Dukas 68, Daniel Vi Garcia 298, Stuart Westmorland 132

**Getty Images / iStock**: Adventure_Photo 24-25t, Adventure_Photo 317crb, aimintang 294-295, Dov Ben Amram 58, Aneese 273, benedek 16cra, benedek 494-495, benedek 84-85, benedek 96-97t, benedek 274-275, benedek 292, Bkamprath 39br, blazekg 80-81bl, bpperry 28b, Megan Brady 10t, BruceBlock 32bl, Cavan Images 17clb, cchoc 439tr, Harry Collins 18t, Gerald Corsi 8cla, dentok 75, Matt Dirksen 231bl, Xu DONG 12t, Shunyu Fan 112-113, Jon Farmer 189tl, Tiago Fernandez 48-49tr, ferrantraite 30-31, Fokusiert 268b, GeorgiosArt 35cla, Cindy Giovagnoli 356bl, gmcoop 23cl, Tonya Hance 13t, Jordan Hinsch 366-67, jaredkay 432-433t, JeffGoulden 16b, jenifoto 78, july7th 122-123, kellyvandellen 114-115ca, kellyvandellen 288bl, Kenneth_Keifer 425, krblokhin 30b, Sanya Kushak 360cr, kwiktor 241, kwiktor 319, Laser1987 382-383, Jon Lauriat 376-377t, lavin photography 245, Sandra Leidholdt 231cr, Brittany Limberakis 204tl, lucky-photographer 16tl, mantaphoto 154-155, Greg Meland 188-189ca, MicheleVacchiano 314crb, MNStudio 473t, NaturesThumbPrint 172bl, NetaDegany 362, NNehring 202-203br, PapaBear 20bl, PatrickPoendl 61, Sean Pavone 360bl, pchoui 279, pchoui 354-355bs, PictureLake 23b, David Radzieta 357, Cheryl Ramalho 204b, RichVintage 314cl, Rmiramontes 81t, RomanKhomlyak 119, romrodinka 17t, romrodinka 402-403ca, Anita Sagastegui 42, sarkophoto 168-169t, SeanXu 226-227b, SL_Photography 335, Spacewalk 130, spates 232, sprokop 45cla, StefaniePayne 13br, Dennis Stogsdill 19b, TalbotImages 490, William Teed 134-135b, thinair28 120-121, tobiasjo 320-321, Stefan Tomic 77b, traveler1116 254-255b, travelview 31cr, wanderluster 29br, wanderluster 328, YayaErnst 12-13bc, YayaErnst 102-103b, yhelfman 90-91, YinYang 20-21tc, YinYang 466crb, zrfphoto 106

**Grand Canyon Conservancy:** 270br

**Great Lakes Shipwreck Historical Society**: 370clb

**NPS:** 183br, Jacob W. Frank 191br, Brady Richards 28t, Submerged Resources Center 371tr naturepl.com: Jim Brandenburg 369tl

**Robert Harding Picture Library:** Colin Brynn 45tr, Adam Burton 55, Christian Kober 138, Michael Nolan 147, Michael Nolan 148-149

**Shutterstock.com:** Tobin Akehurst 17br, Alisa_Ch 311, Galyna Andrushko 146, Galyna Andrushko

336-337, Georgi Baird 326, Chris Blashill 308-309, A. H. Bowman 104tl, Checubus 192t, Steve Cukrov 26b, Damsea 487br, Danita Delimont 116, Danita Delimont 322b, Everett Collection 270clb, EWY Media 387cr, Zack Frank 398, Lijuan Guo 128-129, Steve Lagreca 369br, Kit Leong 374t, Lost_in_the_Midwest 99, LouieLea 286-287t, Doug Meek 342, Doug Meek 347br, Raisa Nastukova 140crb, peransz 214t, Lukas Proszowski 392br, RozenskiP 374ca, SCStock 486-487t, Iuliia Sheliepova 470, Alexey Stiop 394, STS Photography 72crb, sumikophoto 277tr, Edwin Verin 33c, Weidman Photography 33bl, Anna Westman 361crb, Margaret Wiktor 32br, Wirestock Creators 400, Lynn Yeh 54, Colin D. Young 233, Jay Yuan 199

**Unsplash:** Jan Bller 211t, Joshua Earle 47, Madison Oren 377br, Alexander Simonsen 300, Lori Stevens 438

**Cover images:**
Front and Spine: **Getty Images:** Matt Anderson Photography;
Back: **123RF.com:** f11photo t; **Alamy Stock Photo:** SuperStock / Max Seigal cl; **Getty Images:** Matt Anderson Photography b; **Shutterstock.com:** Damsea c;
Front Flap: **Alamy Stock Photo:** Design Pics Inc / Alaska Stock / Doug Demarest cla, Michael Greenfelder bl, robertharding / Neale Clark t, Witold Skrypczak cra; **Getty Images:** Daniel A. Leifheit br, Jordan Siemens c

All other images © Dorling Kindersley Limited

All illustrations © Dorling Kindersley Limited

MIX
Paper | Supporting
responsible forestry
FSC™ C018179
www.fsc.org

This book was made with Forest Stewardship Council™ certified paper – one small step in DK's commitment to a sustainable future.
Learn more at **www.dk.com/uk/ information/sustainability**

### A NOTE FROM DK

The rate at which the world is changing is constantly keeping the DK travel team on our toes. While we've worked hard to ensure that this edition of National Parks in the USA is accurate and up-to-date, we know that park access changes, trails and roads become impassable, and standards shift. So, if you notice we've got something wrong or left something out, we want to hear about it. Please get in touch at travelguides@dk.com

**Contributors** Stefanie Payne, Eric Peterson, Charles Usher, Edward Aves
**Senior Editor** Zoë Rutland
**Senior Designers** Vinita Venugopal, Laura O'Brien
**Project Art Editor** Ankita Sharma
**Editors** Keith Drew, Alex Pathe, Aimee White, Charlie Baker
**Proofreader** Kathryn Glendenning
**Indexer** Hilary Bird
**Picture Researcher** Marta Bescos
**Publishing Assistant** Simona Velikova
**Jacket Designer** Ankita Sharma
**Jacket Picture Researcher** Simona Velikova
**Senior Cartographers** Subhashree Bharati, Mohammad Hassan, James MacDonald
**Cartography Manager** Suresh Kumar
**DTP Designers** Tanveer Zaidi, Rohit Rojal
**Technical Prepress Manager** Balwant Singh
**Image Retouching** Pankaj Sharma, Ashok Kumar, Nityanand Kumar
**Senior Production Controller** Samantha Cross
**Managing Editor** Hollie Teague
**Managing Art Editor** Gemma Doyle
**Senior Managing Art Editor** Priyanka Thakur
**Art Director** Maxine Pedliham
**Publishing Director** Georgina Dee

First edition 2024

Published in Great Britain by Dorling Kindersley Limited, DK, One Embassy Gardens, 8 Viaduct Gardens, London SW11 7BW, UK

The authorised representative in the EEA is Dorling Kindersley Verlag GmbH. Arnulfstr. 124, 80636 Munich, Germany

Published in the United States by DK Publishing, 1745 Broadway, 20th Floor, New York, NY 10019, USA

Copyright © 2024 Dorling Kindersley Limited
A Penguin Random House Company

24 25 26 27 10 9 8 7 6 5 4 3 2 1

A CIP catalogue record for this book is available from the British Library.

A catalogue record for this book is available from the Library of Congress.

ISSN: 1542 1554
ISBN: 978 0 2416 8210 4

Printed and bound in Canada.

www.dk.com